Epidemic Empire

Epidemic Empire

Colonialism, Contagion, and Terror, 1817–2020

ANJULI FATIMA RAZA KOLB

THE UNIVERSITY OF CHICAGO PRESS
CHICAGO AND LONDON

The University of Chicago Press, Chicago 60637

The University of Chicago Press, Ltd., London

Published 2021

29 28 27 26 25 24 23 22 21 20   1 2 3 4 5

ISBN-13: 978-0-226-739212 (cloth)
ISBN-13: 978-0-226-739359 (paper)
ISBN-13: 978-0-226-739496 (e-book)
DOI: https://doi.org/10.7208/chicago/9780226739496.001.0001

Library of Congress Cataloging-in-Publication Data

Names: Raza Kolb, Anjuli Fatima, author.
Title: Epidemic empire : colonialism, contagion, and terror, 1817–2020 /
    Anjuli Fatima Raza Kolb.
Description: Chicago : University of Chicago Press, 2021. | Includes bibliographical
    references and index.
Identifiers: LCCN 2020026469 | ISBN 9780226739212 (cloth) | ISBN 9780226739359
    (paperback) | ISBN 9780226739496 (ebook)
Subjects: LCSH: Terrorism in literature. | Postcolonialism in literature. |
    Imperialism in literature. | Diseases in literature. | Literature, Modern—
    19th century—History and criticism. | Literature, Modern—20th century—
    History and criticism. | Terrorism. | Imperialism.
Classification: LCC HV6431 .R393 2021 | DDC 303.6/2501—dc23
LC record available at https://lccn.loc.gov/2020026469

FOR MY PARENTS

Contents

Figures

Preface: Politics and Scholarship in a Time of Pandemic

This book was going to press when the COVID-19 pandemic struck North America in March 2020. I was teaching in Canada at the time, and my family was across the border in the United States. My parents, one recently retired and one still working, are doctors. Three of my cousins and four of my aunts and uncles are doctors. Another one of my aunts is a nurse, one is a retired medical technician, and another cousin is in school for medical tech. Every one of them has infinitely more to offer our immediate collective welfare than I do. In these last few weeks, every scholar or writer I know has questioned the point of our endeavors, the usefulness of our skills. As I complete this book from quarantine—a practice whose racial and economic history I spent many years studying—I vacillate between feeling "on-call" for the first time in my life and doubting the necessity of scholarship, enraged at the structure of the humanities at present, and fearful for my colleagues, students, and the future of higher education.

For me, the pressure behind these concerns has never been greater, but I have also been writing this book about colonialism, race, and contagion for a long time. My research has its origins in my experience of September 11. I was in college in New York when the towers came down, and I watched with horror as the language of politicians and the media wrapped the events of that day in both Islamophobia and the figural vocabulary of contagious disease: the so-called epidemic of radical Islam and terrorism. These past few months have shown us new dimensions in the cynicism of this discourse. Not only did the framework of contagion serve to further dehumanize Muslims around the world and instigate the longest war we've known as a nation, but it also actively siphoned resources away from public health, preventative care, and disaster preparedness, in order to arm us against what we were told over and over was a more pressing, a more existential threat.

As the coronavirus death toll in New York State crossed the three thousand mark, and then doubled and doubled again—as mass graves

were dug on Hart Island in the Bronx to bury the unclaimed dead—
comparisons to September 11 came hard and fast. Governor Andrew
Cuomo repeatedly invoked the memory of the terrorist attacks. The
similarity, for Cuomo, was in the seeming "randomness" of both events;
he called the pandemic "a violent explosion that ripples through society
with the same randomness, the same evil that we saw on 9/11."[1] I do not
believe these violences ripple randomly. The fallacy of this bidirectional
analogy has deep roots; it is those roots I trace, historicize, and assess
in this book.

Even before September 11, government officials, journalists, cultural
critics, writers, filmmakers, police chiefs, scholars, and policy experts
favored the epidemic metaphor for terrorism and Islamist extremism.
Over the course of researching this book, I have found that the metaphor
of epidemic applied to insurgent and nonstate violence connects many
nonterrorist and non-Islamist genera as well, but in a less patterned and
more ephemeral way. We are prone, as Susan Sontag wrote in *Illness as
Metaphor*, to liken the unknown to the known, as a way to domesticate
and cognize it.[2] The habitual tethering of deliberate and widespread acts
of violence to plague shows the extensibility of this truth, binding one
terrifying unknown to another, creating all manner of epistemic and
hermeneutic confusion that ossifies into policy and shapes the world
order in ways that are scientifically, analytically, and morally incoherent.
At the same time, this policy, this world order, is remarkably like that
of European colonialism and its design of racial and economic brutality—in other words, extremely consistent. In this way, a figural operation
that seems to obscure meaning and understanding through "randomness" also serves extraordinarily stable goals, namely the abandonment
of the poor, the racially othered, the disabled, the surplus of the global
body politic.

In the early weeks of the pandemic, journalist Paul Elie wrote against
this stubborn figural habit and returned, as so many of us have done,
to Sontag. In "(Against) Virus as Metaphor," Elie writes, "Sontag's work
suggests that metaphors of illness are malign in a double way: they
cast opprobrium on sick people and they hinder the rational scientific
apprehension that is needed to contain disease and provide care for
people."[3] Speaking in his conclusion of this "hindrance," Elie points out
what is to me the most important insight of the first COVID-19 months,
namely that

[O]ur disinclination to see viruses as literal may have kept us from
insisting on and observing the standards and practices that would prevent their spread. Enthralled with virus as metaphor and the terms as-

sociated with it—spread, growth, reach, connectedness—we ceased to be vigilant. Jetting around the world, we stopped washing our hands.[4]

I agree entirely with the first part of Elie's claim, but taking a slightly broader view—one that includes the history of the terrorism-as-epidemic metaphor and its future ramifications—I would go farther. This figural operation didn't just keep us, passively, from observing the practices and standards that would prevent a pandemic; it pointedly suppressed these priorities in the belief that the immense wealth of the new imperium would by some trickle-down method keep "us" safe from diseases afflicting the poor, the brown and Black, the hungry, and the weak.

How does the War on Terror intersect with what very quickly became known as the War on the Virus? In the early days of compulsory terrorism talk in the West, one heard incessantly the warmed-over Orientalist association of Buddhists, Hindus, Asians, Asiatics, Arabs, North Africans, and Muslims with fatalism and a drive toward death.[5] Images of hopeful *shahids*, or martyrs to jihad, blurred with the visual assault of pitiable women in hijab—look how these women are already entombed in life, they seemed to say, see how their husbands and sons race toward murderous suicide. Social theories that posited suicidal and life-negating cultures or "ideologies" attributed their spread to qualities of contagion, rather than to economic and political disenfranchisement, occupation, harassment, or outright war. Muslims or Islamists were themselves understood nearly universally to be the vectors of this contagion. In 2018, the Chinese government "quarantined" over a million Uighur people in internment camps in Xinjiang to combat what it described as an "infection by an ideological illness."[6] According to current reports and leaked documents, most of these people are still being confined, even amid a national lockdown to contain the spread of the coronavirus.[7]

The effects of twenty-first-century Islamophobia have now reached far beyond the West and are deeply embedded in the global response to the COVID-19 pandemic. In India, the second most populous nation on earth after China, the pandemic came in the midst of massive nationwide protests against Narendra Modi's Muslim ban, which effectively bars any person even suspected of being ethnically or religiously Muslim from seeking citizenship in India, ostensibly a secular democracy. As Arundhati Roy has pointed out, Modi's Bharatiya Janata Party (BJP) has seized on the pandemic to further vilify Muslims, particularly Delhi's domestic and menial workers:

The mainstream media has incorporated the Covid story into its 24/7 toxic anti-Muslim campaign. An organisation called the Tablighi

Jamaat, which held a meeting in Delhi before the lockdown was announced, has turned out to be a "super spreader." That is being used to stigmatise and demonise Muslims. The overall tone suggests that Muslims invented the virus and have deliberately spread it as a form of jihad.[8]

The global pandemic media landscape has proven just as capable of accommodating Islamophobia as it has discursive histories of yellow peril and myths of East Asian weakness and infirmity. As Mehdi Hasan reports, invocations of "corona jihad" reinforce COVID-19 as a "Talibani crime" in India while click-bait stories in Britain imply that madrasas, "secret mosques," and Muslim gatherings are viral hubs.[9] Newspapers in France and the United States published stories worrying about Muslims' capacity for maintaining distancing orders and positing Ramzaan (Ramadan) and Eid al-Fitr as further health catastrophes in the making.[10] The consequences of this discourse have been immediate. On the first day of the holy month, a mosque in Salt Lake City was vandalized and an Islamic center in Missouri was burned down in apparent hate crimes.[11]

It will be years before we are able to see anything like a comprehensive picture of this moment in time, and how it will recast our understanding of early twenty-first-century history. It will be a defining pivot in how we understand the operations of isolationist empire both in contrast to the territorial expansions of earlier forms of colonialism and as an extension of their corporate and profiteering logic. Donald Trump's decision in mid-April to withhold contributions to the World Health Organization may be the clearest sign of how imperial dominance is no longer predicated on even the fiction of internationalism.[12] The White House pantomime that confers on corporate "leaders," like the CEOs of Target, Walmart, and ExxonMobil, the status of government actors reminds us that private companies have for centuries practiced economic and political dominance in the name of therapeutic empire.[13]

The impact of the pandemic on working-class Americans and the new demographic of "essential workers," the vast majority of whom are people of color enjoying few if any benefits, has already been colossal.[14] At a time when these workers are hailed as "heroes" and asked to sacrifice their health for a fiction sold as the "greater good," it is worth recalling that Europe's imperial powers also mobilized the mythology of duty and sacrifice to a putatively shared endeavor that would lead to greater prosperity for all.[15] It is a cruel irony that the demand for martyrs to the so-called "war" against the pandemic comes from the same mouths that have sought to pathologize "martyrdom" as a behavior of religious fanatics and radical extremists since 2001.

What I imagined would be the end of this project feels once again like a beginning. Theorists of resurgent events like disease, famine, and war have taught me to be careful about anchoring cultural analysis in what appear to be discrete events, but the pandemic still feels like a shock. The chapters that follow trace the "panic and neglect" cycle that recent writing about COVID-19 has identified in "diseases" both literal and metaphorical.[16] Regarding the perennial metaphor of the terrorism epidemic, my hope is that facing a viral threat that has already overwhelmed us all and put a stop to the regular functioning of capitalism will also put a stop to the deployment of disease metaphors and the racial and economic injustices they proliferate. In a few years' time, a generation of scientists and scholars will grapple with what we are living through now. My students are already seeing things more clearly than I can, and I have faith in what they will teach us. I hope something in this book helps them to make sense of the 2020 pandemic not as an isolated disaster, but as a turning point in the history we want to write and the world in which we can live.

"Islam," Terrorism, and the Epidemic Imaginary

He falls, and does not know in the daze of his folly.
Such in the dark of man is the mist of infection
that hovers, and moaning rumor tells how his house lies
under fog that glooms above.

AESCHYLUS, *THE EUMENIDES*

An old physician told me in confidence with a mixture of surliness and solemnity, that the "colonized do not know how to breathe."

ALBERT MEMMI, *THE COLONIZER AND THE COLONIZED*

In the summer of 2018, the United States Supreme Court upheld the "extreme vetting" protocol of Presidential Proclamation 9645, colloquially known as the "Muslim ban."[1] The Court's deliberations hinged on the relevance of Donald Trump's intentions—documented on the campaign trail, in informal conversations, and in Tweets—regarding Executive Orders 13,769 and 13,780, and whether these intentions were fueled by racial animus and religious discrimination. In her dissenting opinion, Justice Sonia Sotomayor alerted the Court to Trump's repeated references to the apocryphal tale of General John Pershing suppressing the Moro Rebellion in the Southern Philippines (1899–1913) by killing Muslim insurgents with bullets covered in pig's blood.[2] Though few remarked on it at the time, Trump's campaign trail rhetoric was pointedly grounded in a history and mythology of anti-Muslim violence at the root of American imperialism—the war in the Philippines, it should be recalled, was the subject of the most famous literary document of the colonial era, Rudyard Kipling's 1899 "The White Man's Burden," a poem the author sent to Teddy Roosevelt as an encouragement to expand the American empire.[3]

Sotomayor also lays out the careful elision of the word "Muslim" in Trump's discourse as it was replaced with the less overtly discriminatory term "terrorist."[4] Of the eventual bill's less incendiary title, "Protecting the Nation from Foreign Terrorist Entry into the United States," Sotomayor notes, "As he signed it, President Trump read the title, looked up, and said 'We all know what that means.'"[5] By expunging the word "Muslim" from his campaign rhetoric—a double emptying of the already-empty category of "Islam" in the American political lexicon—Trump's seemingly random and careless utterances point suggestively to the space they leave behind, equating "Islam" with danger, anti-Americanism, lawlessness, and terrorism as if their conflation is a secret he and his constituents share. Indeed, if we have to know what "Foreign Terrorist Entry into the United States" means, it is because the persistently collapsing political meaning of terrorism and Islam has been the most consistent driver of American foreign and domestic policy for the better part of two decades. This slippage did not emerge ex nihilo on the afternoon of September 11, 2001. A longer view of the colonial record reveals that the Muslim ban and the Supreme Court's decision to uphold it are the culmination of extremely specific and durable ways of thinking that tie the idea of contagious disease to the conceptualization of Islam as an anti-Western, antimodern, and rapidly proliferating ideology.

Written by Chief Justice John Roberts, the majority opinion of the Court trades in this terminological slippage, which has profoundly shaped over 150 years of colonial and neoimperial history: the metonymic relation between a Western idea of Islam and the terror of a global pandemic. To illustrate the necessity of presidential authority in matters of immigration and national security, Roberts writes:

> On plaintiffs' reading, [the executive orders] were beyond the President's authority. . . . Nor would the President be permitted to suspend entry from particular foreign states in response to an epidemic confined to a single region, or a verified terrorist threat involving nationals of a specific foreign nation, or even if the United States was on the brink of war.[6]

In Roberts's analogy epidemic, terrorism, and war find themselves in a familiar series, bringing the Muslim ban into focus as both ideological inoculation and a quarantine operation—one that no witness of Trump's public rhetoric can disaggregate from his incessant likening of refugees and migrants to an "infestation," and Islam to a "malignant cancer."[7]

Terrorism is a disease. An infection. An epidemic. A plague. We have heard these phrases thousands of times since the attack on the World Trade Center in 2001. They are spoken in Paris, in London, in Nice, Boston, Barcelona, Mosul, Islamabad. As the reference to the war in the Philippines demonstrates, this favorite figure did not originate in the twenty-first century; it is a thoroughly colonial metaphor—one whose translation and circulation between times and places is isomorphic with the reach and endurance of the vast empires of the nineteenth and twentieth centuries. In his 1850 essay "The Romance of Indian Warfare," British historian of India John W. Kaye, surrounded by ordinary fevers and a raging cholera epidemic, worried nevertheless that "nothing is more contagious than rebellion."[8] He was not alone in his thinking. Chroniclers of the Indian Mutiny of 1857 would follow Kaye's rhetorical lead, calling the uprising an "infection," an "outbreak," and an "epidemic," even as waves of so-called "Asiatic" cholera, the first global epidemic, spread from the Indian colony to Europe and East Asia, and onward to American shores. Both in the pre-Raj British empire and in the present—as well as many turbulent moments between—the dual figure of the Muslim insurgency and the terror epidemic function as philosophical paradigms of extremity that enable the consolidation of imperial power from the very highest levels of government to the most granular structures of feeling to which this power owes its social, cultural, and material longevity.[9] It should not surprise us, then, to witness Trump, at campaign rallies, intoning arrhythmically the lyrics to civil rights activist Oscar Brown's "The Snake," in which a kindly woman nurses a sick snake back to health and is bitten for her kindness. To Trump, this is a parable about "Syrian Refugees entering the country," their "sickness" being both their fault and their feint.[10]

In its current political form, the idea of "Islam" that "we all know" is not a religion or a culture, not a set of beliefs and practices, not a history, not the Qur'an or the Hadith. It is a dialectical foil for the West, and a racial category stitched loosely together from the remnants of an Orientalism requisitioned in the service of resource-exploiting colonialism. It is a function of racial capital and nineteenth-century counterinsurgency. This "Islam" comes to us from the nineteenth century, the high point of European colonial expansion and also the moment at which European shipping companies globalized the practice of hajj. Old ideas about the premodernity of the Orient, the decadence of the Mughal rulers of India, the flabby and moribund Ottoman Empire, the poor hygiene of the Arab quarter, and the paradigmatic "failed state" of postcolonialism feed easily into this tenacious and politically expedient "imperialist fantasy."[11] The twenty-first-century construct "Islam" in the Anglophone and Francophone worlds—and by extension in global internationalist discourse—is not just "barbaric," as in the language of the Middle Ages, but also contagious. Specifically, it is shaped by rhetoric around poverty, disease, and revolution in the British and French colonial holdings, by the metropolitan fear of the colonies and the Orient coming home to haunt and infect the heart of whiteness. Trump's repeated allusions to Pershing's use of pig's blood as ethno-nationalist apotropaic paints the corporeal terrors of the racial other in mythopoetic tones, suggesting the durability of a logic of not just quarantine but also inoculation against ideological infection. This abstraction carries the figure's force from the realm of workaday policy matters like immigration to the very ontological foundations of empire.

The medical antecedents and evolution of this mythos of the body are, I will argue, specific to the British and later French colonial and US imperial contexts. The association of Islam with irrational and fanatical forms of violence becomes particularly dominant after the 1857 Indian Mutiny, in which the terror of an anti-imperial uprising against Britain was bound to an image of Muslims as crazed murderers and vectors of ideology akin to the actual epidemics that were at the same time decimating the British Army in India. The chapters that follow uncover the history of this undead figure that has imagined insurgent violence as epidemic for nearly two centuries in the service of naturalizing and circumscribing its political dimensions. These are metaphors that turn, that begin to go in reverse, harden, and become irrevocably material. They are not just mechanisms of the mind, but of politics. To invert a phrase from the canonical work of linguists George Lakoff and Mark Johnson, they are metaphors we die by.[12]

Epidemic Empire makes two connected arguments. First, that the imperial disease poetics that casts insurgent violence as epidemic is grounded in narrative and scientific practices central to the management of empire and neoimperial formations; and second, that a comparative historical study of the rhetorical commingling of colonial science and counter insurgency can offer us urgently needed lessons for reading the global political and public health landscapes of today. In our putatively postcolonial moment, we continue to observe the wedding of terrorist violence to the epidemic imaginary in the use of this figure by writers, public intellectuals, lawmakers, scientists, and policy experts along the political spectrum. For Donald Rumsfeld, terrorism is a "cancer on the human condition," for journalist Hans Magnus Enzensberger it's a retrovirus, "a pathological copy of the organism it attacks," for Boris Johnson, it's a "plague," for Jacques Derrida it is "a suicidal autoimmunitary aggression."[13] In 2002, W. J. T. Mitchell observed "the invisible figure of terror spreads like a virus . . . as surely as the powdered toxin of anthrax circulates through the U.S. postal system."[14] Philip Bobbitt, former director of the Center for National Security Law, framed his book *Terror and Consent*, with an introduction titled "Plagues in the Time of Feast" and a conclusion titled "A Plague Treatise for the Twenty-first Century." Tony Blair suggested that it should be "required reading for political leaders."[15] The

United States Institute for Peace, under the leadership of policy experts Paul Stares and Mona Yacoubian, suggested in 2005:

> Given the dynamic, unpredictable nature of Islamist militancy, we are drawn to an "epidemic" conception as a way of thinking. . . . This approach draws on the scientific principles and practices of epidemiology as well as insights from a growing body of research on social contagion phenomena such as fads, rumors, and civil violence. Indeed, social scientists increasingly look to epidemiology to understand a variety of contagions, and here, Islamist militancy is no different . . . [I]t too can be deconstructed using the classic epidemic model.[16]

For the Department of Homeland Security and the FBI's Countering Violent Extremism program, the language of prophylaxis and rehabilitation and the intelligence-gathering tools of epidemiology have become a productive method for analyzing, combatting, and securitizing against "terror," a phenomenon understood to be virulent, shapeless, and evasive, but that nevertheless remains the object of the longest war in US history.

In addition to the rhetorically dehumanizing effects of imperial disease poetics, the actual outcomes of practices like quarantine, the implementation and policing of sanitary borders, national and international vaccination programs, a broad conception of conflicting immunities, and a terror of global pandemic have continued to serve protectionist and West-centric interests, even and perhaps especially during the first months of the actual global pandemic of COVID-19. The figure of the terror epidemic looks to the promise of data collection and rational study of the microbe, the individual, and the population as a means of eradicating the threat of irregular warfare, just as infectious diseases, we were told unconvincingly at the dawn of the twenty-first century, were defeated by the tools of demography, cartography, hygiene, and the study of immunization.[17] On the other hand, the mythopoetics of infectious disease from the Abrahamic scriptures to the present also point toward the divine, the occult, the unknowable, gaps in data and textual lacunae, and the inevitability of natural forces of destruction and sublime phenomena, even when they are cast in explicitly nonreligious terms. This latter is the function of the figure embedded in the literary and political history of the term "terror," a poetic and narrative manifestation of the affect of horror that encompasses both natural and political events and the narrative forms to which they give rise.

In this book, I ask how the idea of a "terrorism epidemic" had become so pervasive in the first decades of this millennium that it all but ceased to register as figural. Where does it come from, what has it meant, and how has it ceased to mean? How have literary and cultural production held this idea both in and out of view of Anglophone and Francophone readerships for more than two centuries? How do such texts—fictional tellings and journalistic ones, political utterances, films, philosophy, think pieces—influence and transform the practical applications of medicine, diplomacy, and war? In addition to rising alarm about climate change in the first two decades of the twenty-first century, the fear of global jihad and the global migration "crisis" have thrown into ever-sharper focus the real and perceived bodily risks associated with the increasingly untrammeled movement of people, animals, and biological materials across borders. The infectious spaces of the Global South—hot, dirty, and teeming with illiterate and unhygienic bodies—have been represented by many health experts, policy makers, and popular science writers as out of sync with the supposed hypersmooth, sanitary space of the Western metropolis. In these ways and more, the post-9/11 era has been inscribed in a variety of discourses with an increasingly acute sense of the failures of rational modernity to protect citizens of sovereign nations in the developed world from anachronistic and illogical forms of harm.[18] If the distant zones of Asia and the "Muslim world" weren't already perceived to be existing in a past out of joint with Western notions of development, the US would remind them that they could, at any moment, "bomb them back to the stone age."[19] To illuminate the rhetorical history of this present—shot through with fears of counterdevelopment, global crisis, and the stagnation of waning empires—I assemble in this book a diverse archive of literary, medical, administrative, legal, military, and visual documents from colonial India and Ireland, imperial Britain, French and independent Algeria, the postcolonial Islamic diaspora, and the neoimperial Unites States. This archive reveals in the colonial encounters of the nineteenth century a genealogy of the concept of epidemic terror emerging from the very heart of Anglophone and Francophone letters.[20]

Terror and Terrorism in Literature and Law

Contemporary legal and agency definitions of "terrorism" are freighted with a great degree of indeterminacy and strategically rely on the permeable boundaries of the terms "terror," "terrorism," and "terrorist" in order to defend policies of surveillance, harassment, and war that impinge on civil liberties, human rights, and national sovereignty. In spite of this indeterminacy, the Department of Homeland Security, in a 2008 memo titled "Terminology to Define the Terrorist: Recommendations from American Muslims," insists:

> Words matter. The terminology that senior government officials use must accurately identify the nature of the challenges that face our generation. . . . We are facing an enemy that holds a totalitarian ideology through force across the globe. We must resist complacency. The language that senior government officials use can help to rally Americans to vigilance.[21]

The memorandum does not define the proper terminology for terrorists beyond calling them "terrorists," though it does suggest the term "death cult" as an alternative.[22] According to the *Dictionary of International and Comparative Law*, terrorism is "the use of arbitrary violence against a defenseless population; [it is] often difficult to draw the line between terrorism and legitimate struggle."[23] A 2004 United Nations Security Council Resolution includes the "purpose to provoke a state of terror in the general public" in its general definition and condemnation of terrorist acts.[24] As we can see in even the briefest of overviews, these definitions' most consistent feature is their expansive instability, resulting in a largesse that is at once taxonomically capacious, riddled with the language of fear, and extremely challenging to parse in terms both literary and legal. As David Simpson argues in his study of Romantic terror, "*Terror* has colonized a part of the lexicon that has, over the years, been occupied by a range of other words—*horror*, *dread*, *fear*, *panic*—and it has displaced them all."[25]

In relation to more contemporary articulations, literary critics Elleke Boehmer and Stephen Morton strive to fill what they understand to be a gap in postcolonial studies' treatment of "terror" as both a tool of colonial power (state terror) and a fact of postcolonial existence (largely antistate terror). In their view, "postcolonial studies has to date largely neglected the back-history of today's colonial or late colonial terror."[26] In the introduction to their *Terror and the Postcolonial*, they highlight a "free floating, liberal understanding of terrorism" as the operative concept in academic approaches to terrorism and terrorism studies as discipline (6). "A system of terror," in this definition, is one in which "a person or a group adopts a policy of intimidation intended to strike with terror those against whom it is adopted" (6). This chiastic and decontextualized précis, they write, "denies the fundamental point that terrorism as political violence is the ground upon which sovereignty is in many cases defined in the colonial present" (6). The editors query the persistence of "familiar orientalist metaphors," and the "ways in which terror may be mediated to consciousness through metaphor," but they do not offer a sustained reading of figures of terror or Islamist terrorism, despite the fact that they earlier wonder whether terror "is a historical force that flashes up at moments of crisis," or is instead a figure that is "heterogeneous and chameleon-like, a form of autoimmunity" (13, 6).

While terrorism has become a compulsory topic in the contemporary American and global political spheres over the last two decades, what terror and terrorism mean culturally, legally, taxonomically, and phenomenologically in the postcolonial era is a definitional problem that long predates September 2001. Eqbal Ahmad's is one of the most important voices in the effort to elucidate the definitional complexity and political bi-directionality of the term. In his 1998 lecture, "Terrorism: Theirs and Ours," he illustrates the semiotic sterility of the term in the post-Vietnam moment, citing former secretary of state George Shultz's tautology on the subject from a speech given in 1984: "terrorism is a modern barbarism that we call terrorism."[27] Shultz's utterance does not serve to incite any outright military action, but it does signify a persistent reliance on Orientalist projections of violence undertaken by nonstate actors as barbaric, and tightly delimits this barbarism as an immutable identity by way of an interpretive tangle that folds back on itself to define terrorism, uselessly yet broadly, as terrorism. Reaching back to this moment with Ahmad reveals a longstanding tactical imprecision in defining what has now become an ever more vague enemy in an unending war.

Italian philosopher Adriana Cavarero has proposed dispensing with the term altogether and replacing it with the even less legally specific "horrorism," which she sees as a more adequately conceptual vocabulary for highlighting the de-individuating effects of such violence on victims and perpetrators alike, who are linked on a continuum of vulnerability.[28] Martin Amis used the same term in the title of his three-part essay, "The Age of Horrorism," written on the occasion of the fifth anniversary of the 9/11 attacks. "Suicide-mass murder is more than terrorism," he writes, "it is horrorism. It is a maximum malevolence," a "pathological cult," and "a poison that might take—might mutate, like bird flu."[29] Despite their shared obscurity and incoherence, definitions of terror and terrorism reliably betray a unifying, if enigmatic shift from observable acts and events perpetrated by human actors to something more atmospheric and ontological, something distinctly at odds with the human. We can see this clearly in Amis's invocation of the "pathological cult," violent acts as the "pollution of Western cities" and the "poison . . . like bird flu" that render Muslim, third-world, and nondeveloped space breeding grounds of toxicity and pathogenicity, of "maximum malevolence."

In *American Islamophobia*, legal scholar Khaled Beydoun distinguishes private, structural, and dialectical forms of animus toward Muslims as outgrowths of both American chattel slavery and Enlightenment-era Orientalisms.[30] He sees private, hate-based Islamophobia as something of a red herring; attacks on Muslims and Muslim-appearing people make headlines, but the institutional and legal frameworks that assume all Muslims everywhere are a national security threat are far more pernicious (36). Dialectical Islamophobia is "the very thread that binds the private and structural forms together . . . the process by which structural Islamophobia shapes, reshapes, and endorses views or attitudes about Islam and Muslim subjects inside and outside of America's borders" (40). For Beydoun, private views and attitudes come into being in relationship to the state's endorsement—through legislation, prosecution, and surveillance and security measures—of "popular tropes" (40). Dialectical Islamophobia, we might argue, following Beydoun, is a literary effect, and writers—novelists, lawmakers, journalists, and academic experts—are its agents. As fraught and objectionable as the term "Islamist terrorism" is, I use it in this book in deference to its lived existence in contemporary discourse and to distinguish it from what I see as the largely discontinuous history of anarchist and revolutionary terrorism at the turn of the twentieth century. As a figure of pathogenicity, the trope of Islamist terrorism as epidemic must also be read through the narrative sciences of health, demography, and sanitation in the colonial sphere—disciplines that, as anthropologist Bernard Cohn argues in his indelible *Colonialism and Its Forms of Knowledge*, "formed the basis of [the British] capacity to govern" its overseas holdings.[31]

Reading Epidemiologically

This book offers a sustained critique of a discipline and form of knowledge that originates in colonial science, but my reading method has also been responsive to and influenced by an epidemiological mode of reading. Epidemiological approaches to public health are social, transverse in both time and space, and multifactorial. In contrast to the clinical scene, which is typically limited to the physician and the tissue, patient, or group of patients, and takes as its object of analysis the individual body and the symptoms expressed on or in it (we might think of this as a kind of close reading), epidemiological studies additionally investigate scenes of behavior, labor, migration, and social intercourse, and move out into the nodes, patterns, and convergences that constitute the social. Synoptic and multivocal descriptive studies play a particular role in tracking and understanding the distribution of epidemic events, systematizing and fixing the anecdote as a form of data in the study of adverse health events that may have occurred at some distance from one another in time and space. Such a bifocal mode of information assembly and reading preserves an important space for the undecidability of representation and the role of the specific case in the creation of broader narratives. Particularly in early epidemiological studies, which persistently strive to project a composite picture of the intersecting lines of origin and transmission in broad-distribution health events, the extrapolation from a tightly delimited scene to a region, disease, or system models practices of reading that seem at odds with the depth-interior hermeneutics of suspicion we associate more regularly with the medical and the medical gaze. In these ways, epidemiological reading shares foundational methods with comparative, interdisciplinary, and postcolonial discourse analysis, especially those studies that aim to compass discontinuous events across large swathes of history and geography.

From the disease mappers and shoe-leather physicians of the nineteenth century, I draw a belief in the actual existence of multiemergent phenomena, in both health and in broader material senses. Understanding such phenomena necessitates a shuttling reading practice that is comparative in temporal and geographical terms, localized in particular sites of close analysis that function exemplarily (bacteria, viruses, tissues, symptoms, local outbreaks), and posits narrative—written narrative in particular—as being, itself, a genre of data interpretation. Some of the most moving moments in my research came when I was least prepared: the notebooks, journals, reports, and letters of Victorian and Indian physicians struggling and elaborately failing to understand the horrors of contagious disease and its relationship to empire's territorial expansions, trade protocols, and demographic and environmental modifications. This archive, riddled with the rhetorical violence of colonial bureaucracy, elicited nevertheless an uncanny sense of kinship for the ways in which much public health work, especially international public health, strives to orient itself toward social justice. This orientation remains a mark of today's most committed epidemiologists, whose work is motivated not by a sense of misguided paternalism, but rather by a desire to right the abuses of global capital—largely American corporations and the global medical economy—and their hold on the pharmaceutical industries, national and international governments, and trade organizations. As Paul Farmer writes in his minutely researched *Pathologies of Power*, "The argument that the afflicted deserve access to care for these ailments is an argument for social and economic rights."[32]

Given this orientation and the increasingly global scale of public health work, epidemiology's methods, motives, and practices of reading are well suited to postcolonial and globalization critique. But it is crucial to note that these hermeneutic models resemble each other so closely because they emerge from a set of conditions that followed a post-Enlightenment ameliorative settler colonialism wherever it went. At the same time as I draw from epidemiological insights and optics, therefore, I am also sharply critical of the disciplinary and discursive history of epidemiological science, its related fields of study, and their literatures. The epidemiology of terrorism in particular, now a flourishing subfield, returns the discipline to some of its most unsavory assumptions, motives, practices, and programs. Although recent work attempts to keep the deep relationship between epidemiology and humanitarian imperialism in view, cautioning against the "diversion of resources from essential public health programs to the 'war on terror,'" funding streams and collaboration with government antiterrorism agencies has made this area of research dependent on the perception, even the manufacture, of ongoing security threats.[33] Terrorism epidemiology thus maintains and justifies military and policing programs designed to prevent the very causes of morbidity and mortality it studies.

This is not a dissimilar friction from the one we find at the discipline's origin. Established in 1850 during the second major outbreak of Asiatic cholera in England, and launching a professional journal in 1859—just a year after the Government of India Act and Victoria's proclamation "bound" England "to the natives of [her] Indian territories by the same obligation of duty which bind[s] [her] to all [her] other subjects"—the Epidemiological Society of London was born of colonial contact.[34] The discipline's very first articulations of its aims are acutely conscious of the necessity of reading and rereading its own methods in this expanded frame of investigation:

> To institute a rigid examination into the causes and conditions which influence the origin, propagation, mitigation, prevention, and treatment of Epidemic diseases—to collect and promulgate, with relation to these subjects, such facts as appear to be established on a sound and sufficient evidence—and to point out those methods of investigation by which the misleading influence of false or deficient evidence may be best avoided.[35]

In its first century, epidemiology remained largely rooted to the study of epidemic disease. In keeping with the prevailing concerns of the day and the vast industries that sold bogus preventions, treatments, and cures, the society also prioritized assessing and controlling the dissemination of inaccurate information, striving to produce its own narrative in the public interest. This practice began with etiology, an investigation of origins akin to philology—also reborn in the early nineteenth century Anglosphere as a function of Britain's relationship with India—but also moved outward to a study of demography and dissemination in terms consonant with those of then-contemporary colonial policy and imperial liberalism, specifically "isolation" and "intercourse."

> In the investigation of Epidemic diseases the aim will be to trace them up to their causes, to examine each cause thoroughly, and to ascertain whether they admit of prevention, and if so, by what means. . . . The spread of Epidemics will form another subject of inquiry; and under this head, the influence of isolation and of unrestrained intercourse will be particularly investigated.[36]

Benjamin Guy Babington, then president of the society, establishes here the dual reading practice embedded in an epidemiological mode of inquiry: it is a paradigm that operates equally and simultaneously in the thorough and rigorous detection of origins, and the interrogation of social effects.

The contemporary practice of global epidemiology has been most lastingly and influentially stabilized by the charter, mandates, and ongoing projects of the United Nations World Health Organization. Continuing the legacy of the International Sanitary Conferences that began during the Paris cholera outbreak of 1851 and the creation of a postwar international order in the League of Nations, the World Health Organization's establishment in the UN's original charter 1948 places the study, protection, and improvement of world health at the heart of twentieth-century structures of internationalism from their inception in the periods of overlap and transition between colonialism, the world wars, and globalization. The WHO currently defines epidemiology as follows:

> Epidemiology is the study of the distribution and determinants of health-related states or events (including disease), and the application of this study to the control of diseases and other health problems. Various methods can be used to carry out epidemiological investigations: surveillance and descriptive studies can be used to study distribution; analytical studies are used to study determinants.[37]

The WHO remains the world's largest international health system, "providing leadership on global health matters, shaping the health research agenda, setting norms and standards, articulating evidence-based policy options, providing technical support to countries and monitoring and assessing health trends."[38] As such, the organization serves as a site of gathering and compromise for an incredibly wide range of public and private health rhetorics, practices, and theories, which often reflect competing interests and ideas about what is urgent, what constitutes "best practice," what constitutes the public and the "world," and how these practices should be implemented. From this diverse set of viewpoints, the organization sets priorities and standards of global health surveillance and care, and putatively enforces these standards in the context of governmental internationality. In this crucial way, the WHO differs from nongovernmental and other research organizations both in its powers of enforcement (although they are limited) and in its function as an extension of international governmentality, rather than a replacement or adjacent structure.[39] For the WHO, whose intergovernmental goals include "quietly protecting the health of every person on this planet, every day," epidemiological thinking not only implies but is explicitly framed as comparative and international, if not governmental.[40] Secondly, although epidemiology can be and very often is practiced outside the framework of governmentality, it is my goal here to excavate the particular relationship between a conception of epidemic and a conception of terrorism, a specifically nonstate and increasingly international phenomenon that is being "fought" by both state and international governmental and nongovernmental means.

The WHO definition of epidemiology shows us certain features that will appear again and again across the archive I study in this book, inflected in different ways by different political and historical contexts. Chief among these is the distinction between health-related states or events and the subcategory of disease. While "epidemic" is used colloquially to suggest illness, communicability, contagion, and transmission, equally robust subfields of epidemiology are engaged in the study of presumably noncommunicable health problems and causes of mortality, the most obvious being chronic illnesses like asthma, cancers, diabetes, and heart disease. Equally valid epidemiological studies investigate patterned events detrimental to health and life, including war, substance abuse, gun violence, traffic accidents, and psychiatric events. This expanded focus has brought about important developments in the uses of epidemiological tools of "surveillance," "descriptive studies," and "analysis" for public health outside of infectious and viral disease, the ground on which epidemiology was founded. Such a capacious view of emergent phenomena brings a massive number of facts of lived existence under the aegis of what we can read through the lens of epidemic. A small number of investigators have specifically pursued the epidemiology of terrorism: these studies tend to be strictly defined assessments of the risks of injury and death by acts of terrorism, however, and do not equate terrorist ideology with the epidemic imaginary, apart from bringing mortality by terrorist acts within the ambit of epidemiological investigation.[41] The breadth of adverse health and mortality events that can be studied in this way, however, proved important in setting norms for the concurrent breadth of surveillance and intervention that can be undertaken in the interest of "health," and the mobile metaphorical language that assists in the projection of global space as the body biopolitic.

The challenges of epidemic representation and interpretation (epidemiology, but also reading writ large) carry over into the figuring of terrorism as epidemic, compounding one incomplete form of mediation with another. Rarely does an epidemic projection of violence, Trump's, Rumsfeld's, or otherwise, posit an analogy or equivalence between its two terms in a detailed way. Rather, the figuring of terrorism as epidemic opens up epistemic and practical convergences between health security and pervasive, seemingly organic forms of violence that escape other existing hermeneutic frameworks. In horizontalizing and proliferating signification, the epidemic figure also disrupts metaphorical systems' customary relationships between the sign and the referent, surface and depth. The mobile legibility of terror epidemics thus bespeaks a reading practice always in excess of, and nevertheless inadequate to, its object. I'm interested in how this discourse, local and purposive but not necessarily intentional, becomes practice at a global scale.[42] I now turn to a brief discussion of some of the ways in which critics and theorists have taken up narratives and figures of epidemic and illness in recent years, in order to historicize both this deficiency and the theoretical and practical surplus it engenders.

Pathotropism: Theory after 9/11

A full account of the efflorescence of biopolitical theory since the start of the new millennium is beyond the scope of this book. I am interested here in a particular inflection of the body politic in the age of globalization by way of the pathogenic imaginary, which has held special sway on the literary and political theoretical side of the spectrum. Following Jacques Derrida's putative "political turn" and the galvanizing role of autoimmunity in his late thinking, we can observe a cluster of pathotropic theoretical works that address themselves to terror and terrorism in the wake of Giovanna Borradori's timely and now-classic *Philosophy in a Time of Terror*. In her interview with Derrida, he considers the novelty of the September 11 attacks, staged on the territory of a nation that imagines itself to play a "sovereign role among sovereign states."[43] To illustrate this novelty and its departure from other political forms and acts of speech, Derrida renews a theory of autoimmunity developed in his earlier essay "Faith and Knowledge," explaining that "an autoimmunitary process is that strange behavior where a living being, in quasi-*suicidal* fashion, 'itself' works to destroy its own protection, to immunize itself *against* itself."[44] For Derrida, as for Roberto Esposito, who takes up similar questions in his 2002 *Immunitas*, the concept of immunity is crucially grounded in religious practice, borrowed from the language of those who were protected from arrest—immune to prosecution because they had taken sanctuary in sacred spaces.[45] Also crucial for Derrida is the extent to which a politics of autoimmunity disrupts the ordinary functioning of the epidemic metaphor as an extension of a xenophobic logic that insists on violent incursions such as the September 11 attacks as originating in extramural and noncivilizational space. Instead, autoimmunitary logic works "in a loop," and "comes as from the *inside*."[46] Moving away from the frontal-conflict model of sovereign warfare, suicidal autoimmunity insists on the ways in which the body politic can attack itself, be responsible for its own vulnerability and harm through overreaction or misplaced, weaponized immune response.

A political theory of autoimmunity therefore inheres the sense of body as archive and arsenal, and discharges injunctions according to its own deconstructive rules: in this sense, it, too, "never forgets." Derrida uses autoimmunity in this inflection to recall

> that the United States had in effect paved the way for and consolidated the forces of the "adversary" by training people like "bin Laden," . . . and by first of all creating the politico-military circumstances that would favor their emergence and their shifts in allegiance. . . . This force will have been *adjusted* with an extraordinary *economy* . . . [I]t will have targeted and hit the heart or, rather, the symbolic head of the prevailing world order.[47]

The double suicide Derrida speaks of here is framed in explicitly anticapitalist and antimilitaristic terms; his aim is to illuminate the course of self-destruction upon which American imperialism seems fixed, even at the level of arming its own future enemies. This is a familiar argument by now. Derrida's conception of autoimmunity thus avows the *mondialisation* of politics as always-already-global in the age of American empire and capital (this section of the interview is framed via the Cold War), and also imagines the global body politic as progressively self-cadavering.

What he does not do in this interview, which profoundly influenced the theoretical left in future thinking on the problem of terrorism, is interrogate the consequences of requisitioning a social concept that is nevertheless routed through natural history and medical discourse to look, once again, at the social. Difficult questions about the logical basis and theoretical ramifications of autoimmunity either do not interest Derrida or exceed the scope of the urgent conversation of the moment. The moral and the ethical dimensions of this theory become particularly worrying if we reverse the paradigm, though it seems clear that we are not to imagine actual autoimmunitary disease in the individual body as punishment, retribution, or an urging to suicide based on our previously imperialist behaviors. Less agile and rigorous critics also take up Derridian autoimmunity—with Derrida's politics as a ready alibi—in troubling ways, returning by way of the autoimmune thesis to a more ordinary virological vocabulary of terror and fanaticism. W. J. T. Mitchell's *Cloning Terror* is an important example of this unfortunate effect. In Mitchell's chapter on autoimmunity, which praises Derrida's interventions, he suggests "a reframing of terrorism as a public health crisis rather than a war."[48] Like the humanitarian imperialism of the nineteenth century, this reframing allows for a total departure from the politics of the War on Terror and a suppression of the ferocious military response and infinitely defensible surveillance undertaken in racial, ethnic, and religious terms as "preventative" care. Though Mitchell's stated goal in reclassifying terror as a "public health crisis" is to offer a "positive alternative" to the war, he misunderstands the process of autoimmunity as an already overactive immune response, and quickly descends into the liberal muddle of therapeutic empire and its proliferation of dehumanization, justification, and prophylactic quarantine measures:

> It would mean . . . strengthening the immune system, a refinement of tactics for determining the difference between friends and enemies, hosts and parasites, natives and immigrants, and a strengthening of that other central biopolitical component of the body politic, a "healthy constitution." It would mean strong doses of *preventive* medicine in the form of a world system that had strong institutions of international justice . . . [I]t would . . . treat[] terrorism realistically as a matter of political criminality for which the appropriate treatments are to be found in the body politic's own immune system, its police and intelligence systems, its judicial institutions, its ability to provide a decent standard of living for its own people.[49]

It is easy to see how this kind of thinking can stand as a defense of policies like the Muslim ban, upheld by the highest court in the nation, and enforced by the "surveillance," "intelligence," and "police" forces in

whom Mitchell puts so much faith to deliver the "strong dose of medicine." In its unreconstructed forms, empire's disease poetics shapes
colonial history and historiography and solidifies the intractable association between violence and epidemic. In so doing, the epidemic thesis produces an "inhuman," natural enemy in order to negate political
demands, and to justify a global security apparatus in defense of "humanity," a category that is constituted by its exclusion of phenomena
perceived as contagious: like terror, like Islam.

Mitchell's thesis and other studies of disease metaphorics owe a great
deal to Susan Sontag's pair of essays, *Illness as Metaphor* and *AIDS and
Its Metaphors*. In the first of the two, Sontag argues that the experience
of illness is poorly served, even perverted, by metaphors that both seek
to describe it in other terms—a primary example for her is the "fight,"
"battle," or "war" against cancer—as well as those that seek to describe
other forms of antipathy through figures of particular illnesses—war can
as easily become a "plague," a "cancer," or an "epidemic" in her account.
Sontag suggests that these mobile and dangerous metaphors are vehicles
"for our justified fears of the increasingly violent course of history."[50] By
the time she writes the second essay, *AIDS and Its Metaphors*, in 1990,
Sontag has built a more flexible operating definition of "metaphor," and
sees in the figurative deployments and projections of disease a number
of capacities in addition to risks and harms. She identifies in the first
essay a limited Aristotelian concept of metaphor, along with its suspicion of the peregrine transformations of language, and clarifies at the
outset of the second a somewhat softer position on the "seductiveness
of metaphorical thinking," suggesting the impossibility of thinking and
interpreting any shared state without metaphor (93). She considers, for
example, both military metaphors of the body, which figure health states
as protected by a kind of corporeal fortress, and civic metaphors of the
body, which help us to imagine health as a social system in which parts of
the body cooperate in both resistance and vulnerability. She identifies in
the latter family of figures a tendency, in comparing society to a human
body, to "make[] an authoritarian ordering of society seem inevitable,
immutable" (94).

Sontag's position on the inevitability and immutability of an ordering
of society based on an analogy to the human body is a crucial feature
of how I understand the process and outcomes of epidemic figuration.
If certain forms of violence are metaphorized as epidemic, these metaphors render such forms of violence "inevitable" and "immutable," just
as they justify responses to those forms of violence as compulsory and
unassailable. The effect, when we draw this claim through a century of
colonial and postcolonial literature, is that a way of thinking about epi-

demic organizes a way of thinking about terrorism such that the possibility of agency, and with it a certain conception of politics, is obscured,
irrespective of what we might think about the content of that politics.
This happens both in the projection of adversity and in the response to it,
which is consequently made to look like an obligation beyond good and
evil, above politics, namely to protect the health of the imagined social
body whose anatomy is isomorphic with the very globe. In this scheme,
terrorists become subhuman—microbial, cancerous, viral—while their
enemies retain status as a collective human body, projecting and protecting a baseline image of health and integrity.

In the work of Patricia Clough and Jasbir Puar, the "viral" is a form of
relation whose "effect on subjectivity, memory, desire, and history . . .
suggests a move away from identity" as well as "a move away from those
sorts of representational forms or strategies that privilege interiority,
depth, and integrity."[51] This conception of virality gives us new purchase
on the paradox of the postsubject as both free of naïve assumptions about
fixed or essential identity, but also frequently relieved of certain meaningful characteristics of subjectivity, such as desire and history, and, by
extension, the ability to assert political agency. The question of motiva-
tion and desire has been key for certain patterns of representation in
terrorist-themed literature over the last two decades: John Updike, Don
DeLillo, Mohsin Hamid, Martin Amis, Richard Flanagan, Pearl Abraham,
Amitava Kumar, and Claire Messud, to name only the most prominent
of writers who have tackled this topic, have turned to prose fiction as a
space for working out the "psychology" of terrorists, both foreign-born
and American. New questions arise when we carry Clough and Puar's
insights into the realm of literature: How do we approach a metaphor of
contamination and transmissibility whose terms undo the very logic of
depth by which it comes to have meaning? What larger representational
and literary modes does such a figure intersect with or give rise to?

Moving from the broader concerns of political theory that animate
the work of Derrida, Esposito, Mitchell, and Sontag to the more granular
work of literary criticism, my readings in this book build on the scholarship of Priscilla Wald and Cristobal Silva, both of whom consider the
point of contact between an idea of disease and narrative form. For Wald,
epidemiology is first and foremost a discipline of representation; it

> turns an outbreak of communicable disease into a narrative, it makes
> the routes of transmission visible. . . . [T]he epidemiological narra-
> tive is, like the microscope, a technology, and it is among the episte-
> mological technologies that delineate the membership and scale of
> a population.[52]

Even once the "outbreak narrative" has made the invisible visible, this information requires "the story that is told about transmission" in order to make sense.[53] Following Wald, and in my own research in early nineteenth-century epidemic writing, the reading and narrative-making practices of epidemiology constitute their object through narrative at the same time as they make up the interpretive framework by which these narratives can be understood and made useful as predictive and preventative evidence. In this way, epidemiology can be understood as a paraliterary genre that aspires to both social history and scientific prediction.

Similarly, in his book *Miraculous Plagues*, which looks at narratives of illness in colonial New England, Silva approaches the forebears of epidemiology "as a literary critic would a narrative genre" and characterizes its practices, such as disease mapping, as "representations of disease that encode bodies, health, illness, social habits, geographic spaces, communities, and borders into coherent narratives that reveal the progress of epidemics over time in provisionally bounded spaces."[54] Wald's and Silva's examinations of the plots, narratives, and genres of epidemic writing suggest a pervasive if inchoate set of conventions in the literature of epidemic: these include messy, contaminant, or transmissible figuration as a structural element; the use of corporate protagonists and multiple points of view; documentary, pseudodocumentary, or archival forms that determine and perform the pace of revelation and interpretation; an explicit consideration and assessment of the status of data; a close attention to the geography of antipathy; and a layered history marked by both memory and repetition. Both scholars' contention that epidemiology may be read as a form of "emplotting" is fascinating in the limited register of literary study, but it is also powerfully in excess of the literary, unbinding itself from the purely representational and influencing policy, diplomacy, military action, and public health interventions. This form of storytelling, in which metaphors become markedly material, as Heather Schell has put it, makes it "an extremely powerful tool for creating master narratives about the world."[55]

Postcolonial Critique and Epidemic Materialism

Postcolonial critique is committed to dismantling such master narratives, first and foremost by understanding where and how they are promulgated—the method is historicist, comparative, and oriented toward the political present. My own work is also firmly in line with Saidian discourse analysis.[56] *Epidemic Empire* is intended primarily as a contribution to postcolonial criticism and theory and to reading the disease poetics of empire as they undergo various crises and sublimations in the geopolitical landscape that has come into focus in the twenty-first century, a period in American and imperial history that has consistently stretched and redefined the meaning of the most foundational terms of the political: war, enmity, sovereignty, security, and health. One of the main goals of this book is to look at the relationship between these shifting epistemologies, narrative form, and imperial strategy. A connected through-line maps what becomes of the biologistic and organicist conception of the state as the very notions of biotic life and the purview of the organism undergo no less radical redefinitions than the concept of the nation itself, providing the conceptual underpinnings for a subsequent biomorphic conception of the globe. In the face of the growing institutional power of "world literature" as a depoliticizing scholarly paradigm, I insist here on the ongoing necessity of postcolonial reading methods that are adequate to the long history of racial capital, global health, and the postcolonial geographies of the "Islamic" world.

What this looks like, in the architecture of this book, is somewhat out-of-joint with more traditional literary histories grounded in narrower times, spaces, and literary traditions. The global project of European colonization brought noncontiguous polities, cultures, and histories into contact with one another and in spaces of translation (literal, conceptual, and metaphorical) in ways that would radically impact later political and narrative formations in addition to disrupting the building of national literary canons. Barring the fact of subjugation, there is no homogenous experience of colonialism, and even less so of anti- and postcolonialism. Nevertheless, networks of military, political, and biopolitical management, as well as the broad rhetorics of justification including education, religion, and political ideology as vehicles of imperial expansion bring disparate scenes into relationship with one another in a way that impacts both political and cultural forms. Even as I argue for such juxtapositions, and borrow Rabindranath Tagore's critique of historiography and the "'pedantic historians' who have narrowed down history in its scope," I am also mindful of his warning about "literary critics who 'wander about so extensively' in history as to rob it of all specificity."[57] In the specifically Tagorean tradition, which is to say an anticolonial poetic and hermeneutic tradition, I also want to make a case for the "marriage of literature and historiography so that the creative insights of one can enrich the other."[58] My impulse to continue in this anti- and postcolonial vein is reparative, and is grounded in the observation that in the hands of their most capable practitioners, subaltern history and comparative postcolonial approaches always resist the homogenizing impulse of both Eurocentric comparative literature and the center-periphery models of imperial power and the vehicular languages of empire. I follow this critical practice because it is committed from its inception to the possibilities and promises of a global resistance to economic and political exploitation, crystallized in early and mid-twentieth-century international efforts to repudiate colonialism.[59]

The chapters that follow thus reconstruct emergent and broken lineages, tropes, plots, and figures that are smuggled into imaginative and literary presents by way of recurrent and novel diseases, illnesses, and contagions and the historical discourses that proliferate Orientalist and counterinsurgent inflections therein. Across the body of texts I've read preparing this book—colonial and postcolonial, but also well beyond these designations—literary recourse to a mythopoetics of disease and to the concept metaphor of epidemic invariably serves as a portal to a variety of histories on a range of different scales. That is to say, epidemic fiction always draws into its orbit the cultural and social memories of outbreaks and crises past. The epidemic is, in this sense, a kind of archive, shaped by and responsive to colonial expansion. The comparative postcolonial dimensions of this book are subtended by a way of thinking about the emergent and resurgent aspects of epidemicity as a structural paradigm for a literary historiography in ways that also draw on Walter Benjamin's writing on historical materialism and philosopher of science Michel Serres's topological conception of time. Notwithstanding the suspicion with which he looks on the purported scientific objectivity of materialist history, Benjamin affirms in "Theses on the Philosophy of History" the revolutionary imaginary enabled by the dialectical "leap" into history, or the "blast" of history into the present, each of which promises to shatter the phantasm of history's progressive linearity.[60] The object of this history is not an empirically discernable past, but the iterative relationship between the past as it is constituted in the present and the future. In the space between the scientism of Marxist materialism and the Gothic haunting of a juxtapositional history that seems to instantiate "profane illumination," we can begin to see how pandemic might function within a Benjaminian paradigm as a different kind of disaster and a different point of access to the thinking and writing of history.[61] In undoing social relations, economic growth, and ordinary governance rather than constituting and being constituted by them, epidemic is equally constitutive and interruptive of lived life and of a view of history as the "material things" on which the "Theses" comments. As Serres—also interested in topological and discontinuous time—describes it, "sickness is a noise . . . sickness, of whatever variety, intercepts a function; it is a noise that mixes up messages in the circuits of the organism, parasiting their ordinary circulation."[62] In Serres's terms, epidemic interrupts both a conception of linear time and the normal mechanics of life: it surges out of the past as a symbol of barbarism, darkness, and a time before civilization and suggests the immediate and inalterable cessation of history as apocalypse. In this way, the imaginary of epidemic compounds the pervasive sense of apocalypse that has hovered over narratives of very recent global history, which as a consequence seems to unfold in a series of ever-escalating crises. An epidemic materialist historiography brings into view a nodal temporal map of the shared precariousness of progress and order—the constant threat of something nascent or endemic exploding with new force out of the local and into the global, laying waste not just to the material facts of progress, but also to the very idea of it.

I've organized the book in three parts, each corresponding to a moment of anti-imperial violence in the porous and shifting geography of the "Islamic" world as it is constituted by the lexicon of global crisis: oil crisis, health crisis, the crisis of statehood, terrorist crisis, and so on. The parts can be read serially, to reveal a two hundred–year literary and discursive history, or as standalone contributions to their respective periods and areas. Part 1, "The Disease Poetics of Empire," is grounded in the nineteenth-century British colonial sphere; part 2, "The Body Allegorical in French Algeria," examines the resurgence of the epidemic trope in the struggle for Algerian Independence; and part 3, "Viral Diaspora and Global Security," addresses the globalization of colonial narratives, population management strategies, and discourses of public health, particularly with regard to the South Asian Muslim diaspora. In the first chapter, "Great Games," I juxtapose the narrative of Osama bin Laden's capture in Pakistan in 2011—an operation in which, it has been claimed, a sham public health campaign played a crucial part—with a recapitulation of the imperial politics, colonial sciences, religious pilgrimages, rail and road travels, and epidemic figures at play in Rudyard Kipling's indelible novel, *Kim*. Chapter 2, "The Blue Plague," centers on close readings of nineteenth-century administrative and medical reports on the "blue plague" or Asiatic cholera in India, the Middle East, and Europe. Here, I show how colonial science writing and early epidemiological literature provide a template for later writing about disturbances, disorder, and outright revolt in the colonies. I track rhetorical patterns and literary forms that consolidate a geographically determined, and later a racialized and Islam-identified, notion of contagious vectors attached to religious pilgrimage, migration, and military and trade movements. Part 1's final chapter, "Circulatory Logic," revisits *Dracula* and its relationship to Stoker's minor works, then-contemporary science, the fear of a dissolving empire in Britain, and the politics of migration and global liquidity at the turn of the last century. I argue that the novel is a work of both epidemic and colonial literature, and one that enjoyed an extensive second life in the early years of the global War on Terror, including a veritable culture industry of vampire fiction in television, literature, and film.

Part 2 shifts to colonial Algeria. The fourth chapter, "The Brown Plague," reconfigures our understanding of Albert Camus's great novel *The Plague* (*La peste*) not just as an allegory of the Nazi occupation of France, as has often been suggested even by Camus himself, but rather as a dispersed mosaic of the chaotic postwar period, including, crucially, the acceleration of the Algerian struggle for independence. The Algerian context, though it is only obliquely named in the novel, appears in Camus's journalistic writings on Algeria from the period, which I read as a crucial moment in the genealogy of analytic writing about colonial crisis and epidemicity. Chapter 5, "Algeria Ungowned," extends the argument about colonial crisis and epidemicity into the wartime writings of Frantz Fanon and Algerian revolutionary Djamila Boupacha, illuminating an under-studied antienlightenment scientism in the work of the former and an anticolonial poetics of the body in the latter. This chapter focuses particularly on the relationship between epidemicity and the gendered morphology of the medicalized colonial subject from the anti- and decolonial perspectives, and advances an argument about the centrality of the Algerian precedent to the American War on Terror by way of a reading of Gillo Pontecorvo's *The Battle of Algiers*, famously screened at the Pentagon in 2003.

Part 3 moves into the postcolonial/neoimperial present and a consideration of global Islam and its constructedness in the West by way of some of the most visible narratives hailing from the Indian subcontinent and its Muslim diaspora. The sixth chapter, "Selfistan," begins with the conceptual and political problem of Kashmir and addresses the arc of Salman Rushdie's literary output, the evolution of which from the 1980s to the present indexes an important transformation from postcolonial migration and diaspora fiction to millennial personal security memoir. Documenting the parallel transformations in Rushdie's deployment of epidemic figure and form from *The Satanic Verses* to *Joseph Anton*, I argue that the anthropomorphic globe that emerges in late twentieth-century "world" literature—and Rushdie's work in particular—can be best understood as a neoimperial concept encased in alibis of biological emergency. The final chapter, "Cures from Within," relocates the *9/11 Commission Report*, a surprise bestseller and notably readable government document, as an inheritor of colonial epidemic narrative and colonial state historiography. Pinpointing the rhetoric of contagion, diagnosis, and cure, I demonstrate the discursive and political consequences of conceiving the

War on Terror through the organicizing model of global health security and the sciences that comprised and continue to influence its study. I read these tendencies against the rhetorical and literary decisions in *The Senate Intelligence Committee Report on Torture*, and the meditations on the specialized vocabulary of the War on Terror by contemporary poet Solmaz Sharif. *Epidemic Empire* can be moved through in order, by parts, or by grouping chapters on the literary and the nonliterary materials. My readings of Kipling, Stoker, Camus, and Rushdie (Chapters 1, 3, 4, 6)—founders of discourse, in Roland Barthes's terms, whose impact on literary fiction and the public imaginary has far exceeded their historical and geographic origins—situates these lionized writers in a multivalent epidemic discourse grounded in colonial science. Chapters 1, 2, 5, and 7 deal with these questions by building and analyzing nonliterary and paraliterary archives.

As I finish this book during what we all hope is the peak of the global COVID-19 pandemic, the objects of my analysis are still very much in motion. During any given week in the research and writing of these chapters, new terror attacks, new theories and approaches to violent extremism, new national and international security tactics, new uprisings, bombings, drone strikes, humanitarian interventions, enhanced interrogations, extrajudicial murders, renditions, arrests, detentions, trials, cyber and biological aggressions, legislative measures, and hate crimes came to light. Al Qaeda was eclipsed by the Islamic State, which, at the time of writing, is once again on the rise in Syria. In coming to light, the mobile text of twenty-first-century terror necessitated constant reframing both in public and policy terms, and in scholarly ones. Even more crucially, well after the Declaration of Alma Ata committed global actors to victory over communicable disease, we have seen in the last decade large-scale outbreaks of new viruses like Zika, SARS, Middle East Respiratory Syndrome, rapidly evolving strains of highly infectious and fatal influenzas; multi-drug-resistant tuberculosis in Eastern Europe, India, and South America; and a massive resurgence of older communicable diseases like cholera, polio, and tuberculosis.[63] Our world is currently being utterly reordered by the novel coronavirus. In tandem with these real events has been the burgeoning of the terrorism and apocalypse plots in literature, television, and film; they are and will have been epoch-defining mythemes. From Habermas to Soderbergh, philosophers, critics, authors, directors, and show-runners with a "global" audience found themselves compelled—for mercenary reasons as much as intellectual ones—to produce "content" about terrorism, Islam, catastrophe, contagion, and the intersections between them.

A tonal shift can be observed in the nature of these stories in parallel with the political moments they reflect. What began under the Bush administration as an emotional, nationalist incarnation of the master narrative of East-West incommensurability and conflict gave way during the Obama years to a more rhetorically tempered approach to preventing terrorism and eradicating the "spread" of its ideologies through domestic and international surveillance, a suite of new intelligence programs in collaboration with large, heavily armed urban police forces, and ongoing ground war, assassinations, and surgical strikes against Al Qaeda and ISIS targets and others. We find ourselves now in a full-blooded resurgence of an earlier incarnation of American xenophobia and pandemic anxiety, this time attached to the rise of so-called populism, white supremacy, neo-Nazism, neofascism, state-sanctioned misogyny, anti-Black and anti-Latinx hatred, immigration criminalization, and concentration camps on our borders. If recent observations hold, the literature, television, and film history of the Trump moment is likely to follow the dystopian lead of fictions chronicling life under neofascism, pumped up by the near-total emergency of the COVID-19 pandemic. I've written this book to reckon with the history I have been living, as an American Muslim, since the morning of September 11 in New York. The violent, indefensible response of the country I was born and raised in shaped the course of my career and my research. I close the chapter of my life spent on this project just as we begin to reckon with the distant and proximate effects of an unprecedented worldwide health emergency. I hope, therefore, that this book will inspire further research and provide a solid foundation for those who undertake it.

PART I: THE DISEASE POETICS OF EMPIRE

CHAPTER 1

Great Games

The whole earth is our hospital
Endowed by the ruined millionaire,
Wherein, if we do well, we shall
Die of the absolute paternal care
That will not leave us, but prevents us everywhere.

T. S. ELIOT, "EAST COKER"

I too believe there is some ulterior motive behind the Doctor's agitation.
He talks about the Baths, but what he's really after is revolution.

HENRIK IBSEN, *AN ENEMY OF THE PEOPLE*

In July 2011, about two months after "Operation Neptune Spear" ended with the killing of Osama bin Laden in a residential compound in the Pakistani hill station of Abbottabad, it was widely reported that a key United States asset in targeting the Al Qaeda leader had been a Pakistani doctor, Shakil Afridi.[1] A state surgeon in the Khyber Agency of the Federally Administered Tribal Area (FATA), Afridi apparently supervised a Central Intelligence Agency–backed hepatitis B vaccination program as a cover for the collection of crucial information—including blood samples—in the area where bin Laden was thought to be hiding. The campaign reportedly began in one of Abbottabad's most impoverished districts, where health workers from the region, including Afridi himself, stopped people on the street and knocked on doors to determine the immunization status of the city's poorest residents, offering free tests when necessary. Journalist Matthieu Aikins reported in late 2012 that Afridi's vaccination team was instructed to perform rapid hepatitis tests, requiring a small blood sample, on patients who agreed to the vaccination. Patients who tested negative were to be immunized by injection; nurses would administer the first of three shots immediately, and two more on a one-month and six-month follow-up schedule. Afridi would then collect the used tests, along with the identifying information attached to them, and turn them over to American handlers.[2]

As with many public health campaigns in the area, the team targeted unimmunized children. One of the nurses Aikins interviewed said she gave oral polio vaccines to seven children at the suspected residence of the bin Laden family the year before.[3] According to a similar account by the *New York Times* reporter Mark Mazzetti, US intelligence operatives hoped that it was among these children that they would find genetic confirmation—from blood samples—of the presence of the bin Laden family in Abbottabad before carrying out an illegal military operation within Pakistan's borders.[4] DNA from bin Laden's sister, who died at Massachusetts General Hospital in Boston the previous year, was to be used as the basis for a match. It remains unclear whether such genetic evidence was collected, but the timing of Afridi's team's reported visit to bin Laden's home between April 21 and April 27, 2011, and the directive two days later to carry out the raid that would kill him, has suggested to some investigators that actionable information collected through or adjacent to the fake vaccination campaign likely played a role in the decision to carry out the targeted killing.[5] By most accounts, the vaccination program was abandoned once the operation was brought to a successful close, leaving many patients only partway through a full vaccination course, effectively unimmunized.

Nearly a decade after the fact, there remains a great deal of confusion and conflicting information with regard to Afridi's role in locating and targeting bin Laden. Most of the official record will be classified for years to come, and very few intelligence officials in the US and Pakistan have been willing to speak on the record about what some authorities believe is a long-standing collusion between higher-ups in Pakistani, Saudi Arabian, and US intelligence. A staggering volume of resources has been poured into creating, interrogating, and defending the narrative of the reviled Al Qaeda leader's death as the inevitable denouement triggering what was supposed to be the final act in the War on Terror. Irrespective of its verifiability, the consequences of the vaccination ruse story are profoundly material. Specialists in infectious disease from around the world have noted, in the wake of the CIA-backed vaccination scandal, the exorbitant price paid by those caught in the crosshairs of the War on Terror: in addition to the hundreds of ordinary people abandoned with compromised immunization status, local and international public health workers in Northern Pakistan and Afghanistan, already subject to suspicion and aggression by the Taliban and its affiliate groups, have been targeted by the dozen in the years since the operation.[6] Following these attacks and in the ever-shifting landscape of insurgency and counterinsurgency, the nonlethal "information operations," and putative state-building enterprises undertaken by the US military and its contractors, polio—a disease that had been effectively eradicated—is once again endemic.[7]

Building on Ranajit Guha's foundational work on colonial historiography, this chapter interrogates the War on Terror's farrago of public health operations and military intelligence in Northern Pakistan and Afghanistan by positing the imperialist origins of a concept of global health, born out of the cholera crises of nineteenth-century British India. The discourse of colonial medicine and insurgency from the mid-nineteenth century reemerge and shape contemporary geopolitical narratives, particularly those about Islam and terrorism in South Asia and the South Asian diaspora. The conflation of Islam and anticolonial violence and the association thereof with the mechanisms and metaphors of contagion first emerges in the official, historical, and fictional documentation of the 1857 Indian Mutiny—the First Indian War of Independence, as Karl Marx styled it. It also haunts Rudyard Kipling's enduring novel of the imperial contest over these same regions, *Kim* (1900), which stands as an emblematic text in the association of anticolonial rebellion and epidemic disease. Despite the many doubts and lingering questions about the veracity of the vaccination campaign ruse, accounts of the capture of Osama bin Laden—and the role of public health workers in it—borrow from and exist because of strategies of figuration at play in the historical and fictional record of the Mutiny. The "great game" in which Kipling was both player and chronicler is not only still under way in the northern reaches of the subcontinent, its rules also determine how we have told and interpreted the history of the War on Terror.

Health Imperialism and the War on Terror

Afridi's reported participation in the bin Laden raid did not yield good results for him or for the residents of Abbottabad—not only was the vaccination scheme abandoned before it was complete, but Afridi also found himself in the midst of conflicting criminal charges and a multiyear diplomatic snarl. News of his cooperation with the CIA emerged when he was arrested by the Pakistani Inter-services Intelligence Agency (ISI) and held on treason charges soon after the bin Laden operation. Through the vicissitudes of what a number of news outlets have pointedly described as "colonial-era tribal laws" that are still in place in some areas of the North West Frontier Province, Afridi was tried without a defense attorney or jury. The charges against him were not for treasonous cooperation with the United States, but rather for conspiring with and supplying medical treatment to the militant Islamist group Lashkar-e-Islam, currently banned in Pakistan and labelled as a terrorist outfit.[8] Afridi was sentenced to thirty-three years in prison, and although the conviction was overturned and a retrial ordered in 2013, he has since been held in Peshawar Central Prison on murder charges for the death of a patient he treated in 2005.[9]

For some time, the doctor claimed to have had no contact with CIA handlers, but officials in the US government stated that Afridi had acted on behalf of the United States and that the CIA had planned the hepatitis B scheme in Abbottabad.[10] In 2012, former defense secretary and CIA director Leon Panetta affirmed that Afridi had "helped provide intelligence that was very helpful with regards to this operation" and called his imprisonment "unfortunate," arguing that Afridi had not acted against Pakistan, but had provided crucial assistance in an operation that benefited both nations.[11] In 2013, the Senate Appropriations Committee cut Pakistani aid by thirty-three million dollars per year, reflecting the thirty-three-year duration of Afridi's sentence, in order to remind Pakistan of the economic necessity of its full cooperation in the War on Terror.[12] In a bizarre turn in US electoral politics, then–presidential candidate Donald Trump took up Afridi's cause in an interview in April 2016, declaring that if he were elected, he would achieve Afridi's release "in two minutes."[13] In early 2020, Afridi began a hunger strike to protest his continued imprisonment.[14] Pakistan's Interior Minister Nisar Ali Khan responded, "Contrary to Mr. Trump's misconception, Pakistan is not a colony of the United States of America."[15]

Khan's response is stunningly simple and direct, invoking both the monumental historical fact of decolonization even as it conjures the de facto continuation of empire. It is obvious enough that Panetta and the CIA's discourse of cooperation, alliance, and mutual benefit upholds the fiction that the United States–led wars in Iraq and Afghanistan are in service of a universal humanity, that they benefit the globe, that they seek to preserve everything that is not-terror. Nonetheless, Khan's reply—his recourse to the status of Pakistan as a presumptive colony of the United States—speaks in a not entirely different vocabulary of states' rights, dignity, and political sovereignty, adding that "[Trump] should learn to treat sovereign countries with respect."[16] Khan further elucidates one of the key factors that distinguishes postcolonial neoimperialism from its forebears, namely the ransoming of sovereign politics against foreign aid: "The peanuts that U.S. have given us in return should not be used to threaten or browbeat us."[17] Khan's criticism, in line with many other such statements from Pakistani officials in recent years, points a finger at more than just a powered-up liberalism; here he speaks not only of the conjoined "free-trade" and development complexes, but also of the leveraging of military aid and the intertwining of state, contract, and other security apparatuses in effectively occupied territories.

Such references to the historical present of colonialism, and critiques of the particular interlocking mechanisms of market, military, and development annexation under the ideological guise of "spreading" freedom, democracy, and rights, and respecting sovereignty, are pervasive not only in the statements of Pakistani and Afghani officials, but also in communiqués and media output from Al Qaeda and the Islamic State.[18] In a "letter to the Americans" published online in 2002, Osama bin Laden wrote, for example,

> You have claimed to be the vanguards of Human Rights, and your Ministry of Foreign Affairs [sic] issues annual reports containing statistics of those countries that violate any Human Rights. However, all these values vanished when the mujahidin hit you [on 9/11], and you then implemented the methods of the same documented governments that you used to curse. In America, you arrested thousands of Muslims and Arabs, took them into custody with no reason. . . . What happens in Guantanamo is a historical embarrassment to America and its values, and it screams into your hypocritical faces: What is the value of your signature on any agreement or treaty?[19]

Although neither colonialism nor imperialism are key terms for bin Laden in any of the statements delivered from the mid-1990s to the mid-2000s, he here deploys key moves from midcentury critiques of colonialism and imperialism, seen in the writing of postwar thinkers like Frantz Fanon, Albert Memmi, and Jalal Al-i Ahmad, all three of whom reverse colonialist fantasies of the diseased spaces of the East and South to point back to the destructive and senseless violence of the colonial endeavor.[20] Bin Laden's communiqués also rely on the rhetorical watchwords of US liberalism, citing international human rights regimes, the sanctity of the agreement or treaty, and due process. Over the last decade and a half, canny critics have noted the extent to which the central conceptual terms on both sides of the War on Terror are at times nearly indistinguishable; this, they suggestively note, may be both accidental and strategic.[21] Dignity, rights, reason, the rule of law, economic and political sovereignty, democracy, occasionally (and perhaps unexpectedly) secularism: the vocabularies of "terrorism" (at least in the forms attached to the organized entities of Al Qaeda and ISIS) and liberalism, these critics argue, share many central concepts and positions. We can observe in these overlaps a kind of conceptual analogue or shunting into language of the arms race, where an impoverished political vocabulary expresses the immanence of US imperialist rhetoric and its definitions of statehood, rights, property, and law. Extending this relationship into internal US relations, the online English-language magazine of Al Qaeda, *Inspire*, frames a 2015 article, "The Blacks in America," on police killings of African Americans, in terms of a shared history of colonization and racist dehumanization under British and American colonialism, calling on Black Americans to rise up, promising, "[W]e will take practical steps to avoid targeting you in our operations."[22] ISIS has famously continued this strategy in its online and in-person recruitment, most memorably in the YouTube speeches of US citizen Anwar al-Awlaki, also killed in a targeted assassination by US forces in 2011.[23]

That bin Laden, Khan, Al Qaeda, and ISIS orators and media strategists found recourse in a critique of colonialism to contest American intervention overseas was hardly surprising; this rhetoric is a historically powerful resource in stoking nationalist and other forms of resistance to both settler and nonsettler interference in politics, trade, and daily life. The narrative and linguistic patterns of anticolonial rhetoric, including the kind of cross-racial, trans-geographic, and trans-temporal analogies we see above, have also, for more than a century, galvanized populations not only against colonialism as such, but also against continued exploitation under trade agreements, structural adjustment programs, and the violence and forced displacement of military occupation. What I want to point out in a detailed way is the persistence and political efficacy of the colonial dialectic and its underlying ideology, even for commentators from the anti- and postcolonial world, even after decades of robust critiques of the de-specifying and ahistorical penchant for "crying colonialism" everywhere, which risks overlooking the particular historical and material conditions of historical and actually existing colonialisms.

For better or worse, actors and observers of many persuasions understand the War on Terror as a colonial war.[24] While robust anticolonialisms continue to thrive elsewhere, a preponderance of the revival of anticolonial discourse in contemporary global politics can be seen as emerging from what we can loosely call the "Islamic world." Its fragmented geography has thus consolidated a sense that the entire Islamic world from Indonesia to Dearborn, Michigan, constitutes a new kind of colonized space. Under these circumstances, the global Islamicate in its many forms has sought or occasioned the recentering and redefining of colonialism and its descendants in a manner that at least attempts to be adequate to the supranational aims, financial motives, and ideological scaffolding of the War on Terror. The consequences of such a redefinition are equally promising and threatening. On the one hand, we might imagine a federated *ummah*, the world's most impoverished peoples, a huge proportion of whom are Muslim, rising up against this not-yet-eradicated colonialism. On the other, of course, are ISIS's claims to sovereignty over prenationalist (but so far contiguous) geographies under the guise of anticolonial politics; the promised caliphate of a distant future brought violently into the present in new inflections in Syria and beyond. What is especially interesting about the Pakistani official's refusal to be treated as a colony of the US is that it necessitates both a redefinition and a historiographic return: for Khan, the lived fact of a postcolonial nation's independence appears to be once again in question, casting doubt on the twentieth-century histories of decolonization and raising new questions about what colonialism was or is.

However off-hand or casual his remark may have been, Khan voices a widely held belief among many critics of the global order in the years after September 11, 2001: that colonialism has never truly gone away, that its motives may have taken different forms, its enemies different names, its cartography different shapes, but that the imperial reach of the United States departs only in very superficial ways from the practices of the great nineteenth-century colonial enterprises, particularly those of Britain and France. It follows that the annexation of postcolonial economies by international financial institutions and multinational corporations centered largely in the US, France, and Britain is not some new and monstrous form of liberalism; rather, it is the very brief moment of noncompany rule, if the Indian example can function synecdochically, that stands as a historical anomaly in political modernity.[25] Such contentions have been the daily fare of left cultural and political analysis over the last twenty years, inflected differently from day to day with rage and resignation. In this way, thinking the legacies of colonialism—especially in the Middle East and South Asia, where the US's lengthiest military engagements in history continue to drag on—has also become a surprisingly pervasive feature of the texture of daily life in the years since September 11.

What I want to suggest in this chapter and this book is that the force of such observations lies not in loose analogy, but in the specific mechanisms, both narrative and material, of neocolonial policy and practice. With regard to the specifics of narrative, the story of bin Laden's killing can be understood as an exemplary moment in the War on Terror in a number of ways. First, it represents one of the most decisive single events in an enormously diffuse, and oftentimes illegible set of actions: in this simple story, patterned on the *mission civilisatrice* narratives of nineteenth-century colonialisms, bin Laden plays the villain, the Pakistani intelligence apparatus, medical services, and armed forces the dupe, the Americans the hero. Second, it creates a sharp distinction between the Obama administration's approach to the war and that of the Bush and Trump administrations: where Bush's war was messy, costly, pointless, productive of a world of enemies, Obama's would be clean, smart, targeted, a veritable godsend to the incompetent but necessary ally of Pakistan. Lastly, bin Laden's death was, according to a number of commentators, one of the murkiest and most egregiously fictionalized moments in the war to date. In his 2015 account, "The Killing of Osama bin Laden," Seymour Hersh suggested its absurdity was such that "the White House's story might have been written by Lewis Carroll."[26] The emphasis in Hersh's telling on the mythic, the performative, the "fabrications," "lies," and "covers" offered by White House staff and counterterrorism officials, the "hoaxes," "fairytales," and "political theater" draws our attention toward broader questions having to do with the historiography of colonial warfare and counterinsurgency, to the narratives that are available to describe and also to carry out the War on Terror. I want to suggest that we can see this event—even as it exists in a highly contested discursive space—not just as exemplary in the War on Terror, but also as an expression of longstanding colonial narratives that bind military to humanitarian exploits, particularly medical interventions. This story and this practice impinge multiply on postcolonial sovereignty and contribute to both the actuality and the narrativization of counterinsurgency as a biopolitical, if not an epidemiological practice.

Making sense of the concept and historical event of Islamist terrorism and the military responses thereto requires that we seek not just historical parallels to colonial practice, as many commentators have done, but also attend to the continuities of colonial statecraft, including the management of colonial populations' health, and its inscription in colonial historiography. Such an undertaking promises to illuminate particular moments and patterns in colonial epistemology and rhetoric that have gone unnoticed or remained quarantined from the present, as if they were obsolete effects of a radically different paradigm of governance and an entirely other global order. It is one such area that I want to illuminate here: the discursive and narrative processes by which epidemics and political insurgency come to figure and materially shape one another in a remarkably persistent tautology. If we find the suggestion that forms of imperialism still structure North-South relations and heavily inflect the US's War on Terror to be a matter of tedious fact, then we should be as little surprised by the way in which the CIA employed the vaccination ruse to carry out one of the war's most extravagantly theatrical operations. This is because the conceptualization and epistemological framing first of world health and later of global health emerge from the immunological crisis of colonial contact.[27] The management of global

and potentially global epidemics is not just a figure for competing immunities, a metaphor for the struggle over the robustness and survival of
state forms; it is as central to the praxis of colonialism as is the extraction
of raw materials, the conscription of labor in various forms, the annexation of markets, and cultural hegemony.

Still, leading figures in global health insist on the extrapolitical
status of medical care not as an ambition, but as fact. Responding to
the revelation of the CIA vaccination plot, World Health Organization
spokeswoman Hayatee Hasan remarked, "[H]ealth interventions are by
nature apolitical. . . . We hope that this story does not prevent children
in Pakistan being vaccinated against polio, measles, and other vaccine-
preventable diseases."[28] Given the long and well-documented history of
the mutual buttressing of epidemic medicine and imperial projects, this
statement only makes sense as a normative one. Health interventions are
no more apolitical than epidemic diseases are ahistorical, which is to say,
they are constitutively political. Despite her intention, Hasan's claim for
a "natural" relationship between public health and politics serves most
pointedly to remind us of the long history of their unfortunate intertwining. Historically, public health interventions bear neither a simple nor a
consistent relationship to politics: the hepatitis B vaccination campaign,
whether fact or fiction, finds its place in a centuries-long record of politically motivated schemes that includes recent revelations of the UN's responsibility in Haiti's devastating cholera epidemic, the prohibitions on
religious pilgrimage in nineteenth-century India, the sanitary relocations
of post–Great Stink London, the eugenic and scientific pretexts for Nazi
genocide, the withholding of syphilis treatment in Alabama, Nestlé's
worldwide promotion of infant formula, the panic-laden homophobic
and racialized prevention discourse of HIV/AIDS, the involuntary sterilization of immigrants in present-day Israel. If there is indeed a "natural"
relationship between health interventions and politics, it is that public
health is always already political, precisely because it is organized around
the conceptualization, definition, protection, and betterment of various
"publics," each one of which, including the global public, is constituted
by its outside.

Hasan's indexical claim advances the mandate of the WHO, which
works on the premise that health is a "fundamental right" that ought
not be jeopardized by political aims and actions.[29] Her well-intentioned
sentiment and the terms of her argument were shared by dozens of NGOs
and other medical organizations in their responses to the CIA ruse, most
prominently Médicins sans frontières and the International Red Cross,
as well as by venerable medical and scientific publications like *Scientific American*, the *Lancet*, and the *New England Journal of Medicine*.[30] The

public outcry over the involvement of vaccine workers in the bin Laden raid brought about the end of the CIA's ruse-vaccination program, thus enacting, in a local sense, the norm Hasan sought to articulate.[31] A more pessimistic way to think about Hasan's claim is to understand it as a defense of the "natural" behavior of public health interventions, such that the vaccination campaign attached to the bin Laden capture stands as an exception or unnatural aberration. She wants, in other words, to dispel a belief in what both critics of global biopolitics and militant groups have called "health imperialism."[32] In the wake of nearly half a century of work on biopolitics, the notion that public health "transcends" the political, either as fact or norm, is both theoretically and historically insupportable.[33] Considered in the context of the longer historical frame, it also serves to uphold and revitalize a long-standing representational and semantic practice in colonial writing—both official and personal, administrative and imaginative—that collapses myths and images of natural disaster, particularly epidemic events, with that of political aberration or intransigence, thereby consigning acts of rebellion to a nonpolitics. Hasan's words strenuously insulate the medical from the political precisely because the historical record indicates their thorough collapsing.

Natural History: Irregular Warfare and the Banishment of Reason

In his important essay "The Prose of Counter-insurgency," Ranajit Guha identifies the historiographic strategy of naturalizing insurgency in colonial India as appearing more or less contemporaneously with the historical events themselves, especially in the context of peasant-driven insurrections like the Barasat *bidroha* (1831), the Santal *hool* (1855), the "Blue Mutiny" or Indigo Revolt (1860), and the Maratha uprisings (1875–1876). He derides what he calls the

> myth, retailed so often by careless and impressionistic writing on the subject, of peasant insurrections being purely spontaneous and unpremeditated affairs. . . . The omission is indeed dyed into most narratives by metaphors assimilating peasant revolts to natural phenomena: they break out like thunder storms, heave like earthquakes, spread like wildfires, infect like epidemics. In other words, when the proverbial clod of earth turns, this is a matter to be explained in terms of natural history.[34]

Guha identifies the many ways in which primary and secondary histories of anti-imperial uprising delegitimated peasant consciousness through a series of similes, elisions, and subtle logical leaps, providing obvious discursive cover for first an "aggressive, nervous" defense of empire, and later a "firm but benign, authoritarian but understanding idiom of a mature and self-assured imperialism."[35]

What appears most prominently in Guha's sequencing of the primary documents he reads—two short letters sent by a colonial official (1831) and an employee of the East India Railway (1855)—is a persistent metonymic slippage that belies historiographical objectivity by distributing ideas of motive and reason unevenly between conflicting parties. Insurgents are described as passive, wave-like, meteorological, miasmatic, by contrast highlighting the humanity, agency, and reason of their opponents, both those who fight them in the "present" of history and those who produce the historical record. The phenomenon Guha describes is limited neither to historical texts nor to counterinsurgent prose; it also turns up in revolutionary poetry and fiction. The Chartist poet Ernest Jones, for example, whose epic *The New World* (1851) predicted the rise of India against her oppressors, deploys many of the same strategies to point to the inevitability of a global revolt. The poem, republished in 1857 after the start of the Indian Mutiny as *The Revolt of Hindostan*, leans heavily on the naturalizing metaphors of insurgency throughout, even as it cheers, praises, and articulates the reasons behind the coming insurrection, whose unfolding is the poem's imaginative present. The poem begins with revolution against Europe's oppressors breaking out from America and Mexico to Africa, China and Japan, and finally in "Hindostan," where the "clouds stood gathering, tier on tier," where "thickening thunders" join "volcanic heat" as the people rise. "Scattered wars" are described as coalescing in a "final storm," beating back the British in "fresh waves," the "victorious deluge . . . from a hundred heights / rolls the fierce torrent of a people's rights."[36] These images of vast geologic and climatic consequence are not set up in contrast to reason, or in order to undermine specific grievances; Jones spares little time in imagining a tremulous confession from the colonial generals: "We murdered millions to enrich the few." Still, the revolution he imagines falls apart initially, as famine strikes and greed and hunger for power transfer down the line to native princes, nobles, "smiling traders," and the middle class, indicating both a jaundiced view of postrevolutionary history (in France, England, and elsewhere) as well as a measure of doubt with regard to what we now call the Global South and its capacity to enact a revolution founded in the erasure of class and exploitation. Jones, in spite of his broad enthusiasm for the possibility of a global rebellion against colonial exploitation, cannot, or simply does not imagine a consciousness for Hindostan. His naturalizing figures invoke the power and the majesty of a worldwide rising—indeed the poem is breathless in its desire to witness this inevitability—but they also undermine the agency and local energies of insurgent activity in India by reinscribing the dialectic of history as eternal, universal, natural.[37]

Guha doesn't address poetry or revolutionary writing in his essay, but it is instructive to note the extent to which Jones's poem shares with the rhetoric of counterinsurgency the features Guha describes as he reads the historical record. Looking at these texts together points up the persistence of an absent or deferred agency in the representation of colonial subjects' attempts to claim political autonomy and economic freedom and raises new questions about the difficulty of imagining revolutionary consciousness across racial and cultural divides. To return to Guha's "metaphors assimilating peasant revolt to natural phenomena," it is notable that the essay provides only a couple of specific examples, offering instead a broad account of how, in particular, the inscription of the Santal uprising by both British and Indian historians expunges the possibility of peasant consciousness by attributing the rebellion to the Adivasis' religious fanaticism. Guha writes, in the closing pages,

> it is not possible to speak of insurgency in this case except as a religious consciousness—except, that is, as a massive demonstration of self-estrangement (to borrow Marx's term for the very essence of religiosity) which made the rebels look upon their project as predicated on a will other than their own.[38]

Here, Guha suggests that historians on both sides deployed religious consciousness in a manner akin to the "natural phenomena" that figure all peasant insurgency. Although he lists thunderstorms, wildfires, earthquakes, and epidemics as prominent naturalizing metaphors, it is religion-as-self-estrangement that serves as his primary illustration of the assimilation of peasant consciousness into the unreason of natural disasters. In other words, the sharp and compelling observation with which the essay begins doesn't reappear as such in his reading of the documents except through the natural or naturalizing event of religious fanaticism, a kind of gripping or insurrection of the mind itself. If we stretch Guha's argument about the habit of historians to naturalize insurrection and imagine peasant rebellion as the proverbial turning of the clod of earth, and we take seriously his contention that one of these forms of naturalization is to render political objections a matter of religious fanaticism, we can see quite exactly the discursive origins of an epidemic approach to terror. Religion, cast as a form of natural catastrophe, is reincorporated not as a politics or even an expression of human agency, but rather as an extrinsic force that befalls the populace, grabs hold, spreads fast, must be contained and eradicated.

If epidemic—the last in the series of natural disasters—is an absent presence in Guha's account of the archive of the Santal *hool*, we can see the figuring of rebellion as contagion appearing with alarming consistency in the historical and fictional record of the 1857 Mutiny, where the language of natural disaster and epidemic is so ubiquitous that it ceases to register as figural.[39] Although it would be difficult to argue that what began as a series of military rebellions in the ranks of the sepoys (native soldiery) was, strictly speaking, a "peasant uprising," Guha's observations about the rhetorical mode of counterinsurgent historiography hold in this archive as well. This is true even in texts that forecast the Mutiny. As early as 1849, nearly a decade before the uprisings began, J. W. Kaye, the celebrated British military historian and then officer in the Bengal Army, associated dissent among the Indian troops with communicable disease. In his essay "The Romance of Indian Warfare," a rhapsodic account of the exploits of James Abbott—the same Abbott after whom the garrison town in which bin Laden was captured is named—Kaye writes that Abbott "chafed at the irresolution which pervaded the counsels of Lahore, and yearned for an opportunity to strike a blow at the rebellion which was gathering strength from immunity and rioting without control."[40] What Kaye means by "immunity" here does not obviously include the philosophical adoption of the term as inoculation through exposure or limited incorporation that we associate with it following Derrida.[41] But his sense of the word isn't limited to legal immunity either, as we see in the next sentence, where he first articulates an idea that will endure in his thinking about Indian uprisings and the British responses to them. Here he declares, "Nothing is more contagious than rebellion."[42] In the context of the late 1840s, it is impossible to think this remark apart from the continual waves of epidemic cholera that took millions of lives in the Indian colony and posed a constant threat to British armies and trade endeavors, as well as nearly constant outbreaks of malaria, tuberculosis, and various other fevers. Dealing with cholera, and dying from it, was, from the moment of the 1817 outbreak, more or less a seasonal fact of military life in India, far more so than the suppression of aggression, revolt, resistance, or unrest with which it was symbolically associated. It's an astonishingly durable association, but Kaye, writing before the Mutiny, doesn't make as much of it as later writers would.

Kaye's key successor in the writing of mid-nineteenth century British military history in India was G. B. Malleson, adjutant-general of the Bengal Army in Calcutta, who finished composing and editing the six-volume account Kaye had begun: *Kaye's and Malleson's History of the Indian Mutiny of 1857–8.* This text details Kaye's sense of the causes of the Mutiny, which he attributes primarily to the colonial administration's inveterate Englishness and the actions of a few influential rebel leaders, mostly concerned for their own security and wealth. Again, there is little to suggest widely shared political or economic motives, from the Indian side, for the Mutiny.[43] The first three volumes, written more or less exclusively by Kaye, also continue the line of thinking that associated mutiny with contagion in the 1849 essay, citing, for example, in a section called "Outbreak of the Mutiny," a senior member of the supreme council who wrote of the growing unrest in Oudh, "The sooner this epidemic of mutiny is put a stop to the better. Mild measures won't do it. A severe example is wanted . . . I am convinced that timely severity will be leniency in the long run."[44] In his own independent writings on the Mutiny, Malleson took up the figure of epidemic and highlighted it as a kind of concept metaphor, titling a chapter in his own condensed and wildly popular *History of the Indian Mutiny of 1857* "The Spread of the Epidemic," and referring to a detachment of native cavalry as those to whom "the contagion had not yet extended."[45] In his much-contested but nevertheless widely read "red pamphlet," or *The Mutiny of the Bengal Army*, composed in the immediate aftermath of the uprisings in Meerut and Delhi, Malleson writes of the causes of disaffection in the native troops as stemming largely from what he calls "Hindu fanaticism" and its influence on the Muslim soldiery, proposing "remedies" for the "symptoms" of growing unrest and "outbreaks" of rebellion, specifically the purging of high-caste Hindu and Muslim troops from the native army.[46] Contemporary historians of the Mutiny, especially those imbricated in the military and civilian aspects of the conflict, wrestled to produce a coherent narrative of what appeared to be similar but disparate insurgent events that took place over two years and at vast distances from each other.[47] In the face of this difficulty, the epidemic metaphor offered a ready framework for understanding the relationship between distinct occurrences while also rendering them legible as instances of the same widespread phenomenon.

Writing for a broader audience, Karl Marx and Friedrich Engels observed the events unfolding in India in real time, chronicling in the *New-York Daily Tribune* the attack on Delhi and the siege at Lucknow from official communications and scraps gleaned from correspondents closer to the action. Marx, who penned the bulk of the writings, is characteristically concerned with the causes of the revolt, to which he lends ready support. Although his analysis is peppered with boilerplate racist descriptions of Indians' "undignified, stagnatory, and vegetative life," their "natural languor," their talents as "virtuosi in the art of self-torturing," their deprivation of "all grandeur and historical energies," Marx, unlike most of his contemporaries above, expresses fuller confidence in the reasoning—indeed, grants the existence of a reasoning—behind the sepoys' uprising.[48] He acknowledges but complicates, in his first dispatch of 1857, the familiar scandal of the regulation Enfield rifle, whose cartridges were alleged to be greased with pork and cow fat, as the catalyst for both Muslim and Hindu outrage among the ranks of the sepoys. Like Benjamin Disraeli, whose speeches he cites regularly, Marx understands the revolt not as a local grievance, but as the expression of a far more widespread and mature resistance to British occupation in India, as well as throughout the "great Asiatic nations . . . intimately connected with the Persian and Chinese wars" (36). The articles document the economic and political crimes of the plundering East India Company, both before and after the 1833 Charter Act, when its monopoly on trade was severely curtailed. Although he eschews the tendency of explaining the movement of insurgency in the native troops by way of the epidemic metaphor, Marx's reporting on the events highlights the specter of cholera that hangs over the British response and threatens to rout any plans for containment. Writing in July 1857, he notes the extent to which the British press downplayed the "ravages of this terrible disease," and predicts correctly what he will report two weeks later: that the forces besieging Delhi would be greatly diminished by its virulence, assisted by the summer rains. By September of the same year, he observes that "the present Great Mogul [Bahadur Shah], even more favoured than Napoleon, finds himself able to back the disease by his sallies, and his sallies by the disease" (87). Subsequent articles forecast a drawn-out campaign against the natives' "long and harassing guerrilla warfare," punctuated by the challenges of the "hot rains and swampy jungles" with "dysentery, cholera, and ague follow[ing] every exertion made by Europeans" (128, 154). If Marx did not intend to equate the waves of revolt breaking out across India with the ebbs and flows of virulent cholera, his writing nevertheless tethered the threat of the disease to the strategies and advantages enjoyed by the rebels. In these examples, we see evidence of the extent to which the depoliticizing, derationalizing organic figures of Guha's counterinsurgent prose—particularly the infecting epidemics he invokes—circulated far beyond the self-conscious inscribers of colonial history.

Stranger Than Fiction: Literature of Terror

The discursive and imaginative impact of the Mutiny far outstripped its significance in tactical terms. Its literary manifestations are legion, if the particular texts are largely forgotten; indeed, scholars Patrick Brantlinger and Gautam Chakravarty both begin chapters on Mutiny writing by citing

1.1 Anonymous, "Miss Wheeler defending herself against the Sepoys at Cawnpore" (ca. 1860). Private collection. Photograph: Bridgeman Images.

the same line from Hilda Gregg's 1897 *Blackwood's* essay "The Indian Mutiny in Fiction," which suggests that "of all the great events of this century, as they are reflected in fiction, the Indian Mutiny has taken the firmest hold on the popular imagination."[49] Christopher Herbert, approaching from a recuperative angle the material he believes has been treated with "condescension" and "systematic denigration" argues that "the epochal impact of the Mutiny on Victorian and post-Victorian consciousness can be meaningfully studied only by considering it not as a geopolitical event but as a literary and in effect a fictive one."[50] Alex Tickell cites the 1756 episode of the "Black Hole of Calcutta," in which nearly 150 East India Company employees and their companions were besieged in Calcutta's Fort William as an overture to the "terror aesthetics" of the British empire in India, which extended from that episode through the literary and historical inscription of the Mutiny and later nationalist uprisings and insurgencies, a verso of sorts to the more familiar heroic aesthetics of adventurous and picturesque life in the colonies (figure 1.1).[51]

Upwards of seventy novels constitute the literary archive of the Mutiny, and popular romances on the subject are as persistent in their reliance on naturalizing metaphors and the specter of epidemic as the histories. Philip Meadows Taylor's 1872 *Seeta* stands out as an exemplary triple-decker novel that both Gothicizes and sediments the epidemic trope as a way of thinking about the uprising, bemoaning the difficulty of "check[ing] an evil which is like the cholera or the small-pox, and seizes whom it will."[52] What first appears as an indiscriminate force of nature, the cholera or smallpox "seizing whom it will," later develops a demographic selectivity in the novel, which connects disease explicitly to religious fanaticism, as in the following scene depicting the galvanizing of the rebels:

> [F]rom all quarters of the camp, the Mussulman warriors rushed forward, and the men of the cavalry became infected, and in a short time the Moulvee had a thousand fanatics around him, to whom, standing on a low mound of earth, he delivered a short sermon . . . on the delights in paradise which awaited any who might become martyrs; and was answered by hoarse cries of "Ameen! Ameen!"[53]

Taylor's novel is so extravagantly riddled with cliché and stock phrases that, when read alongside the historical accounts, it is fair to say that the passage above gives voice to a set of shared ideas and perceptions about both the epidemic space of the Bengal Presidency and British India writ large, as well as to the infectiousness of an idea of Muslim "fanaticism."[54] So pervasive was the purported contagion of rebellion that Sir George Trevelyan felt compelled to weigh in on its explanatory value only in order to dismiss it. In his dark epic of the insurgency, *Cawnpore* (1865), in the chapter preceding "The Outbreak," he writes, "[T]he great crime of Cawnpore blackens the page of history . . . [T]his atrocious act was prompted, not by diseased and mistaken patriotism, nor by the madness of superstition."[55]

One might characterize Taylor's depiction of religious fanaticism, disease, and rebellion as prescient, but I want to argue something different: these accounts, produced in the three decades after the most transformative and widespread uprising in colonial India, do not anticipate but rather set the terms and install the attendant doxa for a reading of terrorist violence in the twenty-first century. The trifold representation of Islam, contagion, and insurgency is already a familiar strategy in the last third of the nineteenth century because it was part of the praxis of empire. The particular focus on the terror brought by orthodox sects of Islam, not long-implanted in India but lately imported there, also mark postmutiny fiction in ways that will be familiar to contemporary readers.

Robert Armitage Sterndale's 1879 *The Afghan Knife*, another three-volume Mutiny fiction, identifies Ahmad Khan's Wahhabism as the source of the rebellion sweeping the Bengal Presidency, and describes the growing disaffection as a kind of miasma, or cloud of disease:

The air was full of rumours, the land was unsettled. The faithful were domineered over by an alien race. The sword had been unsheathed at last, and there were not wanting those who loudly proclaimed that the time for the Muslim to awake from his helotism had come, and that he who hesitated was a renegade to his faith and people.[56]

The appearance of the disease metaphor is somewhat attenuated here, but it sharpens when one considers the fact that the novel's sympathetic and loyal native protagonist is a conscientious doctor who heals not just his own fellow Muslims, but also enacts an ideal British Indian universalism in his clinical practice. The presence of the Wahhabi figure as insurgent villain, stoking fanaticism in crowds of otherwise docile natives, is not unique to Sterndale's text; historian Julia Stephens has argued for the long-standing demonization of the figure she calls the "phantom Wahhabi," which "merg[ed] a kernel of reality with overblown paranoia [and] haunted the imperial imagination as the embodiment of the intertwined threats of religious fanaticism and anti-colonial resistance."[57]

Although the resonances with the contemporary narratives of terror are abundant, it is worth noting that what is a stake in these early accounts—Sterndale's, Taylor's, and Malleson's especially—is a far more evidently nationalist or protonationalist struggle than that which characterizes either the *ummah* invoked by Al Qaeda or the "caliphate" or Levantine empire called for by ISIS. And while moments that figure political unrest as epidemic are ubiquitous in British civil servants' histories and late-colonial romances about the Mutiny, it would be a mistake to argue that they are front and center in the thinking of these chroniclers. I don't mean to suggest that Kaye, Malleson, Taylor, Sterndale, and their fellow colonial subjects were engaged in a rhetorical campaign to associate anticolonial rebellions with the various fevers, plagues, and epidemics that befell colonist and native alike. This descriptive habit, rather, points back to the effects of Guha's casual midlevel observer, who belies his objectivity in naturalizing metaphors. We can imagine Pakistani interior minister Nisar Ali Khan and WHO spokeswoman Hayatee Hasan as the contemporary analogues of these semi-witting historians: actors whose modes of understanding and describing the problems of terrorism, postcolonialism, and global health participate in and sediment our ways of knowing. In situating the vaccination scheme and the killing of bin Laden within this frame, we can further see how narratives of colonial and neocolonial conflict project specific kinds of enemies, especially those not associated with a recognized sovereign state, as plagues, cancers, viruses, and infections in order to justify any and all means to eradicate them, as if their vanquishing were not a matter of war, but instead of global health. The consequence of this double naturalization is the depoliticization of conflict. Approaching it from this angle, we can read Operation Neptune Spear as the culmination of a discursive and epistemic history in which the dismantling of a colonial system cannot be delaminated from the development of a worldwide program of public health and its ways of knowing, reading, and narrating.

"An Interesting Allegory": Transmissibility

If I seem to make too much of these minor figures and obsolete texts, I turn by way of conclusion to Rudyard Kipling, a figure of incontestable significance in colonial literature and the imperial imaginary. Hersh and other critics have suggested that the story of Afridi and the sham vaccination campaign sounds quaintly and uncannily like fiction; this is in large part because the contemporary spy games and contests over ragged-edged sovereignty that we see unfolding in the northern reaches of the subcontinent are prefigured not only in the largely forgotten record of the Indian Mutiny, but also in one of the most widely read colonial novels of the early twentieth century, *Kim*. Following Jed Esty's prompt in his reading of *Kim*'s antidevelopmental narrative, I am interested in "famous books—visible islands in a vast sea of unread novels," which "tell us as much about canon formation as about the empirical reading practices or distribution of texts."[58] Where *The Revolt of Hindostan*, *The History of the Indian Mutiny*, the "red pamphlet," *Seeta*, and *The Afghan Knife* indexed the colonial disease poetics of the day, *Kim* consolidates and transmits them into a canon of imperial writing in far more lasting ways (figures 1.2 and 1.3).

Published as a serial in 1901, Kipling's most celebrated book relates a moment in British and Russian imperial machinations following the Crimean War and the Indian Mutiny. The "Great Game," as Kipling calls it, plays out in the same Central Asian and Northern Indian regions in which bin Laden was captured. Kipling's version of this period in colonial history is told through the itinerary of the young orphan Kim, son of a color sergeant in an Irish regiment, who attaches himself to a Tibetan lama and is subsequently conscripted into the service of imperial intelligence and espionage. Early in the journey of the lama and his chela, the two travelers encounter an old man who had served as a native officer on the side of the British during the Rebellion of 1857. The man tells them stories of his service during the Mutiny, and speaks of the evils of the time when "the land from Delhi south [was] awash with blood."[59] The lama remembers hearing rumors of this "Black Year," when violence overtook reason, and asks the old man, "[W]hat madness

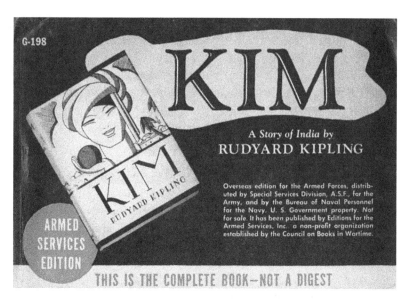

1.2 Rudyard Kipling, *Kim* (1944). Armed Services Edition (front cover). Photograph: Special Collections and Archives, Kent State University Libraries.

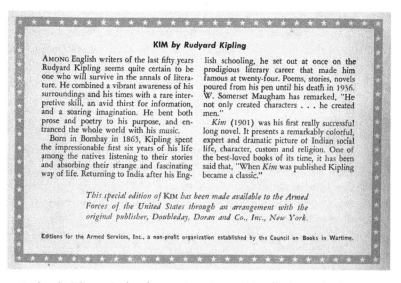

KIM by Rudyard Kipling

AMONG English writers of the last fifty years Rudyard Kipling seems quite certain to be one who will survive in the annals of literature. He combined a vibrant awareness of his surroundings and his times with a rare interpretive skill, an avid thirst for information, and a soaring imagination. He bent both prose and poetry to his purpose, and entranced the whole world with his music.

Born in Bombay in 1865, Kipling spent the impressionable first six years of his life among the natives listening to their stories and absorbing their strange and fascinating way of life. Returning to India after his English schooling, he set out at once on the prodigious literary career that made him famous at twenty-four. Poems, stories, novels poured from his pen until his death in 1936. W. Somerset Maugham has remarked, "He not only created characters . . . he created men."

Kim (1901) was his first really successful long novel. It presents a remarkably colorful, expert and dramatic picture of Indian social life, character, custom and religion. One of the best-loved books of its time, it has been said that, "When *Kim* was published Kipling became a classic."

This special edition of KIM *has been made available to the Armed Forces of the United States through an arrangement with the original publisher, Doubleday, Doran and Co., Inc., New York.*

Editions for the Armed Services, Inc., a non-profit organization established by the Council on Books in Wartime.

1.3 Rudyard Kipling, *Kim* (1944). Armed Services Edition (back cover). Photograph: Special Collections and Archives, Kent State University Libraries.

was that, then?" He replies, "The Gods, who sent it for a plague, alone know. A madness ate into all the army, and they turned against their officers. That was the first evil, but not past remedy if they had then held their hands."[60] The old man's words associate the Mutiny with a plague and a madness, a kind of parasite that "ate into" the army, and might have been "remedied" if the rebels had stayed their hands. Instead, he explains, "they chose to kill the Sahibs' wives and children. Then came the Sahibs from over the sea and called them to most strict account."[61] Here, Kipling figures the mutiny, in fact a series of violent episodes and sieges that began in Meerut and spread throughout Northern India, as a plague and a madness—something natural, like the trembling of the earth, another figure he uses to describe the uprising. But it is also, by Kipling's account, deliberate and human; the rebels "chose" to kill, and the Sahibs "called them to most strict account."

As if to embody the social unrest of his surroundings and the conflicted loyalties in which he is participating, Kim falls ill along with the lama, and it is only upon his healing that he can return to the service of the British. For Edward Said, it is Kim's experience of illness, even his near death, that serves to underscore the cultural liminality of his character—Kim is "like the epic hero," writes Said, "descended into a sort of underworld from which, if he is to emerge, he will arise stronger and more in command than before. The breach between Kim and 'this world' must now be healed."[62] Kim's healing does, indeed, allow him to reenter the world, but to reenter it as a survivor, immunized, as it were, against his own overweening sympathies for the Indian natives, his blind devotion to the lama, his loyalty to his friends over the crown—immunized, in other words, against not just his narrow worldview, but also against the plague of rebellion, the madness of Mutiny. The reward for Kim's intimate relationship with the land and its people, his vulnerability and openness to it, then, is a heightened immunity to its plagues and its politics. With this immunity also comes impunity. Though his loyalties are divided, Kim has positioned himself to be neither chastised nor punished in the ongoing struggles between colonizer and colonized; he is "friend of all the world," a reverse archetype for the medical double agents of today. Such impunity is achieved partly through Kim's alliance with the lama, whose search for transcendence takes him out of the material world, but it is also partly to do with his disavowal of the armed conflict side of colonial praxis. Instead, Kim prefers to move in the presumptively neutral sphere of information gathering, bringing the uncharted regions of the Subcontinent into the ambit of imperial knowledge.

An agent of the British project of mapping and military surveyorship, Kim stands as a proxy for the late-nineteenth-century sciences underwriting imperial power; as he learns his trades of cryptography, surveying, tracking, ethnography, geology, the reader is also inducted into the world of professional colonial intelligence. The elderly lama, whose health deteriorates as the novel goes on, appears and reappears as a kind of moral leitmotif, instructing Kim in the growth of the spirit—an obvious Orientalist's corrective to the hard, cold work of empire building. As Kim's two journeys—the spiritual journey to find the River of Arrow and the imperial quest to forestall a detachment of Russian spies in the foothills of the Himalayas—begin to reach their parallel conclusions, Kim must learn not only how to perfect his craft, but also how to care for the person he increasingly sees as a dependent. In Said's words, "Kipling was one of the first novelists to portray [the] logical alliance between Western science and political power at work in the colonies."[63] I want to extend this observation: it is the particular combination of spycraft and care that makes Kipling's fiction so instructive in an examination of the US's ongoing neocolonial wars. It serves as a striking demonstration of how the cross-pollination of science, insurgency, war, and the function of different forms of healing—both spiritual and bodily—mark narratives of turn-of-the-century colonial conflict as much as they do contemporary tales of counterterrorism.

In spite of the constant question of the lama's failing health, *Kim* is interested in more than just personal events of sickness and healing; the novel's conceptualization of time and space also draws geography, behavior, and politics into the dialectic of health and disease. Colonial-era chroniclers and contemporary historians of tropical medicine in both the East and West Indies have established the connection between colonial geographies and the epidemic imaginary; think, for example, of the environmental theses that motored many nineteenth-century sanitation reforms, or the very name of malaria invoking unhealthy climates—literally "bad air."[64] For most of the nineteenth century, India was strongly associated by the British, both those stationed abroad and at home, with rampant infection, illness, and unreason; even at home in the metropole, the East End of London, rather than the West End, was associated with disease and sanitation catastrophes in ways that seem to double the distribution of ill health in global space. Compounding the scattered uprisings in the colony were waves of epidemic or "Asiatic" cholera, which made their way to Europe from the Gangetic delta by way of British troops and ravaged the global population again and again. Kipling's novel offers a less Gothicized portrait of the land than some of his predecessors in Raj romance, for whom pathetic fallacy was something of an occupational hazard. Still, he registers the enormity of cholera's impact on this period in colonial history by identifying Kim's mother as a victim of the disease on the very first page of the novel. While the father died working on the railway, "the wife died of cholera in Ferozepore."[65] As specters hanging over Kim's life, his parents' deaths by railway and cholera reflect overlapping anxieties about travel and the circulation of both people and disease in the rapidly industrializing networks of colonial space.

Even as it registers a colonial dis-ease, a sense of menace, Kipling's novel maintains a soft-focus approach to the British Raj in India, full of what Said calls "the pleasures of imperialism." Kipling does not seem particularly interested in recording the hard facts of insurgency, or the violent side of the imperial spy games between Russia and Britain; cholera serves as a backdrop for an adventure plot, only reemerging in the soldier's offhand recollection of the Mutiny as a "plague, a madness." The same year *Kim* was published, however, Kipling revisited the felicitous analogy between the practicalities of administering empire and epidemic disease. In a pamphlet titled *The Science of Rebellion*, written for the Imperial South African Association in 1901, Kipling excoriated those British colonialists in South Africa who sympathized with their Boer neighbors in the Second Boer War. In an effort to rouse British support, and taking the view that nothing less than full loyalty to the crown would turn the struggle in the Cape Colony in their favor, he draws a comparison to tribal jihadists in Northern India:

> If you can imagine a Mahsud Waziri rising in fall [*sic*] swing with the heads of jirgas members of the Peshawar Club; the Mullah Powindah himself playing whist with the Commissioner of Peshawar, and all the priests who have preached the Jehad for the past sixty Sundays, calling on the wives of the Civil Service men, you will have some faint idea of the present situation.[66]

These comic scenes of rough tribals cavorting with the native and colonial elite in Peshawar, the mullahs paying a visit to the Memsahibs, are sketched as examples of maximum undesirability, to the point of preposterousness—so chaotic and dangerous as to be unimaginable ("if you can imagine"). Doubling down on his warning in an addendum, Kipling develops an extended metaphor for the "present situation" in Cape Town, under the auspices of what he calls a "sign":

> [T]hey wait, Rebel and Loyalist, for a sign.
>
> February 24
>
> It looks as though that sign had come. We have here a disease called the Plague—a new visitor—the outcome of filth and hidden dirt. It

is caused by rats that seep into men's houses and run about under the floors and presently die; one rat infecting the other. . . . Logically of course, the rat should only be disenfranchised, for Plague does not more than kill the body; and after all the present Municipality's notions of cleanliness are precisely on a par with the late Ministry's notion of loyalty. It is an interesting allegory.[67]

Kipling's "interesting allegory" evinces a more than passing interest in the representation of rebellion through the logics of science, and more particularly narratives of plague. We also see at work in this pamphlet the comparative nature of his thinking as he calls to mind the struggles with tribal warfare and jihad in Northern India. It is worth noting that this reference appears at the precise moment when his public would have been wrapped up in the serial publication of *Kim*, which was released in installments in *McClure's* and *Cassell's* from December 1900 to November 1901.

Later in his career, Kipling would return to the subject of epidemic and language, considering the capacity of words to transmit ideas. In a 1923 address to the Annual Dinner of the Royal College of Surgeons, Kipling confesses,

> I am, by calling, a dealer in words; and words are, of course, the most powerful drug used by mankind. Not only do words infect, ergotise, narcotise, and paralyse, but they enter into and colour the minutest cells of the brain, very much as madder mixed with a stag's food at the Zoo colours the growth of the animal's antlers. Moreover, in the case of the human animal, that acquired tint, or taint, is transmissible.[68]

For Kipling, the transmissibility of words and ideas renders language very nearly a material substance, one capable of acting on the body of the individual or the collective, one that can "infect, ergotise, narcotise, and paralyse." Looked at in one sense, this is why a rebellion can be allegorized as a plague. In another sense, it is why Kipling's own metaphors, and those of his historiographic and fictional predecessors, matter: because they take on a life of their own. "The acquired tint or taint," as he says, "is transmissible." Again, I don't wish to suggest that Kipling or his fellow colonial writers were the architects of a rhetorical campaign to associate either Islam or nationalist violence—or in some cases both—with epidemics. Rather, I want to highlight the self-conscious performance of a scientifically styled rhetoric that would establish the figural chiasm of epidemics and political insurgency that we find so firmly installed in the archive of colonialism and its aftermaths.

While his reputation has understandably diminished in the last half-century, it is important to recall the outsized significance of Kipling as a literary figure, public intellectual, and voice of British colonialism during his lifetime. On the occasion of the publication of the first installment of *Kim*, the editors of *McClure's* rhapsodized,

> Mr. Kipling stands today as the most forceful genius in English literature . . . [*Kim*] is the latest, longest, and most important work from his pen. . . . It is a masterpiece of literature which will make notable in the intellectual world the last year of the Nineteenth Century, so extraordinary for its literary achievements.[69]

Kim's place in the colonial canon has not wavered much since. It enshrines a place in colonial literature for the narrative and poetic possibilities arising from the juxtaposition of colonial space as simultaneously alluring and picturesque, but also insalubrious—a land poised on the verge of some great violence. *Kim* stands as a signal moment in the founding of this discourse, fed into by the primary and secondary documents that came in the aftermath of the Mutiny, and feeding back into the kinds of stories we can now construct about Islamist terrorism and neocolonial operations. In place of the spiritual journey undertaken by Kim and the lama in their search for the River of Arrow, the sham vaccination episode offers us humanitarian health work, antiepidemic care, and vaccination tours as soft covers for hard spy games. In place of Kipling's maps, topographical surveys, rumors, certificates of horse pedigree, Masonic credentials, and letters of introduction—the currency of nineteenth-century colonial espionage—we have public health, syringes, DNA, viral envelope proteins, targeted killing, and remote-control warfare.

Kipling's infectious words loom large, as well, in casual critiques of imperialism. As many critics of the humanitarian alibis for the War on Terror have pointed out, saving Afghani women, vaccinating Pakistani children, "Bring[ing] Back Our Girls" from the Boko Haram kidnapping sprees in Nigeria—these campaigns and their dissemination under US imperial practice and neocolonial warfare appear to be this century's version of the white man's infinite burdens.[70] Historian Alistair Horne begins his canonical account of the Algerian war of independence, the war that crystallized the relationship between Islam, political struggle, and terrorism in the twentieth-century global imaginary, with an epigraph from Kipling—not from *Kim*, but from the indelible poem, "The White Man's Burden: The United States and the Philippines." The epigraph of Horne's *A Savage War of Peace*, which takes its title from the second line below, reads

Take up the White Man's Burden
 The Savage Wars of peace—
Fill full the mouth of famine
 And bid the sickness cease.[71]

Over the last decades, scholars across the disciplines have turned their attention to the systematic effects of cultures of knowledge, narrative, and representation on the everyday practices of imperialism, but few have tracked the tenacity with which colonial encounters are organized around the putatively apolitical burden of "bidding the sickness cease."

A number of questions arise pursuant to this observation: where can we locate the "sickness" of or in colonialism? How do we imagine, or have we imagined, the desire for autonomy and other forms of insurgency, as something that moves or circulates like an epidemic? What are the stakes of the reappearance of this literary and historiographic tradition in contemporary narratives of the War on Terror? These questions teem beneath the surface not just of Mutiny fiction and Raj history, but also of a great many works of colonial, anticolonial, postcolonial, and neoimperial history and literature. In the next chapters, I will show how some of the key works—textual founders of discourse, in Foucault's terms—have responded to and rethought these questions. Whatever facts do emerge about Afridi's role in the bin Laden mission, or the efficacy of the fake vaccination campaign, the proliferating narratives of the War on Terror serve as a constant reminder of the unfinished business of postcolonialism as both a politics and a critical reading practice.

CHAPTER 2

The Blue Plague

Universal rebellion must arise from universal grounds for discontent or from streams deriving from many different sources, but finally merging into one, wide-spreading turbulent water.

SIR SAYYID AHMAD KHAN, *CAUSES OF THE INDIAN REVOLT*

The United Nations deeply regrets the loss of life and suffering caused by the cholera outbreak in Haiti. On behalf of the United Nations, I want to say very clearly: we apologise to the Haitian people. We simply did not do enough with regard to the cholera outbreak and its spread in Haiti. We are profoundly sorry for our role.

BAN KI-MOON, UN SECRETARY GENERAL

When it was first published, a 2017 article in the *New York Times* about new developments in cholera prevention began with a full-screen high-definition looping video: an aerial shot panned along three murky streams into dense greenery, the surrounding treetops darkened by occasional clouds that hung heavy in a gloomy sky. A "teaser" for the piece read "A global pandemic rose from these swamps. Now scientists may have a way to stop it."[1] The article, "Turning the Tide Against Cholera," now liberated from its thriller-like apparatus, nevertheless retains this sensationalist register, borrowing from the genre Priscilla Wald has called the "epidemiological horror story."[2] The gnostic register, the camera pursuing some indeterminate source, the preview-like cadence of the teaser—these details draw from the conventions of the global catastrophe film. Another narrative influence reveals itself in the opening lines, which place the reader on location, as it were, in the tradition of colonial adventure stories and travelogues. It reads:

Sundarbans National Park, Bangladesh

Two hundred years ago, the first cholera pandemic emerged from these tiger-infested mangrove swamps. It began in 1817, after the Brit-

ish East India Company sent thousands of workers deep into the remote Sundarbans, part of the Ganges River Delta, to log the jungles
and plant rice. These brackish waters are the cradle of Vibrio cholerae,
a bacterium that clings to human intestines and emits a toxin so virulent that the body will pour all of its fluids into the gut to flush it out.
Water loss turns victims ashen; their eyes sink into their sockets, and
their blood turns black and congeals in their capillaries. Robbed of
electrolytes, their hearts lose their beat. Victims die of shock and organ
failure, sometimes in as little as six hours after the first abdominal
rumblings. Cholera has probably festered here for eons. Since that
first escape, it has circled the world in seven pandemic cycles that have
killed tens of millions.[3]

An unreconstructed brand of Orientalist horror is immediately apparent
in the Indo-fantastic clichés like "tiger-infested mangrove swamps," in
the invocation of the "deep into the remote" Sundarbans, where "workers" were sent to "plant rice," as if to feed the heart of darkness or the
putatively preagrarian natives, in suppositions that—according with
the timeless, ahistorical East of centuries of European civilizational
Manichaeism—"cholera has probably festered here for eons." More subtly, the writer describes the symptoms of the disease in terms that are
consonant with the landscape he is painting: the "swamps" and muddy
runnels of the swampy jungle presage the "pouring" of bodily "fluids
into the gut to flush it out," while the "brackish waters" that "cradle"
the Vibrio cholerae herald the slowing of circulation, the black blood that
"congeals in [victims'] capillaries." The racialization of the diseased body,
common in earlier medical writing, reappears in the ashen pallor and
sunken eyes of cholera victims, ratifying an overdetermined image of
the colonized other as always already sickened and dissolute. The putative historicism of the article's opening lines is equally marked by inherited narratives of imperialist whitewashing: 1817 was indeed the year
of the first cholera pandemic, but it did not "emerge" or "escape" from
the site of its evolution unassisted. This was also the year that the East
India Company requisitioned the Sundarbans, declaring the mangrove
forests company property and ramping up logging operations, during
the course of which the "workers" mentioned above, actually colonial
troops, spread the infection far beyond its normal endemic region in
their tasks of conquest.

"Turning the Tide Against Cholera" is in many ways an ordinary record
of contemporary global health journalism. It chronicles field-changing
vaccine research that has been taking place in Vietnam and Bangladesh
over the last decades; a 99.9 percent effective treatment protocol, the

article trumpets with an astonishing tone-deafness, "was pioneered here." Infelicitous verbs aside, the *Times* piece offers a sharp example of the tenacity of colonial health rhetoric, shaped equally by bureaucratic observation, imperial romance, tropical medicine, and the epidemic thriller. Upamanyu Pablo Mukherjee has described the formative impact of this colonial practice of meaning-making as "the disaster ideology of empire," which he identifies as the foundational justification for the conceptualization of empire as the "palliative agent that eases the pains of those afflicted" by "natural" catastrophes like famine and disease.[4] Reinvestment in the abandoned disaster zone of postcolonial South Asia led to the creation of the Cholera Research Laboratory in Dhaka (then in East Pakistan) in 1960 by the United States as part of its Cold War–era soft diplomacy efforts. This hospital, now the International Center for Diarrheal Disease Research, is currently funded by the Bill and Melinda Gates Foundation; the cholera vaccine developed there was only recently made widely available after the WHO reversed its position on the benefits of vaccinating against cholera during the 2010 epidemic in Haiti. As is now well-known, cholera, which had been absent from Haiti for over a century, was likely brought to the island by United Nations peacekeepers from Nepal, who were deployed to assist in disaster relief after the earthquake earlier that year.[5]

Following the thread of this exemplary contemporary story, we can see how—even as the "natural" catastrophes and epidemic events that marked the everyday practice of empire and structured its narratives continue apace—the palliative function it correspondingly performs seems to have bisected its two main functions in the wake of decolonization. On the one hand, the "burden" of care—a long-standing justification for empire—has been outsourced to the advocacy and unsystematic benevolence of first-world and global actors operating with varying levels of good faith, even as rampant privatization of public services continues unchecked. At the same time, as the recent rise of neofascist and racist nationalism in Europe and the US reveals, a sense of the ongoing catastrophe that is the impoverished Global South and its incessant disease, failed economies, immigration policies, and policing and judicial systems works to shore up the boundaries of ever more fear-stricken state and multistate forms in the formerly and currently imperial West. One of the doctors responsible for the creation of the new cholera vaccine reflects on the long period in which it languished in the so-called "valley of death"— a period of time in which drugs and other biomedical products, though tested and produced in small quantities, are barred from mass production due to a lack of commercial interest and low or nonexistent profitability. He cites a failure not in medicine or in research, but in advocacy, which is to say, a failure in controlling and promoting the linked narratives of third-world development and first-world responsibility.[6] The ideas of quarantine and "global health" must be understood under the circumstances as both literal and figural.

The 2010 cholera outbreak in Haiti, which would eventually precipitate the mass production of the ready and effective vaccine, was both introduced by UN peacekeeping forces and eventually managed by the WHO and the Gates Foundation's Global Alliance for Vaccines and Immunization (GAVI), which guaranteed support of the production of the cholera vaccine, Shanchol, in India until 2021. In other words, the putative end of empire and subsequent hyperliberalization of global markets, including pharmaceutical markets, has also meant a challenge to palliative imperialism as a viable narrative, even for the United Nations, whose recent admission of responsibility for the Haitian cholera epidemic has raised questions about the advisability of peacekeeping interventions in other locations as well. The destabilized colonial rationale of bettering life for colonial and postcolonial subjects does not, however, mean that promoters of so-called health security have relinquished the insistent projection of postcolonial and failed states as zones of unending systems failure, ill health, and general catastrophe. The result, in the postcolonial moment, is the rise of a simultaneously bellicose and isolationist neoimperial catastrophism, even as the US wars in the Middle East and Central and South Asia drag on.

If the cholera vaccine stockpile continues to grow, cholera is likely to move towards near-total eradication in the coming years. The period of time bracketed by cholera's epidemicity, roughly 1817–2017, may then be understood as also bracketing a certain orientation toward the colonial enterprise, namely a secular form of ministration informed by modern scientific practice, as well as the first phase of epidemiology that was linked so strongly to the British Indian imaginary, and that made possible the idea of shared immunity as a stage in the conceptualization of a public health that could be considered global.

Even in the wake of the extraordinarily rich historical and literary work on cholera that has appeared in the last decades, it would be impossible to attempt a rhetorical and formal reading of two hundred years of cholera writing here. Instead, this chapter assembles an archive of particularly influential—as well as vivid and capacious—cholera literature by colonial administrators and doctors in India, as well as their counterparts in the metropole. My reading of these dispatches and reports show how the discipline of epidemiology is and ought to be broadly reconceptualized as inseparable from the management and inscription of nineteenth-century colonialism and its attendant sciences, both historically and in the present. Simply put, while there were certainly systematic studies of epidemics prior to the 1817 outbreak of cholera in the Bengal Presidency, the discipline-as-such came into being in response to cholera. It is yoked, therefore, to the "tiger-infested mangrove swamps" of the Ganges delta and the imaginary East that glowers and threatens the global body as much as to the famous Broad Street pump and John Snow's iconic morbidity maps of London's Soho. In this way, the science of epidemiology also entails narrative forms and reading strategies that emerge from the practice and poetics of the colonial encounter whether it is explicitly located in points of contact, or telegraphed in the always already peregrine figures of the diseased body and landscape.

In arguing for the constitutive role of Asiatic cholera in the formalization and institutionalization of the study of epidemics and the development of global health regimes from the late nineteenth century on, I mean to extend historian David Arnold's crucial observation that "Western medicine in India was a colonial science and not simply an extension or transference of Western science to a colonial outpost . . . [I]t . . . had grafted onto it ideas and concerns that had their origins in India or in Europe's Orientalizing of India."[7] I mean to suggest that not only is Western medicine in India a colonial science, but global health itself is also an Indian science, where India is taken to be a historical entity—first a corporation, then a colonial state, and finally postcolonial states—separate from both the precolonial empires and the postpartition nations. The narrative modes in which cholera was both produced and reflected are far more central to colonial literary history than has been previously suggested; as I have shown in the previous chapter, epidemic figures were a ubiquitous touchstone of colonial writing about the 1857 Mutiny in India and previous uprisings, and the consequences of this conceptual interpenetration have far-reaching and long-lasting effects. Articulating the relationship between colonial cholera literature and the politics it inscribes is therefore crucial to an understanding of how public health discourse and discourses of health security are deployed today, what presuppositions and histories are encoded in them, and how neoimperial rhetoric carries forward the alibi of healthfulness and a right to health in service of its own political ends and control of global resources and economies.

Sojourn in an Unhealthy Region

The first outbreak of cholera that was recognized as reaching epidemic proportions in India (1817–1821) is now understood to have emerged from the Ganges delta primarily by way of movement into and proliferation within the cities of Jessore and Calcutta, as well as by the East India Company soldiery and its rapid expansion and land acquisition efforts. In the popular imaginary, as in the scientific press, the epidemic would become associated with the "impenetrable and marshy jungles" of the Sunderbans and the "filthy" conditions of life in Bengal's teeming cities.[8] As the first waves of mortality broke out from Bengal all the way to Delhi, doctors and colonial officials struggled against "the constant defeat of their speculations" and attempted with energetic method and little luck to illuminate a subject "over which nature," as if out of respect for the distemper's modesty, had "thrown an impenetrable veil."[9] The earliest efforts to systematically study the outbreaks were particularly focused on atmospheric conditions, refusing to give credence, at least explicitly, to the contamination or contagion theories of cholera, largely due to the disease's surprising habit of breaking out in multiple places at once. Assistant surgeon and secretary to the Medical Board of the Bengal Presidency James Jameson, the so-called "father of Indian cholera literature," produced one of the earliest accounts of the epidemic in the colonial archive.[10] His *Report on the Epidemick Cholera Morbus* sought to ascertain the "hidden causes" of the "disorder," and to effect a "minute research" into what he called one of the most "abstruse operations of nature."[11]

The report begins with a preface recapitulating a brief questionnaire that Jameson dispatched in order to gather information about the early cases and treatment protocols that were undertaken throughout the presidency by army surgeons, European doctors, and unaffiliated Englishmen fond of dispensing medical advice and pet treatments. The text that follows is informed by, and in some cases excerpted from, the roughly one hundred responses. It instantiates a particular kind of corporate authorship in what is arguably the standard bearer of proto-epidemiological writing, drawing as much from the observations and prejudices of lay colonial gentlemen as from military and medical appointees of the East India Company. In synthesizing the voices of many men variously involved in the colonial enterprise, and stamping the dossier with the authority of Jameson's profession and station, the document serves as an exemplary discursive node for many tributaries of "the rhetoric of English India," as Sara Suleri has aptly called it, including the colonial sciences of military strategy, climatology, geography, and infectious disease theory.[12] In this way, the report acted as a crucial conduit, outfitted with the filter of Jameson's own distinctive prose, for the consolidation and further transmission of the rhetorical and narrative modes borne out of the region of cholera's endemicity.

Jameson's questionnaire emphasizes the association of the first epidemic with the movement of company battalions by focusing on the geographies that were brought into being, transformed, and rendered by the military mapping of colonial space. He anticipates the dispersed focus of later epidemiological studies in interesting, if infelicitous ways: rather than gathering information about symptoms or morbidity and mortality rates to start, Jameson's questions first highlight time and space as primary loci of epidemic legibility. The double focus on the location and temporal progress of cholera's appearance causes Jameson to pursue a detailed study not of human travel and intercourse, as would later become standard in the study of contagious epidemics, but rather of the meteorological conditions throughout the Bengal Presidency in the years of the epidemic. The report reflects the influence of miasma theory—the belief that disease spread by way of aerosolized filth from dirty areas—though Jameson engages his predecessors in the field with some trepidation.[13] He begins with a thorough accounting of ordinary and nonordinary weather, observing how the wind in the cold season

> begins to come round to the West and North; and to carry along with it the heavy masses of clouds, which almost constantly float about, and obscure the horizon, during the whole of the Rains. The atmosphere, from being very damp and watery, grows dry and elastic; and the heavens begin to brighten a little. But these appearances are not yet uniform; the sky still at times becomes gloomy and overcast; and heavy showers, accompanied by thunder and lightning, shew that the South East Monsoon has not yet finally taken its leave (xxxi).

The nonuniformity of the weather—the oscillations between its bright elasticity, stormy gloom, and the heavy masses of clouds in constant motion—is a familiar trope of the disoriented traveler's documentation of tropical space. Particularly of note here is the repetition of the "impenetrable veil" Jameson observes in the intellectual and scientific landscape of cholera research and the "obscure[d] . . . horizon" of the epidemic's season. Taken together, these details suggest an implicit understanding about the interpenetration of meteorological unpredictability and cholera's resistance to the tools of empirical science: both are in constant motion, both occasion rapid transformations and gushing deluges, both seem to laugh in the face of data gathering and its predictive function, both, in other words, express the terror of ungovernable space through the observed particulars of British Bengal.

Because of Jameson's conviction that the epidemic was attached to rapid changes in temperature and atmospheric dampness, both the beginning and the ending of the report are marked with a striking pathetic fallacy linking weather and notions about tropical geography and inscribing in the study of colonial disease the particular brand of Orientalist landscape with which the *Times* piece also begins. Compounding what he reads as the relationship between unseasonable weather and the epidemic's routes of transmission is what Jameson believes to be the indisputable preference of cholera to move "almost uniformly from East to West," while seeming to be "so bent on pursuing this Westerly course, that rather than deviate from it in an opposite direction, it would for a while desert a tract of country, to which it afterwards returned under circumstances more genial to its disposition" (96). If cholera indeed had a disposition for Jameson, it was somewhere between the "foul fiend," an indiscriminate "author of mischief spread[ing] universal terror before it" on the one hand, and a more pointed phenomenon that scholars of colonial disease have recently identified as a figure of colonial vengeance, which is prefigured in the report's confounded attempt to grapple with the meaning of the epidemic's Westward tendencies (37).

The second epidemic wave of 1831–1832 reached Europe, and so greatly sharpened the political stakes of the official narratives that would textualize the disease. Writing in 1831, James Kennedy of the Royal College of Surgeons in London sought to synthesize a number of recently commissioned East India Company reports on the outbreak for the general public in the metropole. The tone of his *History of the Contagious Cholera* is consequently less on-the-ground and less scientific than Jameson's, and more interested in cementing a set of causes that would be as little disruptive to British machinations in India as possible—including the priority of free trade—while also offering efficient cures.[14] Kennedy opens his history by repeating and underscoring Jameson and others' Westward progress trope, transforming it from a descriptive effect to the very reason for his work; its transmission to Europe is what piques his attention from London, and makes its application "more imperative" (i–ii). Even in a later section of the history in which he recounts the Eastbound progress of the 1817 epidemic, Kennedy is at pains to remind his reader that the attack "which commenced in 1830 demands the greatest share of attention" because it "overcame the natural and artificial barriers opposed to its progress and eventually succeeded in penetrating to the heart of Europe" (200, 212).

Kennedy borrows as well from two other standard prefatory moves in cholera writing, identifying the ancient aspect of cholera as it "had existed from the earliest ages," as well as the colonial adventurer's dismay upon arriving in the outpost, where "the malarious vapours are seen coiling themselves up from the surface of the land, which presents the unbroken aspect of an endless swamp, covered with low, black, impenetrable jungle" (viii, 2). If this weren't foreboding enough, he notes how the "current of [his] observation flows in a new channel" toward the "thousands of our countrymen [who] have been sacrificed to marsh fever," suggesting a continuity not just between past and present epidemics, but also the permanence of tropical insalubriousness in the form of geographical mortality mnemonics (3). Instead of finding the storied beauty and sublime adventure he expects, Kennedy warns his reader that

> the sojourner in this unhealthy region discovers, sooner or later, that the source of his best enjoyment must ultimately repose on the hope of returning in independent circumstances to his native land; and that the surest way of attaining the object of his wishes is to make himself acquainted with the general character of the Indian soil and climate, in order to avoid, as far as possible, the physical causes of the disease (5).

Enmeshed in this portrait of colonial horror is the metropolitan subject's disdain and pity not just for the natives of the "unhealthy" region, but also for those long-suffering men for whom retreat to cherished England was not and would not soon be possible if predicated on "independent circumstances" (5, 14).

Alan Bewell, in his important study *Romanticism and Colonial Disease*, chronicles the immunological fate of hundreds of thousands of European young men of unfortunate birth or sudden adversity whose health was ransomed for the project of empire, noting the prevalence in Romantic writing of the diseased body as a figure of migration and modernity, the insalubrious wages of economic liberalism.[15] Although Bewell's work locates the sources of the Romantic disease imaginary more firmly in the West Indian sugar islands than in the East, and in tropical fevers and tuberculosis more than in the cold bodily torrents of Asiatic cholera, the connections—especially between colonial writing and ideas of the infectious, florid, or decaying landscape—are for him undeniable in terms of their impact on both fictional and nonfictional writing of the late eighteenth and early nineteenth centuries. Neither do these "tropical" landscapes, which Kennedy records and Bewell analyzes, stay put; one of their most uncanny and disturbing features is the way in which they seemed—to nineteenth-century observers and sanitarians—to infest or inhabit English cities, particularly in the so-called fever-nests of the factory floor and the working-class neighborhood, which were described by both Engels and Dickens, among others, in terms of their warmth, dampness, crowding, and filth.[16]

The moral geography of Kennedy's *History*—where riverine habitats and rotting vegetation become coterminous with putrid habits and irrational beliefs—pervades our own contemporary epidemic literature.

Indeed, Kennedy's very language reappears in the *New York Times* text almost unchanged, as when he reflects on the 1817 cholera by situating its origin in the "Sunderbunds [which] are overgrown with wood, and inhabited only by tigers, reptiles, and such other denizens of the wilderness."[17] The "language employed in describing" this Gothic picture—spun out into a lurid landscape of the dead and the dying—he insists, is "not adopted for any motive unworthy of science, or in the slightest degree an exaggeration."[18] Nevertheless, the literary qualities of Kennedy's text hyperbolize the tendencies of those that fed into its production—the many official reports, largely produced by officers and doctors stationed in the colony—that he cites and summarizes throughout.

Published in London for a decidedly nonspecialist and noncolonial audience, Kennedy's text further enshrines the tropes of earlier reports along the textual transmission routes of empire. What differentiates *The History of the Contagious Cholera* from other contemporary writing on the subject is that even as Kennedy cautions against the ill effects of quarantine and sanitary cordons on free trade both within the empire and outside of it, his text is remarkably insistent on the contagious aspects of the disease, wagering in the very title of his work that the fractious debate between the miasmatists and contagionists that would consume the medical and sanitary fields for the next two decades was already over: cholera was contagious. In light of this conviction, it is the more remarkable that Kennedy's history plays so neatly into the discursive habits of imperial pathetic fallacy that associated the swamps, bad airs, and atmospheric vicissitudes of India with cholera in particular, and epidemics more broadly. Kennedy's text transforms Jameson's systematic study of climate—the predecessor of what would become a long-forgotten and now partially revalidated ecological approach to disease—into a textual atmosphere, as it trembles on the edge of an explosive move toward the primacy of human intercourse in the study of epidemics and other transmissible and broadly distributed morbid phenomena. In this way, Kennedy's text carries the residue of Jameson's epidemic ecology forward into the second stage of epidemiological writing not as scientific practice, but rather as a set of literary effects—images, tropes, and narrative forms— that would proliferate in imperial medical writing as it was conceived in and routed through British India.

Ships, Armies, Caravans, Fugitives, and Pilgrims

The impact of these expressive particulars on the discourse of cholera in the British empire and beyond is difficult to overstate. Reviewing Kennedy's book in the November 5, 1831, issue of the *Lancet*, published at the start of the first cholera epidemic in Europe, the editors of that storied medical journal cite the opening of *The History* as "not [its] least attractive pages . . . devoted to a bold and interesting outline of the topographical peculiarities which arrest the stranger's attention on his passage by the Sunderbunds, his darting through the Hoogly, and his settlement in Calcutta."[19] The review is not just favorable—although it does praise the volume as being "of greater public value than any other which this fertile subject has yet produced" (173)—it also borrows heavily from Kennedy's most evocative moments of prose styling, as well as from his synoptic form, an inheritance from Jameson's report. With the intellectual and scientific weight of the journal behind them, the editors write, in their own words, the story of the two first outbreaks in Jessore and Calcutta in 1817:

> Almost simultaneously with the irruption of violent cholera at Jessore, the capital of the Sunderbunds,—a desolate and marshy abode almost monopolised by the tiger and the reptile—the malady also made its appearance in Calcutta, and effected the most disastrous ravages in the pauper population of the city. (175)

The transmission of this minor trope—the ever-present swamps to which are added the persistent tigers—over the course of two hundred years of cholera writing from Jameson to Kennedy to the *Lancet* to the *New York Times* reveals two interrelated features of epidemic writing in the era during which a global conception of public health emerged: first, that the patterns of disease transmission create the material and bodily conditions under which textual transmission can be seen to follow the course of the disease itself, a discursive "Westward progress" from colonial outpost to metropole, and second, that even before its institutional coming-into-being, epidemiological science was historically, materially, and rhetorically inseparable from the British enterprise in India. To observe the itinerary of the single image from the Sunderbans of 1817 to 2017 is already to bear witness to the contagious behavior of choleric discourse, the machinations of human agency and imperial practice in the construction of the historiographical effect called "cholera." If the *Vibrio cholerae* bacterium had its origins in the climatological conditions of 1817 Bengal, then cholera, the concept, the historical phenomenon, the discursive and epistemological motor of infectious disease science in the nineteenth century, emerged from the "cradle of its birth"—not the eternal swamps, but the East India Company's zones of operation where conflicting immunities and incommensurable sovereignties battled along the sacred river banks at the Eastern reaches of the empire.

Kennedy would become a persistent figure in the translation of colonial medical writing to the capital and its consecration in the annals
of nineteenth-century epidemic literature. Two weeks after it published
the review of his book, the *Lancet*, ordinarily comprising letters, short
reviews, multiple studies and essays, devoted an entire issue to a single
article on Asiatic cholera. "History of the Rise, Progress, Ravages, &ct.
of the Blue Cholera of India," takes "Dr. Kennedy's excellent work on
the pestilence *now* prevailing" as both inspiration and model, signaling
one particular link in the chain of the "mutual refraction of colonial
and metropolitan medical theory."[20] The editors' language is once again
marked by Kennedy's expressive habits: they adopt the anthropomor-
phism of the distemper in his terms, speaking of the "indiscriminate
fury" of the disease, underscoring the insidious terrestrialization of an
enemy that "sow[s] its seeds . . . in every soil," marking the seeming injustice of the disease that makes no overtures, but instead causes such
"sudden seizures" that its victims appeared to have been stricken "as if by
lightning" (242). The Westward infiltration narrative appears once again,
tracking the disease as it pursues "the course of the Ganges and its tribu-
tary streams," its banks and nearby roads littered with the "dying and
the dead" in its "marchings and countermarchings," its "migration . . .
over the gulfs and arms of the ocean which wash the littoral boundaries
of the Indian Peninsula," as it makes "in *one* direction an uninterrupted
tour from the Gangetic Delta to the River Wear" (242, emphasis in the
original). In the *Lancet's* account, the agency of the disease—although
it remains an occult specter with all the features of a vengeful tropical atmosphere—is tempered by an equally confident declaration of the
means by which the "poison. . . . *makes mankind the chief agent for its
dissemination*" (261, emphasis in the original).

The following section of the article is devoted to a proof of the contagious communicability of the disease, outlining the details of the movement of armies, maritime communication, and finally the movement of
pilgrims within and across the borders of India. The last of these moves
from an examination of the "immense multitudes" of Hindus gathered
at "some remarkable festivals," in 1818 and 1820 where the cholera broke
out, and who subsequently "fled in horror to their homes" thereby propa-
gating the disease, to the "furious eruption of cholera [that] commenced
its ravages at Mecca" during the next outbreak—the one that would reach
Europe—in 1831. The movement from abstract atmospherics to abstract
agents to particular groups of persons is evident in a section concerning
cholera's "remote causes": the "irruption of the disease in previously-
uninfected places" is associated with "the arrival of ships, of caravans
of fugitives or pilgrims, of individuals, and with the progress of armies,"

a point illustrated in the subsequent case studies (261). Particularly of note here is the conflation of fugitives and pilgrims (both of whom are perceived as traveling by way of the distinctively Oriental conveyance, the caravan) and the way in which the category of "pilgrims" would become bisected in the case studies along religious lines, where Hindu pilgrims are cited as agents in the earlier outbreaks, and Muslims gathering at Mecca in the later, more far reaching epidemic.

As David Arnold notes, "several nineteenth century epidemics were directly attributed to Hindu festivals and pilgrimage sites," where

> [t]he mass bathing by Hindu pilgrims in a sacred tank or river . . . and the sipping of water as part of the ritual of worship and religious purification provided almost ideal conditions for the rapid communication of the waterborne vibrio. The chain of transmission was further extended by pilgrims bringing back Ganges water infected with cholera for relatives and friends to drink.[21]

G. B. Malleson, author of the influential "red pamphlet" and historian of the Mutiny, would examine thoroughly the impact of the 1867 Haridwar *mela* on that year's outbreak in his *Report on the Cholera Epidemic of 1867 in Northern India*. Then Bengal's sanitary commissioner, Malleson followed his predecessors in observing the topography ("malarious") and the weather ("unsettled") around the gathering, seeking to organize sanitation efforts and surmising about the origin of the "poison" in the "filthy" environs of Haridwar (figure 2.1). But he also noted that from wherever the "specific cause" arose, the "large masses of human beings" made the *mela* "most favorable to its rapid and extensive development."[22] He posited "two facts" in support of the idea that the "people may have been and probably were infected by means of the water," namely that

> the cholera *contagium*, must have been very active on the great bathing day—rain, it will be remembered, fell heavily throughout the 11th, and continued up till noon of the 12th, when the bathing ghat was crowded with devotees, and, secondly . . . that to drink the water of the holy river is no less a part of the pilgrim's object than to bathe his person in its stream.[23]

His report concludes in a strongly contagionist bent—conclusions that had long ago been reached in the metropole—but his sanitation and taxation proposals were not pursued by what was by then the Crown, rather than the company.

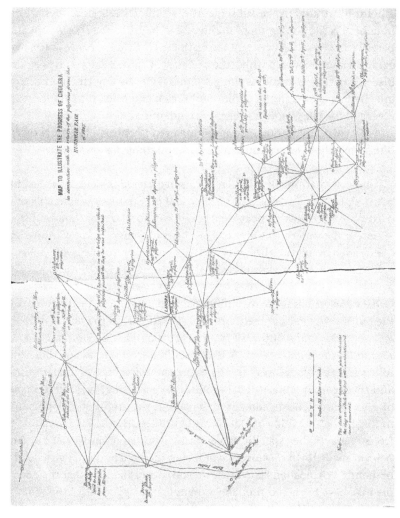

2.1 G. B. Malleson, "Map to illustrate the progress of cholera in connection with the return of the pilgrims from the Hurdwar Fair of 1867." Photograph: Center for the History of Medicine, Francis A. Countway Library of Medicine, Harvard Medical School.

Malleson's focus on the Haridwar *mela* in the 1867 outbreak notwith-standing, in the context of Indian religious syncretism, "Hindu" practices like pilgrimage and ritual bathing refused to break cleanly along what Europeans understood to be confessional lines—indeed many commen-tators noted the dynamic religious practices associated with cholera, in-cluding a possibly retrofitted cholera goddess Ola Bibi, and newer deity Hurdoul Lal, acknowledged and propitiated as promiscuously as the dis-ease itself alighted up and down the riverways, as well as the influence of Hindu pilgrimage on the religious practices of Indian Muslims.[24]

British efforts to manage and sanitize these great gatherings in India were inconsistent. Anglo-Indian writers addressing the subject in the aftermath of the 1857 Mutiny would show particular hesitation with re-gard to any contagionist theory that might be perceived as curtailing religious freedom and, more importantly, the movement of trade and military operations, not to mention cutting British India off from the rest of the world. James Bryden, working as a statistical officer for the Sanitary Commission of India, had also balked at the notion of chol-era's human transmission in his 1869 *Report on the Cholera of 1866–68*, insisting that cholera traveled the "aerial highways" of climate, season, and bad air.[25] Given their prominent positions in the colonial govern-ment and the perceived advantage of observing the epidemics in their "native" territories, later colonial cholera chroniclers like Bryden and Cunningham—following Jameson and Kennedy before them—would keep the prejudices of environmental etiology and the rhetorical forms in which they were expressed in view far longer than prevailing scien-tific opinion would support. Nevertheless, quarantine and sanitation measures were urged on with greater and greater alarm and growing international concern during and after the second epidemic wave in 1831, when focus would shift from Hindu pilgrimage within India to the role of the Muslim hajj—which occasioned the movement across the Middle East of an enormous number of Indian Muslims—in assisting the dis-ease in its transit Westward. If Hindus bore some of the blame for carry-ing cholera from river to river and village to village within the colony in the archive of cholera writings that traveled back and forth between the metropole and the outposts of empire around 1820, it was Muslims and their geographic reach, combined with the explicit doctrinal requirement to gather in Mecca, whom the international community would blame for infecting the world in 1831 and after.[26]

The *Report to the International Sanitary Conference* (the third convening of the body in Constantinople, following the 1851 and 1859 Paris con-ferences) gives scant attention to the endemic conditions that allowed for the emergence and seeming permanence of cholera in the alluvial regions of Lower Bengal. Instead, the commissioners aimed to study the causes of its shift to epidemicity, the most crucial of which, they explain, are "the great *agglomerations and migrations* of men, and particularly the *pilgrimages* which are made at special seasons in many parts of India."[27] The Constantinople report paints scenes of pilgrimage in lurid hues, describing first the gatherings of Hindus whence cholera "breaks out every year":

> The pilgrims arrive from all parts; and, often after a journey of many hundreds of leagues, made almost always on foot, during the hot season, they arrive exhausted by fatigue and misery. Once in the holy cities, their condition is aggravated still more by the horrible agglomeration, by all the causes of infection resulting from it,—bad nourishment, bad water, debauchery; in a word, by a host of circumstances favorable to the development of cholera among them. Then, finally, when the multitudes disperse, they go scattering cholera everywhere on their journey, and become thus the agents more or less active of the propagation of the epidemic. (22)

The very population and movement of Indian people become, in this description, sources of diseased chaos, as in the "horrible agglomeration" of bodies, the "debauchery" associated therewith, the carelessness with which they "scatter" cholera "everywhere" in "more or less active" ways. In contrast to the horizonless skies and marshy swamps of the early nineteenth-century imaginary, patrolled by tigers and fragrant with rotting vegetable matter, the picture that is conjured here, assisted by the larger cartographic scale of the Constantinople report, is that of swarming, indistinguishable brown bodies, insect-like at a distance, tumbling over each other in senseless waves without rhyme or reason, flinging about pestilence in their frantic idolatrous rovings.

Although the commissioners strongly resist the Westward movement narrative of earlier documentation, later sections of the Constantinople report underscore the culpability of Indian people in evidence above by citing "crowding," insistently posited as a permanent condition of life in India, as one of the primary aggravators of choleric epidemic conditions, as well as by diminishing the impact of army and troop movement on the spread of the epidemic, absolving the East India Company from "having allowed to fall into ruin the ancient hydraulic works," and identifying the global epidemics as a result of the "increase of intercourse" with India and "the greater celerity of the means of transport" (24, 17, 26). Specifically, Indian Muslims are to blame for the newly boundary-leaping form of epidemic cholera. As the report pulls back to a regional scale, it draws a comparison between pilgrimages within British India—again largely cast as a Hindu undertaking—and those that exceed its bounds:

> In these descriptions, which are the result of observations made especially in these latter years, do we not find *on a larger scale*, the exact representation of what occurs at Mecca? Here, as at Mecca, cholera does not break out with violence until some days after the gathering of the pilgrims, and it is dispersed and propagated with them in all directions. The pilgrims of India, then, as at Mecca, must be at the same time the foci of reinforcement and the disseminating foci of the disease. (22)

Although the commissioners of the International Sanitary Conference take care to note the key difference that "[a]t Mecca . . . cholera is always imported," its shift in focus toward the global epidemics keeps Muslim pilgrimage as a means of dissemination prominently in view, tracing through dozens of case studies, anecdotes, and contributing reports the appearance of cholera in the immediate environs of the Hijaz as well as Egypt, Java, and beyond, following the hajj season. Persian Muslims bearing corpses to Baghdad are also mentioned as possible agents of transmission, "brought to receive sepulture near the venerated tombs of the great saints of Islamism," complicating a largely hajj-centric model of Westward dissemination from India, and compounding the picture of both Hinduism and Islam"ism" as occult, irrational, and infectious (55).

In *The British Empire and the Hajj 1865–1956*, historian John Slight proceeds from the observation that the hajj "was a unique dilemma of empire," and argues for the centrality of the 1865 cholera epidemic (and the sanitation measures it demanded) to the British administration of the pilgrimage, suggesting:

> [In the] British Empire's interaction with the Hajj . . . the crucial events . . . are the 1856 cholera epidemic, when pilgrims carried the disease from India to Arabia and enabled its spread to Europe . . . and the 1956 Suez Crisis, which forced Britain to temporarily cede control of its Hajj administration in Saudi Arabia to its Pakistani counterparts.[28]

Although he contends that the control and surveillance of religious practice was a focal point of imperial policy, his chapters on the oversight of Hindu and Muslim pilgrimages in Victorian-era India demonstrate what he repeatedly calls an "ambivalence" on the part of colonial officials with regard to intervention in any religious practice, especially after the 1857 Mutiny, which was widely perceived by British officials in the colony and at home as a religiously motivated uprising.

While some commentators in the period concentrated their fears on the consequences of masses of Indian Muslims carrying cholera from the Subcontinent to the Nearer East, others expressed anxiety about the hajj serving as a "catalyst for . . . anticolonial resistance movements" (13). In particular, the Dutch response to the increasing number of Indonesian pilgrims making the journey to the Hijaz in the middle of the nineteenth century was inflected by fears about the decades-long Padri Revolt in Sumatra (1803–1837) and the war between the Muslim Sultanate of Aceh and the Dutch (1873–1913), which marked hajjis as "instigators of fanaticism," and the hajj itself as "the plague of native society" (39, 121). In late-nineteenth-century Russia, Slight observes, "[t]he Hajj was a 'scarcely tolerated evil,' and returning pilgrims were thought to spread 'extremist Islamism,'" while in turn-of-the-century France, whose Algerian holdings were still relatively new, the voyage to and devotions within Mecca were understood to be "a perfect 'breeding ground' for anticolonial ideas," which, when combined with an acute terror about the cholera epidemics, would lead France to suspend permission for its Algerian subjects to participate in the pilgrimage twenty-two times between 1875 and 1915 (46, 43).

Slight illuminates an inconsistent and somewhat trepidatious position over the course of the nineteenth century, a time during which, he argues, Britain could well be understood as a Muslim empire (1). The alarmist, fear-mongering tendencies of some of the period's more florid writing on Islam were a minor strain in the empire's overall discursive construction of and response to the hajj; Slight calls this "exaggeration and hyperbole" "ephemeral" (65). The more dominant position was a laissez-faire attitude with regard to quarantine in the interest of maintaining the open circulation of goods and people that supported British economic liberalism (58, 79). Still, there is an important impact and afterlife of these scientific, administrative, and rhetorical "errancies" that—even as they may not represent the sum total of imperial thinking and action about disease, poverty, migration, and religion in India and the Middle East—persevered in the broader imaginary of empire and contributed to what we might now call Islamophobic discourse. In other words, the hyperbolic and exaggerated accounts of unsanitary, impoverished Indian Muslims, preparing for anticolonial jihad as they streamed out of British-held India and sowed physiological and psychological pestilence in their wake, are just as integral—perhaps more so—to the historical narrative of cholera and empire as the official pilgrimage reports compiled by the British consulate at Jiddah (5).

Black as a Porpus

I've highlighted the prevalence and epistemological effects of two distinctive features of cholera writing in nineteenth-century British India: the first imagines an unbreakable and deterministic continuity between the landscapes of Lower Bengal and the emergence, symptoms, and spread of Asiatic cholera, while the second identifies colonial subjects and their cultural and religious practices as both conduits and metonyms of the disease. These two narrative strategies can be very loosely periodized to correspond to the first cholera epidemic, which spread widely but largely stayed within India (1817–1820), and the second epidemic, which reached Europe (1830–1832); they also map approximately onto a pervasive shift from miasma theory to contagionism that evolved from epidemic cholera's first appearance until about the middle of the century. These narrative practices—both of which primarily developed in observations and diagnoses from and of colonized space—might be best understood as first the Orientalization, and later the ethnicization of "cholera" as a historical and imperial phenomenon. Building on this legacy, cholera writing in the metropole would conscript and synthesize both rhetorical tactics in service of the racialization of the disease, beginning with an imprecise colorism that hammered again and again the blackness and blueness—invoking the popular fascination with images of Hinduism's blue god Krishna—of the choleric body.

Writing in July 1832, less than a year after the first cases of Asiatic cholera arrived in Britain by way of passengers aboard a ship from the Baltic, Samuel Taylor Coleridge took up the subject on many Britons' minds in his minor poem "Cholera Cured Beforehand." He positions the speaker as a sanitary reformer, taking up the popular association of poverty, filth, and indigestion that together make up "The diabolus ipse, / Call'd Cholery Morpus."[29] This devil, "who with horns, hoofs, tail, croaks for carrion to feed him," comes "with this gipsy"—a broad racial epithet derived from the racial catch-all "Egyptian"—"black as a porpus" in the poem's second stanza, to afflict the unsuspecting addressee with dyspepsia, "pains ventral, subventral, / In stomach or entrail." The speaker warns of the "offal-fed vagrant" who "[s]hall turn you as blue / As the gaslight unfragrant," while excrement "gushes in jets from beneath his own tail;— / 'Till swift as the mail, / He at last brings the cramps on."[30] Asiatic cholera's appearance in England lends a new and ubiquitous hue to the anthropomorphized disease: the devil in Coleridge's poem is black as a porpus, unfragrantly blue, and to avoid his wrath, the "lads" are advised to "foreswear all cabal . . . / Wakes, unions, and rows, / Hot dreams and cold salads / . . . And whitewash at once bowels, rooms, hands, and manners!"[31] Curing cholera "beforehand" was a matter of whiteness as much as of washing—avoiding certain foods, gatherings, and unsanitary living carried one so far in one's prophylactic efforts—but the bowels, rooms, hands, and even manners must be made as inhospitable as possible to the dusky invader as well.

Certainly Coleridge's poem was not the only place where the disease and its characteristic chromatics would suggest a link to the race of the colonial subject—from Jameson to Kennedy to Bryden, Malleson, and more, observers of the cholera both medically trained and not were keen to describe its physiological consequences, including the darkened skin, shrunken eyes, shriveled limbs, and coagulated black blood that make an appearance in nearly every official report, whether or not it included dissections and case studies. The *Lancet's* "History of the Rise, Progress, Ravages &ct. of the Blue Cholera of India" was published the year before Coleridge's poem, in November 1831. It brought the poetics of Asiatic cholera to the public in the metropole in very particular terms—legible in the color appended to the disease in the article's title—that emphasized cholera's foreign origin by way of its ostensible racial otherness. It cites at length a report by Drs. Russel and Barry, who wrote up their findings on the outbreak at St. Petersburg, where Russian peasants had been calling the disease the "*black illness*."[32] The symptoms they describe linger upon the wasting, darkening, and mentally disordering effects of cholera on the patient:

> The features become sharp and contracted, the eye sinks, the look is expressive of terror, wildness, and, as it were, a consciousness on the part of the sufferer that the hand of death is upon him. The lips, the face, the neck, the hands, the feet, and soon the thighs, the arms, and whole surface assume a leaden, blue, purple, black, or deep-brown tint, according to the complexion of the individual, varying in shade with the intensity of the attack. The fingers and toes are reduced at least a third in thickness; the skin and soft parts covering them are wrinkled, shrivelled, and folded; the nails put on a blueish pearl-white; the larger superficial veins are marked by flat lines of deeper black. . . . The patient asks only for water, speaks in a plaintive whisper (the "vox cholerica"), and only by a word at a time, from not being able to retain air enough in his lungs for a sentence. . . . If blood be obtained in this state, it is black, flows by drops, is thick, and feels to the finger colder than natural.[33]

External markers of morbidity are joined by a "terror" or "wildness" in the patient, as well as a loss of agency in the form of speech—the suppressed, breathless "vox cholerica" standing as a tragic antonym of the vox populi. Variations fill the pages of London's *Cholera Gazette*, the full six-number run of which appeared by commission of the Central Board of Health in 1832. Each issue of the entirely cholera-focused bulletin considered sanitation measures and published mortality reports and physicians' dispatches from the field, many of which enumerated the now-familiar slate of symptoms. In issue 1, five-year-old Isabella Elliot is recorded as having a "countenance blue [and] eyes deeply sunk," while a patient at Morpeth exhibited "the blueness of the skin . . . the collapse of the features and shriveling of the fingers."[34] Similar language proliferates throughout the inaugural issue. Numbers 2 and 3 repeat these illustrative terms dozens of times, while in number 4, Dr. James Bartlett details four-year-old Charles Connell's demise in a veritable rainbow of suffering:

> He vomited some pale, or whitish thin fluid, and passed at the same time a greenish dark liquid by stool. . . . the hands especially [were] of a blue colour,—the countenance oppressed . . . the temperature of the body much reduced, the colour (of the limbs especially) a deep livid, darkening at the extremities of the fingers, and more particularly under the nails, into a plum colour, while the countenance was more of a dull shade of that purple which it exhibits in some malformations of the heart . . . the eyes sunk into the orbits, almost as inexpressive as glass eyes . . . the tongue had a dry yellowish brown crust.[35]

Bartlett records the boy's slowing circulation, his longer bouts of unconsciousness, "the breathing more oppressed . . . the face and hands more discoloured, the nails of the latter at last looking as if stained by ink" until "he could no longer be said to live."[36] In addition to the child's transformation into a sort of human bruise, Bartlett emphasizes his slow departure from the realm of human recognition by pointing to the inexpressive, glass-like eyes and characterizing his breathing as "oppressed."

Because the darkened, purpled, or blued body of cholera victims was so central to the lay understanding of the disease, it followed almost inevitably that when the trope crossed over into anthropomorphic imaginings, these figures immediately took on an Oriental appearance, sometimes by way of Indian signifiers, as in the lithograph depicting cholera as a turbaned blue intruder breaking through "the wooden walls of Old England" (figure 2.2).

At other moments, cholera appears in a human form marked by signifiers of the Muslim East; an 1883 illustration from *Puck Magazine* depicts the epidemic as a skeletal Ottoman, sporting a fez, an embroidered vest, and a cloth wrapped around his lower body in a style reminiscent of a

2.2 Orlando Hodgson, "John Bull catching the cholera" (ca. 1832) (i.e., defending Britain against the invasion of cholera). Photograph: Wellcome Collection.

salwar, or loose pant typical of Central Asian and Indian Muslim dress (figure 2.3).

Here, an anthropomorphized cholera perches on the prow of a ship flying the Union Jack—a testament to the perception of cholera as a metonym for the human wages of empire—a long crescent scythe on his right shoulder as his unkempt hair sprouts from the top of his fez. These two representative images index the successful movement of relatively

2.3 Friedrich Graetz, "The kind of 'assisted emigrant' we can not afford to admit" (1832). *Puck Magazine*. Photograph: Harvey Cushing/ John Hay Whitney Medical Library, Yale University.

minor and contained racializing descriptions of cholera into the looser space of public conversation and humor not just in Europe, but in the burgeoning American empire as well.

As many scholars of cholera and its cultural history have shown, the disorder's ostensible preference for the lower classes—evidenced, for example, in the address of Coleridge's poem to the "Useful Classes"— was only further accentuated by the way in which the disease seemed to inscribe itself on the body as an accelerated impoverishment: first victims seemed to waste away as if from famine, followed by a darkening or devolution toward the lower races, and finally the thickening of the blood that, in many observer's words, resembled India ink, as if the blood of poor Europeans had been replaced by the staining stuff of empire and its sheaves of bureaucratic documentation.[37] Particularly following the Mutiny, the massive dehydration that thickened the blood into a coagulated black substance suggested the waning fecundity of resources from abroad—the indigo, cotton, jute, tea, and indentured labor harvested in India—as well as the slowly shrinking colonial export market.[38] A bodily rebellion in miniature was thus doubly staged in the evacuated choleric patient: first as a corporeal takeover that turned white people dark, and then as a pathological omen in the wasted alimentary canal and shriveled vessels of the increasingly vulnerable imperial economy. The rhetoric and iconography of cholera depended on a continuity between the destitute masses in the colonies, those that traveled across Asia and the Middle East, and those at home in England, and all three populations were subject to increasingly horrifying caricature in the form of a vengeful racialized monster. As Pamela Gilbert has convincingly argued, "the British came to regard the cholera . . . as a form of Indian counterattack on the Empire."[39]

The shift in perceptual scale that enabled the imaginative oscillation between the individual body and a social whole was central to the development of epidemiology as a discipline. We have seen a variety of ways in which physicians, sanitary reformers, military personnel, and colonial officials sought to study epidemics through morbidity and mortality during the first two cholera epidemics, but the combination of professionalization, the production of a literature, and the pressing public health concerns in London, Paris, and New York that followed from the third epidemic in 1848–1849 contributed to the rapid expansion of a proper discursive field and a self-consciously new discipline called epidemiology. In addition to the diagnostic criteria of clinical medicine, largely focused on the individual patient's progression of symptoms and autopsy observations, epidemiology's tools of interpretation borrowed heavily from the mapping, interviewing, statistical analysis, and narratives that were central to the administration of empire. For doctors, attending to such "distal" or upstream determinants of disease required a massive leap in perception; an anthropomorphizing operation that allowed for the conception of the zones of epidemicity as organ systems in the body of empire.

In his important pamphlet of 1849, *On the Mode of Communication of Cholera*, John Snow, perhaps the most lionized figure in the history of public health, turned his attention to the private plumbing, the neighborhood wells, their attendant networks of drainage and waste containment, and finally the corporate waterworks of London. He begins by declaring forcefully that cholera is "propagated by human intercourse," specifically "by the emptying of sewers into the drinking water of the community."[40] Following in the footsteps of his colonial counterparts, the pamphlet walks through a number of cases, connecting outbreaks spatially as it names the rivers and streams that supply water to the regions where the disease has broken out with particular virulence—the Clyde, the Nith, the Thames, and the Lea—as well as their tidal patterns and filtration and distribution networks.[41] In London, Snow examines wells, interviews residents about their laundry-washing habits, excavates rotten cesspits, observes the gutters that connect houses, and diagrams the results against the number and chronology of cholera deaths. His maps show not an emanation outward from a central point of infection, but rather a transmission patterned on water lines. Later, during the epidemic at Broad Street, Snow would codify this approach to infectious disease research in the so-called "ghost maps" and Voronoi diagrams of local mortality, which he began producing in 1854 on the basis of Edmund Cooper's maps for the Metropolitan Commission of Sewers.[42]

Eventually, these approaches would prove not only the truth of his claim—that cholera was communicated by way of drinking water contaminated with choleric evacuations—but more importantly, the effectiveness of his method, which sought to situate infectious disease in a field gridded by the time and space of public intercourse and infrastructure. Snow's important role in the reorganization of medical knowledge in the metropole—lessons that had been incompletely learned in the context of British India and the migration and pilgrimage patterns of Hindus and Muslims in South Asia and the Middle East—required a significant departure from the clinical orientation of the day, particularly the faith in the legibility of the ailing body and the efficacy of extrapolating the data it yielded from singular to general. That his research revealed how cholera followed the very waterways that also enabled local and global commerce underscored the disease's ominous moniker: the blue plague.

Beginning in 1850, this new method would begin to be codified under the auspices of the Epidemiological Society of London. On the occasion of its tenth anniversary, Benjamin Guy Babington summarized the goals of the society:

> We endeavor, by the light of modern science, to review all those causes which result in the manifestation and spread of epidemic diseases—to discover causes at present unknown, and investigate those which are ill understood—to collect together facts on which scientific researches may be securely based—to remove errors which impede their progress.[43]

Babington articulates and institutionalizes here a new paradigm of medical investigation, gathered from the scattered practices of the previous three decades, but also leans on the military language so prevalent in earlier colonial reports, suggesting that they attend to the "strongholds of our enemies, and their modes of attack, to suggest those means by which their invasion may either be prevented or, if in spite of our exertions they may have broken in upon us, to seek how they may be most effectually combatted and expelled."[44] The language of reconnaissance, invasion, and combat suggests an important overlap between colonial administration and the techniques of surveyorship employed by so-called shoe-leather physicians—the epidemiologists who moved out of the hospitals and into the streets. Such an overlap, it must be recalled, was always more than metaphorical, given the origin of cholera's first epidemic outbreak in the movement of East India Company troops in Bengal.[45]

The full significance of foundational epidemiology's invocation of enmity, war, invasion, and expulsion comes into view when we consider that this speech was delivered in 1860, only three years after the Mutiny. The metaphor of contagion was a ubiquitous figure in Mutiny fiction, but cholera also makes an appearance in political analyses of the uprising. Sir Sayyid Ahmad Khan—jurist, reformer, philosopher, and founder of the Anglo-Indian Oriental College at Aligarh in Uttar Pradesh—was probably the most widely read native commentator on the Mutiny, and certainly the most widely read by his British colleagues because he was a tireless, even shameless advocate of their rule. His long essay *Asbab-e Baghwat-i Hind*, published in 1858 in Urdu and translated as *The Causes of the Indian Revolt* in 1873, considers various theories about the catalyst and origins of the rebellion, from jihad to the annexation of Oudh (Uttar Pradesh), all of which pointed the finger at Muslims in particular.

Ahmad Khan insists that the "outbreak," like all rebellions, was not some homegrown terror, or long-plotted revenge on the part of the displaced Mughal rulers, or an autochthonous eruption of spontaneous violence—somewhat akin to the malodorous landscapes of James Kennedy's writings—but was rather the result of a "policy obnoxious to the dispositions, aims, habits, and views, of those by whom the rebellion was brought about" and that "[t]he men who have ruled India should never have forgotten that they were here in the position of foreigners, that they differed from the natives in religion, in customs, in habits of life and thought."[46] He recalls the conjoined terrors of the Mutiny and the cholera epidemics by invoking the tale fondly known by historians of South Asia as the "chapati mystery," in which bread was thought to be used as a signal or circular communicating plans for the uprising:

> Cholera happened at that time to be raging in Hindustan. Some have imagined that these chuppaties were used as a kind of Talisman to keep off the Cholera, the superstitious Hindustanees being in the habit of using such talismans. The fact is that even at the present day we do not know what caused the distribution of those chuppaties. We may be very sure, however, that they could never have been used with the object of spreading a conspiracy. We have, in Hindustan, I know, a custom of passing messages from tongue to tongue in this way: but with these chuppaties there is no such message passed.[47]

In spite of his disavowal, this peculiar story renders indelible the picture of India as a space where political disorder and public health catastrophe are continuous with one another—chapatis against cholera, or chapatis against the empire, the figural tether between the disease and the uprising remains undisturbed.

Feeding into the association of both disorders with the impoverished classes, Ahmad Khan writes of a growing neglect on the part of a government whose officials no longer seem to want to know "the daily habits, the modes of thought and life, the likes, and dislikes, and the prejudices of the people."[48] Throughout, Ahmad Khan is at great pains to establish poverty—not religious fanaticism or anti-imperialism—as another key factor in many rebels' decision to fight alongside the Sepoys, noting that the difficulty of "getting service" or obtaining employment "pressed most heavily upon the Mahommadans," whom he continually portrays as the most impoverished British subjects.[49] It is especially interesting to note, then, that Ahmad Khan, in addition to likening the rebellion to an explosion that "wanted but the application of a match to light it," also elaborates a naturalizing metaphor that can't—in the context of the late 1850s in British India—help but evoke the horrors of cholera as a "blue plague," a water-borne threat that lurks in tanks and swamps and arrives by ship or river, pump or pipe. "The causes of rebellion are, I fancy, everywhere the same," he writes:

> widely-spread disaffection cannot spring from any solitary, or local cause. Universal rebellion must arise from universal grounds for discontent or from streams deriving from many different sources, but finally merging into one wide-spreading turbulent water.[50]

In the context of discursive flows and the rhetorical commingling of nineteenth-century British imperialism, this beautiful figure, where streams of resistance flow into the turbulent waters of revolution, does not just describe the rising tide of revolt; it also points up how minor, errant, and often forgotten discourses infuse one another, and in turn infuse the epoch-defining works of literature and culture that carry them forward. In the next chapter, I turn to such a work, Bram Stoker's indelible *Dracula*, whose promiscuous incorporation of geographical determinism, Orientalization, and racialization of disease—as well as colonially inflected epidemiological epistemologies—performs exactly such a transmission. Although it had been widely discredited by the time of the novel's publication in 1897 as a viable therapy, it is worth remarking here that one of the primary treatments of cholera in the first half of the nineteenth century was bloodletting.

CHAPTER 3

Circulatory Logic

If anything needed to be compared with the circulation of the blood, it was not the formal circulation of money, but the content-filled circulation of capital.

KARL MARX, THE *GRUNDRISSE*

[W]hat is so dismal as the idea of some invisible agent pervading the atmosphere, and spreading over the world? If the writer's opinions be correct, cholera might be checked and kept at bay by simple measures that would not interfere with social or commercial intercourse; and the enemy would be shorn of his chief terrors.

JOHN SNOW, *ON THE MODE OF COMMUNICATION OF CHOLERA*

In what now seems an inevitable culmination of the logic of post-9/11 terror poetics, London terror suspect Khalid Masood, an English teacher and alleged convert to Islam who, in March 2017, drove a car into dozens of pedestrians on Westminster Bridge and stabbed a police officer, was dubbed by his neighbors "the Vampire."[1] Acquaintances, reflecting afterwards on the man who had moved undetected through their midst, cited his "shifting identity," his propensity to go out at night, his "black Islamic dress and black beanie hat," the way he moved "like a shadow."[2] A familiar racial discourse inherited from imperialism's strategic cultural hierarchies dwells in such statements. There's the retroactive association of the stranger with the mysterious and the monstrous, the moral coding of darkness in skin, dress, and nocturnal habits, the neighbors' fears about the mutability of identity and susceptibility to conversion. This chapter argues that the ease of this reference—Muslim, vampire, terrorist—like other casual articulations of millennial Islamophobia, obscures the complex literary and discursive history of the association, as well as the extent to which fictional and fantastic narratives preserve the social, racial, and ethnic categories of colonialism that continue to shape global discourse, study, and policy on terror.

The vampire terrorist isn't just a cartoonish fixture of the post-9/11 era, though work like Ana Lily Amirpour's film *A Girl Walks Home Alone*

3.1 Still from Ana Lily Amirpour, *A Girl Walks Home Alone at Night* (Vice Films, 2014).

3.2 Still from Ana Lily Amirpour, *A Girl Walks Home Alone at Night* (Vice Films, 2014).

at Night has satirized the insistent association in popular visual culture between the hijab and the cape in smart ways, highlighting the gender slippage that, in his neighbors' minds, takes Khalid Masood from "black Islamic dress" to "Vampire" (figures 3.1 and 3.2).[3]

The vampire terrorist also has deep roots as an object of science in the canon of anticolonial writing. It is a touchstone in Frantz Fanon's essay on the bodily poetics of the Revolution, "Algeria Unveiled" ("L'Algérie se dévoile"), where the vampire appears as a concept metaphor for the dehumanization and pathologization of Algerian Muslims—specifically men, but extendable, through the metonym of the veil, to women as well. Much as the hysterical reaction to sati, or widow immolation, in nineteenth-century India served a broad colonial reform program that sought to discipline reproductive and bodily behaviors in accordance with British norms, so too, according to Fanon, did the criminalization and pathologization of Arab men and their treatment of "their" women serve the French colonial project in Algeria, marking the veil as a backward, irrational fetish—a mnemonic for the entombing of women within life. Against this projected barbarism, Fanon notes how colonial discourse differentiated itself from its object of scrutiny by counterposing its own rationality against the monstrosity of the revolting Muslim natives: "with infinite science, a blanket indictment against the 'sadistic and vampirish' Algerian attitude toward women was prepared and drawn up."[4] Here, the colonial answer to the pathological monster or abnormal subject is the colonizer's "infinite science," a paradoxical concept that both affirms and infinitely defers rationalism and mastery.

In the previous chapter, I argued that the unprecedented cholera epidemics originating in India and spreading throughout the British empire and eventually throughout the world caused literary strategies of representation, oftentimes borrowed from the toolkit of Orientalism, to make their way into colonial medical writing and thence into the wider imperial discourses of sanitation, health, and science. So too did colonial medical surveillance and methods of research bleed into literary space, where they joined a looser set of anxieties associated with empire. In addition to contagion, other fears like rebellion, miscegenation, degeneracy, and dissipation were enormously important drivers of nineteenth-century culture and science. Deriving their figures, language, and generic maneuvers from forms like travelogues, imperial Gothic, Orientalism, and reformist realism, colonial efforts to textualize the bodily problems of empire strongly inflected popular works of nineteenth-century British fiction, especially those that imagined the world beyond Western Europe. These works, even as they traded in the affective coin of the terrors of rebellion and disease in the baleful East, were imprinted with a managerial and scientific rationalism that sought to diminish exotic threats to the imperial body politic by rendering them legible, surveyable, and comprehensible.[5]

An archive of colonial Gothic writing—a more technical and epistemologically experimental side of both Gothicism and Orientalism influenced by the bureaucratic machinery of empire—stretches across the nineteenth century from Charlotte Smith's *The Story of Henrietta* (1800) to Mary Shelley's *Frankenstein* (1818) and *The Last Man* (1826) to Arthur Conan Doyle's Sherlock Holmes stories (1887–1927) to Wilkie Collins and Richard Marsh's Victorian Orientalist mysteries, *The Moonstone* (1868) and *The Beetle* (1897). By far the most enduring and popular novel in this archive is Bram Stoker's *Dracula*, a text so capacious in its allegorical accommodations that it has been read as incorporating nearly every threat and monster of its own time and place—including those I have been tracking in this book, like global epidemic, the shadow of the Ottoman Empire, the Mutiny in India, and the famine in Ireland—as well as carrying them forward into the present where they mingle with our own in what is now a well-documented millennial vampire surge in popular culture.[6] Following Fanon, who invokes the rich mythology of the vampire to point up colonial discourse's specific habits of dehumanization, we can locate *Dracula* in an important archive of colonial writing that sets the "science" of monsters on its infinite course and advances a reading practice that borrows from the surveillance apparatus and epidemic narrative strategies of colonial disease literature.

Because of its extraordinary durability, *Dracula* is a crucial textual conduit in the transmission of minor ideas about the circulation of terror, rebellion, racialized bodies, foreign materials, and communicable disease from largely forgotten nineteenth-century texts and contexts into the common sense of late empire and late capitalism. Although *Dracula* is not a terribly self-conscious, systematically researched, or ideologically consistent text, it is decisive in its effects. The assumptions, ethnographic and scientific gleanings, and obsessive attention to the media of circulation that the novel smuggles into popular culture in the folds of its notorious villain's cape have substantially shaped one of the most important metaphors of monstrosity that remains available for all invasive forms of infamy, including but of course not limited to Islamist terrorism. The first sections of this chapter identify the insistence and importance of *Dracula* in the Islamophobic atmosphere of the US at the beginning of the War on Terror, and reveal in Stoker's textual forebears and his own archive a persistent fixation with the shifting borders of the Orient and the incursion of its materials—germs, dirt, people, blood— into imperial metropolitan space. The latter sections move away from the novel's many specific allegorical systems to examine its staging of material circulation in, across, and at the borders of the East. Circular, mobile, self-reproducing, liquid: *Dracula's* circulatory logic undoes the linear and center-margin geometries of trade, migration, and influence that structure empire. In so doing, *Dracula* also calls for a new kind of materialist reading attendant to the movement of immunities alongside that of commodities. The novel's documentary form teaches us how to read this new kind of threat, and prepares the ground—imaginatively, epistemologically, and morally—for a shift away from the nineteenth century's bellicose conception of enmity toward a depoliticized and ethically neutered global security apparatus. The chapter concludes part 1 of the book by showing how the legacies of the post-Mutiny decades in the British empire establish new epistemological and military norms for twentieth- and twenty-first-century colonialisms. The novel's popularity and critical indefatigability cement its function as a carrier and disseminator of minor tropes—including those that bind the imaginaries and metaphorical systems of rebellion, terror, Islam, and disease—not just at the turn of Stoker's century, but also, improbably, our own.

Vamping Orientalism

In a volume on the Romantic Gothic, Peter Kitson suggests that

> the vampire is the most important gift bequeathed by Orientalism to the Gothic mainstream . . . [It is] the ultimate other for nineteenth-century Britons: exotic, Eastern and supernatural, a demonic inversion of Protestant modernity, with its seductive mixture of forbidden desires and hidden excesses.[7]

Kitson is right about Orientalism's bequest to the Gothic mainstream, and about the consummate otherness of the vampire, but the breadth of his formulation—common in Stoker criticism—masks an important historical specificity in the myth of the vampire, namely the connection to what was then called the Muslim Near East. Reconstructing this history helps us to understand the revivification of Stoker's novel at the beginning of the War on Terror not as an accident of cultural felicity or a randomly grasped-for tale of familiar horror but rather a pointed (if unintentional) transmission of a very specific set of concerns and epistemological strategies that emerged from Stoker's research and background as well as from the broader context of colonial crisis and Ottoman decline in which he wrote.

Scholars of culture and terror have noted the uncanny return of British imperialism's monstrous others in recent years. Working at the intersection of discourses of monstrosity and post-9/11 culture, for example, Jasbir Puar posits the relationship between terrorism studies and the disciplining of sexuality, querying not just "what is terrorist about the queer," but also "what is queer about the terrorist."[8] For her, the "failed and perverse" masculinities evident in the early millennium's homophobic images and flat psychologizations of terrorists' motives (thwarted sexuality, virgins in heaven, etc.) are associated with disease as the infinitely retreating horizon of knowability, an "unfurling, viruslike, explosive mass" whose eradication defines the global security state.[9]

We can understand the effects of the queered terrorist epidemic trope Puar identifies in the same way we understand Guha's naturalizing "prose of counterinsurgency," as a rhetorical depoliticization in the historical record; natural phenomena and perverted psychology are analogous in their effects. Though neither Puar nor Guha pursues the implications of the "viruslike," or "pathological" encoding of insurgent violence, the tension they each describe between the unfathomable and the scientifically manageable is crucially at play in both paradigms, which reach for figures, analogies, allegories, icons, and landscapes to render migratory global phenomena visible, to comprehend and domesticate them while also perpetuating the politically expedient threat they pose. This phenomenon is representational, if not strictly literary. In an earlier article, Puar and coauthor Amit Rai call for an interrogation of the "history that ties the image of the modern terrorist to a much older figure, the racial and sexual monsters of the eighteenth and nineteenth centuries" but their examples don't draw from the literary history.[10] Returning to these texts further sharpens our sense of how such monsters concatenate not just vague racial and sexual terrors but also a very specific set of bodily and political threats to empire.

It's not an uncomplicated history: villains, abnormals, and Orientalist monsters operate not only within a Western discourse of terrorism, but also describe the legacies of militarism left behind by colonialism and revived in neocolonial occupation and the soft annexation of sovereign states by debt structures, contingent aid, and multistate security operations. We see this adaptation, for example, in the Pakistani "Abbottabad Commission Report," completed in 2011 and leaked by *Al Jazeera* in 2013, which points up the promiscuous mobility of such nineteenth-century monsters in representing political landscapes that exceed legibility not just in an East-West framework, but also in theories of sovereignty and just war. To describe the chaotic political context of the tribal areas in Afghanistan in the decades leading up to bin Laden's assassination, the commissioners reach for a familiar Gothic monster:

> [A]fter the Soviet invasion of Afghanistan, the military government at the time had created a Frankenstein's Monster in the shape of militant organizations posing as national liberators. It may have been in the national interest at the time to get so deeply involved in Afghan affairs. But the fact was that the country had paid a massive price for its many unwise decisions and it would take a generation or more to deal with the consequences.[11]

Here, Frankenstein's monster illustrates the ill effects of Pakistan's collaboration with Afghani militants "posing as" rebels during the Cold War. On the one hand, this way of figuring the militants underscores the monster's association with the putatively tribal, unenlightened, violent Islamism and untamable history of the Afghans, as opposed to the Pakistanis. This is not surprising. The association of "Afghanistan" with heightened danger has long incorporated a sense of the biologically unruly. Following the Second Anglo-Afghan War (1878–1880), for example, the region became a recognizable metonym for describing the dangers of bacteriology, a discipline that an 1882 article in *Cornhill Magazine* likened to "an intellectual Afghanistan."[12] On the other hand, the report leaves implicit the history of US pressure on Pakistan to support the militant organizations against the Soviets—a fact that turns the figure backwards, implicating the US in this monstrosity as well. The report's recourse to Shelley's notorious creation points beyond the Frankenstein myth and its presumptive use as a rhetorical tool of a unilaterally Western imperialism. Although the question of Shelley's Orientalism and her precise critique of empire broadly construed—and British imperialism particularly—remains an ambiguous one in postcolonial, feminist, Romanticist, and even Americanist scholarship, what is clear here is that *Frankenstein*, with its antagonist's bodily and reproductive failure, generatively stages the horrors of empire and its uncanny sutures in ways that range far beyond the context of their creation in both time and space, much like the monster itself.[13]

What becomes even more visible in this comparative context is how *Frankenstein* remains a productive touchstone for thinking not just threats to the natural or naturalized bourgeois order of the novel's world, but also for thinking imperial and national geographies as anthropomorphic or pseudo-human bodies; bodies politic, by extension, that cannot cohere or thrive. The analogy in the "Abbottabad Commission Report" between Shelley's creature and the rapid growth of militancy in Afghanistan and Northern Pakistan after the Cold War relocates to the space of the postcolony what was already a pessimistic allegory of empire, even in the first decades of the nineteenth century. In this way, the metaphor doesn't just figure a monstrous body, it also circulates and proliferates like one, becoming a constant presence in the global discourse on terrorism in Britain and the US as well as in Pakistan.

Faisal Devji, in his work on the centrality of humanist and human rights discourse to the global text of Islamist terror, describes an inversion of this paradox by which a shared sense of the human and the non-human (or subhuman) is established across the divide between the West and Al Qaeda and its affiliates. In *The Terrorist in Search of Humanity*, Devji refuses to grant the ideological distinctions upon which a xenophobic and anti-Muslim construction of Islamist militancy rests and works to reveal far more rhetorical and philosophical overlap than the field of terrorist studies and casual commentary on terrorism has heretofore allowed. "Militant rhetoric," he argues, "can no longer remain something traditional or foreign . . . [I]ts global influence is based precisely on stereotypes that are shared across the planet."[14] The planetary figure that serves as the epigraph of Devji's book—the figure that defines the problem of the human and the nonhuman in his thinking—is none other than Shelley's monster, evading the creator who "ever follow[s] in his track" in the "wilds of Tartary and Russia," leaving his mark to be found—"the print of his huge step on the white plain."[15] Elaborating the analogy, Devji suggests that like Frankenstein's monster, "modern man's humanity remains abstract and dislocated, despite the fact that every part of him is human."[16] The tragic figure illustrates the rude conjoinings that constitute an abstract global humanity—comprising humans, but not itself entirely human. Following the logic of Devji's epigraph, the monster—our monsters—must become fugitive, absent, or expelled in the face of a limited humanity that cannot encompass its others, even as they make themselves known, leave their traces in the snow. The final pages of *Frankenstein*, from which Devji's epigraph is drawn, are crucially ambiguous. Shelley leaves open the question of the monster's survival, the possibility of his reproduction, the as-yet-impossible "race of devils" the doctor trembles to imagine. Still, *Frankenstein*'s epistolary form, the isolation of its characters, and the singularity of its protagonist and his experiment foreclose to some extent the reproducibility of the monster's sorrow and rage, the horror of his existence. He is, in the end, alone and far away.

As productive as Shelley's tale has been in transmitting the literary monsters of the nineteenth century as well as their Gothic and Orientalist underpinnings into the present of geopolitical allegory, *Frankenstein* doesn't provide an apt mythologem for the "viruslike explosive mass of the terrorist network" that Puar invokes so forcefully. Another story composed in Geneva during the infamous year without a summer might be better understood as the genesis of pathogenic, viral monstrosity that would later ramify in representations of the global threat of terrorism: "The Vampyre." The story was originally published in the *New Monthly Magazine* in 1819 under Byron's name but quickly attributed to his young companion, the physician John Polidori, who accompanied Byron and the Shelleys on their sojourn in the Alps. Along with Robert Southey's long poem *Thalaba the Destroyer* (1801), a significant work that garnered fewer readers, Polidori's tale established the vampire in British writing as a Romantic Gothic figure whose relationship to that era's Orientalism was attenuated but persistent.[17]

Polidori's vampire, Lord Ruthven, is described in racializing terms that resonate with the descriptions of cholera victims in the contemporary literature of medicine—a profession, it bears repeating, in which Polidori was trained. Like the victims of cholera that peopled the *Cholera Gazette*, Polidori's vampire is possessed of a "dead grey eye" that falls "like a leaden ray" on that which it observes, and a face that sports a "deadly hue . . . which never gained a warmer tint."[18] The landscape and visual vocabulary of the story reinforce the relationship to the Near East. Polidori styles his story's first victim as an Oriental painting, situating the young Ianthe in Athens and associating her grace and beauty with that border space and its darker races—she "might have formed the model for a painter wishing to pourtray on canvass the promised hope of the faithful in Mahomet's paradise, save that her eyes spoke too much mind for any one to think she could belong to those who had no souls."[19] Ianthe here is almost but not quite the houri of an infidel heaven, the presence of which presses on the border of Europe in the form of Ottoman proximity to Greece. But for the presence of mind evident in her eyes, Polidori tells us, she could almost be a harem girl, both hapless victim and already part-monster.

The Orientalist trifles of "The Vampyre" are more a matter of atmospheric effect than a major thread in the story. A commonplace-looking English girl is also vampire-possessed by the end, and the protagonist dies from a vague malaise more akin to depression than contagious affliction. Neither is the threat a public one: the vampire in Polidori's tale circulates in an intimate suite of spaces. The story's sense of enclosure—its sick rooms and parlors, its ships and tombs—is redoubled by various details: the desperate intimacy of the first-person narrative, the secrets and oaths that structure the plot, the portraits, hidden like clues in lockets close to the heart. Like Sheridan Le Fanu's later, more famous vampire story *Carmilla* (1872), Polidori's "The Vampyre" shares more characteristics with Shelley's Romanticism and Byron's Orientalism than with its most famous literary inheritor, remaining an example of the relatively closed system of the Gothic, even as it flirts with an idea of the pathological or infectious villain.[20] Later in the century, Richard Burton's translation of the Sanskrit tales collected as *King Vikram and the Vampire* (1870) would add to the archive of claustral vampire tales, this time in the aesthetic sphere of classical Hindu writings.[21] The fiend that stalks Burton's tales loans some traits to later vampires: he is a demon, another species, and, in Burton's translation, an ancient menace from far away.[22] He is also a shapeshifter, sometimes a bat, he animates corpses, but his condition is not transmissible. One of the most notable texts on the infectious side of Romantic experiments with terror is Mary Shelley's third novel, *The Last Man* (1826), in which the entire population of the earth is wiped out by a plague originating in Constantinople.[23] This novel, with its "curse of Allah" descended on and spreading out from "Stamboul," broadens the concerns of *Dracula*'s literary predecessors to a global stage, making a bid for infectiousness and contagion originating in the Muslim East as primary motors of a universal history.[24] In Stoker's hands, the germ of Polidori, Southey, Shelley, Le Fanu, and Burton's Orientalism remains, but the vampire moves differently, contaminating the very circuits of the social, where his infectious incontinence and endless appetite circulates freely alongside information, currency, property, even thoughts.

Stoker's uses of Orientalism are, in keeping with his time, looser and more faddish than those of his predecessors, but his personal archive and research materials reveal an important focus for the study of *Dracula*: a menacing sense of the influence of the "crescent," or Islamic incursions into Europe. Despite Stephen Arata's formative reading of *Dracula* as a novel of "reverse colonization," Stoker's interest in the Ottoman advances in Eastern Europe and the presence of the Islamic empire as a metonym for racial and ideological difference has remained largely unremarked upon in the scholarship.[25] This buried thread in the origin story of *Dracula* illuminates a great deal about the specific ways in which the novel's textual history intersects with both colonial-era fears of the Eastern other and, more importantly, those that mark our present moment, upholding the novel's popularity and relevance in a study of the afterlives of imperial-era monsters.

When Bram Stoker's personal library went to auction in 1913, it included multiple volumes pointing to his long-standing interest in Orientalism, the Near East, and Egypt, the last of which would provide the fashionable setting for his 1903 novel, *The Jewel of the Seven Stars* (figure 3.3). In addition to two copies of Omar Khayyam's *Rubaiyat* (the FitzGerald translation), Stoker's library included two large multivolume histories of Egypt, F. D. Millet's *The Danube from the Black Forest to the Black Sea* (1893) and *Egyptian Tales* (1895), Kipling's *Jungle Books* and *Out of India* (1895), *The Ordnance Surveys of Great Britain* (1848, etc.), Budge's *Book of the Dead* (1895), Norden's *Travels in Egypt and Nubia* (1757), and a personally inscribed presentation copy of *Arabia, Egypt, India*, by Isabel Burton (wife of Sir Richard Burton).[26] The Second, Third, and Fourth Reports of the Wellcome Research Laboratories at Gordon Memorial College (Khartoum, Sudan)—penned by Andrew Balfour, a giant of tropical medicine and an assiduous student of malaria, mosquitos, sanitation, and urban water infrastructure—were added to Stoker's library after the publication of *Dracula* between 1906 and 1911. According to biographer Barbara Belford, Stoker also drew on his younger brother George's travel narrative, *With the Unspeakables; or Two Years' Campaigning in European and Asiatic Turkey*.[27] If these texts influenced Stoker's thinking as he was composing *Dracula*, others had a more direct impact.

According to Stoker's research notes, the settings and local color details that shape the novel's Gothic overture in Transylvania are largely

CATALOGUE

OF VALUABLE

PRINTED BOOKS

AUTOGRAPH LETTERS

AND

Illuminated & other Manuscripts

INCLUDING

THE LIBRARY OF THE LATE BRAM STOKER, ESQ.

Days of Sale.

FIRST DAY ... Monday, 7th July .... Lots   1 to 317
SECOND DAY . Tuesday, 8th July .... Lots 318 to 625

1913.

ILLUSTRATED COPY.—PRICE ONE SHILLING.

3.3 Sotheby, Wilkinson & Hodge, *Catalogue of Valuable Printed Books, Autograph Letters, and Illuminated & Other Manuscripts, Including the Library of the Late Bram Stoker, Esq.*" (1913) (front cover). Auction catalogue. The Rosenbach, Philadelphia (EL3 .S874d MS 45b).

adapted from three books not present in this collection, one of which was E. C. Johnson's *On the Track of the Crescent: Erratic Notes from the Piraeus to Pesth*. Johnson's volume recounts his experiences in the regions of Eastern Europe that had for a time "fallen into the hands of the unspeakable"—a dysphemism for the Turks that also appears in the title of George Stoker's personal narrative.[28] The crescent whose track Johnson follows casts its lurid Islamic light over the territories that become not just a vague "East," as previous scholarship on *Dracula*'s geographic imaginary suggests, but a specific locus of pastiched belief, bloodshed, and mixed heritage. The Carpathian rocks Johnson describes echo with the cries of "Allah-Il-Allah!," an invocation that punctuates the "spirited" Romanian victory poem Johnson includes in his text.[29] Stoker translates Johnson's exoticism and historical musings into Dracula's deeply accented English and his reflections on his heritage, particularly his vociferous rejection of the implied Islamic stain on his heritage, in spite of his admission that, for a time, "the flags of the Wallach and the Magyar went down beneath the Crescent."[30] The tangled bloodline Dracula claims thus preserves the possibility of a monstrous blood mingled with the Turks'. Stoker's *Dracula* notes also include citations from Isabella Bird's *The Golden Chersonese*, a travel narrative based in and around Malaysia about local devils, one of whom is a "storm fiend who rides the whirlwind, and spirits borrowed from Persia and Asia. It almost seems," according to Bird, "as if the severe monotheism [of Islam] to which they have been converted compels them to create a giant demonology."[31] In an episode that captivated a number of critics at the time of the novel's publication, *Dracula*'s young solicitor Jonathan Harker witnesses his host descending the walls of the castle "face down . . . just as a lizard moves along a wall."[32] If the rigors of Islam, as Bird believed, "compelled" its adherents to invent fiends and fantastic creatures, the British empire's control of vast swathes of Islamic territory necessitated a reciprocal chimerical inventiveness—Stoker's own demonology drew on these folkloric traditions to join the djinns and phantoms of Orientalism to those of a more pressing cosmopolitan haunting.

In the final text of *Dracula*, Stoker's interest in the Ottoman history of Eastern Europe is quiet but persistent. Jonathan Harker's register of observations during his imprisonment in the castle, for example, is overdetermined by what he confesses in a parenthetical note: "Mem., this diary seems horribly like the beginning of the 'Arabian Nights' for everything has to break off at cockcrow. . . ."[33] The elusive, disappearing horizon of knowability in which a diurnal infinitude, borrowed from Scheherazade's life-preserving tales, defies interpretation and accounting, draws attention to Harker's sense of metanarrative, of the circulation and superhuman life and geographic spans of stories, myths, narrative forms. More interestingly, the novel appears to consign to its opening Gothic frame an antiquated sense of what the Islamic East might mean, narratively, culturally, interpretively. Following Harker's return to London, Dracula seems to leave behind not just the fantastic atmosphere of a Transylvania steeped in the spectral presence of the Islamic world and its myths and stories, but also the interpretive modes proper to reading those Eastern texts and their didactic mysticism. In other words, the appearance of *The Arabian Nights* as a doubly suppressed or missing text—one that is abandoned as an analogue once the tools of rational accounting become available in London—registers Stoker's interest in the movements and spread of the "ghoul stories" of the Near East and Islam's extended geography, even as it seems to quarantine this narrative mode from that which will follow.

Nevertheless, the putative distance between the novel's antique East and contemporary West, layered and loosely significatory as they are, is perpetually threatening to contract. The atmosphere of *Dracula's* far-flung overture leaks into the home-space of London in text and body, figure, and form in ways that belie the distance between geographies. In a moment that marks the shift, for example, from the early terror of collective victimhood to the ensuing investigation-and-sterilization plot, Dr. Van Helsing refers to Arthur Holmwood's suffering—he has lost his wife Lucy to vampirism, and now has to decapitate her and drive a stake through her dead body—as the "bitter waters" through which he will have to pass "before we reach the sweet" (189). The phrase appears twice more in the novel, once in a letter to the younger doctor, Jack Seward, about Holmwood's plight ("he must pass through the bitter waters to reach the sweet") and again just before the Lucy beheading ordeal ("[y]ou are now in the bitter waters . . . [B]y this time tomorrow you will, please God, have passed them, and have drunk the sweet waters . . . [T]ill then I shall ask you to forgive me") (236). The Sweet Waters of Europe, mentioned in Stoker's notes toward the novel, was the name given to a famed stream in Constantinople—the consummate site of Eurasian mixing—which began in the hills just outside the city and emptied into the Bosporus by way of the Golden Horn inlet, where it met another such stream from the East: the Sweet Waters of Asia. In an account written for *Harper's* magazine in 1873, the banks of the stream that flowed from the Asian hills framed a picturesque scene of cultural intermingling, with ladies of the harems taking their picnics alongside a group of Western tourists and restful Sabbath takers: an idyll of the pleasures of East-West intercourse.[34]

The count employs a menacing variant of this language of confluence in describing the history of conquest that marks his native land:

"In our veins flows the blood of many brave races who fought as the lion fights . . . [h]ere in the whirlpool of European races" (31–32). He invokes the Hungarian "flood" that sweeps eastward: first their capitulation to the Turks, then their vigilance at the frontier, where Turkish soldiers have imparted a martial proverb to their foes: "water sleeps, enemy is sleepless" (32). This phrase, gnostic and aphoristic, stands alone on a typewritten page of Stoker's research notes for the novel, crystallizing the false wisdom the story dismantles as it incorporates and deflects nameable forms of violence, and tries to grapple with the as yet unnamable scourge that arises from the blood-soaked soil of post-Ottoman Eastern Europe. Water, in fact, may be the novel's most sleepless medium of all, and liquidity the greatest terror it explores. As I have shown in the previous chapter, public waterworks and sewage systems became the focus of a great many public health campaigns and reforms, not just in India, where the great cholera epidemics originated from the Ganges delta, but also across Europe. It is of more than passing interest, then, to recall that the Ottoman Empire was widely referred to in the latter half of the nineteenth century as the "sick man of Europe"—a coinage contemporaneous with the third global cholera epidemic.[35] In his earliest notes for *Dracula*, Stoker constructs his monster as a "plague," and assigns a pair of doctors to its discovery and eradication.[36]

Choleric Pretexts: Charlotte Stoker's Letter and "The Invisible Giant"

If the management of the British colonies was as much a matter of statistics, bureaucracy, and data collection as it was of brute force, then horror stories like Stoker's, which hyperbolized the bodily threats of free trade, commercial liquidity, and mobile populations, would also reconceive enmity in less dialectical and more multivalent terms. *Dracula*, in both theme and form, registers the terror of the circulatory logic of empire, and concentrates this terror in the circulation of disease. For this reason, and because its villain stalks the very streets of the metropole, *Dracula* is the monstrous text that most menacingly embodies—and, in its investigative plot and synoptic form, also theorizes—its own late-colonial moment, and points most clearly toward the monstrous metaphors that define our own. Stoker's inflection of the colonial Gothic is preoccupied, as major readings of the novel have noted, with the technologies of capital, bureaucracy, and science.[37] *Dracula*'s experimentation with these technologies, particularly those used to investigate the symptoms of illness and the mechanisms of contagion and infection, evinces Stoker's curiosity about advances in medical science. This interest is evident in his library, which in addition to its Orientalist holdings, contained a number of scientific texts like George Harley's *The Life of a London Physician*, as well his correspondence with his brother, Thornley Stoker, chair of anatomy at the Royal College of Surgeons in Ireland and frequent contributor to the *Dublin Journal of Medical Science*.[38] As any careful reader will note, *Dracula* is also full of tropes of medical horror familiar from the colonial Gothic, as in Kipling's "The Mark of the Beast" (1890) and other popular mystery, detective, and sensationalist fictions, emblematized by Arthur Conan Doyle's Sherlock Holmes stories, a number of which deal explicitly with medical detection, tropical disease, and even vampirism.[39] The disease poetics of *Dracula* are more specific than in these other works: they emerge from a double transposition of the infectious landscapes of the Ottoman Near East and British-held India by way of Stoker's marked interest in cholera over the course of his career. Previous scholarship has certainly noted Stoker's interest in infectious disease and epidemics, as well as the novel's brand of Orientalist horror.[40] What has not yet emerged from the generative extant scholarship is the extent to which these two paradigms are tethered to and dependent upon one another, the way their comingling in the novel telegraphs the presence of India and the British Islamic empire in the heart and guts of London.

How the vampire moves through the ways and passages, the capillaries and the tides—his routes of arrival and evasion, and the narrative shape they lend to *Dracula*—offer the novel's most obvious link to Asiatic cholera and the new science of epidemiology as it was practiced and theorized from the 1850s through the 1890s. In his *Cholera: The Biography*, Christopher Hamlin suggests that the disease was understood by its two most prominent "Asianizing" theorists as "an unfortunate byproduct of bringing India into the world," and argues that cholera as an idea, as much as an empirically observable phenomenon, "grew up in conjunction with Enlightenment liberalism, nationalism, imperialism, and the rise of the global biomedical science[.] [I]t was most problematic in precisely those places where these darlings thrived."[41] According to this account, the risks of systematically extending the global economy and circulation of goods into and from India was the insalubrious confluence of immunities and pathogens, health histories understood to be embedded in—indeed native to—European and Indian bodies respectively. The link Hamlin underscores between cholera and the material epistemologies of liberal imperialism is causal: the disease spread because of colonial trade and discourse networks. This argument foregrounds the extent to which the contact zones in which cholera became "most problematic" were not necessarily those in which it took the most lives. Its greatest mortality was confined to Asia and the Middle East.[42] Rather, cholera made itself known as a "problem" for Europe in the cities and ports that served as nodes in (and facilitated the expansion of) these networks. Such spaces amplified the spectacular horror of cholera's rapid onset and high death rates because the large, mobile, and economically diverse populations that circulated in these spaces posed the greatest challenges to containment, existing medical facilities, and the disposal of the dead. Scenes of suffering, death, and decay played themselves out in terrifyingly public theaters across Europe, deeply influencing social reform and hygiene movements as well as scientific practice and cultural production. Although such scenes were equally devastating across the better part of the globe, epidemic cholera struck a parochial European population with the force of something cruelly new, collateral for the rapid expansion in Asia. In the medical and popular literature, the cholera epidemics produced a robust lexicon to describe the novel horrors of the new disease layered over long-since stabilized fantasies about the horrors of the Orient.

Stoker's preparatory work for *Dracula* began in the 1870s, just as London was recovering from the devastating, nearly decade-long cholera epidemic of 1852–1860, and another, smaller outbreak in 1866. Stoker biographers have tended to highlight the formative impact of Bram's mother, Charlotte Stoker, on his imaginative writings, particularly her grisly stories of the famine and the 1832 cholera in the seaport town of Sligo, where she lived as a child.[43] Charlotte Stoker sent a letter to Bram in 1873 describing her family's flight from Sligo—"a provincial town in the West of Ireland . . . long before the time of the railroads and (I think) of steamboats"—at the first warning of cholera.[44] Sligo may have been provincial, but it was not isolated: roadways, carriages, and mail allowed enough intercourse with the world outside that town officials warned of the "terror," and tracked its progress from Germany to France, and finally to England. "In a very few days," she writes,

> the town became a place of the dead . . . [M]any people fled, and many of these were overtaken by the plague and died by the way . . . [M]ost of the clergy of all denominations fled, and few indeed were the instances in which the funeral service was read over the dead. (413)

The letter describes Charlotte and her family decamping to Ballyshannon, where they encounter a "half-mad doctor," who leads a pitchfork-armed assault on the family for violating quarantine. As the family moves on to Donegal, Charlotte reports being met with the cries of a riotous mob, screaming for "Fire to burn the cholera people!" (417). On returning to Sligo, they find "the streets grass-grown and five-eighths of the population dead" (418). The letter also recounts two cases of live burial: first, a woman thrown from the hospital into a mass grave, where she is later found by her husband and taken home to a full recovery, and second, a very tall sergeant thought to be dead of cholera until gravediggers attempt to break his legs in order to fit his body into a hastily made coffin (414). Charlotte Stoker's detailing of disease, exile, panic, violence, mad doctors, states of undeath and pseudo-death, the radically changed landscape in the wake of a natural disaster, and the desolation and terror of the experience, turn up transformed and modified in Bram Stoker's novel and other fictions. Other details required no modification: her phrase "mad doctor" appears alongside Stoker's addition "mad patient" in his earliest notes toward *Dracula*.[45]

In his own writing, Stoker imagined a terrible disease emerging from the stagnant marshes of an unnamed city. He began exploring ideas about communicable disease in an 1882 short story called "The Invisible Giant," published in *Under the Sunset*, a collection of macabre tales for children. This story, written some fifteen years before his more famous novel, provides a more straightforward allegory for the twinned maladies of poverty and disease than *Dracula*, while also establishing the ways in which urban infrastructure can become the target of sabotage by malevolent forces that limn both apprehension and comprehension. Like the spectral anticolonial insurgents in India whose fanaticism was associated with the cholera outbreaks, Stoker's "invisible giant" corrupts, contaminates, and sabotages the spaces of social intercourse. The story follows an orphan child, Zaya, who raises alarm when she reports that she has seen a menace invisible to everyone else—the self-absorbed and materialistic residents of the City Under the Sunset—in "the form of a Giant, hanging dimly in the air" (figure 3.4).[46]

As her neighbors and friends begin to fall sick, Zaya's warnings attract the attention of a solitary old medicine man, who accompanies the girl into the center of the city, where they observe the symptoms of the "Giant-plague."[47] These symptoms follow tropes associated with the textualization of cholera, including the sudden darkening of the body: the first victim "cried out in great pain, and screamed horribly . . . [H]is face grew blacker and blacker, and he fell down before them, and writhed a while in pain, and then died."[48] Soon the streets are filled with the dead, and the living flee to the countryside. The old man eventually succumbs to the disease, its last victim. In addition to the plague allegory, the story, dark and didactic, sketches out many of the character archetypes and concerns that would later preoccupy Stoker in his longer narrative fictions.

3.4 W. V. Cockburn, "The Invisible Giant" (1882). From Bram Stoker, *Under the Sunset* (first edition). Photograph: © The British Library Board (akg5309687).

In the form of its mists and fogs—the allegorical "giant" that "hang[s] dimly in the air"—the story draws on and anthropomorphizes miasma theory, the now discredited but long-prevailing conjecture that cholera and other epidemic diseases were spread through the atmosphere in sickening fogs and clouds rather than through germs and viruses, which were only just being discovered and investigated.[49] Scholars have also read Stoker's engagements with communicable disease theory as a loose staging of the politically fractious debate between Britain's miasmatists and contagionists, tracing the development in Stoker's thought from the miasmatic underpinnings of "The Invisible Giant" to contagionist and germ theory imaginaries at work in *Dracula*.[50] In addition to allegorizing miasma theory, "The Invisible Giant" hints at detection strategies associated with more contagion-oriented cholera investigations in London during the second and third outbreaks, especially the concerns about transmission through food and drink. The girl is attended by a flock of "little bird friends" who "tell her when there is danger . . . flutter before her and try to impede her, and scream out in their own tongue 'Go back!'"[51] Like the proverbial canary in the coal mine, the birds "pecked of her bread and drank of her cup before she touched them. . . . Often it happened that, even whilst it pecked at the bread or drank of the cup, a poor little bird would fall down and flutter its wings and die."[52] The story's concern with the alimentary, so prominent in the inquiries into cholera following Snow's and Koch's discoveries of the role of water and the presence of the *Vibrio cholerae* bacterium, takes a distinctly experimental bent here; the birds serve as a verifiable measure of the suitability of food and drink.

Reflecting the shifting focus from air to water in matters of public health and sanitation, Stoker organizes the space of "The Invisible Giant" around a central fountain, which provides a stage for the rapid onset of symptoms, and for numerous and spectacular deaths. The story concludes with the old man expiring there in terror, redoubling the fountain's function not only as a social node in the center of the marketplace, but also as the tale's clearest locus of infection, the place where the Giant reveals himself to the unseeing. Like the Broad Street pump, which proved in John Snow's investigations to be the epicenter of a major cholera outbreak in London's Soho in 1854, the fountain is the site at which the disease is most forceful and apparent—a nexus of infectious intensity, if not its cause. In its relationship to prevailing debates in social welfare and public health, "The Invisible Giant" brings together uses of narrative, chronology, morbidity statistics, disease mapping, and environmental factors in ways that suggest more than a passing interest in communicable disease theory. If the short story is built on a straightforward symbolic economy that associates threat with disease, and proposes "innocence and devotion" as its best medicaments, *Dracula* works by degrees of greater subtlety that correspond to the novel's more complex representations of antipathy, where seduction joins with revulsion, and infection is a matter of intimate precision rather than a blow that fells an entire city.

Earthly Envelopes: Dirt, Blood, Ink

Contrary to the Turkish proverb Stoker trumpets in the novel's overture—
"water sleeps, enemy is sleepless"—*Dracula* shows us that waters and
bloods, like histories and networks, do not sleep. They are transmitted,
they live on and replicate. Each can become, under the right circumstances, the sleepless enemy itself: the night stalker, the invisible killer.
In place of the center-margin geometry that shapes so much Stoker
criticism, I want to suggest that the circulation of matter, material, and
media is the dominant logical system in *Dracula* precisely because it is
the dominant logical system of late empire.[53] Consequently, liquidity
shapes not only the novel's motifs, landscapes, and detective plots, but
also its figures and its form. The novel's detour-retour plot bears this
thesis out: Dracula doesn't just emigrate to London from the "geographical pivot of history," as the geographer Halford John Mackinder dubbed
the circulatory "heartland" of Western Asia and Eastern Europe, he also
returns there, and in returning implies many such circuits of travel over
the course of hundreds of years of hemophagic life.[54] Like the germ and
the mutineer, Stoker's vampire embodies the dangers and confabulation
of that which falls outside imperial dialectics and monodirectional development narratives: he is both settler and migrant, mobility and shifting countenance, free-floating allegiance and thwarted recognition. The
vampire's contagious dissemination from Transylvania—his one body,
his many bloods—indexes the threat of such an unaccustomed enemy,
one who can move lines of engagement at will, can take many shapes
simultaneously, can slip into urban space undetected, hide in plain sight,
kill its victim from within.

Just as the common name "cholera," from drain or duct, points to both
the material and conceptual registers of flux or flow, so too do *Dracula*'s
central figures—blood and vasculature—hyperbolize the behavior and
function of metaphor itself as "transfer," the imaginative conduit of an
idea, carried from one place to another in a new disguise. *Dracula* both
is, and is about, metaphor as transfer point, co-touching as contagion.
At the same time, the novel's play with ontological instability, rendered
spectacular in the form of blood transfusions, both stages and works as
an extension of metonymy, the figure that best characterizes its interest
in the sliding metamorphosis of form.[55] If the material successes of the
British empire can be attributed to the ever-greater mobility of commodities and the removal of all barriers, physical and legal, in their unim-
peded circulation, then *Dracula*'s horror strikes at the heart of this order
while also revealing the horrors of an unfettered liberalism through literalizing metaphors of material transfer. In this sense, the novel's ap-

parent sexual conservatism and cultural isolationism also share facets of a robust and, at the time of Stoker's writing, mature anticolonialism emerging from the author's native Ireland and beyond.

Because it is insidious, slow, and nonfrontal, the vampire's infiltration and corruption of London's infrastructural systems is akin to both the classical forms of anticolonial insurgency (disruption of military operations, train track bombings, power grid disturbances) as well as contemporary Islamist terrorists' attacks on urban infrastructure (roads, bridges, checkpoints, train stations). Stoker's apparent and successful translation of an abiding myth of distant monstrosity to the spaces of industrial modernity goes some way toward explaining why the figure has been so close to hand in contemporary political discourse. The novel also usefully suggests the possible limits of a Victorian encyclopedism by destabilizing late nineteenth-century imperial urbanism's connected epistemological frameworks. Dracula's arrival in England throws into crisis knowledge practices, including the ability to read signs and figures, to recognize danger, to prevent and remedy it, even as he liquidates the bodily health of individuals—Lucy, Mina, and the mental patient Renfield—and the social body, by contagious extension. As Dracula's metaphors and media proliferate, they grow increasingly slippery and wide-ranging, producing a secondary circulation of metonymic material as a complement to the circulation of the vampire. Such allegorical and figural involution highlights the insufficiency of both realist and Gothic modes in recording the colonial world as its fracture and fragmentation begin to outpace its building and consolidation. In light of this abundance of mobile signifiers, we see how figure itself, in Stoker's hectic, haptic text, becomes another name for contagion writ large at the turn of imperialism's most anxious century.

The novel's most evident register of play with fugitive metaphor is the vampire's shapeshifting, which untethers metaphor from a stable portrait, and disrupts a notion of the one-to-one correspondence between literary image and that which is figured. In Harker's Transylvanian overture to Dracula, we are introduced to the familiar shape (borrowed from the Romantic vampire texts) of the pale, effete, Semitic count—"a tall, thin man, with a beaky nose and a black moustache and pointed beard"—but the vampire also manifests as a man-sized reptilian, creeping down the walls of the castle, as well as "quaint little specks of dust floating in the rays of the moonlight," which "gradually materialized from the moonbeams," and finally the "three ghostly women to whom [Harker] was doomed."[56] Later in the novel, Dracula's embodiments, portents, and familiars include a "dog, which landed when the ship struck" (89); an escaped zoo wolf named Berserker (150–151); the beautiful "Bloofer

Lady . . . known to the writers of various headlines as 'The Kensington Horror,' 'The Stabbing Woman,' or the 'Woman in Black'" (196); a bat, "perhaps some wild specimen from the South" (216); a fog "like smoke, or with the white energy of boiling water . . . concentrated into a sort of pillar of cloud" (287); "thousands of rats with their eyes blazing red" (310); and finally as a celestial light: "He slid into the room through the sash, though it was only open an inch wide—just as the moon herself has often come in through the tiniest crack, and has stood . . . in all her size and splendour" (311). As Van Helsing has it, "It is no common enemy that we deal with!" (312).

Alongside this list of animal, celestial, and meteorological species is the gurgling liquidity Van Helsing associates with Dracula's origins, suggesting an autochthonous confluence between the polymorphous count and the tumultuous flow of the Transylvanian landscape:

> The very place where he have [*sic*] been alive, Un-Dead for all these centuries, is full of strangeness of the geological and chemical world. There are deep caverns and fissures. . . . There have been volcanoes, some of whose openings still send out waters of strange properties, and gases that kill or make to vivify. (355)

The eruptive geological features of Dracula's home—liquid and gaseous emissions, deep caverns, bubbling fissures, and strange waters—project a geological nativity continuous with the attributes of the vampire, whose primary characteristic is that he is eternally bleeding out. Taken in conjunction with Van Helsing's invocation of the bitter and sweet waters, where Asian streams mixed with the springs of Europe, Dracula's many manifestations, from miasma-like "specks of dust" and "pillars of cloud" to long-feared animals like rats and bats "from the South," point to the novel's sustained experimentation with the poetics of contagion, tropical disease, and choleric symptomatology. They also establish the novel's world as one thoroughly determined by mediation and material transmission—a troubling prospect for the group of Londoners as they try to fortify their collective domicile.

Dracula's narrative morbidity map charts not just the movement of bodies but the movement of the earth itself, and it is the inoculation and sterilization of the vampire's sleeping boxes that leads, ultimately, to his demise. As Harker discovers in one of his numerous attempts to escape the castle, the count sleeps in coffins full of native soil: "There, in one of the great boxes, of which there were fifty in all, on a pile of newly dug earth, lay the Count!" (53). These boxes, built by the Romani laborers in the weeks leading up to Dracula's emigration to England, are the weird cargo of the ghost ship wrecked at Whitby. A clipping from the *Dailygraph* pasted into Mina's journal reads:

> The sequel to the strange arrival of the derelict in the storm last night is almost more startling than the thing itself. It turns out that the schooner is a Russian from Varna and is called the Demeter. She is almost entirely in ballast of silver sand, with only a small amount of cargo—a number of great wooden boxes filled with mould. (89)

Between the silver sand ballast and the boxes of mold, the schooner is wholly and exclusively freighted with earth. Mina's clipping, and its inclusion in the investigative dossier, highlights the disarming strangeness of encountering earth itself, perhaps agricultural civilization's most enduring figure of nation, people, and home, as a waterborne, liquidated, deterritorialized substance, forcing a recognition of the earth's potential—and potentially monstrous—flow.

Beyond the enduring and haunting image of the ghost ship, unpeopled and drifting at the mercy of the waves and the winds, the shipwrecked Demeter telegraphs a number of different histories that colored late nineteenth-century Irish writing.[57] During the height of the potato famine in 1847, the vessels on which the starving Irish populace emigrated were dubbed the "coffin ships" for their high mortality rate, a result not only of famine, but also of disease.[58] Sligo in particular, the site of Charlotte Stoker's cholera horror, was known as an infamous port of embarkation toward death.[59] Though his Anglo-Irish family, of professional class and comfortably situated, was mostly shielded from the devastating effects of the famine, Stoker was born in November 1847, the year known as "Black '47" for its high famine-related mortality rate, in a house overlooking the Dublin bay, with its near-constant shipping traffic.[60] The famine and the upheaval it occasioned—the riots, looting, and beatings of those abandoned to starvation and those that abandoned them—impacted the family enough that they moved from Dublin to Clontarf. Presaging *Dracula*'s central terror of hematophagy, tales of cannibalism were rampant during the famine in Ireland. These often capitalized on anti-Catholic sentiment by way of vulgar literalizations of Protestants' derision of transubstantiation, the supposed barbarity of eating the body and drinking the blood of Christ.[61] This fear, too, was bound to the ship and the shipwreck. A parliamentary session in 1849 occasioned the reading of a letter from a Protestant vicar in Ireland who alleged that he had seen "a shipwrecked human body . . . cast on shore: a starving man extracted the heart and liver, and that was the maddening feast on which he regaled himself and perishing family."[62]

Starvation, class unrest, and epidemic were often linked in the press, as in an account from the *London Times* in 1845, which called for the need to "prevent, as much as possible, the horrors, the high prices, and extortion of a famine," and later in 1846 when the paper warned again of the "certain and immediate perils of famine, plague, and pestilence."[63] The diseases afflicting the famine victims were numerous, but as historians Leslie Clarkson and Margaret Crawford note, in the final year of the famine, 1849, Ireland was "assaulted by cholera . . . an exotic visitor from Asia [that] had not been a feature of earlier famines."[64] On the side of botanical pathogens, which in the case of the Irish famine increased susceptibility to human epidemics, the fungus-like oomycete that caused the potato blight was likely brought to European shores in one of the innumerable shipments of bat guano harvested in the Andes. This served to fertilize Northern Europe's increasingly exhausted wheat and potato fields, the latter of which subsistence crops was itself an import from the New World in earlier centuries.[65] If *Dracula*'s ghost ship Demeter renders surreal the famine's notorious coffin ships, bound to the New World from Ireland, peopled with refugees carrying the diseases of the Orient, then the vampire's dirt boxes, their rough sides pierced with holes like a crude planter, suggest the presence of a pale and poisoned tuber, the white, necrotic thing lurking in imported earth, the infected fruit in the wooden womb.

The Demeter's foul, moldy wreck makes vivid the potential of the very earth of foreign lands to arrive on the shores of England. In *Dracula*'s fictionalized universe of a multivalent colonial unease, even more worrying than the arrival of immigrants is the delivery of the soil of Ottoman conquest, soaked in many bloods and awash in the light of the crescent, returning as the very ground of former East-West conflict to wreak its revenge. It functions, therefore, as a hypotyposis and extension of Arata's reading of *Dracula* as a novel expressing the anxiety of reverse colonization. Revisiting this forceful reading, I would suggest instead that the novel's interest in medium, mediation, figuration, and transfiguration point up the extent to which the movement of colonial goods is always already an undoing of the center-periphery model of colonial dialectics. Rather than expressing an anxiety that the colonized will soon flood into the metropole, in other words, *Dracula* unfolds in the queasy knowledge that England, both England proper and its Empire, is from the very moment of its inception lousy with the pathogenic "goods" of foreign lands. Stoker's vampire condenses this knowledge into a horror story on a legible scale. And because dirt, disinterred as it were from its native locale is a hyperbolic figure of mere matter—earthly stuff with no purpose but to be a medium, as in the boxes of mold, or simply weight, as in the case of the silver sand ballast—it renders visible in the simplest possible terms the materiality of empire's seemingly conceptual circulatory system. In this way, the Demeter's sand and dirt cargo also manifests the terrestrial interruptions of a purportedly aqueous economy, not just a shipping industry, but also liberalism's fantasy of an increasingly weightless, liquid, symbolic global trade scheme.

This economy and the shifting class structure inherent in it is indexed, for some Marxist critics, by the evolution of the vampire's stone- and gold-bound fortune—a landed aristocratic inheritance—to a paper one associated with the rise of the merchant classes and the bourgeoisie, visible in the solicitors' tasks of letter writing, credential gathering, and securing paper deeds for Dracula's properties scattered throughout London.[66] Following this reading, the making liquid of Dracula's fortune in the form of paper and ink, contracts and certificates, allows for his mobility, and therefore allows his condition to spread beyond the scope of an endemic violence into the realm of the epidemic, where speed and spread overtake origin and cause. As the vampire begins to fade from view—he is ultimately a poor subject for deep narration, motiveless and overdetermined by too many myths, incoherent in his many affiliations, collapsible in form and nearly inapparent—it becomes clear that the novel has no determinate or singular villain. Its horror, instead, is in the proliferative material of contagion. As it navigates towards its conclusion, *Dracula*'s focus shifts from persons to media, raising questions of hospitality, domain, and lair.

The distribution of coffins of dirt in London, and the location and sterilization of each of them, ultimately leads to Dracula's retreat from English shores. Following the pattern of the morbidity or "ghost map," the boxes of mold serve as consummate sites of contagion, disease vectors or host bodies that sustain the sickness the count carries with him. For the vampire hunters, the process of containing the threat Dracula poses is one of mapping and of counting these boxes, eliminating the contaminated sites from which he might launch his attack. The scattered boxes prefigure and prejustify a strategy of terrestrial inoculation undertaken by the medical men, who seek to "sterilize the lairs . . . of his earthly envelope" with communion wafers, "a portion of the host."[67] If the host stands in for the holy body against the unclean, it also evokes its liturgical companion—the blood of Christ—a drink bound for the veins as much as for the stomach and the soul. Here, Stoker redoubles the registers of mediation, illuminating the parallelism between a Christological understanding of spirit, housed in the material substrate of the wafer, and global epidemic disease, whose invisible operations between people can begin to be understood only by way of the material exchanged between them.[68]

The investigators know from the shipping bill of the Demeter that there are fifty such "foul lairs" distributed throughout the city on both sides of the Thames. The dispersed shape of this network is replicated in miniature by the collection of papers they discover at one of the count's properties. This miscellany includes the newspaper story of the shipwreck at Whitby, the Demeter's shipping bill and manifest, the arrangements for the purchase of the house at Carfax, and Dracula's personal notes. Laying in "a sort of orderly disorder . . . there were title deeds of the Picadilly house in a great bundle, deeds of the purchase of the house at Mile End and Bermondsey; notepaper, envelopes, and pens and ink."[69] These tools of contractual art highlight not only more definite sites of vampiric incubation at Mile End and Bermondsey, but also the evolving liquidity of the count's fortune from a castle filled with gold to London townhouses commandeered with paper. Complicating the existing map of terror, the as yet unused notepaper, envelopes, and ink point to the potential of further spread, an ever-greater network of invisible battlements. Completing the lurid still life is "a jug and basin—the latter containing dirty water which was reddened as if with blood."[70] In their juxtaposition, Dracula's accessories of communication, his paper, pens, and ink, reveal a slant but important likeness to the novel's substances of infectious transfer, namely dirt, water, and blood. The hastily abandoned tableau of his unlived-in home reveals a filthy basin standing in for the villain himself, as traces of pathogenic blood disperse back into the very water that carries "earthly envelopes" of infected dirt, the ink of future envelopes standing at its side.

The horror of invisible permeability and rampant, untraceable dissemination haunts every register of disease literature, particularly in the cholera age, when the porousness of national boundaries and riverways seemed to amplify the fatally absorptive capacities of lung capillaries and bed linens.[71] Between these two levels—the body's interior and the borders of nations—is the anxiety *Dracula* manifests about increasingly elastic interpersonal relationships, especially ones in which bodily fluids are exchanged, whether by choice or by force. Pamela Gilbert connects the late Victorian preoccupation with liquidity to the racial and gendered imaginaries, suggesting that British middle-class masculinity was

> predicated on the control of a "liquid, pulpy" sense of the undisciplined body and on the rigid control of desire. . . . If that liquidity and uncontrollable desire was projected onto the female and colonial male

body, then cholera was the disease that most clearly symbolized that lack of control.[72]

Gilbert pinpoints undisciplined liquidity as a threat to British masculine selfhood—an anxiety shared by the protagonists of Stoker's novel, who are compelled by their circumstances to pour out discomfiting streams of emotion and desire, the affective flip side of the lashings of blood they are terrified of losing.

Lucy, Stoker's "first girl to die," is perhaps the greatest example of the Victorian tendency toward feminizing the pulpy (I would add, in both textural and generic terms) and the liquid (again to add, the liquidity of both capital and fluid states of matter). Her promiscuous circulatory system duplicates the miscegenated soil of Transylvania on which so many bloods were spilled over centuries of conflict between the Cross and the Crescent.[73] Lucy is subject to blood contamination not only from the vampire, but also in the form of transfusions from her betrothed, Arthur, as well as the two doctors, Jack Seward and Van Helsing, and finally from the American Quincy Morris.[74] This multinational hematological gang bang serves as contrapasso for her barefoot, free-roaming ways, and for her wish to "marry three men, or as many as want her!"[75] Lucy's language, in letters to Mina, gushes with breathless enthusiasm, rich with figures of torrents and their risks, from her "sympath[y] with Desdemona when she had such a dangerous stream poured in her ear, even by a black man," to her account of Dr. Seward "pouring out a perfect stream of love-making," and "bursting into tears" at the end of her "very sloppy letter."[76] Lucy's fluent register carries over into Seward's own account of his suffering following her refusal of marriage. Despite his syntactical efficiency, "ebb-tide in appetite today," he begins his phonographic journal, too, in low-water terms (67). *Dracula* frames Lucy's need for blood in the language not just of lack, but also of desire, pointing up the "loose" distribution of affections that give the character her name. "She wants blood and blood she must have or die," explains Van Helsing, "we are about to perform a transfusion of blood—to transfer from full veins of one to the empty veins which pine for him" (134). In her pining and her wanting, Lucy is suffused and inhabited by no less than four men, underscoring her promiscuity, in a manner that Arthur will later describe, in spite of her untimely death, as having made them "really married" (192).

A counterpoint to the melodramatic register of the novel's early love and entrapment plots, Van Helsing performs the operation "with swiftness . . . with absolute method," delivering a "blood so pure that we need not defibrinate it" (135).[77] Stoker's allusion to "defibrination," or blood purification, then a relatively rare procedure, reveals a keen interest in contemporary medical advances, terminology, and praxis.[78] The prevalence of technical medical language increases acutely in the second half of the novel, as the narrative unfolds more and more in the voices, notes, and conversations between Drs. Seward and Van Helsing, the men of science who jointly endeavor to diagnose the ills befalling their companions. In spite of the certitude of the diagnostician, however, the novel's many scenes of transfusion are not without traces of the uncanny return of the monstrous. *Dracula* lingers over and returns again and again to blood transfer as a spectacular performance of the invisible process of infection, highlighting the lurid strangeness of opening one's veins to another, and watching the life pass from body to body.

In his 1859 *The Physiology of Common Life*, philosopher and amateur physiologist George Henry Lewes begins a chapter on "the structure and uses of our blood" with an invocation: "Blood is a mighty river of life," even as "[b]y some the Blood is regarded as the source of all diseases."[79] This same paradox—equally applicable to water and air, in the contagious and miasmatic imaginaries—is ever present in *Dracula*'s mythobiological treatment of blood. The vitality of the substance itself, blood's materiality, fully transfused with its metaphorical and spiritual value, is celebrated in the novel by the enthusiastic enunciations of the mad patient Renfield, who declaims in crescendoing tones after weeks of accumulating animal matter in the form of a few kittens, themselves having fed on birds, who fed in turn on spiders, who eat still more flies, "[T]he blood is the life! The blood is the life!"[80] Such celebrations do not render the process of transfusion ontologically uncomplicated, quotidian, or without fascination. At the time of Stoker's writing, transfusion was heavily overwritten by anxieties about sharing blood, a process that was understood to be tantamount to sharing something essentially personal between giver and receiver.[81] The communicative capacities and dangerous valences of circulating fluid are ubiquitous in *Dracula*, and, in keeping with Gilbert's thesis, it is the women in particular whose health degenerates, who become vessels of pathologic incubation as they nurse at the breast of the monster.[82] In its figures of miscarried reproduction, monstrous transmission, and insemination without gestation, *Dracula* capitalizes particularly on the feminine bodily horrors of menstruation and lactation.[83] The climactic scene depicting Mina's near-demise is composed as an inverse pietà, with Dracula "forc[ing] her face down on his bosom" like "a child forcing a kitten's nose into a saucer of milk to compel it to drink."[84] As she swallows, Dracula invokes the vows of marriage: "[Y]ou are now to me . . . blood of my blood . . . my bountiful wine-press for a while . . . [N]ow you shall come to my call. When my brain says 'Come!' to you, you shall cross land or sea to do my bidding."[85] Mina's mind and spirit are thus opened to the count at the moment of their bodily confluence. Van Helsing calls this her "baptism."[86]

Recognizing her compromised condition, Mina asks to be hypnotized in the hopes that a stethoscopic knowledge of the vampire in her veins will open another level of hearing, one in which she might sense Dracula's movement through sound. As Mina follows "the current of her thoughts . . . the lapping of water," she notes that "it is gurgling by, and little waves leap," and her companions glean that the count is on a ship that it is weighing anchor as they speak (347). As her infection advances, Mina's access to Dracula's sensorium grows stronger. She intones the pulse of his retreat: first "the waves lapping against the ship, and the water rushing by," then "water swirling level with my ears and the creaking of wood . . . on a river in an open boat . . . the banks are near, and it is working against stream" (371, 393). Like Lucy before her, Mina is spent by the labors of mediumship, both physical and psychical, that she has performed by bearing this information to the encouraging murmurs of so many male spectators. Placed as evidence alongside the newspapers, deeds, and shipping manifests in the vampire hunters' investigative dossier, Mina's telepathic information draws together the "medium" of late nineteenth-century occultism—frequently a female figure or a racially othered man—with the everyday media of detection. In some senses, the novel ends here, as the map of information comes together and throws the ordinariness of Dracula's operations into high relief.[87] The group corroborates her report with a battery of train and boat schedules, rounds of map consultations, and interrogations of the Slovak dock workers in charge of the "box" containing the vampire's body.[88] Splashing for a few moments in a "puddle" of information, the doctors and their companions conclude that the vampire has been chased off of English shores and has secured his passage home to Transylvania. In split crews on land and sea, they beat the enemy back into the place of his perennial retreat.

The novel's ending is notoriously abrupt and disappointing: the undoing of circular and circulatory logics transpires all too rapidly through the conceit of liquid telepathy. When the group descends on the villain in a field that spans the riverbank and the castle's ramparts, the vampire's end is fast: "[A]lmost in the drawing of a breath, the whole body crumbled into dust and passed from our sight."[89] In this feint of a happy ending, no blood is spilled back into the ancient soil. For all the heroic striving and well-coordinated research marshaled in service of understanding this foreign enemy, the final scene vaporizes every mark and sign of Dracula's violence, returning him to a species of miasma, a slant version of dust-to-dust. In this sense, his demise also holds out the promise of a return, a sequel, a rising. This is not merely a matter of pulpy serialism.

As Friedrich Kittler notes in "Dracula's Legacy," an essay written on the occasion of Jacques Lacan's death, the way Dracula's body crumbles into dust in the final confrontation renders impossible the definitive death-by-staking required to finish him once and for all. Like Lacan's tapes, Kittler reminds us, the vampire is disseminated. And like the atomized, atmospheric Invisible Giant before him, he will remain dormant and unseen until favorable conditions for his self-perpetuation arise.[90]

Colonial Modalities and Documentary Form

In the preceding sections, I have located within the novel as well as in Stoker's research and sociopolitical milieu a set of Orientalist and epidemic materials that appear more and less explicitly in *Dracula*'s final form, and that, in either case, become part of that novel's perennial cargo—the historical and figural material it persistently deposits in the minds of readers in the century and a quarter since its publication. Any study of British literary production in the 1880s and 1890s would reveal dozens of popular works inscribing and allegorizing similar historical events, similar concerns. These decades saw Marsh, Doyle, Collins, Wells, Haggard, Stevenson, Conrad, and more set free an earlier, more scholastic Orientalism in a pulpier style. Each marshaled exoticism, peregrine objects, Eastern sublimity, "premodern" ontologies, and a sense of the ever more rapidly encroaching East to illustrate the anxieties of late-colonial Britain, ranging from sexuality in crisis to the famine, infectious disease, pollution, and sanitation to the aesthetic and spiritual fascinations of a rapacious and tottering archipelago of lands and cultures conquered. I have also insisted that *Dracula* is a unique entry in this corpus, both because of its ongoing influence on popular culture and neocolonial orientations toward the monstrous unknown, as well as for its singular form: an Orientalist Gothic overture followed by an investigative dossier comprising diaries, reports, clippings, medical notes, and phonographic recordings. In this section, I show how Stoker's approach in compiling this dossier is shaped by colonial narrative form as a fundamentally remedial undertaking that invariably sought to expose if not fix perceived pathologies in colonized subjects and spaces through meticulous recording—a feature of what historian of early colonial India Bhavani Raman has called the Raj practice of "bureau rule."[91] Specifically, the novel's use of multiple optics is indebted to theories and practices of synoptic epidemic investigation and inscription, which during the time of Stoker's writing were becoming codified and institutionalized as a discipline inextricable from colonial surveillance and population management. *Dracula* not only thematizes the ontological crisis of late colonialism through its figures of liquidity, its circulatory logic, and its map of communicable disease, it also performs colonial epistemology by plotting collation and interpretation as self-sustaining activities of empire. *Dracula* therefore unfolds both the Orientalist sublime and its undoing by rendering the study of imperial epidemics as a social-realist horror story, foregrounding the role of data collection, reading, narrative production, and interpretation in more sophisticated and lasting ways than any other novel of its time.

Bernard Cohn, in *Colonialism and Its Forms of Knowledge*, defines the knowledge-gathering projects of the British empire in India, the largest and most deeply embedded of the nineteenth-century colonies, as follows:

> As a part of the imperial settlement project after the repression of the Indian uprising of 1857–1858, the Government of India carried out a series of censuses which they hoped would provide a cross-sectional picture of the "progress" of their rule. By 1881 they had worked out a set of practices that enabled them not just to list the names of what they hoped would be every person in India but also to collect basic information about age, occupation, caste, religion, literacy, place of birth, and current residence. Upwards of 500,000 people, most of whom were volunteers, were engaged in carrying out the census. The published census reports not only summarized the statistical information thus compiled but also included extensive narratives about the caste system, the religions of India, fertility and morbidity, domestic organization, and the economic structure of India. The census represents a model of the Victorian encyclopedic quest for total knowledge.[92]

I cite this description at some length to capture both Cohn's periodization of this "encyclopedic" undertaking—importantly systematized after the 1857 uprising and extending into the last decades of the century—as well as the chiastic structure of the endeavor. The shift from Company rule to Crown rule was marked by a bureaucratic form of poiesis that required colonial officials and settler volunteers to produce, reproduce, and reproduce again an archive of knowledge and fact shaped specifically to justify the continuation of the colonial project. That the census reports were designed to "provide a cross-sectional picture" of "colonial progress" conscripted both survey design and the adjacent "extensive narratives" into a predetermined project. A record of imperial progress distilled from surveyable life burgeoned between a set of fixed coordinates, including name and location, fertility and morbidity. At the same time, the more prismatic and holistic a picture of British India could be drawn, the greater the resources that could be marshaled to administer, control, and extract resources and levies from it.[93] In Cohn's terms, the colonial "theater of power" put enormous textualization projects center stage, and in so doing "created and normalized a vast amount of information that formed the basis of [its] capacity to govern."[94] Buttressing this archival project was the "fact," whose form, according to Cohn, "was taken to be self-evident, as was the idea 'that administrative power stemmed from the efficient use of these facts'" (4).

The stakes for the producers of this knowledge were existential; the data they produced had to both implement and make a case for their own method, logic, and ongoing necessity. Consequently, many such reports began with remarkable offerings on the theory of imperial information, and the status of knowledge and fact as crucial building blocks of the colonial project. This was especially true when the fundamental principles of empire and liberalism were under threat from different knowledge communities, as in the case of James Bryden's *Report on the Cholera of 1866–68*, which offers this commentary on its own facticity:

> Such opinions which I have recorded, have been arrived at after many previous misconceptions, and no one can be more aware of the fact than I am, that every year and every epidemic teaches us something new, and throws a different or a clearer light on the conceptions derived from former experiences. I have tried to dispose the facts and figures in such a shape that it is open to everyone to draw his conclusions from them, and these may be corroborative of my views, or they may not. I have tried to give shape to the study, and I have little doubt that some at least of the inferences which I have made, will be found available in the future when the laws of the cholera of India shall have been framed into a system.[95]

Bryden sketches out the map of territories from which his morbidity and mortality statistics on cholera outbreaks, going back to 1817, are derived, giving context to his data, then describing the folded logic by which he hopes to build his case: "these data I therefore propose to give as an essential introduction to the conclusions to be based upon them."[96] Compare Bryden's remarks to the prefatory instructions to the reader in *Dracula*, which outline the novel's form as a documentary collection with its own internal logic, that will supposedly emerge in the reading of them. The preface assures the skeptical reader:

How these papers have been placed in sequence will be made clear in the reading of them. All needless matters have been eliminated, so that a history almost at variance with the possibilities of latter-day belief may stand forth as simple fact. There is throughout no statement of past events wherein memory may err, for all the records chosen are exactly contemporary, given from the standpoints and within the range of knowledge of those who made them.[97]

The unnamed narrator here—possibly Mina, possibly some later inheritor of the archive—makes no claim to a synthetic or totalizing account from a single perspective or a unified narrative voice, but rather puts their faith in the multiplicity of generic forms and perspectives that will follow. The frame, in keeping with the tradition of the Gothic authenticating preface, serves to both ratify and cast doubt on the provenance of the manuscript, to render more surreal, more mysterious, more challenging to the ordinary physics of diachronic narrative that which will follow. Indeed, on the facing page, the reader is alerted to the fact that Jonathan Harker's journal, the first set of texts, is transcribed from shorthand, and that, in the novel's opening lines, we are "leaving the West and entering the East . . . among the traditions of Turkish rule" (1). If the passage from West to East was not enough to signal to nineteenth-century readers that knowledge, fact, and observation were about to be overturned, the preface's instability is underscored by the novel's final "note," written in Harker's hand, which promises that "in all the mass of material of which the record is composed, there is hardly one authentic document! Nothing but a mass of type-writing . . . [W]e could hardly ask anyone, even did we wish to, to accept these as proofs of so wild a story" (421).

These framing notes reveal from the outset that *Dracula*'s suspense will not be in its drama or plot. There will be little confusion about who is to blame. The vampire's rough shape and predilections were already known quantities—the Victorian vampire fad stretched back at least to Polidori. If at some point the novel inspired anxiety about who or what the horror of the monster was, it certainly cannot now. Narrative force and mystery emerge instead from the gaps in memory and understanding, the spaces between the texts and the memos in the dossier, and from the almost total absence of the vampire in the novel that bears his name. The documents tell their story not only through their "simple" facticity, a chiastic structure akin to that of the colonial census—but also from their organization and the social and professional status of those who have written them. Although the epistolary form and the complicated nesting prefaces were pervasive features of both Victorian Orientalism and colonial adventure tales, *Dracula*'s formal apparatus moves far beyond the ordinary indications that what will follow is strange and foreign, sensational and dangerous; by contrast, Stoker's other major novels and most of his short stories are narrated by a single young man of professional standing. *The Jewel of the Seven Stars*' Malcolm Ross is a young barrister; *The Lair of the White Worm*'s narrator closely approximates the perspective of the enterprising Adam Salton; "The Burial of Rats" is told by an unnamed young man biding his time abroad while his engagement's probationary period comes to an end. It would be one-dimensional to suggest that *Dracula*'s staying power should be attributed solely to the novel's formal innovations, but it is instructive to consider what the documentary form ultimately captured about Victorian and colonial epistemology—and about the prominence of contagion as a then-contemporary concept—and why the vampire hunters' records have provided a more fruitful archive for future transformations than, say, *The Jewel of the Seven Stars*' barrister's diary about an odd-smelling cat mummy.

Beyond imitating specific forms of colonial and Gothic writing, *Dracula*'s textual assemblage is a literary analogue to Cohn's colonial encyclopedism, juxtaposing different forms of evidence and communication dispersed in social space from multiple perspectives in a manner like what I have called the synopticism of epidemic writing. Friedrich Kittler's reading, cited in brief above, highlights the novel's epidemic backdrop, situating Stoker's "sterilization" plot as a legacy of Adrien Proust's (Marcel's father) 1830s cordon sanitaire at the borders of the Occident. For him, the quarantine operation makes "*Dracula* . . . no vampire novel, but rather the written account of our bureaucratization."[98] It's a bit of a feint—he suggests later that "anyone is free to call this a horror novel as well" (73). Rather than simply calling *Dracula* a horror novel *as well* as a written account of our bureaucratization, I want to insist that the novel's semi-archival form shows us how—in the colonial scene—the two are mutually constitutive, how horror becomes a fundamental aspect, a framework of imperial bureaucracy. Stoker's textualizing project, similar to those Cohn describes, neutralizes the Eastern foreigner through description and encyclopedism even as it trades in and advances xenophobic tropes of Gothic horror. In so doing, *Dracula*'s investigations set a literary precedent in the nineteenth-century effort to square older forms of terror with epidemicity as an epistemological problem, a reading practice, and as a set of specific bodily and social symptoms brought about by the everyday practices of empire.

The parceling out of the narrative into distinctive genres highlights the novelty of what Kittler calls a "new paradigm of science" exemplified by "Edison and Freud, Sherlock Holmes and Van Helsing"—its freshness, its departure from existing regimes of empiricism—in the nearly unnarratable transition from Harker's Gothic overture to the documentary narrative that takes shape afterwards (68). Harker's time in the "thunderous atmosphere," among the "frowning rocks" of Transylvania stands as a Gothic text within a text—its horizon limited in opposition to the evidentiary omnibus that follows.[99] After days in the castle, he tries in vain to locate the beginning of the story in another genre's terms: "Let me begin with facts—bare, meager facts, verified by books and figures, and of which there can be no doubt. I must not confuse them with experiences, which will have to rest on my own observation or my memory of them."[100] In her early work on the Gothic, Eve Sedgwick posits the difficulty of reading and interpretation as the central textual features of Gothic writing, pointing to the "massive inaccessibility of those things that should normally be most accessible, the difficulty the story has in getting itself told."[101] She also writes of the "rarest of all" Gothic novels: "the book . . . without a pseudonym and an elaborate account of the provenance and antiquity of the supposed original manuscript."[102]

In its explanatory prolegomenon and in its first chapters, *Dracula* evolves the ubiquitous authenticating preface of Gothic literature according to new technologies of disenchantment, modelling the movement from illegibility in Gothic reading practices to a belief in legibility proper to "science," sited geotemporally in an urban modernity stitched into a wild and vast empire.[103]

These newer concerns may help to explain why the novel occasionally turns clinical medicine and pathology (narrowly defined as the study of tissues) into a set piece for frailty and human foibles.[104] For Michel Foucault, in *The Birth of the Clinic*, pathology created a space of interpretation and reading wherein the body became legible to science, and, by extension, to the institutions of knowledge upheld by and that reciprocally upheld the state. If pathology was the cornerstone of nineteenth-century medicine, it was organized by way of the sightlines that gridded the clinical encounter: the doctor with his sight-enhancing apparatus turned his gaze to the body of the patient, her parts and her tissues becoming text. When he speaks of the anatomist examining the brain, looking for "grain of things," Foucault gestures toward a secret braille buried in the skull, sketching the contours of a period in medical history in which disease could be thought in terms of its thingliness, or the thingly changes it occasioned in the body.[105] Under the conditions of what he names the "flexion" between the classical clarity of the enlightenment and the clinical optic of the nineteenth century, truth becomes once again coterminous with sight—"as it opens, the eye first opens the truth"—and coterminous as well with presence, with the singularity of the sick body.[106]

A surgical episode late in *Dracula* demonstrates the limits of the pathological gaze and its extractive procedures, recalling the abuses of the clinic recounted in Charlotte Stoker's letter; how the nurses in the cholera hospitals saved time waiting for the sick to die by "dragging the patients down the stairs by the legs with their heads dashing on the stone steps, before they were dead."[107] In one of the most horrific and critically neglected episodes in *Dracula*, Stoker layers his mother's memory of medical misconduct during the cholera with a neurophysiological note on head trauma that he receives from his brother, Thornley, sometime in the early 1880s (figure 3.5).

The scene takes place near the novel's climax; Dr. Seward stands aghast in the doorway of the mad patient Renfield's room in the lunatic asylum, the locked doors and windows of which admit no entrant:

> I found him lying on the floor on his left side in a glittering pool of blood. When I went to move him, it became at once apparent that he had received some terrible injuries. . . . As the face was exposed I could see that it was horribly bruised, as though it had been beaten against the floor—indeed it was from the face wounds that the pool of blood originated.[108]

In the novel's logic, Renfield's madness indexes a different, deeper kind of infection and inhabitation by vampirism—unlike Mina, who mostly feels tired and dissipated, and Lucy, who simply dies too quickly, his entire cognitive apparatus is overtaken by the count. His injuries are accordingly more spectacular. When Van Helsing arrives, he concludes, contrary to Seward, that "the wounds of the face were superficial; the real injury was a depressed fracture of the skull, extending right up through the motor area."[109] What follows is an irruption of technical and medical jargon and surgical theatrics that attenuate the lead-up to the novel's most spectacular scene: the forced feeding of Mina at Dracula's breast. As he lies bleeding on the floor of the lunatic asylum, Renfield's cell is suddenly transformed into an operating theater whose finale is the trephining operation performed by Van Helsing in order to "reduce the [cranial] pressure and get back to normal conditions."[110] Delivered in Van Helsing's awkwardly foreign cadence, the scene is easy to read as comic.

These terms, and the description of the operation, are taken directly from the memo written by Thornley Stoker in answer to Bram's query about the symptoms and treatment of depression fractures some fifteen the surgeon opportunity to remove the blood clot might give instant relief. I have seen a patient in profound coma, begin to move his limbs and curse and swear during the operation. The more recent the injury, the more rapid the relief. A patient dying of these conditions would be profoundly comatose, and stertorous in years prior to the final publication of the novel. Thornley's memo instructs: "If a depressed fracture the symptoms would probably be immediate . . . [T]rephining to remove the depressed bone, or to give the surgeon opportunity to remove the blood clot might give instant relief."[111] In *Dracula*: "We shall wait . . . just long enough to fix the best spot for trephining, so that we may most quickly and perfectly remove the blood clot; for it is evident that the haemorrhage is increasing."[112] It's revealing that trephining—one of the oldest surgical procedures in evidence in which a small burr-hole was drilled or scraped into the skull—was for much of its history used for psychiatric disorders including seizures, madness, depression, and loss of speech. In the parlance of the early modern period, it was the preferred method of extracting the "stone of madness."[113] Renfield's suffering repeats in medical spectacular terms the perpetual hemorrhaging from which all of Dracula's victims suffer. The doctors' heroic efforts on his behalf are motivated in part by their belief that he has some crucial piece of information about the vampire, a stone of madness, as it were, secreted in his wounded brain. In the novel's arc, however, the trephination operation is one that fails, and its failure stages the tension between the optics of clinical pathology and other forms of medical knowing that expand the ecology of study beyond the individual patient. Before dying, having recovered from the "stertorous breathing," Renfield lets loose a stream of disappointing information that the reader and inquiring doctors already know: the vampire can atomize himself into dust, rats, a death's-head moth, a "red cloud," he is on his way to Mina, Renfield's own wounds are simply a diversion.[114] In spite of its interest in multiple models of medical investigation, the novel thus telegraphs the limits of a depth-based approach to contagious phenomena and moves toward the surface currents of the social, even as it sketches them out in a haphazard and inchoate fashion.

Stoker's experiments with the clinical scene in *Dracula* constitute an important part of the novel's advancement of the sciences proper to a pathological empire, which, in its extended geography, harbored tendrils of cholera, of blight, of typhus, and of horrors unknown. If Renfield's brain operation can be understood as a set piece inviting the reader to consider the limits of a vertical relationship between knowledge and its extraction—information about and as contagion that can simply be plucked from where it permanently resides—then its failure points, too, to the failure of the clinical scene in an allegory in which vampirism as an epidemic phenomenon might also contain the key to its own firm and final meaning. Instead, *Dracula* explodes what Michel Foucault understood to be the nineteenth century's signal experiments with individual bodies, which fail in every case to stand as accurate indices of the social whole, in favor of a multiple, metonymic representation of social simultaneity as the proper figure of a circulatory empire—biopolitics in advance of its theorization. Although both are legacies of nineteenth-century sciences of state, and both persist as foundational knowledges of statecraft in the twenty-first century's new empires, the divergence of their visions is precisely the representational maneuver that distinguished an epidemiological approach from a clinical one.

The failure of the trephining operation also points up the limits of allegory as a depth-based model of reading. The history of *Dracula's* popular and critical reception shows clearly that it has endured in part because it works as an efficient allegory for any number of social ills and political maladies. Extant scholarship accordingly identifies Stoker's vampirism as a successful projection of a range of Victorian anxieties: the poverty of the rural masses arriving in London; migrants from Eastern Europe; moral degeneracy and untamed sexual desire; a diffuse "decadence" as well as the aesthete who performs it; miscegenation in the colonial periphery and the heart of the metropole; the Jew as usurer and occult capital maker; the exhaustibility of natural resources and foreign markets—mineral, vegetable, human—in Britain and abroad; rebellion and nascent nationalism in both Ireland and India; homosexuality (Stoker's, as well as that of his close associates Wilde, Whitman, and Henry Irving); and the inevitable dissolution of the British empire presaged by Ottoman decline in Eastern Europe.[115] These are just a few of the more compelling and frequently invoked historicist keys to Stoker's promiscuously interpretable text. Indeed, the symbolic breadth of *Dracula* has led some critics to note a critical propensity to read the novel as "an all-purpose allegory."[116]

As a consequence of this allegorical habit in the criticism, readings of *Dracula* have tended to hold apart the novel's various symbolic vocabularies by favoring one strand—illness, capital, sexuality, communication, technology, and so on—and suppressing others. Such readings invite us to read the novel's terrors as symptoms of some social ailment observable in the historical context of its composition. The figural potential that has defined these historicist readings as well as the novel's historical impact—the inexhaustible logic of the vampire-as-*X*—reflects epistemological and literary developments that respond to the massive increase in the flow of bodies and goods over the course of the nineteenth century.[117] It is possible without abandoning these insights to follow *Dracula's* formal features as they lead us away from isolated social symptoms and toward an understanding of the novel's allegorical elasticity through the circulatory logic that links its investigations of both mediation (textual, financial, extrasensory) and contagion (sexual, narrative, psychological). In other words, *Dracula*'s poly-allegorical features stage the hyperbolic fluidity and untrammeled circulation of goods, bodies, and ideas along the shifting borders of the Orient and the British empire. The novel's form is in advance of itself—it is more than a matter of period-appropriate genre mixing. *Dracula* offers, I think, an epistemology attuned to the social whole and the currents of exchange proper to late imperial political and immunological sprawl, beginning with its depthless characters and culminating in the continual thwarting of efforts at deep knowledge gained through observation and deduction.

Voluntary Bloodletting and 9/11

In the preface to the 1765 edition of *The Castle of Otranto*, Horace Walpole complained that "the great resources of fancy have been dammed up by a strict adherence to common life."[118] Eddying through Stoker's undammed Gothic distortions, his dramatist's preference for melodrama over psychological realism, the arcana of the decadent, there is the evident insistence of common life. The triumph of the novel, as infuriating and messy as it is, is the triumph of the systematized study of a contagious phenomenon arrived from afar—the demystifying domesticating practice of naming, mapping, and charting things, the compiling of data, the technological force of the typewriter, the phonograph, the telegram, the deed. A strict adherence to common life, to science and empiricism, lends a new and terrifying shape to the vampire myth borrowed from Romanticism and its Orientalist leanings. If the pathologization of the twenty-first-century Islamist terrorist draws on the historical and narrative traditions of eighteenth- and nineteenth-century monsters, we can see not just how the fantastic morphology of the Gothic monster serves as a projection screen for the full battery of Victorian social anxieties, but also that the terror of the colonial other, the bodily risks entailed in managing a liberal empire, was already embedded in the enormous threat of infectious disease and the narratives and figures that represented them.

The broader point to draw from the foregoing analysis is that the Orientalist monsters of the nineteenth century are still very much with us today, and that far from being a caprice of history, the extraordinary renewed interest in the vampire myth after September 11 has a great deal to tell us about the culture of Islamophobia and imperial disease poetics in the West, both in terms of its origins and in terms of its future. *Dracula*'s particular geography of East-West conflict, and Stoker's conscription of a biopolitics avant la lettre and the imperial science of epidemiology in the telling of his vampire tale place his novel firmly within a canon of colonial narratives that have profoundly shaped the easy association of Islam, violence, and epidemic in the twenty-first century. Stoker reinvents the vampire, and invents its undoing through forms of knowledge necessitated and upheld by the colonial encounter and global trade. With "infinite science"—to return to Fanon's term—the novel lays traps for the vampire's defeat, and conscripts surveillance technologies at the cutting edge of late-nineteenth-century biopower to save the soul, body, and blood of the population under threat. The origins of a self-evident relationship between, on the one hand, a vampirish Islamist monstrosity, rendered cartoonish by the depiction of the hijab of the Algerian woman or the "black Islamic dress" of the Westminster terrorist as latter-day Dracula capes, and compounded by a pervasive sense in the West that "they" both "hate our freedoms" and also "want what we have," and on the other hand sickness, disease, contagion, and imperial epidemiology, have been largely ignored in studies of our foundational colonial fictions because to acknowledge this relationship requires that we overlook the most thrilling moments of terror, suspense, and violence in novels like *Dracula*. The drama of learning how to read this violence is far more ordinary than the Gothic overture would have us believe, but it retains the fantastic moves of the imagination whereby the urban infrastructural vasculature, itself a microcosm of global circulatory logic, can be envisioned as an organ system of an anthropomorphic planetary public health.

An arresting and illustrative example of the force of this imaginary serves as one of the opening examples of Catherine Waldby and Robert Mitchell's study, *Tissue Economies: Blood, Organs, and Cell Line in Late Capitalism*:

Within hours of the terrorist attacks on the World Trade Center, the U.S. Department of Health and Human Services, the American Association of Blood Banks, and the American Red Cross issued calls for people to donate blood. Supplies were low throughout the state of New York. . . . In the chaos following the attacks, health authorities could not estimate how many people were injured, or what quantities of transfusion blood they might need. Immediately thousands of people came forward to give blood. They waited in line for hours. The New York Blood Center, which supplies most of the city's hospitals, collected more than five thousand units of blood and fielded twelve thousand phone calls in the first twelve hours. In Washington, after the terrorist attack on the Pentagon, blood was collected at hospitals, makeshift centers, and a building next to the White House. When the collection centers closed, many people queued through the night. . . .

This overwhelming desire to give blood was not limited to the citizens of New York and Washington: all over the United States, similar scenes were played out. In the weeks following September 11, more than 475,000 units were collected for the victims, but only 258 units were used for them, and much of the blood had to be discarded.[119]

Waldby and Mitchell suggest that this immediate outpouring of blood donation springs from "a model of the body, and of relationships between bodies, that we take for granted in the twenty-first century: one body can share its vitality with another through the redistribution of tissues, from donor to recipient, through biotechnical intervention."[120] As I have argued in the first part of this book, this "model" of the body is one that arose in part to deal with the imaginative challenges of conceiving and representing imperial space in the late nineteenth century, in relationship to the rapidly evolving challenges to social immunity brought on by colonial expansion, military intervention, and trade. Stoker and others participated in the experimental textualization of this model, naturalizing the very notion that vitality might be both shared and stolen through the material of the body, coextensive with the material of international trade. Diseased people and diseased artifacts could also be revitalized by healthy bodies, infusions of foreign goods and money, not to mention attitudes, beliefs, and habits. In this way, the notion of the "body" of empire, comprising relationships between colonies-qua-bodies, served as a precursor to the aid economy and third-world debt structures of postcolonial internationalism.

If, as these theorists argue, the impulse to give blood as a gift "promote[s] the optimum form of circulation to maintain the body politic of the welfare state, by creating a certain kind of civil intercorporeality," then one must necessarily ask what determines the limits of this civic body and the population it incorporates. The Manichean cast of the Islam-versus-the-West binarism that has only strengthened its hold in the last two decades makes it clear that the borders of the welfare state are mere heuristics assigned to the long-standing extramural status of the barbarian, the nonperson, the Muslim, the monster, the terrorist. The fall of the World Trade Center towers has been cast in loose psychoanalytic terms as an American castration, with the obvious parallel of the cloud-reaching hubris of the World Trade Center and the phallus. The destruction of 9/11 heralded, among other things, the end of an unchallenged US imperialism following the Second World War. The immediate impulse to give blood, however reflexive and warm-hearted it may have been, invites us to reimagine this simple story in more complicated terms. Urged on by the charitable institutions that supported

an ever-more pathological health care system, Americans read the terrorists' theft of life as a theft of blood. In order to keep the wounded state
alive, they lined up like so many Sewards and Van Helsings to share of
this vital resource, and in so doing silently ratified the securitization of
the coming War on Terror in the terms of public health, as if such a construct had ever been or could ever be free of its colonial history.

PART II: THE BODY ALLEGORICAL IN FRENCH ALGERIA

CHAPTER 4

The Brown Plague

War, to sane men at the present day, begins to look like an epidemic insanity, breaking out here and there, like the cholera or influenza, infecting men's brains instead of their bowels.

RALPH WALDO EMERSON, *MISCELLANIES*

In 1828, when our great-grandfathers crossed the Mediterranean for the operation that was to end in the conquest of Algeria, Algeria was an archaic country. So was France.

GERMAINE TILLION, *ALGERIA: THE REALITIES*

In his notebooks of 1942, as Albert Camus was drafting his second major work of fiction, *The Plague* (*La peste*), which would be published to great acclaim by Gallimard in 1947, he wrote, "science explains what happens, not what *is*" (*la science explique ce qui fonctionne et non ce qui* est).[1] The tone is characteristic of the notebooks, where one finds many of the big ideas that will appear dispersed in his variegated writings as aphoristic keys for the general abstraction of the oeuvre. The point is almost certainly to distinguish the flat-footed pedantries of scientific observation from the deeper, more permanent truths to which fiction, theater, or lyric essay—Camus's own means of thinking and knowing—presumably give us access. Literature, it can be inferred, shows us that which *is*, eternally, essentially, while science simply records observed events—what happens, works, or unfolds as a function of time, in mere sequence. Indeed, Camus has been celebrated for generations as the paradigmatic philosophical novelist of the twentieth century: a reliable purveyor of deep, universal human truths, if not always of a liberatory politics.

A different way of understanding this maxim, however, is to look at how Camus's writing—marked by a striving for balance and objectivity, presented from journalistic, medical, lawyerly, and testimonial points of view—represents the dynamics of what unfolds in life-before-our-eyes, and in so doing, complicates a notion of what *is*, what is true, or what ought to be. Camus's statement suggests that his work contains not just a meditation on the metaphysics of epidemic, but also an as yet un-interrogated interest in a scientific or phenomenological depiction of postwar upheaval, including the threat of a nationalist ideology that appeared increasingly dangerous, virulent, and contagious as it took hold in the French and British colonies, and in Algeria in particular. Reading the statement in this way doesn't tell us much in terms of establishing a more consistent reading of Camus's practice of representation—and even less so what he thought about science, a topic that very little of his work engaged explicitly. What it does do, I think, is illuminate how and why *The Plague*, the most explicitly scientific and historical of Camus's fictions, allegorizes political violence through a chronicle of epidemic. Approached in this way, the novel is less a coherent tale of a communal existential crisis, and more a social and scientific experiment, unfolding from multiple perspectives the difficulty of understanding what happens *as it happens*, oftentimes in the absence of reliable knowledge of what it, in fact, *is*. The plague itself, for example, remains unnamed until well after its arrival in the Algerian city of Oran, and is identified only because an elderly doctor recognizes it from his days in China. Even then, it seems impossible; the doctor deems his own diagnosis "hardly credible," placing the preposterous anachronism of the illness—what it *is*—under the sign of uncertainty.[2]

Instead of investigating the plague's identity and origins, much of the story revolves around the workaday efforts of a group of men to observe and cope with the sickness and its "reign of terror" (199; 181). The focus on the topography and social behavior of disease in a populous colonial city, rather than its microbial or symptomatic identity determined in the clinic or the morgue, reflects the broader epistemic shift at the end of the nineteenth century from pathological etiology to colonial epidemiology as a data-gathering and narrative enterprise—key practices in what Bernard Cohn called colonialism's forms of knowledge. In the voice of his narrator, Dr. Bernard Rieux, Camus admits that his band of brothers are neither heroic nor memorable: "the grim days of plague do not stand out like vivid flames, ravenous and inextinguishable, beaconing a troubled sky, but rather like the slow, deliberate progress of some monstrous thing crushing out all upon its path" (179; 166). Camus's approach is the banality of evil avant la lettre; instead of the spectacular imagery associated with plague narratives and art—corpses, buboes, the distinctive beaked mask of the medico della peste—the novel favors a depiction of the slow, deliberate progress of the disease, its transmissibility between people and places, its geometric growth, its steady calculus of mortality, the boredom of quarantine. In these particulars, *The Plague* insists that "nothing is less sensational than pestilence . . . [B]y reason of their very duration, great misfortunes are monotonous" (179; 166). We can hear in these words not only a premonition of Arendt's analysis in the Eichmann trial, but also a reflection on the bureaucratization and institutionaliza- tion of power under the aegis of education, military and intelligence service, population management, sanitation, and public health, each of which sought to bring colonial subjects into the statistical and adminis- trative orbit of global humanity.[3]

To meet this threat as it comes, the work of The Plague's protagonists is equally slow, statistical, observational, and bureaucratic. Camus's in- vestigation of "science" as a literary perspective troubles a distinction be- tween observable events and symptoms on the one hand and the deeper, more persistent metaphysics of disease and violence. To stage this un- certainty, The Plague displaces the Nazi occupation of France (the novel's title puns on "la peste brune," referring to the Germans' brown uniforms) to the more ambiguous space of French Algeria, a colony populated by a different kind of brown body, and teetering on the edge of drastic politi- cal change that Camus was documenting elsewhere in his journalism.[4] In displacing the allegory of Occupation and Resistance from Europe to Af- rica, the novel hypothesizes the contagious nature of ideology, and links the past events of the Second World War to the threat of a mimetic future in Algeria. The Plague as text is also readily transposable and translatable; abstract enough to be relevant to a great many contexts of extremity. Like The Stranger (L'Étranger), it has enjoyed a long life not just in French letters, but also in the British, American, North African, and so-called "world literature" canons. In a November 2001 essay on the timeliness of a then-new translation of The Plague, critic Tony Judt framed the novel in relationship to the events of September 11. "Today," he wrote, "The Plague takes on fresh significance and a moving immediacy," arguing that Camus's "depiction of instant ex cathedra judgments—'My brethren, you have deserved it'—will be grimly familiar to us all."[5] Again in 2020, during the novel coronavirus pandemic, sales of The Plague skyrocketed.[6]

For the first two decades after his death in 1960, Camus scholarship oscillated dramatically between condemnation on political grounds, exemplified in Conor Cruise O'Brien's forceful Albert Camus of Europe and Africa (1970); hagiographic recovery on biographical and humanist grounds, a key instance of which is Herbert Lottman's Albert Camus: A Biography (1979); and trauma theory and historicism, paradigmatically in the witness-oriented reading of The Plague by Shoshana Felman (1989).[7] In the mid-1990s, following Edward Said's provocation to study Camus's body of work in light of French colonial cultural production in Culture and Imperialism (1993) and the publication of the unfinished manuscript of The First Man (Le premier homme) in 1994, both devotees and critics sought to resituate Camus's novels and stories in the broader context of his life and political and journalistic writings, as well as in interpretive frameworks beyond that of postwar existentialism, including postcolonialism, surrealism, and the aesthetics of violence. The intensity of this project has only grown in the years since 2001, decades marked by a sharply increased interest in the historical roots of the intersection of global Islam and terrorism, which many readers associate with the Algerian War of Independence.

Accordingly, a number of new scholarly and popular works on Camus's writing have appeared in the last years. In the context of a North American Camus, the long-awaited English translation of the *Algerian Chronicles* by Arthur Goldhammer in 2013 joined David Carroll's *Albert Camus the Algerian* (2007) and Robert Zaretsky's *Albert Camus: Elements of a Life* (2010) in signaling a return to Camus scholarship in the new millennium, specifically a critical reappraisal of Camus's writings and politics in light of the global War on Terror.[8] The centenary of Camus's birth in 2013 occasioned a flurry of events and publications, an excitement compounded by the sense that Camus's "spirit has hovered over the Arab Spring."[9] Following the publication of Kamel Daoud's important novel *The Meursault Investigation* (*Meursault, contre-enquête*) in 2014, millennial readers in Algeria, France, and abroad have begun to recognize that to claim Camus exclusively in the French literary tradition, or to refuse to recognize him as an Algerian writer during the period of decolonization, is to miss a great deal about what makes his work consequential with regard to the shifting parameters of the human and the political during his most productive years in the postwar period. In some ways, this new moment echoes and builds upon the Algerian recovery of Camus during the "*décennie noire*" or black decade of the 1990s, which Alice Kaplan and Emily Apter have both noted as an important counterpoint to the rejection of a serious postcolonial legacy in Camus's oeuvre.[10] Kaplan and Apter both describe the ways in which Algerian intellectuals, under the threat of a repressive Islamic regime's censorship, exile, and even execution, reclaimed Camus as a North African secular humanist, and recast him as a prescient observer of the threat of *fascislamisme* that soured the dream of national independence about which Camus expressed such skepticism. In the contemporary North American context, Camus has begun to be similarly recovered from his reputation as an unwavering colonialist—myopic to the point of hypocrisy, blind to the very existence of non-European Algerians—and refashioned as an important early observer of the painful realities of decolonization in North Africa, and the cyclical, ineradicable scourges of political violence and totalitarianism. These critical movements register the extent to which *The Plague* holds new significance in a global conversation about epidemics, the history of terror, and the aesthetics of violence; it is a function of hexagonal criticism's failures that it hasn't always been read as a novel about Algeria.

The Unthinkable

Camus's fictional plague emerges in colonial Algeria in the year 194-, a future anterior wedged between the end of the war and the beginning of the end of French possession, marked by the massacre of Algerians at Sétif on May 8, 1945, a date celebrated throughout the world as Victory in Europe Day. The novel's final pages reveal that it has been narrated by a physician, Dr. Bernard Rieux, who emphasizes the simple facticity of the story, and favors grand abstractions more in keeping with contemporary descriptions of postwar politics than twentieth-century discourse about epidemics: he calls the narrative a "record of what had to be done, and what assuredly would have to be done in the never-ending fight against terror" (199; 308, 279). As the outbreak progresses, Rieux takes to calling it "an abstraction" (91; 88). Even medical discussions of the plague are marked by silence and uncertainty: when the older physician, Castel, drops in to discuss the terrifying symptoms and cases he has seen, he builds his diagnosis around the negative space of plague, its space-opening status as taboo or terror.

> "Naturally," he said to Rieux, "you know what it is."
> "I'm waiting for the result of the post-mortems."
> "Well, *I* know. And I don't need any post-mortems. I was in China for a good part of my career, and I saw some cases in Paris twenty years ago. Only no one dared to call them by their name on that occasion. The usual taboo, of course; the public mustn't be alarmed, that wouldn't do at all. And then, as one of my colleagues said, 'It's unthinkable. Everyone knows it's ceased to appear in western Europe' [*l'Occident*]. Yes, everyone knows that, except for the dead men. Come now, Rieux, you know as well as I do what it is." (35–36; 39–40)

Castel's circumlocutions first identify the plague obliquely: as something one sees in China, that, in Paris, one wouldn't dare to call by its actual name, as an unthinkable anachronism that has "disappeared from the Occident"—the only people who can attest to its unseasonable return are the dead. "It's hardly credible," Castel continues, ". . . but everything points toward its being plague" (40; 44). In a sleight of hand that imagines Oran, a coastal Algerian city as "temperate" and "the Occident," Castel's disbelief highlights how the imaginary of disease—not just what happens, but where, and to whom—is profoundly culturally, historically, and discursively mediated. Plague cannot be in Oran because Oran is full of Frenchmen, because Algeria is France.

Naming the plague as "plague" is something of a taxonomic feint; it is both specific—historically and geographically—and metonymic, standing in for all disease, malediction, catastrophe. The novel, as a result, veers wildly between allegory and medical realism. Following the moment at which "[t]he word 'plague' had just been uttered for the first time," it is immediately equated with war—"there have been as many plagues as wars in history"—but it is also rendered in more scientifically precise, evolving rapidly from a zoonotic disease to a bubonic form in humans, and finally to a more contagious pneumonic form (41; 45). A concern with what is namable—say the detection and discovery of a virus or bacterium, or the location of a point of origin or index case for an outbreak—was, by the 1940s, only one part of the study and management of communicable disease as it evolved from the period of the great epidemics of the nineteenth century.[11] By the end of the First World War and the ravages of the 1918 influenza pandemic, an understanding of epidemic disease as socially, geographically, and behaviorally contingent had largely replaced older models, instantiating a new era of international public health that was equally concerned with what *happened* in disease events as it was with what *was*, in terms of pathology and microbiology. The novel's abstraction, denuded language, and rampant silence route these epistemological changes through a vocabulary of midcentury phenomenology at odds with what the townspeople observe: "they were humanists: they disbelieved in pestilences," they think of it instead as "a mere bogy of the mind, a bad dream that will pass away" (37; 41).

An alarming proportion of the novel is devoted to this problem of naming, and further debate about the epidemic opens onto the colonial history of communicable disease that has gone largely unnoticed in the scholarship. Long after Castel and Rieux have agreed that they're under occupation by the black plague, an asthma patient comes to see Rieux:

> "Well, Doctor, it's cholera, isn't it?"
> "Where on earth did you get that idea from?"
> "It's in the paper, and the radio said it, too."
> "No, it's not cholera. . . . Don't you believe a word of it." (61; 65)

This moment is wonderfully revealing in the way it marshals two histories of East-West immunological contact. Plague—with its undertones of medievalism, its visibly painful buboes, and its connotations of the wound, the lash, the curse, the bite of the pest or vermin; its habitually inseparable connotation of blackness; its genesis in the East, and its slow march on the backs of rats and men along the Silk Road toward Europe—serves up a different set of Orientalist myths and presuppositions than cholera, which also traveled by way of trade and military routes from Asia to Europe during the golden age of imperialism. Although Camus's doctor dismisses this possibility immediately, his patient's assumption serves as a point of contamination through which nineteenth-century colonial history and discourse leak into the flat temporality and homogeneous population of the novel's indeterminate 194– French Algerian settlement. By invoking the memory of the Asiatic cholera pandemics—and by extension the range of exotic ailments familiar to Western European and *pied-noir* populations—the patient accidentally reveals the dual character of the colonial city that seems to linger between times and places. Populated by two peoples engaged in the making of increasingly divergent histories, Oran is at once located in the pestilent, unruly East, and also separated from the vastness of the Algerian landscape and its manifold threats by fortress walls that will soon shut the city off from its environs.

Although cholera is only mentioned once in the novel, many critics believe that *The Plague* drew on the legendary cholera outbreak not of 194–, but of 1849, which decimated Oran nearly twenty years after the French conquest.[12] As in Britain's colonies, infectious diseases played an important role in the establishment of colonial dynamics between Algeria and France, as well as in the foundation of the modern state's relationship to public hygiene and health systems in the metropole and the territories. François Delaporte, a historian of medicine and student of Foucault, documents the massive 1832 cholera outbreak that ravaged Paris just two years after the French seizure of Algiers. Describing the significance of the cholera epidemics in the creation of new forms of state population management and revisions of the postrevolutionary social state, Delaporte writes

> The cholera that swept across Europe demonstrated the vulnerability of an ancient system of defense . . . [T]he epidemic of 1832 surely marks a historical watershed: the moment when the need to *import* into the civilized class a health apparatus forged by and for the bourgeoisie became evident.[13]

The ancient system of defense included military measures such as the troop-based cordons sanitaires and economic measures—both to curb trade from abroad to limit the possibility of new contamination—as well as the sequestration of cities and towns, which slowed internal commerce to a near halt. The new "health apparatus" would replace the primacy of state interests as well as refocusing away from prevention, quarantine, and closure toward the lived health of the bourgeoisie. Delaporte notes the tendency over time of nineteenth-century sanitation and hygiene sciences to abandon social reform in favor of a less service-oriented preservation of biological privilege (paralleling economic privilege), emphasizing in his history the imbrication of power and biomedical management that was the hallmark of his teacher's work, and of that of Foucault's own teacher, Georges Canguilhem (200).

French hygiene and sanitation experts, like their British counterparts, assigned blame for the devastating epidemics first to their impoverished cohabitants in the cities of France and elsewhere in Europe, who were understood to be a distinct race of persons less possessed of the moral fortitude that would dissuade the epidemic from carrying them off. Later, with increasingly sophisticated means of mapping epidemic spread, these same observers would also point the finger at their darker-skinned compatriots to the South and East. Delaporte's history draws attention to the slippery analogy enabled by this shift, whereby the economically disenfranchised and the foreign become commensurable, in some instances indistinguishable, citing nineteenth-century economist and statesman Michel Chevalier's plaintive observation that "the admirable people of Paris, who are so heroically confronting the cholera of poverty . . . were not made to serve as fodder for the cholera of Asia and to die like slaves in pain and terror" (2). This impassioned comment condenses a great deal that was essential to the development of the social state in post-Revolutionary France. The "cholera of poverty" identifies the ailment as one that afflicts the poor, while that poverty itself is depicted as a kind of fever or rage, *la colère* as much as *le choléra*. Chevalier's "cholera" is a general distemper abstracted from the material conditions of life, labor, and infrastructure that enabled its spread, while also materializing from poverty and slavery, as a "natural" phenomenon or racial characteristic.

Chevalier's insistence that the people of Paris "were not made . . . to die like slaves in pain and terror" thus analogizes the suffering of cholera with laboring in the tropics, with the brutal history of plantation slave labor, yoking both to the terrors of post-Revolutionary France and the Haitian revolution. Implicit in such a statement is the sense that there may be some who are *more* deserving than the people of Paris to suffer in this way. For other commentators of the period, those people certainly included the Algerians, who were, in France, the most proximate figure for denizens of uncivilized places, burdened with insalubrious climates, and teeming with autochthonous diseases. By the height of the new imperial enterprises in the 1890s, both cholera and typhus posed an enormous threat to the health of the citizenry and state sovereignties of Europe. Historian Andrew Aisenberg, in his work on health management in nineteenth-century France, cites a particularly striking example of what is evident in dozens of colonial-era writings about sanitation and epidemic: that epidemic diseases were routinely associated with the barbarous races, and that this connection was used as a justification for the necessity of colonial surveillance in order to keep the movements of the natives in check and quarantines strictly enforced. Achille Kelsch, for example, a theorist of latent germ behavior following Pasteur, "blamed the 1893 [typhus] epidemic on Algerian immigrants who had in his view served as carriers of the germ."[14] Drawing on the popular ethnomythology around the Arab-Berber people's hospitality (in this case to the germ, which they harbored and unleashed on others who were not immune), Kelsch "used the example of these immigrant carriers to illuminate the mechanism of latency [by] identif[ying] microbe-carrying Algerian 'nomads' as posing a permanent danger to French society that could be addressed only by placing them under constant surveillance."[15] Aisenberg explains how the hypothesis of latency, which would shape the cultural mythology around the spread of typhoid fever in the early twentieth century, "dissociated . . . etiology from a politics of social regulation centered on the home," and instead reached out beyond the insular cartography of determinants and into the geographical and temporal space beyond.[16] This reorientation toward distal determinants of disease was complicated by the contemporary advances in microbiology pioneered in Robert Koch's discovery of the *Vibrio cholerae*, which, combined with statistical and mapping approaches, produced the new epidemiology in the last decades of the nineteenth century. Kelsch's own words demonstrate how this shift reconstituted the colonial subject both in and outside of the "population" for which public health exists:

> I am inclined to believe that these nomadic groups, which are so dangerous for the population but not for themselves, do not have typhus but carry the cause within them. The vigilance of public hygiene is needed not only in regard to those vagabonds suffering from typhus, but also those who are not.[17]

Professionals in the sciences of life and morbidity in metropolitan France sought to bring the life practices of the Algerian people under the control of the state, simultaneously criminalizing their migrancy within Algeria as well as their emigration to France. As healthy, or asymptomatic, carriers of the disease, these "nomads" also represent the threat of undetectable assimilation and invisible intercourse between races in the form of contagion, as well as the specter of a reverse colonization. Such anxieties contributed to the consolidation of fear around various assimilation proposals after the Second World War that would bring Algerians into full French citizenship, and thus tip the population balance to outnumber the French ten to one.

In addition to pointing beyond the boundaries of the metropole and its people, the new discourse of disease occasioned by the modern epidemics also pointed outside of the immediacy of the present. Even in the middle of the nineteenth century, when cholera was still a novel and little-understood disease, commentators in France understood it as out of sync with the march of civilizational and scientific progress, and like the plague in Camus's novel, an anachronism in the post-Enlightenment age—an unaccountable blemish on the sanguine nationalist projection of a sanitary and healthful body politic. The rhetoric of sanitation and its relationship to morality in midcentury France is more emphatic more florid than in Victorian England, where reformist tracts, particularly with reference to the urban poor, tended over time toward self-conscious restraint, objectivity, and scientism, even as they drew on the rhetorical habits of sentimentalism. Delaporte recounts how the public reacted to this affront:

> [W]hat was surprising was that an affliction like cholera, which reminded people of the great medieval epidemics, should have appeared in an age of progress. Hence, the devastation caused by the disease came as a shock, especially to members of the bourgeoisie, who with all the resources of civilization at their disposal never dreamed that they would have to contend with such a frightful calamity . . . [A]ncient obsessions seemed to well up from the depths of the Middle Ages. (49)

Given this reaction, which we have witnessed again in 2020, it becomes clear how the epidemics of the nineteenth century were marshaled in service of a medievalization of the colonies, continuous in the cases of India and Algeria with the existential threat posed by Islam.

Literary accounts also play a role in Delaporte's genre-defining history, particularly Heinrich Heine's recollections of the colorful scenes of suffering in the homes, courts, ballrooms, and avenues where subjects of the new July Monarchy entertained themselves. In *De la France*, an account of his early years in France, Heine tells an arresting story about the high-spirited Parisians who scoffed and postured to overcome their fear of the disease by mimicking it, "Parisians danced with even more gaiety than usual on the boulevard, where one saw masks whose sickly pallor and deformed features mocked the fear of cholera and the disease itself"

4.1 Alfred Rethel, "Death the Strangler" (1850). Photograph: The Cleveland Museum of Art (1939.620).

(quoted in Delaporte, 133–134). As the dance halls fill up on a temperate spring evening, Heine's companions dance and drink to banish their well-founded fears, when "suddenly, the sprightliest of the harlequins felt cold in his legs, ripped off his mask, and to everyone's astonishment revealed a face that had turned bluish-purple in color" (quoted in Delaporte, 134) (figure 4.1). The harlequin's spectacular end is made more lurid by his joyous playful outward appearance—a special horror reserved, in Heine's account, for the mimetic expiration that reveals a death mask beneath the actor's costume.

The victim here is racially indeterminate like his English brethren, whose chromatic obsession with cholera I discuss in chapter 2, his blue-violet skin indexing the easy adoption of racialized pseudo-Hindu gods and amalgams of Muslim stereotypes in cartoon depictions of the epidemic. Although Camus doesn't cite Heine's writings on cholera specifically, he was reading the *Ideas* and possibly the memoirs during the years when he would have been drafting *The Plague*; he cites Heine a number of times in *Carnets IV* and *V*, which run from January 1942 to April 1948.[18]

The Plague stages a scene very like the one Heine describes above, in which the lead player in a production of Gluck's *Orpheus*—already a visitor to the land of the dead—succumbs to the illness onstage during his climactic duet with Eurydice. The first act goes off without incident, apart from "some tremolos not in the score" and "some rather jerky movements he indulged in."[19] Later, the plague will be anthropomorphized in similar terms, "progressing with its characteristically jerky but unfaltering stride," exhibiting the same kind of bodily incontinence that it visits on its victims (258; 233). In the third act, Orpheus is overcome: "He chose this moment to stagger grotesquely to the footlights, his arms and legs splayed out under his antique robe, and fall down in the middle of the property sheepfold, always out of place, but now, in the eyes of the spectators, significantly, appallingly so" (201; 182–183). If there is any doubt as to whether the young singer requires assistance or a coffin, it is dispelled immediately—no one rushes to his side. The orchestra stops playing, and the audience rises slowly to its feet, "like worshippers leaving church when the service ends, or a death-chamber after a farewell visit to the dead" (201–183). Calm gives way to panic, and "the crowd stampeded toward the exits . . . pouring out into the street in a confused mass, with shrill cries of dismay" (201; 183).

The narrator is heavy-handed here. Apart from this scene, and one that follows, in which a young boy dies after being administered an experimental serum, the novel is rigorously and studiously unbeautiful. Or at least, it insists that it is, telling us from its opening pages that it is a "chronicle" set in a town without passion—a document, or act of witness, more than a story or *roman*. Rare moments of sensory richness dissipate into flat actional language almost immediately. The much-loved scene in which Tarrou and Rieux escape the plague-locked city to go swimming in the sea, the "gentle, heaving expanse of deep piled-velvet, supple and sleek as a creature of the wild," for example, ends abruptly when the two swimmers encounter a chilly current, and after a final thrash of freedom, prepare to "set their shoulders to the wheel again" (256–257; 231–232). After their companions flee the opera house, Cottard and Tarrou

> had merely risen from their seats [and] gazed down at what was a dramatic picture of their life in those days: plague on the stage in the

guise of a disarticulated mummer, and in the auditorium the toys of luxury, so futile now, forgotten fans and lace shawls derelict on the red plush seats (201; 183).

Like Heine's harlequin, the young man expires in the midst of a pageant; the visual joke is the mummer, or mime (*histrion*), becoming quite literally disarticulated (*désarticulé*) and inarticulate, collapsing the fiction in which he plays. The novel doesn't linger on this scene or give it the kind of space Camus does in his notebooks; leading into the episode, the narrator explains dispassionately that he has found the account in Tarrou's notes, and that it "re-creates as nearly as may be the curiously feverish atmosphere of this period" (199; 181). The novel's restrained descriptions of the monotony of life under extreme conditions expunges affect, detail, texture, and emotion in favor of clear-sighted, rational action—a tempered, masculine optimism. And yet, at particular moments, this tone is set against a more baroque register that ruptures the studied flatness of the novel's surface. These moments articulate points of contact with the more distant histories the allegory seems to disavow, particularly those having to do with earlier imaginaries of plague and cholera, each tinged with its respective period's Orientalism.

In its manifest symbolic overdetermination, the *Orpheus* scene points also to the spectacle of the diseased or suffering body in the context of political violence—specifically the German occupation—by way of biographical detail. Camus attended a production of Corneille's last play, *Suréna*, in which a princess named Eurydice dies onstage, in November 1943.[20] After seeing the play in Paris following the culmination of a season of intense Allied bombings across France, as a consequence of which the tide of the war had begun to turn, Camus writes in his notebook,

> *Suréna*. In the fourth act, all the doors are guarded. And Eurydice, who up to now has struck such wonderful notes, begins to be silent, to search her heart without being able to express the word that would deliver her.[21]

This was also the month Camus had begun to work as an editor at Gallimard and was living comfortably, entertaining friends and going out in the midst of a city under siege. This experience appears to have been an inspiration for the Orpheus scene: the guarded doors of the stage, which point beyond the doors of the theater to the guarded doors of Oran, and the punctuation of muteness and death to end a song of suffering. A few pages later in the notebook, Camus writes, "Plague. End up with a motionless woman in mourning announcing in sufferings what men have given in lives and blood," and later in the same entry, "a theatrical company is still playing: a play about Orpheus and Eurydice."[22]

I want to ask pointedly about the effects of transposing this scene from 1943 Paris—still in the grip of the Occupation—to Oran in 194-, a city under a different kind of siege. In abandoning Europe for Africa, does Camus abandon his responsibility to a specific history? What becomes of the reflective woman figure who bears witness and mourns by "announcing in sufferings what men have given in lives and blood?" For Roland Barthes, who challenged Camus to defend the "ahistorical ethic" of his novel, the absent presence of this feminine figure is an unforgiveable abstraction, she is *la terreur, la peste, la déesse inconnue.*

La Déesse inconnue

Generations of readers have celebrated and puzzled over the singularly blank effect of Camus's prose—its smoothness, its authority, its odd lack of detail.[23] The ubiquity of tragic forms and archetypes, like Orpheus and Eurydice above, contributes to this effect, which, in *The Plague*, is amplified by the characterlessness of the city and the lurking presence of silent and absent subjects, not just women, but also Arab Algerians. Francis Jeanson, the then-untested young critic whom Sartre would later allow to review *L'Homme révolté* for *Les Temps modernes* described Camus's tone as "noble and haughty" and characterized him as "against history" and "in favor of a metaphysical rebellion against the human condition."[24] Where Jeanson took issue with Camus's self-seriousness and limited political vision, Camus's most vocal critics in postcolonial criticism— Albert Memmi, Edward Said, and Conor Cruise O'Brien—have all registered the impact and political implications of this frictionless tone and absence of geographical, political, linguistic, and cultural specificity in his work. Memmi, in a 1957 essay, called him a "well-meaning colonizer," Said wrote that he was "a novelist from whose work the facts of imperial actuality, so clearly there to be noted, have dropped away," and O'Brien judges that in considering Camus's utopian dream of Mediterranean unity, "including the Arabs [but] based on the Romance languages, it is not excessive to speak of hallucination."[25] O'Brien also comments on the aphoristic quality of the mechanics of justice in *The Stranger (L'Étranger),* and accuses Camus of trucking not in a grand interrogation of responsibility, but rather in the impossible fantasy of a colonialism in which all subjects are reduced to equal blankness: "The presentation in this way of a court in Algeria trying a crime of this kind involves the novelist in the presentation of a myth: the myth of French Algeria . . . [I]t implicitly denies the colonial reality and sustains the colonial fiction."[26]

Indeed, the sparseness of *The Plague*—the empty landscapes, the attenuated plots, and the bombed-out interiorities of its characters—points most obviously to a generalized human condition, a feature that earned Camus a reputation as both a hero of postwar humanism and as an embarrassing peddler of adolescent pabulum from his less sympathetic readers.[27] Other critics have dismissed this "naïve humanism" as an inaccurate depiction of Camus's open-work style, suggesting instead that the elements of his fiction are intentionally depleted. It was Camus's writing in *The Stranger* that was one of Barthes's central models for writing degree zero, which he calls, in his book of the same name "basically the indicative mood . . . amodal."[28] In these words, we can hear echoes of Camus's own description of scientific explanation from the 1942 notebooks—an account of "what happens" that is indicative, observational, amodal. Unlike Said and O'Brien, Barthes saw in *The Stranger*'s striving for neutrality and flatness

> a style of absence which is almost an ideal absence of style . . . a sort of negative mood in which the social or mythical characters of a language are abolished in favour of a neutral or inert state of form . . . [T]hought remains wholly responsible, without being overlaid by a secondary commitment to a form of History not its own. (77; 56)

Barthes further identifies an "attempt towards disengaging literary language"—a colorless, transparent form of speech that has discarded the whiplash of opposites for a "third term . . . a neutral term, or zero element" (76; 55–56). For Barthes, at least initially, these praiseworthy features of Camus's writing are situated within a broader project that aims to displace literary expression in the mode of ritualized platitudes, which Barthes saw as serving and embodying the "bourgeois myth," in order to make room instead for what he calls the "biological" or "biographical" presence of style in writing that makes itself apparent through form, rather than through the impositions of history (11–12; 17). In this kind of writing, this "[l]iterature reduced, so to speak, to being its carcass," Barthes imagines the achievement not only of a writing scrubbed of ideology, but also of the vitalist underpinnings of art—an "Orphean dream: a writer without literature (5; 9–10)." *The Plague*'s details, perhaps more than *The Stranger*'s, give on to a form of history or histories that are not properly its own by intersecting with both medieval and colonial discourses of disease. It is also clear how the morbid reduction and silence of Camus's texts—perhaps even their neutrality and biologism, the sense that, like Orpheus, they have returned from a place beyond life—are historically bound up with the depleted conditions of living through, after, and in the presence of mass death in wartime Europe. Notwithstanding *The Plague*'s atmosphere of total negativity, its engagement with biology and plague specifically as an abstracted, neutralizied, and naturalized allegory of Nazi violence renders antipathy a problem of nature, rather than of action, in very much the same way we have seen in the historical record of the Indian Mutiny. This observation, coupled with Camus's accelerating distaste for Algerian nationalist movements, destabilizes what Barthes once praised as Camus's "wholly responsible thought," his refusal to allow improper forms of history to pollute the "negative mood" and "inert state of form" in his writing.

If Camus's banishing of myth and figure in favor of biologistic neutrality in *The Stranger* was a virtue for Barthes in *Le degré zéro de l'écriture*, it was a related but misplaced objectivity and a frustrating lack of historical specificity with regard to what exactly *The Plague* was allegorizing, and what the implications of that allegory were, that made Barthes question the ethics of Camus's second novel on the same grounds as he offered his admiration of the first. Their conversation on this matter proceeds from the question of the historical referent, but involves other factors as well, including a consideration of what is possible, historically speaking, when geographical and subjective transpositions have taken place. In his own version of a Gothic preface, Camus borrows the words of Daniel Defoe to set the tone of his novel and present the paradoxes of historical representation in which he is interested, and in so doing also presents the tensions implicit in the novel's allegorical form: "It is as reasonable to represent one kind of imprisonment by another, as it is to represent anything that really exists by that which exists not."[29] This line comes not from the expected place in Defoe's body of work—*A Journal of the Plague Year* would be the obvious intertext for Camus's own plague narrative— but rather from the third narrative featuring Robinson Crusoe, a series of moral and pseudo-anthropological essays. For Camus, representing the sense of imprisonment, separation, and isolation occasioned by the arrival of the plague and the subsequent quarantining of the city were some of the earliest motivations for the writing of the novel, motivations that reflect a greater interest in the experience of life disrupted by pestilence than in the character of the pestilence itself. In his notebooks of 1942, for example, he writes, "Novel. Don't put 'the plague' in the title. But something like 'The Prisoners.'"[30] While the thematic resonance of *A Journal of the Plague Year* remains oblique in *The Plague*'s epigraph, the *Crusoe* citation explicitly highlights how *The Plague* flirts with but refuses to name historical referents, and marshals the narrative position and literary forms of "reasonable" and "serious" observation and reflection, while also claiming status as a multifaceted allegory.

By Camus's own account, given most definitively in an open letter to Barthes published in the magazine *Club* in 1955, the novel was written to chronicle the activities of the Resistance in France, which Camus joined in 1943, and whose underground newspaper, *Combat*, he edited from 1943 to 1947.[31] In response to what Barthes identifies as the novel's ahistorical ethic Camus writes,

> *The Plague*, which I wanted to be read on a number of levels, neverthe-less has as its obvious content the struggle of the European resistance movements against Nazism. The proof of this is that although the spe-cific enemy is nowhere named, everyone in every European country recognized it. Let me add that a long extract from *The Plague* appeared during the Occupation, in a collection of underground texts, and that this fact alone would justify the transposition I made. In a sense, *The Plague* is more than a chronicle of the Resistance. But certainly it is nothing less.[32]

Although his claim that he "transposed" the chronicle from France to Algeria in order to avoid persecution and censorship makes sense, there is something slippery about Camus's defensive position here, especially the logic that because "everyone in every European country recognized" that the novel was about the Nazi occupations in Europe, their recogni-tion serves as proof that it was. Surely a writer as sophisticated, well-read, and well-traveled as Camus was by 1955 would recognize that for other readers in other times and places, the plague would reflect their own sense of injustice and crisis. In fact, he claims to have striven for this very figural excess and extrapolation, commenting that *"The Plague* is more than a chronicle of the Resistance," a point he reemphasizes later when he says explains that "terror has several faces."[33] It is precisely the broad applicability of the novel's moral geometry that makes Camus feel as if he is "living by and for a community that nothing in history has so far been able to touch" rather than "feeling installed in a career of soli-tude."[34] Nevertheless, his insistence that the novel depicts the Resistance to Nazi occupation in its most simple form has been adopted more or less whole cloth as a slogan that places the text squarely in the historical canon of European and modernist writing about the Second World War.

Because of its allegorical parameters—including its setting in Algeria, instead of in France—it is most often read as a philosophical and ethical rather than testimonial account of the war, although there are notable and important exceptions that take the text's silence with regard to its real-world referents as an important point of departure. The conversation between Adorno and an absent Célan about poetry after Auschwitz stands firmly at the base of the mute-testimony defense of Camus's novel, which from this perspective becomes a fable about silence and the impossibility of witness. The effort to approach the war and the Holocaust, even obliquely, as early as 1947 is an aspect of Camus's text that critics have commended. Particularly helpful in establishing this reading was Shoshana Felman's 1989 essay "Narrative as Testimony: Camus's *The Plague*," in which she posits history as a negotiation between events and narrative to argue for the novel's capacity to bear witness indirectly, yet faithfully, to the Holocaust: "Camus's testimony is not simply to the literality of the history but to its *unreality*, to the historical vanishing point of its unbelievability."[35] Felman elaborates what she identifies as Camus's construction of an "event without a referent," a situation partly achieved through the anachronism of a plague that had largely receded from the shores of Western Europe.

Still, Camus insisted repeatedly and under increasing duress from his social circles that the event he described did have a very specific referent. In addition to the reference to the Nazi occupation as *la peste brune*, the novel also draws on the pervasive sense of German fascism as both unspeakable and "inhuman," a term that became nearly synonymous with the death camps.[36] The asymmetry between human actors and inhuman violence is hyperbolized in Camus's allegory as both more and less existential than ordinary warfare. This is precisely what is wrong, in Barthes's view, with *The Plague*, a novel by a writer he deeply admired— the writer whose "neutrality," "responsibility," "transparency" and attention to form inspired him to explore the zero degree of writing as an ethic.[37] In "*La Peste*: Annales d'une épidémie ou roman de solitude?," Barthes's first critique of *The Plague*, published as an open letter in *Club*, he argues that the novel's dehumanization of the enemy obstructed a serious consideration of responsibility and insulated Camus's story from the more difficult questions of human evil. He suggests that Oran in the novel constitutes "a world deprived of History" and characterizes the plague as an "unknown goddess who fulfills her inhuman role like a destiny as immured as an ancient prophecy" (*presque aussi clos que le Fatum antique*).[38] Barthes continues to challenge what he sees as the quietism of Camus's position by further characterizing the goddess of plague in terms of transcendence and sublime unknowability. He remarks,

> One knows nothing of her except that she *is*; one is ignorant of her origin and her form; neither can one assign her any adjective, which

would be the first way of taming her; she is absolute Evil, and as such, cannot be qualified by that which she overpowers; she is visible, evident, and nevertheless unknowable; at the very least, there is no other knowledge possible but the recognition of her absoluteness.[39]

Barthes sees an insufficient political and historical seriousness in Camus's allegory—a mystification of evil in the form of a divine feminine that exceeds description, become instead simply enormous, "absolute." Such a departure from the realm of the human is also, for Barthes, necessarily a departure from the practical difficulties of facing evil in its human form. Moreover, a nameless faceless enemy—an enemy without agency—cannot be held accountable or brought to justice for his crimes. Barthes insists on this point in both of his letters to Camus on the subject of the novel in 1955, concluding the second with the following lines:

> To defend oneself against plague . . . is a matter of conduct more than of choice. But to defend oneself against men, to be their executioner so as not to be their victim, this begins when the plague is no longer just the plague, but an image of evil with a human face.[40]

For Barthes, Camus's plague precludes not only accountability, but also choice; the plague cannot but reduce the respondents' actions to a matter of what Barthes calls "conduct." Barthes sharpens his point by borrowing Camus's own terms, *bourreau* and *victime*, from the renowned series of essays published in *Combat* in November 1946. In "*Ni victimes ni bourreaux*," Camus had argued strongly for a refusal to identify either as victim or as executioner in the postwar harrowing; he worried that a hysteria for revenge against collaborators was simply legitimating murder under the mantle of justice. An earlier piece he wrote for *Combat* drew attention to the uses of sanitary language during this period. In August 1945, a little less than four months after Victory in Europe Day and the infamous massacre of Algerians at Sétif, Camus warned that

> the word "purge" itself was already distressing . . . [T]oo many people clamored for the death penalty, as if imprisonment was an inconsequential punishment. By contrast, too many others screamed "terror" when sentences of a few years were meted out to those guilty of denunciations and other dishonorable acts.[41]

In an effort to undo the binary logic that made the choice out to be an either-or proposition—you either kill or you die—Camus offered neither-nor: to maintain a rigorously ethical stance, one must acknowledge the necessity of choosing, and nevertheless strive to transcend the choice by being neither victim nor executioner.

A good deal of writing about Camus's legacy, especially in casual and popular criticism, depicts his relationships with his critics in static and oppositional terms: Sartre and Camus were enemies; Camus hated Simone de Beauvoir for her transparent caricature in *The Mandarins*. Most locate a turning point in these relationships on the occasion of the publication of *L'Homme révolté*, which Sartre invited Jeanson to review in *Les Temps modernes*; it was not a kind review. In light of these quarrels and the way in which they have entered into the history of postwar intellectual life, it is important to note that Barthes's criticism came rather late, nearly a decade after the publication of the novel. By this time, the immediacy of the Occupation and the war had given way to a more analytical distance, and the stakes of the conflict in Algeria had become clearer—a public intellectual's position on the conflict was as solid a metric of left engagement as involvement in the Resistance had once been. The response from Camus is accordingly personal, wounded, and more than a little scolding. He reminds Barthes that he had, in fact, come face to face with the occupiers, and that the question of how to confront this kind of evil was, for him, a far from hypothetical one. In Camus's words,

> [T]he question you ask: "What would the fighters against the plague do confronted with the all-too-human face of the scourge," is unjust in this respect: it ought to have been asked in the past tense, and then it would have received the answer, a positive one. What these fighters, whose experience I have to some extent translated, did do, they did in fact against men, and you know at what cost.[42]

In a rhetorical crescendo, Camus promises not to lay down his pen: "They will do it again, no doubt, when any terror confronts them, whatever face it may assume, for terror has several faces"; he defends his decision not to name the plague so as to preserve its flexibility as a signifier: "[s]till another justification for my not having named any particular one [terror] in order to better strike at them all."[43] The tone is characteristic of the way Camus would routinely extrapolate his politics in later years—particularly in reference to the question of Algerian nationalism—from the experience of the Resistance and the early journalism that both inspired, and to an extent, constituted this involvement.

With reference to the political extrapolation from the early years, Alice Kaplan suggests that Camus's 1939 "The Misery of Kabylia" series about the famine on the Algerian plateau and the French government's shameful abandonment of its victims "contributed to the shutting down of

[his] newspaper [*Alger républicain*] and to his blacklisting by the French government in Algeria. He was unable to find a job," she writes, "and he was forced to leave the country." She calls this his "first exile," and illuminates how it shaped his self-image: "For the rest of his life, he believed he had risked everything for his anticolonial activism."[44] The hagiographic (and autohagiographic) approach Kaplan critiques here explains a lot about the stonewalling that Camus's readers, including Barthes, faced when they called his commitments into question. Camus's response— that the question about how one *might* face an enemy with a face that is all-too-human is moot, and that Barthes need only look at Camus's own personal record to find his answer—bears this out. By 1955, he had been more or less backed into a corner by politically engaged artists on the left, and his public comments on Algeria especially are characterized by a marked defensiveness, frustration, and melancholy.

After returning to Algiers, Camus makes multiple attempts to parse the terms "terrorism" and "militancy" in formal and informal texts, including *Le Premier homme* and "L'Hôte," the short story set in the lonely, windswept plateau of Kabylia that would appear in the 1957 collection, *L'Exil et le royaume*.[45] Reprising his use of *terreur* to refer to the Nazi atrocities in the letters to Barthes in 1955, at time when he was also working out—in his notes—the full implications of both the terrorist activities of the FLN and the French counterinsurgency, Camus elides the considerable historical and political differences between the two in what would become a persistent mistake that marred his last years as a public intellectual. Given the range of historical and discursive intertexts at play in *The Plague* and Camus's postwar and Algerian writings, I want to suggest two new ways of thinking about the debates that erupted over the historical referents of the novel that find their genesis in the conversation between Barthes and Camus above. The first is that there is a more complex historical specificity in Camus's novel than Barthes allows, important strands of which predate the World War II context and reach back to the colonial inflection of contagious disease in the nineteenth century, particularly through the misprision of cholera in the novel and its setting in the North African colony. The second is that in suggesting that in Camus's novel "one knows nothing of [the plague goddess] except that she *is*; one is ignorant of her origin and her form . . . she is visible, evident, and nevertheless unknowable," Barthes identifies the powerful way in which Camus's novel stands as an important moment in the reconfiguration of radical antipathy in the space between science and literature. What might have been depicted as a frontal event in which the healthy city faces the enemy of plague, like so many soldiers approaching from just beyond the horizon, is instead represented as an emergent event that can be known only through its effects, and may not yet be namable, may even, as we have seen, be unthinkable.

In order to approach such a problem, the novel's form complements the synoptic investigative point of view as another omnibus or archive: a collection of anecdotes and data points from multiple perspectives. This experiment cannot be thought apart from the French experiments with phenomenology that straddled the war and inflected every philosophical conversation from Paris to Algiers. These details constitute the basis of phenomenological knowledge and of practice, if not a pathological or microbial understanding of the disease. Although Barthes points to this epistemological difficulty as a failing of Camus's text, specifically its treatment of history, he also unknowingly identifies a crucial function of Camus's novel, namely that *The Plague*, one of the most widely read literary fictions of the twentieth century, yokes a phenomenology of infectious disease to a phenomenology of terror.

Blank Maps and Rats

Two elements of the novel's allegorical architecture invite further inquiry: the setting in Oran, and the absence of Algerian subjects. The opening pages of *The Plague* describe Oran as a "thoroughly negative place" that "turns its back on the bay, with the result that it's impossible to see the sea, you always have to go look for it."[46] For the young Camus, the Mediterranean's classical legacy pointed to a recuperable cultural unity of the Romance language–speaking peoples along its shores and adjacent territories—the dream that Conor Cruise O'Brien calls a "hallucination" for the way it imagined away the presence of non-Hellenic cultures in the vast and variegated Algerian population. For Camus, wounded by his multiple departures and exiles from Algeria, and suspicious of the growing violence on both sides of the colonial conflict, the idea of Mediterranean humanism amounted to a remedy: a reattachment of the colonial prosthesis in which a confederacy of citizens stretching from France in the North to his beloved Algiers and beyond would flourish. That the novel begins with Oran "turning its back on the bay" signals that the space of the colonial city is symbolically cut off from this dream—a condition made worse by the quarantine. When Alice Kaplan asks pointedly "why does the setting for *The Plague* look more like Marseille than Oran?" the answer is simple: it looks like Marseilles because it intends to be about France and the French, and the text seems everywhere blind to its Africanness.[47] Still, it is Oran—an Algerian town without suspicion, perhaps, but one that turns its back on Camus's dream of a lively Mediterranean land above nationalism, "full of games and joy."[48]

Oran is depicted as a place cut off not only from the sea, but also from history, from beauty, even from itself. Rieux describes a "town without intimations. . . . completely modern. . . . its life is not particularly exciting. . . . Treeless, glamourless, soulless, the town of Oran ends by seeming restful, and, after a while, you go complacently to sleep there."[49] Wavering indecisively between descriptions of Oran's situation in a "unique landscape" without equal and its quality as a "thoroughly negative place," its complete modernity and its soulless complacency, Camus's narrator unfolds a tension between the concreteness of place and the cognitive blankness of the quintessentially modern, exemplified in the town's lack of intimation or suspicion (6, 3; 13, 11). Without glamour, devoid of the "beat of wings or the rustle of leaves," *The Plague*'s Oran is set up to work as a space of open signification and interpretation—like so many colonial spaces erased by arriving cartographers' refusal to see what is already there, it has no history (3; 12). The ahistorical character of Oran in Camus's hands, particularly as it intersects with a tradition of writing into the presumed historical emptiness of the colony, makes the town a difficult place in which to die, even to die, as the narrator puzzlingly puts it, a "modern death" (5; 13).

At the time that he was composing *The Plague*, Camus had been involved in theater for more than a decade. Though he wrote vigorously for newspapers in the early years of the 1940s, he was at the same time tending increasingly toward the classical tragedy—its formalism and constraints—which he associated with Algeria as the site of a "solar tragedy," a place veering between light and unreason. What is curious about the unsympathetic depiction of Oran in the first part of the novel is that it turns out to be the city itself—and the collectivity it embodies—that is the subject of this tragedy. In the opening lines of part three, Oran itself is in extremis, and the fate of the city has become the fate of its inhabitants:

> [B]y this time, mid-August, the plague had swallowed up everything and everyone. No longer were there individual destinies; only a collective destiny, made of plague and the emotions shared by all. Strongest of these emotions was the sense of exile and deprivation, with all the crosscurrents of revolt and fear set up by these. (167; 155)

The crisis of contagion here becomes ontological, turning the city of lazy, entitled pleasure seekers, individualistic merchants, and businessmen into a single organism whose habits and characteristics are subsumed by their collective status as tragic hero and victim alike. In its capacity for self-reproduction and the way in which it preserves, as an open question, the topic of its character, the plague remakes the city in its own image; Oran itself becomes pathogenic. Unlike in *Dracula*, there is no suggestion that the plague has arrived from anywhere outside of Oran, it rather emerges from *beneath* it, or inside of it. Sketching place-as-character allows Camus to explore a dramatic climax in the novel without psychology or the spectacular suffering of an individual. The chronicle makes this structural feature explicit: "the narrator thinks this moment, registering the climax (*sommet*) of the summer heat and the disease, the best for describing, on general lines, and by way of illustration, the excesses of the living, burials of the dead, and the plight of parted lovers" (167; 155). The state of crisis is one that belongs to the social whole, casting Oran as a classical tragic protagonist in the mold of Orpheus, while also continually undercutting this abstraction with the particularity of Algeria and the dis-ease associated with colonized space—the eruption of an epidemic that has long retreated from European shores. Even as it works toward abstraction, then, the novel seems incapable of not reproducing the paradigmatic colonial city as hot, sick, and ancient.

Understanding the novel's dual setting—Algerian and allegorical—requires us to think about how colonial representations of morbidity intersected with the discourses of morbidity, extermination, and sanitation in the Second World War. The literature of plague and cholera consolidated for centuries around the threat of racial others as both carriers of illness and as walking embodiments of death, while early-nineteenth-century descriptions and caricatures of Asiatic cholera borrowed from the iconography of the black plague, using the ligature of color-disease as a handy way of rendering it foreign. What became known as *la mort bleue* gained a menacing dimension by recalling the medieval terrors of *la peste noire*. The astonishment with which onlookers encountered the withering of the body and the darkening of the skin of white European cholera victims from a *bleu violet* to black dovetailed with a growing anxiety about reverse "colonization" of the white body by dark-skinned others.[50] These darkened bodies and faces were viewed not just as uncanny replicas of the uncivilized and underdeveloped Orient, but also as manifestations of death within life. François Magendie, widely considered the founder of experimental physiology, dubbed cholera's effect on the body "cadaverization" to explain the way in which

> the cadaver-like appearance . . . was sometimes more pronounced in living patients than in actual cadavers: among the signs were dryness and slackness of the skin due to lack of blood in the capillaries; facial changes, especially hollowness in the cheeks; eyes that appeared sunken and bluish; and a loss of transparency in the cornea,

which appeared to be folded or collapsed back on itself and opaline in color.[51]

The closed-off and translucent appearance of the eyes suggested a corresponding absence of subjecthood that resonated with depictions of colonial subjects as intellectually inert and emotionally impassive, characteristics that the city of Oran shares in Camus's hands.

In Paris, the epidemic waves brought with them a terror of hordes of cadaverized people nearly indistinguishable from the dead, whose numbers created enormous logistical problems for the state. The unthinkable calculus of mass death, and the challenges of dealing with potentially infectious corpses, pervades nearly all of epidemic literature; many of the canonical texts are organized around the point at which ordinary death, mourning, disposal, and last rites must be abandoned because there are simply too many bodies. This crisis—in Defoe and Camus in particular—represents the nadir of common experience, the de-ritualized disposal of human bodies as waste. A long section of *The Plague*'s third part is devoted to this narrative feature of the genre. At the worst point in the epidemic

> [t]he hospital . . . made use of five coffins . . . [A]t the cemetery they were emptied out, and the iron-gray corpses put on stretchers and deposited in a shed reserved for that purpose . . . [T]he empty coffins, after being sprayed with antiseptic fluid, were rushed back to the hospital and the process was repeated as often as necessary. (175; 162)

Later, Rieux describes bodies being flung directly out of ambulances into mass graves, one for men and one for women. Soon there are enough dead clogging up the city and the ambulances that this courtesy, too, must be abandoned, and the bodies are piled altogether in heaps outside the city limits. These scenes, so vivid in their echoes of the horrific mechanics of murder in the German camps, were, at the time of the novel's publication in 1947, irrefutable evidence of Camus's effort to record something of the horror of the war, however successfully or unsuccessfully he managed to do so.

The plague camps stand as another inchoate feature of Camus's allegory—in the novel, they are not explicitly *for* death, punishment, labor, and dehumanization, but rather for the preservation of life in the still healthy population of the city. Still, the Nazi discourse of sanitation, purification, and bodily health, which justified the cleansing of the national body, can be heard in the sanitary agenda that supports the existence of the quarantine and isolation camps, overseen by "commandants" during the plague. While Camus depicts the practice of quarantine as an extension of care that necessarily entails the sorrow of isolation, rather than as an expression of the radical evil of plague, the two different valences of the camps merge through the figure of the camp-person, a shred of a human being reduced to an ambling vector of pathogenicity. These "unfortunates" or "inmates"—the forgotten—are reduced to a silence so absolute that upon his visit, all Tarrou can hear are the flies buzzing about the tents (237; 224). The novel's infected recall the most dehumanized prisoners in the extermination camps, whom Primo Levi identified by the then-common name of the *Muselmänner*, or Muslims. Although other critics have suggested that the term's genesis was in the bodily incapacity of these prisoners, which rendered them unable to stand, and in a state of prostration or genuflection resembling Islamic prayer, Levi gives little by way of background or reflection on the term. Giorgio Agamben takes it up in *Remnants of Auschwitz*, providing a fuller context for its adaptation and a terminological history—some notable synonyms are "staggering corpse," "mummy-men," "donkeys," "swimmers," "cripples," "camels," "tired sheikhs," and "*Muselweiber*" or female Muslims—which in his view reflects a general European view of Muslim fatalism and Oriental submission.[52] Agamben calls the term "deprecatory" and dehumanizing, a "ferocious irony." In the chapter named after this figure, "The Muselmann," he writes,

> At times a medical figure or an ethical category, at times a political limit or an anthropological concept, the *Muselmann* is an indefinite being in whom not only humanity and non-humanity, but also vegetative existence and relation, physiology and ethics, medicine and politics, and life and death continually pass through each other. (48)

The Muselmann's capacity for the relational is both diminished and magnified here; his eviscerated being negates all possibility of intersubjective understanding, while at the same time embodying the threat and potential—the infectiousness or possibility of transfer—of this very condition to others. Agamben describes this condition as a "third realm," which serves as "a perfect cipher of the camp, the non-place in which all disciplinary barriers are destroyed and all embankments flooded" (48). He defines this "third realm" of the Muselmann, suspended between life and death, as constitutive of the very definition of life, a logic that mirrors the way in which the state of exception determines the "normal legal order" (48). Although Agamben writes specifically about the conditions in the camps, his comments raise important questions about Camus's absent subjects in *The Plague*; not those whom we see in quarantine, or even in mass graves—the Muselmänner of a different sort—but those who we don't see at all: the "Arabs."

It is evident how postcolonial critique might regard the problem of the absent Arab in Camus's second novel: as naïvely universalist, hysterically blind, flatly racist. As in many of his works, Algerian subjects are part of the landscape, plot devices, or occasions rather than subjects. I am largely in agreement with these positions: Conor Cruise O'Brien and Edward Said are the best known of these critics in the North American and Anglo-Irish tradition of Camus scholarship. More recently, Emily Apter has revisited this question, calling Camus's depiction of Algeria "Made in France."[53] For Alice Kaplan, it was an encounter with an Algerian scholar that gave her pause in her thinking about Camus's legacy in a postcolonial context:

> [W]hat she said may have been familiar to everyone in the room, but it was completely new to me: "It's true that Camus was banished for a long time, by critics, readers, etc. I don't think it's *The First Man* that brought him back. It was the situation, the terrorism we experienced in the period we call our civil war (1990s). . . . Those Algerians in the 1990s recognized themselves in Camus . . . the constant vacillation, the hesitation, the not being able to figure out what is going on or take a clear position. Since we were experiencing those same hesitations, we read him again in a new way."[54]

The unnamed scholar (her husband had been murdered in the dirty wars) expresses precisely the opposite of the kind of politically unilateral postcolonialism that comes under fire by staunch defenders of Camus, who are impatient with what they understand to be anachronistic and revisionist rejections of his work. What's evident here is a new interest in the relationship between the politics legible in Camus's political writing and the absences in his fiction in light of the specific failures of nationalism and democracy in Algeria and the increasingly untenable situation for those who resist the state's form of Islam. The climate of terrorism in Algeria in the 1990s occasioned a reconsideration of Camus's refusal to support the forms of violence that subtended the Algerian nationalism he perceived to be taking shape in the 1950s—forms which already involved the use of extreme and irregular forms of violence that, by the 1990s, appeared to have become "epidemic" in independent Algeria.[55] Since 2001, this concern has become a pointedly American one as well, as Kaplan demonstrates in her preface to the *Algerian Chronicles*, which after more than fifty years has become available to an English readership.[56] These recent reevaluations of what have long been understood as the reactionary lacunae in Camus's work emerge specifically in light of the rise of global Islamist violence and terrorism not just in postcolonial Africa but also in South Asia and the Middle East, Western Europe and North America.

Although there are important disagreements over how to interpret the absence of non-European Algerian subjects in Camus's writing, Francophone and postcolonial scholars have been increasingly interested in recent decades in looking very carefully at those absences across his body of work. O'Brien deals with this issue throughout his monograph *Albert Camus: Of Europe and Africa*. For Camus, he suggests, it was unimaginable that there may have been

> Arabs for whom "French Algeria" was a fiction quite as repugnant as the fiction of Hitler's new European order was for Camus and his friends. For such Arabs, the French were in Algeria by virtue of the same right by which the Germans were in France: the right of conquest. . . . From this point of view, Rieux, Tarrou, and Grand were not devoted fighters against the plague: they were the plague itself.[57]

O'Brien's simple reframing proliferates the already-slippery questions about Camus's allegorical arithmetic. If for the Arabs, the doctor and his sanitation squads are the plague, how might the settlers' terror be explained? As a fear of themselves? Of the depredations of the colonial enterprise, in the spirit of later critics like Albert Memmi? Does the novel offer a precursor to the Derridian autoimmunitary paradigm? Is anyone agential in this logic? Are all events "merely" natural or reflective? Is there a theory of revolution or resistance, as Camus seemed to imply in the exchange with Barthes?

O'Brien's reading doesn't exactly relocate a recognizable "subject"—a type Camus was already dismantling in earlier work—in the disappeared Arabs, but tethers the Arab population to the novel's visible indexes of disintegration: the dead, the dying, and the city itself. We've seen how Camus's strategies of representing illness intersect with the colonial history of epidemic management in the nineteenth century, but a twentieth-century imperial disease poetics also inflects two other pressure points in the novel that tell us more about its absent and dehumanized presences: first, the tethering of sanitation rhetoric to the Nazi death camps, and second, the biopolitical tactics of the French colonial government against Algerian nationalists, including medical surveillance, provision of care, and the stockpiling of pharmaceutical and surgical resources.[58] When examined in a twentieth-century biopolitical frame, the novel unveils itself in dimensions better suited to our moment, and better capable of explaining its durability in twenty-first-century critical discourse. That is to say that the plague metonymizes the entirety of the problem of Algerians in colonial Algeria for Camus—the incommensurability of Algerian prosperity and self-determination with the survival of the *pied-noir* population. It is easy to imagine this version of the fable, since the bodies of Camus's Arab Algerians are already expunged from the text—already, as it were, shipped off to the quarantine camps, where they stand both as death and as the vectors of the threat of death's slow and steady growth.

In this way, the absent natives align with another class of disappeared life in the novel: the rats of Oran who teem from the city's underbelly in the novel's opening pages as a portent of the plague. Along with the more recent history of Asiatic cholera, there was a plague in Marseilles in 1720. The last of its kind in Europe, the epidemic killed more than 100,000 people, and stands as an important antecedent for the novel's geography of terror, as it was sourced to a ship that had arrived from Lebanon by way of Libya. Like *Vibrio cholerae*, the rats that carried *Yersinia pestis*, the plague bacillus, were a species native to India; the black rat known as *Rattus rattus* had almost entirely replaced European species after the return of the Crusaders from the East.[59] When *The Plague*'s young journalist, Rambert, asks Rieux about the "sanitary conditions" and "living conditions prevailing among the Arab population," he's instructed by the doctor to forget about the Arabs, "if he was out for curious stories for his paper, he might say something about the extraordinary number of dead rats that were being found in the town just now. 'Ah!' Rambert exclaim[s]. 'That certainly interests me.'"[60] In the pages that follow, the rats take the place of the asked-after Arabs, littering the hallways of the doctor's building, interrupting the ordinary operations of domestic life. Their emergence from the city's underbelly and death "out in the open" constitute the beginning of the plague:

> From April 18 onwards, quantities of dead or dying rats were found in factories and warehouses . . . [F]rom the outer suburbs to the center of the town, in all the byways where the doctor's duties took him, in every thoroughfare, rats were piled up in garbage cans or lying in long lines in the gutters. (15; 22)

A key aspect of their horror is the flagrancy of the rats' public death, how the residents of Oran are forced to *see* the rats "coming out of their holes" and dying "all over the place," "a particularly disgusting nuisance" (13–14; 21). The novel lingers on two particularly graphic scenes in the opening chapter to underscore the perversity and shamelessness of the rats, who, "from basements, cellars, and sewers . . . emerged in long wavering files into the light of day, swayed helplessly, then did a sort of pirouette and fell dead at the feet of horrified onlookers" (15; 22). In their death throes, the rats are not only offensively visible, but also audible: "at night, in the passages and alleys, their shrill little death-cries could be clearly heard" (15; 22).

As the infection accelerates, the problem of corpse disposal and hygiene compounds their aesthetic inconveniences:

> In the mornings the bodies were found lining the gutters, each with a gout of blood, like a red flower, on its tapering muzzle; some were bloated and already beginning to rot, others rigid, with their whiskers still erect. . . . People out at night would often feel underfoot the squelchy roundness of a still-warm body. (15–16; 22–23)

The city is forced to develop a rodent corpse removal and incineration program, prefiguring how human fatalities will later be dealt with at the height of the plague. The rats' expulsion and removal from the social body of the city establish the parameters of plague as metaphor of purgation and expression or suppuration that resembles the "outbreak" prose of Guha's counterinsurgency:

> It was as if the earth on which our houses stood was being purged of its secret humors; thrusting up to the surface the abscesses and pus-clots that had been forming in its entrails. You must picture the consternation of our little town, hitherto so tranquil, and now, out of the blue, shaken to its core, like a quite healthy man who all of a sudden feels his temperature shoot up and the blood seething like wildfire in his veins. (16) (comme un homme bien portant dont le sang épais se mettrait tout d'un coup en révolution! [22])

Here, the city is represented by a healthy, tranquil man pierced by a sudden elevation of temperature, which Gilbert translates as "wildfire in his veins," but which in the original appears in more politically evocative terms as a *"révolution."* The Algerian revolt isn't too far off, temporally or, I would suggest, metaphorically. The novel's sanitary service, or *service dératisation*—a rhyme with the practice of *ratissage* or *raton-nage*, a raking or sweeping operation that would later come to describe the "pacifying operations" of the French against Muslim villages and revolutionaries in Algeria—seems to quell the *révolution de sang épais*, at least as it is expressed in the regurgitation of rats from the bowels of the city.[61]

The rat crisis in *The Plague* swaps out the absent Arab bodies Rambert asks about for those of the detested rodents, whose mass death—or sacrificial disappearance—provides an overture to "human" infection, which in the novel's logic means the death of white people. Returning to the moment of Rieux and Rambert's conversation allows us to see the novel's expunging of Arab subjects as an undoing of the putatively "French" allegory right at the start. The reason the Rieux gives Rambert for his silence on the question of the living conditions in the Arab quarter seems to be Camus's reason for largely disappearing Algerian Arabs in his fiction as well, at least in a charitable reading; Rieux asks Rambert if the paper would be willing to "publish an unqualified condemnation of the present state of things," whether "the journalist would be allowed to tell the truth" about the Arab living conditions (12; 18–19). Rambert replies, "Unqualified? Well no, I couldn't go that far," and the doctor falls quiet, refusing to speak, even when goaded by Rambert: "You talk the language of Saint Just" (12; 18–19). Rieux's feelings harmonize with Camus's own jottings and essays on the exhaustions of injustice: "the language he used was that of a man who was sick and tired of the world he lived in—though he had much liking for his fellow men—and had resolved, for his part, to have no truck with injustice and compromises with the truth" (12; 19).

This moment telegraphs the question of Arab Algeria as both massively important in Camus's thought, and yet, of necessity, unapproachable through the approximate, compromising media of both speech and writing. Much has been made of Camus's own silence on the Algerian question beginning in 1956, after which he entered a "29 month silence" that, Kaplan has suggested, "became a metonymy for cowardice."[62] During this period, the perception of his cowardice and hypocrisy was compounded by the 1957 mess over the Nobel interview in which *Le Monde* reported him to have said "I believe in justice but I will defend my mother over justice."[63] To set the record straight, as many critics have suggested in recent years—or to attempt to recuperate his foundering reputation— Camus released *Chroniques algériennes* the following year, with a new essay "Algérie 1958," that closed with the haunting final line, "This is the last warning that can be given by a writer who for the past 20 years has been dedicated to the Algerian cause, before he lapses once again into silence."[64]

It is entirely understandable that the novel's author and predominantly metropolitan readers mistook its dis-ease about an oppressed population and its growing agitation against colonial rule for a more digestible condemnation of the injustices of Nazi violence. If *The Plague* refuses to speak directly to the shamefully overlooked and neglected lives of Oran's Arab inhabitants—worthy, in a doctor's opinion, of total condemnation—it displaces the conversation to the other population that marks time in corners of the city between the visible and invisible, silence and the wail of suffering. *La peste brune* is here differently literalized, through Rieux's transposition, as a plague of dehumanized brownness, a hazy, dirty, "murky" or "shadowy" atmospheric threat that lurks outside the fortifications of the city; a plague not of brown cloth, but of brown skin. In its studied imprecision, the novel teases this reading right from the start, very nearly calling Arab Algerians a plague by deflecting a question about their lives with an answer about the rats. Given the state of affairs between the French colonial government and the growing Algerian resistance after the massacres at Sétif and Guelma in 1945, during which time Camus was both drafting the novel and writing about the colonial situation, this reading is not unthinkable at the time of the novel's publication, and certainly in the decades after. O'Brien approximates this position toward the end of his chapter on *The Plague*—which he calls both a "masterpiece" and an "allegorical sermon"—with the claim:

> Eight years after the publication of *La Peste*, the rats came up to die again in the cities of Algeria. To apply another of Camus's metaphors, the Algerian insurrection was "the eruption of boils and pus which had been working inwardly in the society." And this eruption came from precisely the quarter in which the narrator had refused to look: from the houses which Dr. Rieux never visited and from the conditions about which the reporter Rambert never carried out his inquiry.[65]

The Plague's body-snatching allegorical system reveals the tension between Camus's avowed commitments and his unavowed prejudices and fears. The novel strenuously objects to the injustices of fascism—perhaps including that of the French government in Algeria—but in his larger body of work, and in his critical disagreement with Barthes, Camus seems far more traumatized by what he understood to be the threat of expulsion for the million Algerian-born *pieds-noirs*. For O'Brien, this is a repressive operation for both writer and reader: "the source of the plague is what we pretend is not there."[66] Even as "what we pretend is not there" shifts over time, the novel energetically skirts the most obvious brown plague in its pages—that of the Algerians—and renders the fraught relations between the two publics as a horror that cannot be seen.

Dirty Ink

In his 1966 essay, "Depth and Complexity," Pierre Macherey discusses a fallacy of then-contemporary criticism, suggesting that it is "easy to find [the text] *deep*, like an enigma or mask behind which lurks some haunting presence; this is but one more way of representing the text as a smooth and decorative surface, deceptive in its perfection."[67] Instead, he suggests that the text is present, "entirely *readable*, visible, entrusted," whereas "interpretation simply offers a reductive explanation by identifying just one of [the writer's] choices" (112–113). The sole example Macherey offers in this brief essay of such a fallacy of depth is that of Sartre's interpretation of Camus's first novel, *The Stranger*—he calls the explication a "simple procedure" that Sartre "applied" to the novel (113). Macherey wants readers to receive the text, to attend to the simultaneity of its activities. Thinking with Camus, Macherey's intervention insists that we attend, almost scientifically, to what *happens* in the text, "examin[ing] the work in its real complexity," rather than reducing our understanding to an argument about what *is* by way of what he calls its "mythical depth" (112). If Camus's fictions invite such readings, and *The Plague* in particular does so, as in the quarrel with Barthes, it is precisely because the writing attempts to negotiate the space between a phenomenology of epidemic and a metaphysics of evil and remains silent on so many of the points that might pin it to a particular history, or a particular interpretation, even a particular villain, as obvious as the Nazi answer may seem. Macherey offers a theory of such absences in the conclusion of his essay, exhorting readers to move toward an awareness of "the *reason* of [the text's] process" (113). He writes:

> It is not a question of perceiving a latent structure of which the manifest work is an index, but of establishing that absence around which a real complexity is knit. Then, perhaps, can be exorcised the fallacies which have bound literary criticism to ideology: the fallacy of the secret, the fallacy of depth, the fallacy of rules, the fallacy of harmony. Decentered, displaced, determinate, complex: recognized as such, the work runs the risk of receiving its theory. (113)

If *The Plague* is ready to be at risk, to "receive its theory" once again, as Judt, Kaplan, and others have suggested in resituating the novel and its ancillary texts in the era of millennial terrorism, then perhaps it is in the very absences, complexities, deformations, decenterings—the extent to which "the book is always the site of exchange," as Macherey puts it—that its substance lies. Like *Dracula*, *The Plague* knits complexity around the absent presence of epidemic; it also knits complexity around the absent presence of Algeria.

This absence is more notable for Camus's voluminous journalism about the crimes of France in its colonies. Both prior to and during the time Camus was drafting *The Plague*, he was also publishing multiple series of articles on living conditions and political movements among the non-European inhabitants of Algeria for the radical socialist paper *Alger républicain* and *Combat*, the French resistance paper he edited for a time. In 1939, when Camus was just twenty-five, he published the series of articles called "The Misery of Kabylia" (*La Misère de la Kabylie*) on the woeful economic conditions afflicting the inhabitants of the Kabylia region. A later series for *Combat* entitled "Crisis in Algeria" (*Crise en Algérie*) appeared between May 13 and June 14 in 1945, just days after the end of the war was marked by Victory in Europe Day on May 8. In keeping with the metaphorical landscape of *The Plague*, Camus's use of the word "crisis" in the title carries with it connotations of ill health, its Greek root *krisis* describing the turning point in the progression of a disease or malady.[68]

This series, Camus announces in the first essay, was to be an objective account of the conditions in Algeria that made possible the uprisings in Sétif and Guelma days earlier, which ended with the massacre, according to modest estimates, of at least six thousand Algerians by the French military and the foreign legion in the raking-over of Muslim villages known as *ratissage*.[69] As for the "political dimension" of the series of essays, Camus writes, "I want to remind people in France of the fact that Algeria exists . . . I want to point out that the Arab people also exist . . . that hundreds of thousands of Arabs have spent the past two years fighting for the liberation of France."[70] In some ways these statements are utterly unheroic—it is, after all, no great accomplishment to point out to French readers the mere existence of millions of people who were not only inhabitants of France but directly suffering for the enrichment of the metropole. But these lines from the May 1945 essays are crucial for two reasons: first because the timing of their publication suggests that for Camus, the end of the war only increased France's already formidable debt and responsibility to Algeria, and second because they serve to reopen questions about the absence of Arab Algerian subjects in Camus's writing. John Foley, for example, reads "the absence of Arabs from Camus's *La Peste*" as "neither malicious nor miraculous, it is meticulous . . . [T]he political and social questions which would be raised by their appearance . . . would likely overwhelm the more abstract moral questions."[71] Foley's claim, like those of many before him, suggests that the minutiae of particular politics would get in the way of, rather than constituting, more lofty moral and philosophical considerations. Notwithstanding this blunt reduction, his comment invites consideration of what a meticulous expunging might mean, as opposed to a malicious or miraculous one, especially if we think back to Camus's own differentiation between what science—and perhaps other more putatively objective forms of writing—explains, namely that which happens, and does not explain, namely that which is.

This does not require that we blind ourselves to what Camus did say about Algeria, and about colonial dynamics more broadly, in his articles of the 1930s and '40s. The articles make plain that Camus believed he was performing a critical service as a liaison between a French public at home and a forgotten population in the colony. The content of these articles sheds a complex historical light on the figural universe of *The Plague*, evincing an abiding concern and sense of responsibility on Camus's part for the living conditions of Arab Algerians, even at the risk of alienating the colonial government. The 1939 series illuminates what Camus sees as the French government's responsibility in prolonging and failing to take realistic measures to remedy massive famine and destitution in the overpopulated Kabylian region of Algeria. These essays advocate for the political empowerment of the Kabyle people, for "greater independence and self-rule" for a people from whom Camus believed his readers "could humbly take lessons in dignity and justice."[72] But they also establish what will prove to be an enduring obstacle for Camus in years to come. Even as he disavows the French colonists, who he believes may never act to improve the conditions of their cohabitants in Algeria, he calls on metropolitan France to "step in," arguing in the penultimate article in the series that "a system that divorces Algeria from France is bad for France . . . [W]hen the interests of Algeria and France coincide, you can be sure that hearts and minds will soon follow" (80; 935). Whether Camus's privileging of what is good for France here is simply a cynical attempt to win his audience or reflects where his sympathies truly reside remains ambiguous. In a melancholic turn, he names the "meaning of [his] investigation" in the series' conclusion: "If there is any conceivable excuse for the colonial conquest, it has to lie in helping peoples to retain their distinctive personality. And if we French have any duty here, it is to allow one of the proudest and most human peoples in this world to keep faith with itself and with its destiny" (83; 938). There is no absence of humanity in the essays on the conditions of Algerian peasants that make up "The Misery of the Kabylia." On the other hand, these essays are shot through with both a romanticizing depoliticization of these people as noble and simple, and a firmly entrenched belief that their best hope for survival, even happiness, was fuller incorporation into the French legal system rather than independence. Like Aimé Césaire in Martinique, Camus advocated, for a time, for a kind of departmentalization.[73] Another way of putting this is that Camus believed there was one road to the full realization of the Arab Algerians' humanity, and it was through the patrimony of the French nation state.

On May 10, 1947, Camus circled back to the confluence of crisis and sickness in an essay for *Combat* called "La Contagion." It was not, as one might imagine, given the close proximity of *The Plague*'s publication that summer, about either Algeria or the war, at least explicitly. The essay is about the "stupid and criminal malady" of racism in France, which Camus locates in the biased press coverage of an attack on Joseph Raseta, a deputy from Madagascar who was assaulted in the Palais Bourbon, but who was nevertheless called by the papers "Raseta the murderer," for his ostensible role in the anticolonial riots in Madagascar beginning in April of that year.[74] Of the uprisings, Camus writes that he feels nothing but "equal repugnance for the methods of both sides," namely the French and the Malgache, but that, since no allegations have been proven, and no reliable account of the atrocities in Madagascar have been given, the French press calling Raseta a murderer expresses a blatant disregard for balance and objectivity in favor of hate-mongering and sensationalism: "[N]o journalist," he writes, "would have dared to use such a headline if the alleged murderer had been named Dupont or Durand" (290; 321).

Camus situates this example of the malady of French racism in a broader context, illuminating the conflation of colonial immigrants and criminality by way of a lurid anecdote that recalls Meursault's shocking absence of humanity in *The Stranger*. Alluding to a recent police inquiry into a murder in Essonne, he writes that

> [n]o one is surprised to learn that the unfortunate student who killed his fiancée used the presence of "sidis" as they say, in the forest of Sénart to divert suspicion from himself. If Arabs go for a walk in the woods, it cannot be simply because spring has arrived. It can only be to murder their contemporaries. (290; 321)

"Sidi" is used in this context as a slur for brown Muslim immigrants, most of them from North Africa. Their presence as criminal scapegoats in France's cities, however, is not enough, in Camus's view, to remind their French cohabitants either of the Arabs' humanity, or of France's own recent traumatic history under occupation—an analogue, in this particular moment in Camus's writing, for an oppressive colonialism. He draws a stark comparison between the events in Sétif, which he had sought to explain in the 1945 series "Crisis in Algeria," and their aftermath in the uprisings and subsequent inhumane treatment and torture of Algerian prisoners on the one hand, and the terror tactics visited on the citizens of Europe by the Germans on the other.

> One year ago in Algeria, methods of collective oppression were used. And *Combat* recently revealed the existence of the "spontaneous confession chamber" in Fianarantsoa . . . [T]hree years after being subjected to a policy of terror themselves, Frenchmen are reacting to this latest news with the indifference of people who have seen too much. Yet the facts are there: the clear and hideous truth: we are doing what we reproached the Germans for doing. (291; 322)

Here Camus clearly aligns the terror of the Nazi occupation with the colonial situation in both Algeria and Madagascar. Although he does not go so far as to bring Algerian anticolonialism and nationalism into this comparative constellation, both French and German terror tactics are coded as "contagious," while the violence on the Malgache side inspires "equal repugnance," suggesting that the Malagasy, too, have caught this contagion. Following the comparison to the Germans, Camus writes, "I am well aware that we have been offered an explanation, namely, that the Malagasy rebels have tortured Frenchmen" (290; 322). This statement clarifies further what he means by the contagious logic of both action and discourse in the use of asymmetrical violence on the part of the colonists, who inspire violent retaliation, and so on, in a cycle of mutually reinforcing contagion. By extension, the same victims who were tortured by the French in Fianarantsoa are equally susceptible to this contagion, and may soon, if they haven't already, join the Malgache and the French in being repugnant carriers, if not the most egregious dispensers, of this terror.

In the essay's penultimate paragraph, Camus draws Algeria into this cycle of contagion, working explicitly through the logic of racial hierarchy and processes of dehumanization that makes such violence and racism possible. This moment serves as one of the clearest articulations in Camus's writing of how he understands the pathologies of both nationalism and colonialism as transmissible phenomena:

> If the Hitlerians applied their shameful laws to Europe, the reason was that they believed their race to be superior, hence the law for Germans could not be the same as the law for enslaved peoples. If we French revolted against their terror, it was because we believed that all Europeans were equal in rights and dignity. But if Frenchmen can now hear of the methods used by other Frenchmen against Algerians and Malagasies and not react, it is because they are unconsciously certain

that we are in some way superior to those people and that it makes little difference what means we choose to demonstrate that superiority. (291; 322)

Here, Camus brings together the prismatic historical referents that inform the depiction of plague in the novel as both a particular occurrence wedded to a particular state of crisis under the occupation, but also as a messy, flexible signifier that reflects the potential contagiousness of this crisis into other spaces, and through other means. As such, this moment in the essay "Contagion" lends itself readily to a broader interpretive apparatus that helps make sense of the way in which Algerian absence functions in *The Plague* as a space of open anxiety, of potential infection or corporeal vulnerability, and of dread for the horrors that may return unbidden through the touch and exchange of colonial contact and the virulent nationalisms he fears it will engender. This essay, it is important to note, was published just three months before Pakistan and India would achieve independence from Britain in one of the bloodiest mass migrations in modern history.

Camus's position on Algeria—which never really entertained the possibility of an independent state—became entrenched in the years leading up to and following the official start of the Algerian war of independence in 1954. Even as he continued to defend the dignity and humanity of the Arab Algerian people, his writing expressed an increasing anxiety about the status of other native Algerians; Algerians like his mother, whose life of toil and poverty, he insisted, was equally deserving of dignity and humanity. There is the now-famous utterance that Camus made during a discussion with students after accepting the Nobel in 1957 that still rings discordantly for many readers; the last line especially is often cited as a reason to dismiss an inveterately colonialist Camus. *Le Monde* reported Camus' statement as follows:

> I have always supported a just Algeria, where the two populations must live in peace and equality, I have said and repeated that we have to bring justice to the Algerian people and grant them a fully democratic regime . . . I have always condemned terror. I must also condemn a terrorism that is practiced blindly, in the streets of Algiers, for example, and which one day could strike my mother or my family. I believe in justice, but I will defend my mother before justice.[75]

Although the statement was a paraphrase, Camus defends it in a letter he sent subsequently to the paper, writing "I was willing to state publicly to that young Algerian . . . personal explanations that I had previously kept to myself and that your correspondent reported accurately."[76] In this letter, he remarks further that the young Algerian who had asked him the question that prompted this response was someone to whom he "[felt] closer . . . than to many French people who speak about Algeria without knowing it." He continues, "[H]is face reflected not hatred but despair and unhappiness. I share that unhappiness. His face is the face of my country."[77]

Earlier, in a 1948 essay, "The Exile of Helen," Camus gives shape to this sense of shared unhappiness and tragedy, drawing together the feeling of loss that had come to mark his experience of both Algeria and France with the story of another plague in another time that ended with the death of another beautiful city of the East. Drawing on the Homeric song of Ilium, he speaks of the exile of beauty in the Mediterranean as the exile of Helen. This tragedy is not hidden or obscured, but plainly visible in the bright light of heroic antiquity. He writes, "The Mediterranean has a solar tragedy which has nothing to do with mists. . . . In this golden sadness, tragedy reaches its highest point."[78] In marked contrast to this idealized past, a past in which the face of the young Algerian, like the face of Helen, might stand plainly for the beauty of homeland that cannot be shared and a sorrow that must, a face unclouded by the mists or miasmas of pathology, Camus writes of his own time: "the despair of our world—quite the opposite—has fed on ugliness and upheavals" (148; 853). The language of filth and contagion are pervasive in this period of Camus's writing—it is not just *la peste brune* that emerges in the postwar fiction, but also the crisis, contagion, and malady of colonial violence and terror tactics on both sides that we see surging out in the journalism and essays. This period also marks the beginning of what will come to be seen as Camus's unseemly phase by committed leftists and anticolonialists in both Algeria and France, a moment in which the ugly parochialism of his politics would sully a shining record of political engagement. Camus seems aware of this disappointment lurking on the horizon in the essay on Helen, remarking obliquely on the inadequacy of writing to strike at the heart of the present "despair," "ugliness," and "convulsions." He laments, "Our miserable tragedies have the smell of an office, and their blood is the color of dirty ink" (148; 854). For the contemporary reader of Camus, these lines are an uncanny reflection of the way in which the journalism, essays, and comments on Algeria have come to be read: as so much dirty ink spilled in defense of a colonial power of which Camus was a privileged member.

The indelibility of these words, and their connection to the blood and suffering of the people, are reflected in the permanent threat of plague articulated in *The Plague*'s final moments. Here, the novel finally tells us something of what the plague *is*: it arrives not from a geographical afar but from a temporal afar. It is a slow and patient dread that, in the words of Dr. Rieux, who has by the end of the novel revealed that he is its chronicler, "bides its time in bedrooms, cellars, trunks, and bookshelves."[79] In the early conversations between Rieux and Castel, Castel has tried to remind his younger colleague that there is nothing novel or shocking in the arrival of the epidemic, just as there is nothing novel or shocking in the perpetual outbreaks of war that count out the time of human history. He remarks, "Everybody knows that pestilences have a way of recurring in the world yet somehow we find it hard to believe in ones that crash down on our heads from a blue sky. There have been as many plagues as wars in history; yet always plagues and wars take people equally by surprise" (37; 41). The final sentence of the novel reprises the older doctor's warnings, this time in the voice of Rieux, who has learned that the ending of this chronicle is no ending at all, at best, it is only a pause:

> [T]he plague bacillus never dies or disappears for good . . . [I]t can lie dormant for years and years . . . [P]erhaps the day would come when, for the bane and the enlightening of men, it would rouse up its rats again and send them forth to die in a happy city. (308; 279)

I want to return to the essay "Contagion," published the same summer as the novel, because the final lines of that text illuminate the confounding absence of Algeria in the chronicle that Camus claimed was an allegory, at least, for the inhumanity of Nazi violence and the struggle staged against it. That piece begins by diagnosing an epidemic of racism in France, but it ends on a very different note that suggests that colonialism, too, breeds pathology. Camus writes,

> If it is accurate to say that the colonial problem is the most complex of all the problems we face, and if it is going to shape the history of the next fifty years, it is no less true to say that we will never be able to solve it if we allow the most pernicious of prejudices to influence our judgment.[80]

In spite of the absence at its heart, *The Plague*, an immediately proximate text of contagion, speaks not only to what happened in the Second World War, but also to the epidemics of colonialism, which, if we read this pair of closing lines together, begin to reveal themselves as continuous with the pathological nationalism of the Third Reich. Like the plague bacillus, which Rieux predicts will rise again from beneath the happy city, the "colonial problem" will shape the history of the next fifty years, reemerging in moments of intensity as various forms of terror in Algeria, in France, and beyond. At the risk of oversimplifying a vast number of contributing factors, the problem of colonialism—in Camus's moment as in our own—is also at the heart of the problem of the kind of violence we call terrorism.

Recall Tony Judt's resituating of *The Plague* in 2001, in light of the overwhelming preoccupation with the events of September 11: there, he suggests that "[Camus's] controversial use of a biological epidemic to illustrate the dilemmas of moral contagion succeeds in ways the writer could not have imagined. Here in New York, in November, 2001, we are better placed than we could ever have wished to feel the lash of the novel's premonitory final sentence."[81] These displacements are as central to a reading of the novel as any search for a single historical referent may be. The logic and structure of contagion, of epidemic, and of plague are forceful precisely because they deconstruct and dismantle the artificial separation and quarantining of places and times, rendering all space vulnerable to its ravages. If Camus did not write a novel that deals ethically with history, as Barthes suggests, and if his text naturalizes human violence as both subhuman in the form of a microbe and superhuman in the form of an unknown goddess, he nevertheless offers a figure of epidemic violence that has remained central to an understanding of terror for more than half a century.

CHAPTER 5

Algeria Ungowned

Those boys who blew themselves up, boys like that were beating their sisters.

NADEEM ASLAM, "VIGIL IN A DARKENED ROOM"

It is not unfair to say that in 2003 most Army officers knew more about the U.S. Civil War than they did about counterinsurgency.

JOHN A. NAGL, "THE EVOLUTION AND IMPORTANCE OF ARMY / MARINE CORPS FIELD MANUAL 3–24"

When the Office of Special Operations and Low-Intensity Conflict screened Gillo Pontecorvo's 1966 film *The Battle of Algiers* at the Pentagon in late summer 2003, the objective was to provide a useful primer—historical, strategic, and, I will argue, broadly epistemological—for the practice of counterinsurgency in Iraq. A Defense Department official suggested that the film "offers historical insight into the conduct of French operations in Algeria and was intended to prompt informative discussion of the challenges faced by the French."[1] In an interview about the film's relevance for the American war against terrorism, Richard A. Clarke, former national coordinator for security and counterterrorism, made a causal link: "I'll be happy to guess that Al Qaeda has watched this movie, that the Palestinians have watched this movie."[2] As if touting its own anachronism and obsolescence along the bending arc of history, the flier advertising the Pentagon screening read, "How to win a battle against terrorism and lose the war of ideas." This glib framing of both the film and the events it describes confirmed the cynicism, false optimism, and tone-deafness of the Bush administration and its adjuncts and appointees in national security, effectively trumpeting the operations in Iraq not only as a colonial occupation, but one that would this time succeed. In a summer of profound perversities, following the historic spring during which thirty-six million people across the globe took to the streets in protest against the Iraq and Afghanistan wars, here was the revolutionary reel, requisitioned for a new age of imperial right.[3]

Implicit in the Pentagon's framing was not only an identification with the French occupying forces in late-colonial Algeria, but also a categorization of the insurgency in Iraq, if not as an explicitly anti-imperial undertaking, then something very like it. Now, as the War on Terror reaches toward its second decade, as American imperialism becomes the de facto framework for understanding the global order in the twenty-first century, as the revelations of decades of illegal detention, rendition, and torture have been confirmed by the very architects of the war in state-sponsored reports, declassified documents, and histories-by-committee, the "how to win a battle against terrorism and lose the war of ideas" line reads more like a confession than a warning. The copy that followed this headline on the flier has been quoted by a number of scholars and commentators since the film's timely re-release the next year in October 2004, when it was newly packaged with a wealth of historical materials, including the interview with Richard Clarke and former State Department coordinator for counterterrorism Michael Sheehan, by the prestige film distribution company the Criterion Collection. The invitation to the screening read

> Children shoot soldiers at point blank range. Women plant bombs in cafes. Soon the entire Arab population builds to a mad fervor. Sound familiar? The French have a plan. It succeeds tactically but fails strategically. To understand why, come to a rare showing of this film.[4]

Here, Pontecorvo's frequently misunderstood film—funded in part by the Algerian government, produced and heavily influenced by the writings of Yacef Saadi through his company Casbah Films, touted as "La Première grande production algérienne" in the opening credits—is presented as both an unmediated history lesson as well as a warning that contains its own simple solution. Even as they avow the resonances between the Algerian struggle and the insurgency in the Sunni Triangle in the summer of 2003 ("sound familiar?"), the screening's organizers seem to anticipate the limitations of military might. Making the public relations risks of asymmetrical warfare explicit, Sheehan suggests that in the urban theater, "terrorism is usually a tactic to provoke . . . a heavy-handed response" and that the lesson to be learned from the film is that "if you allow them to pull you into open warfare . . . you're being sucked into a losing strategy."[5] Perhaps someone at the Pentagon wondered momentarily about culture, messaging, a longer game, forgetting the moral ground that would inevitably be ceded to their opponents by drawing on colonial history as a model for the War on Terror. Reflecting on the timeliness of the screening, Sheehan mused, "I think it's a good thing."[6]

The Pentagon screening in 2003 was not the first reappearance of Pontecorvo's film in the official planning of America's War on Terror. On

September 20, 2001, nine days after the attacks on the World Trade Center, Christopher Harmon, a professor of international relations at the U.S. Marine Corps Command and Staff College, described the difficulty in identifying and mapping "a militant Muslim international" by referring to its "remarkable" mobility. "They operate well in Europe," he stated,

> which is rich, which has many media outlets, which is generous to them and gentle in most of its immigration laws. Now, they use a cell structure which has never been better explained publicly than in the famous film, *The Battle of Algiers*, in which is shown the way in which a clandestine organization can form and operate and, while never impenetrable, reduce some of its counterintelligence problems.[7]

When marshalled to these ends, what *The Battle of Algiers* ostensibly demonstrates is that even in the face of unthinkable violence—children gunning down police officers in the streets, women conscripted into violent and deadly assaults on civilians, an entire populace whipped up into a "mad fervor"—there can be a "strategy" to win "the war of ideas," which is separate or separable from tactical success. It is the failure of this "strategy" by French forces, a coda to the tactical and strategic failure in Indochina earlier the same year, that the screening's organizers hoped would serve as a negative example, would provide lessons for how to manage the increasingly unmanageable ground operations in Iraq and Afghanistan.[8] The screening, it should be noted, occurred less than three months after then-president George W. Bush, in combat drag, stood in front of a banner declaring the American undertaking in Iraq a "mission accomplished."[9] In spite of Clarke's, Sheehan's, and the Office of Special Operations' claims that the film shows how battle tactics can succeed at the expense of broader claims to legitimacy, it is difficult to imagine a reading of *The Battle of Algiers* that would provide useful information or warnings about anything *but* tactics during a summer when Saddam Hussein was still at large, the frequency of IED and mortar attacks was approximately twelve per day, and nearly 600 US troops were wounded in three months, a number that doubled from September to December 2003.[10] Even the film's central counterrevolutionary military strategist, modelled in part on the French general Jacques Massu, does not mistake tactical successes in Algiers for an effective suppression of a nationalist movement—his jaundiced view of the undertaking is pitted repeatedly against the dual demands from the metropole that the colony be maintained at all costs and from the *pieds-noirs* that the maximum possible punishments be inflicted on Algerians who dared to rise.

The irony of this dual demand is forcefully revealed in the film's opening scene, in which a weeping informant sits in his white undershorts, glaringly lit in the center of a tiled room as a camouflage-clad soldier rubs his shoulders with a damp cloth and another washes chains— instruments of a just-completed torture or threats of a future interroga- tion—in a sink behind them. A counter reminiscent of an operating table and the gallery of lurid metal tools laid out at the right edge of the frame complete the shot's slant quotation of the torture chamber as surgical suite, a fantasy wherein information functions as pathological tissue to be extracted for the good of all, discrete truths prepared for surgical removal and examination under the microscope of counterinsurgency intelligence. "He finally came clean," says one of the torturers. Played by a man imprisoned for petty theft who was kept under close guard dur- ing the shooting of the film, the subject of the interrogative operation transforms into the therapeutic subject, the patient. He is offered a cup of coffee and told not to worry. "Drink this, you'll feel better," the inter- rogator says as he holds the cup to the trembling informant's mouth and pats him gently on the back. A fellow soldier joins him and together they, fully clothed, lift the stripped and weakened man in a gesture of intimate care that recalls, at once, pietà and exemplary bedside manner.

The conceptual and visual juxtaposition of torture and care in the film's opening scene reveals the extent of martial proceduralism's dis- abling of politics. This is familiar to us from the naturalizing metaphors of epidemic insurgency in the nineteenth century, here refigured as the scrubbed and sanitized site—the well-lit chamber—at the other end of the ticking-time-bomb scenario. The association is not merely atmo- spheric. In her preface to the republication of Henri Alleg's shattering 1958 memoir of torture in Algeria, *The Question*, Ellen Ray points out the historical link between "medical complicity" in the Algerian war of independence and current practice in United States detention facilities and black sites:

> Military doctors, including psychiatrists, are an integral part of these operations. They advise interrogators on new ways to be more success- ful in extracting information . . . [T]hey observe and report on torture sessions, in violation of the World Medical Association, to which the American Medical Association is a signatory.[11]

The prior question, from which Alleg's question (interrogative torture was referred to in his time as *la question*) must follow, of whether France ought to stay in Algeria at all, is suppressed in the film for historical rea- sons and in technocratic terms, a point to which I will return. It is also suppressed, and made useful in its suppression, in the film's revival as a teaching text for the War on Terror. Quite apart from the fast-shifting tides of elected officials and their influence on foreign policy and military strategy, the film and its revival reveal the continuity of more permanent concerns of career officers, diplomats, and security strategists—these deep state structures both buttress the project of imperialism and remain remarkably immune to the influence of smaller-scale disturbances, like who is president and what the latest brand of Islamophobia looks like. In this way, the longue durée of imperial statecraft finds its perfect match in the depoliticized vision of the epidemic and its perennial return that is nevertheless a permanent emergency.

To return to *The Battle of Algiers*, the success of both film (minor) and revolution (world historical) are already inscribed in its title sequence which lists both prizes and national cultural institutions as its opening gestures: Lion d'Or, XXVII Festival International de Venise, 1966; Grand Prix de la Critique Internationale, 1966; Prix de la ville de Venise, 1966; Casbah Films; Première grande production algérienne. These details frame both the battle and the film, historically and rhetorically, as a revolution won. Were the viewers of the film at the Pentagon screening supposed to hope for a different outcome? In order to reconcile the Pentagon screening's confounding avowal of neocolonial warfare as the proper horizon of the War on Terror with the film's more subtle gestures and messages, it is crucial to tease out the way Pontecorvo stages the transition from brute vengeance, crystallized in the Commissaire's bombing on the Rue de Thèbes in the casbah, to the more dispassionate intelligence operations that arrive with the film's most sympathetic antihero, Colonel Philippe Mathieu. Like Clarke and Sheehan, Mathieu, played by the famous stage actor Jean Martin, is not only a literate, humanistic warrior, but also a kind of technocrat, much of whose work in the events depicted in the film is to effectively quarantine the FLN's activities and to organize and interpret data on the structure of the organization. In a scene immediately following the hearts-and-minds-style distribution of baguettes by French soldiers in the native quarter, he likens the terror cells in Algiers to a *tenia*, a tapeworm: "Any of you ever suffer from tapeworm? It's a worm that can grow infinitely. You can destroy its thousands of segments but as long as the head stays, it reconstitutes itself and proliferates. The FLN is organized in the same manner."[12]

As he says this, Mathieu stands facing his working diagram, the famed "Organisation Rebelle D'Alger, 3ième Sect" (figure 5.1). On the board, he has outlined the pyramidal structure of the FLN and its agents, where no member of the organization knows more than two people: the one who recruited them, and the one they in turn recruited. Mutual knowledge at the level of the horizontal is foreclosed entirely, even as the cell structure

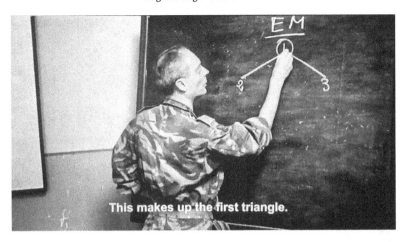

5.1 Still from Gillo Pontecorvo, *The Battle of Algiers* (The Criterion Collection, 1966). Col. Mathieu (Jean Martin) diagrams the triangular organization of terrorist cells for French paratroopers.

proliferates. "That is why we don't know who our enemies are," explains Mathieu, "because, in point of fact, they don't know each other. To know them signifies their elimination."[13] Characterizing the FLN membership as a radical fringe, unconnected with the will of the people, he insists that the work of the paratroopers will be to "isolate and destroy this minority. . . . The only information we have concerns the organization's structure. Let's start from there."[14] In addition to the cordon sanitaire approach, he proposes to "isolate and destroy" known revolutionaries. The resonance between the terror-cell diagrams and the archetypal disease map—one of the epidemiologist's foremost tools—was a feature of the French suppression of Algerian liberation activities right from the start.[15] Intelligence officers at French army headquarters in the spring of 1954 "maintained what was known as the 'smallpox chart,' marking up the occurrence of fresh outbreaks of violence, and the blotches were beginning to spread rapidly."[16]

The striking formal similarity has not been lost on filmmakers in the twenty-first century. Steven Soderbergh's epidemic thriller *Contagion*, released two days before the tenth anniversary of September 11 (the visually significant date 9/9/11)—spliced, therefore, in viewers' minds with commemorative footage of the crumbling Twin Towers—cites Pontecorvo's diagramming scenes exactly. In *Contagion*, the transmissibility of a flu epidemic originating in the jungled wilds outside Macau is mapped on a white board by a CDC "epidemic intelligence service officer," played by Kate Winslet, here softened along the moral continuum of care in gendered terms (figure 5.2). The key number the doctor hopes to isolate,

5.2 Still from Steven Soderbergh, *Contagion* (Warner Brothers, 2011). Dr. Erin Mears (Kate Winslet) diagrams viral agents for Minnesota public health officials.

the R-o, is the virus's basic reproduction rate—"for every person who gets sick, how many other people are they likely to infect?," a question that points back to Pontecorvo's scene as one that unfolds the FLN's transmissibility as well as its structure. The epidemic intelligence officer's boss back in Atlanta tells assembled reporters that their first step is always "to find Ground Zero," the phrase an uncanny hybridization of epidemiology's archetypal "patient zero" and the site of the World Trade Center collapse.[17] In *Contagion*, Pontecorvo's terror-mapping antecedent finds its legacy in its own buried epistemological framework, the plague returned to itself through the allusive metaphorical tethering of terrorism and epidemic. In other words, global pandemic, in Soderbergh's hands, allegorizes the war against terrorism in a visual vocabulary that was already allegorizing "Islamist" terrorism as a smallpox outbreak.

In an interview reflecting on the film's legacy in the present, Soderbergh confessed, "*Battle of Algiers* is a movie that . . . I stole stuff. I stole stuff and made it ours."[18] Thanks to Soderbergh, the post-9/11 terror of global pandemic, too, is now entangled with Pontecorvo's legacy. It is the persistence of the epidemic metaphor, muted as it may be, that allows Pontecorvo's film to function simultaneously as a confession of neocolonial warfare and also as a text that can be repurposed, in its recourse to long-standing discourses of necessity in the unendingly catastrophic space of the colony, to fundamentally eclipse the political content thereof in the guise of imperial care.

The Pentagon's decision to screen *The Battle of Algiers* made material a history that was already pressing at the conceptual and ethical edges of the War on Terror. The understanding of this history of Algerian terrorism—visually consonant with a Western image of "the Muslim world" as a veiled, chaotic space—shuttled in the American public imaginary between, on the one hand, righteous violence against colonial occupation and a faith in the community shaped by underground resistance, and on the other, the cultural and psychological black box of Muslims committing acts of terrorism, made more incomprehensible in our own moment by the movement toward suicidal martyrdom. Algeria became the twentieth-century linchpin for a twenty-first-century understanding of terror from a Muslim place—the kernel that would evolve, unlike models from the IRA or early-twentieth-century anarchisms, into a conceptual and hermeneutic model for "Islamist terrorism" in the years that followed. The 2006 republication of Alistair Horne's classic 1977 history of the Algerian liberation struggle, *A Savage War of Peace*, by New York Review of Books, a boutique press with a left-sympathetic audience, confirmed the centrality of the Algerian precedent across the political spectrum and in multidisciplinary terms. The cover of the new edition bears a blurb, backgrounded in splashy orange: "Anyone interested in Iraq should read this book immediately."[19]

In this chapter, I am interested, as I have been throughout this book, in the meeting point of content and form in the figure of epidemic, the medicalized body as both individual and national corpus, and the discipline of epidemiology as a colonial endeavor as it transitions uneasily but persistently into the epoch of neoimperialism, both as a health practice and as a method of imperialism, as territorial annexation and de facto governance. In the highly mediated materials I study in this chapter—an Italian director's take on an Algerian revolutionary's memoir, an Antillean psychiatrist's embedded reflections on the role of women in the Algerian uprising, and the publication under Simone de Beauvoir's name and under the sign of Picasso's portrait of the lesser known but once again important memoir by Djamila Boupacha of her rape torture at the hands of French military interrogators in Algeria—the figure of colonial epidemic transforms and grows attenuated, but persists in ways that shape the foundations of an American response to terrorism in material, narrative, and epistemic terms (figure 5.3).[20]

Pontecorvo's, Fanon's, and Boupacha's engagements with contagion and the sciences of medical inscription and interpretation color a multidisciplinary understanding of colonial and postcolonial history. In our moment, *The Battle of Algiers*, Frantz Fanon's 1959 essay "Algeria Unveiled," and *Djamila Boupacha: The Story of the Torture of a Young Algerian Girl* (1962) invite careful reexamination built on earlier scholarship in feminist and postcolonial studies. The three brief readings in this

5.3 Pablo Picasso, *Portrait of Djamila Boupacha* (1961). © 2019 Estate of Pablo Picasso / Artists Rights Society, New York.

chapter will seek to reorient our understanding of these texts in light of the reemergence of the Algerian paradigm in the War on Terror, and recover a largely unnoticed strand of anxiety about the medicalization of insurgency and the rebel's body that links them. If we have written and read too much about the naïveté of Pontecorvo's and Fanon's visions of women, if we have registered the disappointments of class- and gender-based liberation after the midcentury's independence struggles, we have not yet appreciated the complex interactions between the art of war and the science of rebellion that come to us from this crucial moment of Algerian struggle, the postwar analogue of the Indian Mutiny.[21]

Contagious Revolution and the Shape of Counterinsurgency

Barring the obvious fact of *The Battle of Algiers*'s position on the side of the revolution—confirmed in countless interviews with Pontecorvo—its value as a text that might have provided a useful point of entry or historical context for insurgent activities in Iraq raises a number of crucial questions.[22] These questions are not just about the vision of the fronts of the War on Terror as latter-day colonial outposts, but also about *The Battle of Algiers*'s techniques, generic maneuvers, its influences and arguments, as well as its life in the world of both anti-imperial and counterinsurgency discourse. Foremost among these questions is whether such lessons are to be drawn from the events depicted in the film itself or rather from its own fraught role in the war of ideas and their dissemination, a problem Pontecorvo and his screenwriter Franco Solinas theorize in important scenes of discourse production. In one such scene, reporters are told explicitly that the outcome of the war will depend on them, that the UN is too "far away" to be influenced by actual events on the ground. Without the reporters, how will they be able to assess the magnitude of the FLN's general strike, on what grounds will they be able to offer moral or material support? The camera's position in this scene replicates the reporters' line of sight, interpellating the viewer and the film itself as coproducers of "*une volonté politique*," a political will, even after the fact of the revolution's success. The conversation turns to specific nodes of ideological influence, including the intellectual left. "Just do your reporting and do it well," says former Resistance hero Mathieu, fresh from Dien Bien Phu, "it's not warriors we need."[23] Pressed further, Mathieu asks, "What did Paris say yesterday?" "Nothing," says his interlocutor, "another article by Sartre." The colonel pauses, turns to the door of the Cabinet du Prefet next to him as if to carry what he has gleaned into the offices of decision making, then swings his head around with a smirk, "Who can tell me why the Sartres are always born on the same side?" "So you like Sartre, then?," replies the suited man, "No, but I like him even less as an adversary," says the colonel as he enters the office.[24] In this scene and throughout the film, Pontecorvo lays bare both the instrumentalization of the press and the role of public intellectuals in the conflict as well as the historiographic parameters of his own film as a mock piece of journalism, shot in the grainy, newsreel style that carries neorealist conventions to their limit. The film's famous hyperrealist effects, which Pontecorvo employed to make it look like "a stolen historical record of events," recommends *The Battle of Algiers* to precisely the kind of viewing that would elevate it above the fictional and into the realm of information, of archive, a problem the film theorizes in surprisingly sophisticated terms to destabilize the positivist, empiricist view of history writ large.[25] The many scenes of writing as it relates to power—secret messages and official communiqués in addition to news—make this point a central one in the film's approach to historiography. *The Battle of Algiers*, in other words, seems simultaneously to balk at the cynicism of the "war of ideas" not as an adjunct to but as the center of modern warfare, and also to deploy its own medium to these ends with self-conscious finesse.

Not all of the film's explorations of narrativity and mediated evidence are centered on the creation of public opinion through journalism, literature, and philosophy. Surveillance, too, plays an important role. An earlier scene shows paratroopers attending an informational briefing about security in the casbah, where police footage of a checkpoint is being shown. "Note the cameraman's hunch," remarks Mathieu, musing on the "futility" of checkpoints and gesturing at the teaching screen as the camera zooms in on a hapless man in a *djellabah*, "he's sure there's something in that box."[26] The man drops the box, and a litter of white mice skitters out. A child bends down to assist him in gathering his fleeing goods. The camera pans across the darkened room where the newly arrived paratroopers laugh. "There might have been a false bottom with a bomb inside," adds the grim colonel. "We'll never know."[27] This moment, and many others like it, reveals not just the historical record, but specifically the filmic record as one of profound undecidability, even manipulability, within the scope of the battle for Algiers and the independence movement. Though Pontecorvo distinguishes between the work of his own images and that of the surveillance footage presented above as a text for military analysis, the line between the two is rent powerfully and purposefully when one of the three famous women bombers flashes a smile across the flickering screen of Mathieu's teaching reel.[28] A background figure whose role in recent acts of terror is already known to the film's viewers, but not to the soldiers, her presence, her beauty, her smile register what Lindsey Moore calls the "manipulation of scopic and sexual regimes by the colonized."[29] When asked about the coward-ice of using handbaskets (*paniers*) to carry bombs at a press conference alongside Mathieu, resistance leader Ben M'Hidi responds, in one of the film's most famous lines, "obviously planes would make things easier for us. Give us your bombers, sir, and you can have our baskets."[30] Soon thereafter, Mathieu calls the press conference to a close: "C'est terminé, le spectacle?," asks Ben M'Hidi. "Oui, il est terminé," replies Mathieu, "avant que nous produisions un effet contraire."[31] In light of the film's self-consciousness about mediation, rhetoric, the spread of ideas, and the structure of collectivity, we must wonder anew what military strate-gists and civilian advisers hoped to glean by watching *The Battle of Algiers* other than a paranoid confirmation of the worst fears organizing the ground operations, namely that every Iraqi—even those transporting mice, or flowers, in their proverbial baskets—were probably also carry-ing improvised explosive devices.

Not only does *The Battle of Algiers* theorize the central role of photogra-phy, radio, loudspeakers, journalism, film, and literature in revolutionary and counterrevolutionary practice, it also positions itself immediately as a part of this archive, with a commission from the Algerian government and coproduction credits held by FLN member Yacef Saadi's company Casbah Films.[32] In the tradition of third cinema, the film constantly re-minds us of the camera's role "as a weapon in nationalist struggle and revolutionary violence." To put it in Saadi's terms, "I have substituted a camera for a machine gun."[33] In spite of winning the Golden Lion in Venice in 1966, the film, politically radioactive even after Algerian in-dependence was granted in 1962, was banned in France for five years after its release, amplifying its status as a dangerous object. Jean Martin, the actor who plays the cool-headed Mathieu, recalls that the day before the film was set to premier in Paris, the theater was firebombed and the screen slashed.[34] And, as even casual viewers of *The Battle of Algiers* know, the film has been compulsory viewing for insurgents, revolutionaries, and anticolonial freedom fighters since the moment of its release, with poor prints circulating in and between revolutionary organizations from women's groups to the Black Panthers, the Palestinian Liberation Or-ganization to the IRA, making its mark on both the practice of violent resistance and the public relations attached thereto.[35]

In counterpoint to depictions of the French project of rhetorical man-agement and the role of the press in swaying public opinion in France, Pontecorvo's film also furnishes numerous scenes of media hijacking on the part of the revolutionaries. In one memorable moment, a young boy reels in a microphone being used by a French gendarme to blast warnings over a loudspeaker that the general strike will not stand, that

5.4 Still from Gillo Pontecorvo, *The Battle of Algiers* (The Criterion Collection, 1966). Le petit Omar steals the army's microphone.

the denizens of Algiers must return to work or face the consequences. The boy, le petit Omar, one of the central cluster of insurgents the film follows, announces from a hidden corner of the public square, from behind jumbled concertina wire, "Take heart!" The crowd, moving like an organism, stops dead, the ambient noise of the quarter's activity falls away. The boy, now invisible to both the police and the film's viewers, continues, "The FLN tells you not to be afraid. Don't worry, we're winning. The FLN is on your side" (figure 5.4).[36] That these words issue from the same loudspeaker that has just declared, "The FLN wants to stop you from working. . . . The FLN is forcing you to close your shops. . . . The FLN wants to starve you and condemn you to poverty. . . . Residents of the casbah, France is your motherland!," the same loudspeaker used to incite the residents of the casbah to "resist the FLN's orders" and return to work, illuminates how the film resists an incommensurability model of civilizational conflict—one that presumes the Algerian's desires are neither self-evident nor reasonable, are utterly beyond the legibility of Republican values—and insists on both the general strike and revolutionary affect as a spreading phenomenon, if not a contagious one.

As the camera captures the crowd's reaction, this mimetic effect is forcefully enacted in the canon of liberation cries "Tahi'al Jazair! Tahi'al Jazair!" and the women's crescendoing chorus of ululations. The boy and the residents of the casbah to whom he speaks are as adept at hijacking the media of disciplinarity as they are at reorienting the counterinsurgency's metaphors of plague, smallpox, epidemic. The FLN's communiqués, as the film presents them, borrow Camus's specific term from *The Plague: fléau*.[37] In one of the film's voice-overs, meant to replicate the revolutionary radio dispatches detailed in Fanon's essay "This Is the Voice of Algeria," the FLN announces the moral degradations of the *pieds-noirs* as a plague or a scourge:

> People of Algeria! The colonial administration is responsible not only for the poverty of our people and their slavery, but also for corrupting and degrading many of our brothers and sisters who have lost their dignity. The FLN engages an action to eliminate all these plagues (*fléaux*) and calls on the help of the population in this endeavor. As of today, the clandestine authorities of the FLN assume responsibility for the physical and moral health of the Algerian people, and therefore will ban the sale and use of alcohol and drugs, prostitution and procuring. Violators will be punished. Recidivists will be put to death.[38]

The function of the proto-state as giver of care is what launches it into the realm of a believable governance, an organized authority that can replace the French state, will issue decrees, will back them up with sovereign action. The assumption by the "clandestine authorities" of responsibility for the "physical and moral health of the Algerian people" becomes the signal, in other words, for the preparedness of the revolution to accede to legitimate authority. As this announcement is read, the camera follows a down-on-his-luck drunk as he is chased by a group of children and kicked mercilessly down a flight of stairs, evidence of the violent consequences of the "cleaning up" that resistance leader Jafar called for in the previous scene. The FLN's requisitioning of the counterinsurgency's language of sanitation is underscored by a symmetrical announcement from the French government that appears a few scenes later in the form of a voice-over:

> The governor general of Algeria decrees: First Article—purchase of pharmaceuticals for gunshot wounds will be dispensed by the sole authority of the prefecture. Article 2—responsible parties at health establishments will make known to the authority of the police any admission of wounded patients who wish to be treated.[39]

This well-known tactic on the part of the colonial authorities to limit access to medical supplies and enlist caregivers as informants in the fight against the revolution reveals itself in this moment to be a site of intense contestation—public health holds a central place as both metaphor and literal battle site.[40] Immediately following the reading of this decree, a further voice-over—this time on behalf of the prefecture—announces the sealing off of the Arab quarter, as soldiers carry barricades heavy with barbed wire to be placed in front of stunned-looking women and children. Although the film does not use the favored term of the period, "cordon sanitaire," it hovers over the scene.[41]

Mathieu's recourse to the organicizing metaphors of parasitism (*le tenia*), and the film's fine-textured engagement with imperial disease poetics and its appropriability by the FLN, cleans up the work of counterrevolutionary violence in the terms of sanitation, disinfection, *ratissage*, and public health. As we have seen, framing political rebellion through the metaphors of natural disaster is almost always a depoliticizing device—one that is waged at the level of rhetoric while effacing the profound effects of that rhetoric's persistence on an empire disguised as kindly transnational caregiver. In the face of such a durable paradigm, *The Battle of Algiers*'s position on whether the colony ought to remain or give way to national independence may hardly matter. We do not have to exercise too vigorous an imagination to guess that the Pentagon audience might have nodded sagely in agreement at one of the film's most damning speeches. Mathieu, embattled, taking on liberal opinion in France, articulates his position as a double-bind:

> The problem is this. The FLN wants us out of Algeria, and we? We want to stay there. And now to me it seems even with the slight nuances there are, you are all in agreement that we must stay. When the FLN's rebellion began, there was no such nuance. Every newspaper, even the Communist press, demanded that it be smothered. We are here for this. And we, gentlemen, are neither fools nor sadists. Those who call us fascists forget that many of us did a lot for the Resistance; those who called us Nazis don't know that some of us survived Dachau and Buchenwald. We are soldiers and we have the duty to win. To be precise, let me ask a question. Should France stay in Algeria? If you still respond yes, you must accept all the necessary consequences.[42]

In the broken logic of a Republican empire on full display in Mathieu's burnished, rational comments, we recall his earlier conclusions about the situation in Algiers, the "*tenia*," or parasitic form of the FLN's leadership, and what these challenges call for—"all the necessary consequences," in his words. "The basis of this work is intelligence," he says point blank, "the method is interrogation."[43]

Mathieu's comments in this crucial confession—one that seems likely to have spoken in particularly poignant ways to the Pentagon audience— point us back to the film's representation of torture and the torture chamber in its opening scene as a horrifying double of the operating theater. In light of *The Battle of Algiers*'s persistent returns to metaphors of illness, epidemic intelligence processes, and outright embargoing of medical supplies and expertise in the fight to suppress the FLN, the opening scene takes on new dimensions as an image of clinical coercion, remedial violence, a kind of political chemotherapy that hypertoxifies in order to heal. Observers on the side of Algerian revolution were canny about this—the omnipresent Sartre, for example, a thorn in even the fictional general's side, would appropriate the favored figures of imperial disease poetics in his preface to Alleg's *La Question*, a memoir about the widespread use of interrogation methods imported from the Nazis and from the struggles in Indochina. Here, perhaps in a passive-aggressive form of homage to his estranged friend Camus, Sartre writes of torture as a "plague infecting our whole era . . . a semi-clandestine institution," that, even when the causes are different, "betrays the same sickness."[44] In parallel with Pontecorvo's pointed depiction of the FLN's reversal of normative health poetics—an epidemic of colonial immorality rather than of anticolonial, revolutionary, fanatical, Islamist violence—Sartre's framing of Alleg's sensational text participated in a growing discourse that would medicalize the struggle in Algeria in epistemic terms beginning with the publication the next year of a collection of torture testimonials under the title *La Gangrène* and reaching into the anticolonial writings of Frantz Fanon in *L'An V de la révolution algérienne* (*A Dying Colonialism*).

Unveilings

One of the most prominent voices in the struggle for Algerian independence as it unfolded before his eyes and in his clinical practice, Frantz Fanon was acutely aware of the spiraling complexities attached to the revolution and its iconographies and metaphorical systems, which were derived from and in turn impacted material realities of the conflict. Pontecorvo had read Frantz Fanon's essay "Algeria Unveiled" ("L'Algérie se dévoile") and discussed it with his screenwriter Franco Solinas in preparation for making *The Battle of Algiers*, and he relied on it particularly heavily in developing the famous scene of the three women bombers' transformation from traditionally dressed Algerian women to modern cosmopolitans, the centerpiece of some of the most sensitive critical writing on the film by scholars.[45] "Algeria Unveiled," often dismissed along with the chapter on Mayotte Capécia in *Black Skin, White Masks* as evidence of Fanon's misogyny—at worst—or at best lack of understanding of the intersection of gender, feminism, and liberation movements, is to my mind one of the most fascinating and frequently misread parts of Fanon's difficult oeuvre.[46] The essay famously centers on the shifting signification of the veil in the Algerian struggle for independence, first as a surface of resistance to the erotic, power-laden gaze of the colonizer, and later as an armor of double-woven dissimulation—one that could be stripped in misdirection, as the women in *The Battle of Algiers* do, to create the illusion of Western assimilation, a disguise for ease of movement, and also used as a kind of drag by men seeking to transport weapons and messages into and out of the casbah and across various checkpoints that quarantine the residents of Algiers. Pontecorvo cites these latter sections of the essay as well in his film, which shows Jafar and Ali La Pointe racing up and down the casbah's alleys and stairs with machine guns beneath their robes and kerchiefs covering their rough-shaven faces. As Fanon writes:

> To the colonialist offensive against the veil, the colonized opposes the cult of the veil. What was an undifferentiated element in a homogenous whole acquires a taboo character, and the attitude of a given Algerian woman with respect to the veil will be constantly related to her overall attitude with respect to the foreign occupation. The colonized, in the face of the emphasis given to this or that aspect of his traditions, reacts very violently.[47]

The significatory proliferation of the veil—like any object overdetermined by colonial mores and legal dictates—occurs, through the agency of the Algerian women, as a function of "her attitude with respect to the foreign occupation." This attitude, and the actions she bases upon it, also function here as forms of violence. Careful readers of Fanon will note that the violence that appears here somewhat incidentally links the political, sexual, religious, and militant resignification of the veil to the work of violence he would outline in *The Wretched of the Earth* in the notorious and often decontextualized chapter, "On Violence." Here, he writes of violence as "the absolute praxis" and identifies the militant as "one who works."[48] To work, he explains "means to work toward the death of the colonist" (44; 118). Inasmuch as the militant must perform an irreversible act, and equally, the revolutionary group is constituted though the possibility of return, violence becomes for Fanon "the perfect mediation" (la violence est ainsi comprise comme la médiation royale) a version of the postcolonial subject's *détour-retour* itinerary through the metropole (44; 118). There are a few important details to note here. First, the text scrupulously does not delimit what constitutes "an irreversible act," but it does frame revolutionary violence in terms of praxis, work, and mediation. Second, the uncertain status of both key terms in this passage—violence and mediation—can't be understood without the supplement of the text's unfolding, particularly its suggestive shift to the literary, which helps to ground the meaning of the concepts that precede it.

This shift brings Fanon to a long extract from Aimé Césaire's *And the Dogs Were Silent* (*Et les chiens se taisaient*), which culminates in the Rebel, the play's enslaved protagonist, murdering his master where he sleeps:

> The master's bedroom was brilliantly lit, and the master was there, very calm . . . and all of us stopped . . . he was the master . . . I entered. It's you, he said, very calmly. . . . It was me, it was indeed me, I told him, the good slave, the faithful slave, the slave slave, and suddenly my [*sic*] eyes were two cockroaches frightened on a rainy day . . . I struck, the blood spurted: it is the only baptism that today I remember.[49]

The irrevocable act presented in this scene is quite literally *staged* in Fanon's text, even as it is presented graphically. The citation of Césaire's poetic work, rather than his nonfiction, or an anecdote from Fanon's own knowledge of revolutionary violence in Algeria, whose parameters he outlines on the very next page, reveals the complex layering of what Fanon understands as the relationship between work, mediation, and violence. In addition to the overdetermined and ritualized—and therefore performative, choreographed, mannered—baptism in blood, Césaire's Rebel is denatured and denaturalized by his repeated adjectival experiments: "le bon esclave, le fidèle esclave, l'esclave esclave." His entrance into the master's brilliantly lit inner chamber is a gesture, then, of mythic fulfillment, one that cannot be understood as any kind of direct or pure act, even within the bounds of the play, and certainly not in its textual incorporation into Fanon's own prose. Offered to the reader as the paradigmatic example of the mediating work of violence, the Rebel's infiltration of the "bedroom" both unveils the master to reveal the master ("et le maître était là . . . c'était le maître"), still playing a role in his denuding, and also constitutes the Rebel in a rebirth, *un baptême*, of ritual performance. Césaire's, too, is a kind of operation in both senses of the term, both a surgical procedure and a tactical act. The meaning of Fanon's "work," the work of killing the colonizer, the work of passing irrevocably beyond re-incorporability into the colonial system, stretches between the poles of writing and performance where imagination stands alongside acting, staging, writing, and dress as an analogue for killing, or at least for "killing." That the "mediation" takes place through Césaire's words deepens the sense that Fanon understands violence as the processual return-to-self modeled in so much of his teacher's writing, particularly in the imaginative apocalypse that concludes the *Notebook of a Return to the Native Land*. I suggest this critical revision in how Fanon's relationship to violence is understood in order to make sense of how agency and performativity are conjoined to produce gender as a form of militant work in "Algeria Unveiled," where the woman's attitude with respect to the veil is a matter of "very violent" reaction. Coming into visibility at a slight angle to the unveiling of both Algeria's women and the nation itself, the ungowning of the revolutionary body in the space of the medical examination will become both an unworking of the militant struggle and also its uncanny preservation.

Fanon narrates the battle against French colonial forces in "Algeria Unveiled" as a cultural and epistemological one that must address itself to the colonizer's "infinite science" with which "a blanket indictment against the 'sadistic and vampirish' Algerian attitude toward women was prepared and drawn up."[50] The fetish object, the transhistorical sign of such an indictment, is of course the *haïk* or veil behind which the Algerian man, the Muslim man, imprisons his wife, his daughter, his mother. This veil, in the mind of the colonizer, also introduces a barrier he finds intolerable. Fanon writes,

> This woman who sees without being seen frustrates the colonizer. There is no reciprocity. She does not yield herself, does not give herself, does not offer herself. . . . The European faced with the Algerian woman wants to see. He reacts in an aggressive way before this limitation of his perception. (44; 23)

The revision Fanon proposes of Hegelian reciprocity in the master-slave dialectic in the penultimate chapter of *Black Skin, White Masks* here achieves its specific revolutionary apotheosis in women's mastery of the full range of revolutionary tools—her body and its covering included. What functioned as an obstruction to the complete adoption of Hegel's dialectic in Fanon's famous footnote in "The Negro and Recognition"— that the master wants no recognition from the slave, wants only his work—appears recast as the violation of the Muslim woman's body. The colonizer does not want her assimilation, he wants her maidenhead. "The rape of the Algerian woman in the dream of a European," writes Fanon, speaking as a clinician and analyst of dreams, "is always preceded by a rending of the veil. We here witness a double deflowering" (45; 25). What short-circuits this refusal also defetishizes the fetish, makes a new fetish of the Algerian woman's skin, her body becoming text. This is the rending of the veil recast as the patient's ungowning, which precedes a doctor's examination. Fanon writes, again, as a clinician reflecting on his practice,

In a medical consultation, for example, at the end of the morning, it is common to hear European doctors express their disappointment. The women who remove their veils before them are commonplace, vulgar; there is really nothing to make such a mystery of. One wonders what they are hiding. (44–45; 24)

This largely unremarked moment in Fanon's essay anchors the through-line on the fugitive signification not only of the veil, but of gender itself as a kind of mediation, a labor, one that is performed even in and through scenes of radical vulnerability. Given the infectious energy of the three-women scene in Pontecorvo's film, scored with driving war drums and edited to quicken the heart, it is important to note that Fanon emphatically disavows the overdetermination of the Algerian revolutionary's behavior as a mode of "play, of imitation, almost always present in this form of action when we are dealing with a Western woman." It is not, he continues, "the bringing to light of a character known and frequented a thousand times in imagination or in stories. It is an authentic birth in a pure state, without preliminary instruction" (50; 30). For many critics, particularly Diana Fuss, who cites them in dismay, these last lines about authenticity amount to a derogation of responsibility to both Algerian (she writes "black") women in the struggle, and to the relational ontology Fanon is at such great pains to develop in *Black Skin, White Masks*.[51]

The kind of "pure" birth Fanon writes of here, however, has to be understood through his persistent return to the themes of alienation as both terror and inevitable condition of psychic existence under colonialism, of mediation, and means, of instrumentality, of the Césairian *retour*, and the Hegelian dialectic. I'm inclined to read this passage about the authenticity of the revolutionary's choreography and inhabiting of gender as a corrective rather than an absolute statement. Particularly in his ironizing of Orientalism's favorite cycle of tales, the *Thousand Nights and a Night*—the rejection of "character known and frequented a thousand times in imagination"—we see in Fanon's lines an insistence on the agency, rather than the colonial mimicry of the Algerian woman. Her "authentic birth in a pure state" is thus best understood under the flexion of the powerful image of natality that erupts into the auto-theoretical narrative of *Black Skin, White Masks*, when the speaker finds himself, on a white winter's morning, born in the violence of a self-autopsying. This moment—as is well known to readers of Fanon—follows the French child's monstrous hail, "Look, a Negro!" Fanon writes, "[M]y body was returned to me spread-eagled, disjointed, redone, draped in mourning. . . . The white man is all around me; up above the sky is tearing at its navel; the earth crunches under my feet and sings white, white."[52]

The Algerian woman, swaddled in the whiteness of the colonial city, rather than the white *haïk*, the only instrument of violence apparent to the colonist's gaze, may be seen to follow the same circuit of return, her "authentic birth" mediated by the reality of the colonial theater. Before the colonial official, certainly before the public, the colonial doctor is the first to experience the disappointment of her unveiling, which reveals not the essential secret he sought, but rather something already processed, resistant. His patient's unveiling, her subsequent ungowning, reveals neither the proper cause of exoticism and mystique, nor a body that will submit to the forced racial dynamics of colonizing caregiver and colonized care receiver. Instead of difference, the physician finds sameness, and in this sameness, banality, frustration, and disappointment. Such an encounter liquidates the terms of the power-laden contest on which colonial psychodynamics, especially gendered colonial psychodynamics, are premised. Because desire has been routed, the colonized woman's assimilation is no longer a prize to be won. Her unveiling, in Fanon's paradigm, does not manifest any ontological modification—or modernization in the colonist's terms—but rather stands as an authentic tactic, the pure pursuit of national liberation. In this way, the erotic dimensions of the veil are obviated, and the veil itself transforms into precisely the kind of "mediation" Fanon would go on to describe in *The Wretched of the Earth* in close proximity to his discussion of the particulars of the Algerian struggle as it came to a close.

In Fanon's essay, and in the structure of his collection, which moves toward a double conclusion with the rarely considered "Medicine and Colonialism" and an essay on Euro-Algerian supporters of the FLN and national independence, it is the medical gaze that makes this deflating realization possible. Consequently, the doctor's experience of revelation is also associated with the loss of a symbolic order that upholds the colonial project in aesthetic and hermeneutic terms. Extrapolating from the unveiled woman's "commonplace" appearance, her share in the commonwealth of worldly womanhood, we can see how the difference that scaffolds even the most intimate of encounters in colonial space begins to fall away and reveals not just the ordinary sameness of the body, but also, perhaps, the ordinary sameness of that body's political demands. In place of inscrutable and insurmountable ontological, cultural, and political difference, the "vulgar" body of the Algerian woman functions as an overture to what is for the colonizer a vulgar, disappointing historical truth: namely a national consciousness that looks surprisingly like Republicanism. Unveiling in these terms begins to take on cataclysmic dimensions beyond the immediate issue of the Algerian struggle and the women in it, pointing beyond itself, beyond even the North African

Muslim world, to an eschatological fulfilment of French destiny as the end of the Fourth Republic and of empire altogether.

What I want to suggest in revisiting Fanon's essay, so influential for the development of Pontecorvo's symbolic lexicon and so frequently read alongside the film, is that the medicalization of the revolutionary body, both individual and national, is deeply rooted in both texts, and gives onto an apocalyptic vision that helps us understand their reemergence on the syllabus of the War on Terror's early years, as American officials, intellectuals, and bureaucrats sought to cast the rise of Islamism as a global harrowing. To return briefly to Pontecorvo, *The Battle of Algiers*'s final scene is enacted in parallel to Fanon's narrative as a crucial dilation from women to the nation. It is orchestrated specifically as an unveiling—one that is far more nuanced and ontologically destabilizing than either Fanon or Pontecorvo is credited with in readings that focus on the more thematically available scenes of transformative disrobing. This unveiling follows what the film identifies as the spontaneous upsurge of revolutionary activity in the fall of 1960, the parting of a historical fog, which the film manifests as a rising curtain of cloud and smoke behind which throngs the populace. Or, as Fanon puts it in an earlier essay usually appended to "Algeria Unveiled," the coming into "full daylight [of] a tactic acquired, and solidly reinforced, in the heyday of the Franco-Moslem period" (65; 47). In this piece, Fanon gives an even more precise formulation of the epistemic disturbances for which the *haïk* stands, noting wryly that "[a]mong things that are 'incomprehensible' to the colonial world the case of the Algerian woman has been all too frequently mentioned . . . [S]he is 'inaccessible, ambivalent, with a masochistic component'" (64; 46–47). The visual cue that marks the break in the narrative, then, between the end of Ali La Pointe and his compatriots in the casbah—the period of the war known as the Battle of Algiers—and the coda in 1960, when evidence of the revolution became incontrovertible not just in the colony but in Paris as well, may be read as an elaborate play with Fanon's metaphorics of the veil. The intervening years of revolutionary activity are corollarily obscured behind presuppositions of enigma, mystery, inaccessibility. This conceptual scaffolding allows the revolution, in turn, to appear to French observers as spontaneous, organic, a broken dam or a flood of humanity whose face is that of the dancing, ululating woman.

The Battle of Algiers's conclusion as national unveiling follows directly on a sequence, narrated in a voice-over that approximates the tone of the film's earlier French journalists, in which the speaker puzzles over the seemingly random resurgence of revolutionary activity, as if it emerged spontaneously, overnight. Over shots of the growing crowd that emerges out of lens-flared beams of light that pierce the alleys of the casbah, the voice-over struggles, like a live commentator at a race, to translate what is before him in the deliberately obscurantist terms Fanon outlines above:

> For some unknown reason, due to some obscure motive, after two years of relative quiet, the war contained mostly in the mountains, the disturbances broke out again without warning, and nobody knows why or how. . . . This morning for the first time, out came the flags with crescent and star, thousands of flags (*drapeaux*), probably made overnight. "Flags" is hardly the word, more like torn bedsheets, shirts, rags, but flags nevertheless.[53]

Here, the blistering, seemingly contagious spread of nationalism under the radar of colonial surveillance and its checkpoints and cordons is encoded as a mystery akin to the veiled woman's body—a site of incomprehensibility, of incommensurability, of radical difference. The voice remarks on the "unintelligible, rhythmic cries" of the Algerian women. A broadcast announcement in the casbah insists on incomprehension: "Return to your homes! What is it that you want?" ("Retournez chez vous! Qu'est-ce que vous voulez?").[54] To read this voice-over alongside the incomprehensibility, inaccessibility, and ambivalence of Fanon's Algerian woman in the eyes of the colonizer is to confront the gendering of colonial space, of Algerian space in particular, as Muslim woman. In this final scene, Pontecorvo gives the viewer the double of the earlier revolutionary makeover montage, now reimagined as the coming-out of the nation. It is a powerful—and when read alongside Fanon's essay, a dreadfully prurient—visual pleasure to bear witness to the nation's unveiling, to feel the elation the film evidently offers and also its violent collateral, as it calls back elliptically to the colonist's forcible denudings. Though it is jubilant, this revelation when witnessed from the position of the colonizer, or in our moment, the Pentagon official, is an apocalyptic one.

Reinscribing the bedsheets, rags, shirts, and especially the *haïks* that have served as a cover for machine guns and bombs as a heraldic symbol of nationalism, the people of Algiers render visible in the film's final moments the contagious, metonymic operations of national self-determination and the alarmingly not-inscrutable motives thereof. The revelation of the FLN's intervening operations, which largely moved out of the city and into the countryside in the intervening years, reveals how, for the French men who look on, this unveiling or clearing of mist is experienced as apocalypse, both in the sense of a revelation, and—as they are pushed out of the frame and losing the focus of the camera to the women with their jubilant cries—the sense of an inevitable end and its belated comprehension. The loss of the colonies here becomes coterminous with the end of the world, while the unveiling of the Algerian nation stands as both revelation and apocalypse. Here we find a crucial entry in the structural paradoxes of the colonial knowledge-making project in the human sciences and otherwise, an enormous epistemological apparatus that insists at once on the availability of truth, of empirically stable fact, taxonomy, and at the same time never fails in its astonishment at the inscrutability of the colonial other, his dwelling place, his modes of prayer, his networks of transmission. It hardly bears repeating what the colonist makes of his wife. The epidemiological approach to terrorism—transmitted to the audience of Pentagon officials by *The Battle of Algiers* in spite of its critiques and complexities—dons this inchoate and obstinate mode of thinking whole cloth. In her important essay, "The Character in the Veil: Imagery of the Surface in the Gothic," Eve Sedgwick posits the veil as that which registers the belatedness of the forensic operation while also carrying the message or messages of the body out and into the world—a spot of blood becomes textual. The veil, for her, is point of transfer.[55] Whether as ink, as medium, as writing—or in the horrific symptomology of torture, the bruises, cuts, and burns—these marks of or on the veil give rise to questions of a clinical sort, perhaps even a diagnostic sort that begins to lead us to the medico-legal evidentiary realm: whose blood? How did it come to be there? What is it evidence of? How is it to be read? With regard to the body of the colonized woman, such questions can scarcely be thought without recourse to the animating incident of Bhubaneswari Bhaduri's suicide during her menstrual period, which gives on to the indelible question of Gayatri Spivak's most important engagement with colonial subjects: "can the subaltern speak?"[56]

A Completed Portrait by Picasso

As in the case of Bhubaneswari's suicide and the multiple erasures under which it was written, the medical space is always a fraught one for the colonial subject and for the colonized woman in particular, irrespective of social class and education, though these factors can certainly compound inaccessibility to avenues of power and legitimacy in the colonial state. The FLN's reversal of imperial disease poetics as it is depicted in Pontecorvo's film, and the adoption of the plague metaphor by pro-liberation French intellectuals, were not without consequences. Particularly as the revelations of torture methods used in Algeria began leaking more widely in France, the status of medical evidence would play an increasingly large and often doubly victimizing role in the transformation of public opinion and later the transformation of French policy with respect to its oldest, most precious colonial holding. The text most responsible for putting

5.5 "Ici on noie les Algériens" ("Here we drown Algerians"). From *L'Humanité* (October 17, 1961).

not just the testimony but specifically the medical testimony and its dossier of scientific proofs and repeated gynecological examinations firmly at the center of the debate in France over the horrors being visited, in Alleg's memorable words, "in their name," in Algeria was the story of Djamila Boupacha. The book was written by her lawyer, Gisèle Halimi, and sold prominently under the name of Simone de Beauvoir, whose introduction to the volume revisited the devastating and politically transformative essay she wrote for *Le Monde* ("Pour Djamila Boupacha," June 3, 1960) about the case on Halimi's prompting. The Paris massacre, in which Parisian police opened fire on a massive pro-FLN demonstration in the metropole, it should be noted, had occurred in the interim.[57] The conflict in Algeria had undeniably arrived in Paris, where threats became public (figure 5.5).

Before turning to Boupacha's memoir, and the pivot of the vaginal examination therein, it is instructive to return briefly to another, less often cited text in Fanon's *A Dying Colonialism*, which calls back in striking ways to the ungowning of the Algerian woman in the colonial doctor's office in "Algeria Unveiled." In "Medicine and Colonialism," Fanon describes the experience of the colonized person as the object of Western medical scrutiny. This encounter, he argues, must be historicized, situated, disburdened of the natural assumption that all scientific progress is good, that to its unassailable goals of providing succor or "easing pain," "no negative reaction can be justified."[58] He begins the essay with "The Algerian Example":

Introduced into Algeria at the same time as racialism and humiliation, Western medical science, being part of the oppressive system, has always provoked in the native an ambivalent attitude. This ambivalence is in fact to be found in connection with all of the occupier's modes of presence. With medicine, we come to one of the most tragic features of the colonial situation. (121; 111–112)

For Fanon, the reality of colonial medicine presents itself as "one of the most tragic features of the colonial situation" precisely because of the promise of care that is as constantly withdrawn as it is grudgingly given. The betrayals of the Hippocratic oath of which he speaks do not manifest solely in the dehumanizing conduct of the European doctor toward his Algerian patients—though this is certainly an important facet of his grim analysis. Fanon is also at pains to note the particularly two-faced role played by doctors in the war through the withholding of care, medications, and confidentiality, in addition to the administration of torture, truth serums (citing Alleg), and their covering up (137; 131).

Motivated by racism, a sense of cultural and professional superiority, and an unwavering desire to maintain their conditions of economic superiority, the European doctors in Fanon's analysis create and work in an astonishingly narrow corridor of hypocrisy. Of particular interest to Fanon is how the colonial encounter invariably creates the Algerian as an insubordinate or noncompliant patient. In his terror at entering "the hospital of the whites, of the strangers, of the conqueror," the Algerian is already locked in a battle with the presumed forms of care and their empirical foundations he will find there, already resistant to its prescriptions and invasions of his body and the broader social fabric that has maintained it in health, and now betrays it in sickness (125; 116). Unlike in "non-colonial" society, where the "attitude of the sick man in the presence of a medical practitioner is one of confidence," the Algerian's attitude is permanently disfigured by the memory of medical abuses in the colonies, such that the "sudden deaths of Algerians in hospitals . . . are interpreted as the effects of a murderous and deliberate decision, as the result of criminal maneuvers on the part of the European doctor" (123–124; 114). To explain this hesitation, to legitimate the colonial subject's resistance, and to preempt the favored sociological explanation, Fanon cites the example of the French army's psychiatric experiments—made on false scientific pretexts—to measure the different races' survival thresholds for induced epileptic seizures. As I have argued throughout this book, these well-founded fears are neither the sign of colonized subject's irrationalism or refusal of modernity, nor are they in our past.

The recalcitrant patient as noncompliant subject emerges in Fanon's essay in parallel to the veiled Algerian woman—inaccessible, ambivalent, a little masochistic—in the collection's first chapter:

> [T]he colonized Algerian proves to be an equally unsatisfying patient . . . [T]he patient plays hide-and-seek with his doctor. The doctor has no hold on the patient. He finds that in spite of promises and pledges, an attitude of flight, of disengagement persists. All the efforts exerted by the doctor, by his team of nurses, to modify this state of things encounter, not a systematic opposition, but a "vanishing" on the part of the patient. (128–129; 120–121)

Life, in this scheme of fugitivity, self-vanishing, and disengagement, resembles for Fanon "an incomplete death" (123–124; 114). Unsurprisingly, neither the European doctor nor the colonial system in which he is employed recognizes the patient's rejection of medical treatment as a "systematic" strategy, part of an organized revolt against the epistemic and disciplinary reach of systematic violence. Fanon posits this rejection "not as a refusal of life, but a greater passivity before that close and contagious death" (129; 120–121). In the face of such refusals, such "monosyllables," the patient's unwillingness to talk, to indicate where it hurts, to describe his life or reveal his past, the European doctor harbors hope in the clinical examination, "thinking," writes Fanon, "that the body would be more eloquent" (128; 120). In Fanon's story, the paradigmatic Algerian patient yields himself neither verbally nor corporeally. To the doctor's dismay, "the body proved to be equally rigid. The muscles were contracted. There was no relaxing" (Il n'y a pas de détente) (128; 120). A more precise translation of Fanon's last phrase directs us to the war unfolding in the clinic: there was no détente.

It was to her credit and her great good fortune that the twenty-three-year-old Algerian woman Djamila Boupacha, arrested on February 10, 1960, on suspicion of planting a bomb in a university café in Algiers and harboring FLN members, recognized the demands of colonial medicine as an extension of the demands of an imperial legal system. From the first day following her horrific experiences of torture (*la question*) in El Biar prison outside of Algiers, where interrogators stripped her, spat gouts of beer onto her body, scotch-taped electrical wires to her nipples, stubbed out cigarettes on her thighs, raped her with a toothbrush and an empty beer bottle, kicked her in the ribs and back, and left her passed out in a pool of her own blood, Boupacha would insist again and again on a medical examination. When they pressed her to identify a handbag found at the site of the bombing as her own and she refused, they told her she will be "taken back for another dose of medicine."[59] Her blood-stained shift, the bruises on her back and torso, her broken displaced rib, she knew, would not be enough. Her vaginal hemorrhaging would not be enough. Although she confessed to an outlandish number of crimes and terrorist acts under interrogation, she retained enough confidence—whether cynical or idealistic—in both the legal and medical institutions in French Algeria to request, repeatedly, to be seen by a doctor, a woman doctor if possible.

As a student in her early twenties, Boupacha's faith in the medical system and its ability to fulfill its responsibilities to the people of Algeria was beginning to waver. Prior to her arrest, Boupacha had been working as a probationer in the Beni Messous hospital, and revealed in her first conversation with her lawyer, the Tunisian-born Gisèle Halimi, that she had stolen medical supplies for the FLN the day after she learned that Muslim girls working in the hospital would not be allowed to take their certificates. The first physician who examined Boupacha after her ordeal, Dr. Lévy-Leroy, noted the evidence of brutal beatings, the rib contusion and burns and bruises, but admitted to the involvement of her sex only insofar as he observed "constitutional menstrual irregularities," in other words, irregular vaginal bleeding. Though he initially admitted that he hadn't properly examined the prisoner, who had not removed her clothes, he would later revise his statement to insist that he had inspected her "completely naked" and could not speak to any evidence of vaginal trauma following her torture, since the girl had not specifically complained of being assaulted sexually and that, in any case, evidence of "traumatic defloration"—the phrase that would later be used to describe her rape—was rather illegible on the self-healing elastic surface of the young woman's vaginal walls. In Boupacha's words,

> Every time I tried to tell him what had been done to me he said "Oh, there's no harm in that, no harm at all." He scarcely examined me at all—the whole thing was over in about two minutes. . . . He felt my ribs and looked at my fingers, saying, "Nothing serious here, nothing to worry about." I didn't even undress! (54; 51–52)

Beauvoir, both in her article for *Le Monde* and later in her introduction to Halimi's book about the case, describes the reaction of the president of the Committee of Public Safety in France, Maurice Patin, to Boupacha's complaints of being raped. Relieved to hear she had not been forced to sit on the bottle, "[he] feared at first that she might have been violated *per anum*, as was done on occasion with the Viets in Indo-China: such treatment results in the perforation of the intestines, and is fatal. But this is something quite different" (9; 2). Beauvoir adds, "[C]learly nothing of the sort could ever happen to *him*" (avec le sourire d'un homme à qui on ne la fait pas) (9; 2fn). Patin would later confess that while he had sympathy for Boupacha's plight, it was difficult for him to empathize with her. She was not a pleasant girl, she imagined herself too easily as some kind of latter-day Jeanne d'Arc (97; 94). French Minister of Justice Edmond Michelet, in response to the Djamila Boupacha Committee's insistence that her case be tried in France rather than Algeria, would diagnose the source of Boupacha's ills rather differently; as reported by Beauvoir he explained, "The Nazis are responsible for this canker (*gangrène*) in our midst. It spreads everywhere, and corrupts all it touches. You can't eradicate it. . . . A canker in our midst" (14; 6).

Two things changed the course of Boupacha's trial and caused it to transcend the thousands of others awaiting some form, or at least performance, of justice in Algeria: these were the transfer of the proceedings to France, tirelessly fought for by Halimi, whose travel to and from Algeria was, like many Parisian lawyers (or as they were known in the colony "FLN lawyers"), restricted and strategically blocked by Algerian authorities, and secondly the resonance of her girlhood and the loss of her virginity for the makers of left public opinion in France, who eventually triumphed in getting Boupacha a new medical examination in late July 1960, five months after her torture. Though they could not attribute her many scars to electrical or cigarette burns without a skin biopsy, which they refused to do, a committee of five doctors, including a woman, Hélène Michel-Wolfrom, would report:

> Granted that after five months the rapid healing of vulvo-vaginal tissue normally makes it impossible to identify the method employed in any particular instance of defloration; and further, bearing in mind the fact that we could consult no other examination of the subject's genital organs made *prior to her arrest*, our answer to the second question remains, nevertheless: *Yes, Djamila Boupacha may well have had the neck of a bottle inserted into her vaginal passage.* At the date of examination, 28th July, 1960, it is impossible to specify either the date or the exact method of her defloration with any precision; but the tightness of the vaginal passage, the thickness of the hymen, and the narrow localization of the actual perforations (analogous to those observable in the case of surgical defloration (*défloration chirugicale*), which involves a single dilation of the speculum) all might well argue *in favour of traumatic defloration* (*défloration traumatique*). (126; 140)

Michel-Wolfrom followed the physical examination with a psychiatric assessment, and observed that Boupacha seemed constitutionally incapable of dishonesty, as well as noting that she had clearly suffered a mental trauma in the course of her rape, to which she returned during their conversation in an "obsessional" manner. Michel-Wolfrom, who spoke repeatedly of her disinterest in the "politics" of the case, attributed Boupacha's obsession with virginity to the fanatical hyperinvestment of purity in Islamic culture (127; 119). Although Halimi concedes the legal necessity of Boupacha's reexamination in France, titling the book's dramatic culminating chapter "Fresh Medical Examination" (*La contre-expertise médicale*), she is also pained by what she understands as her infliction on Djamila of successive interviews and inspections. "They involved," she reflects, "a double humiliation (*une double humiliation*): being obliged to undress, and having her word doubted" (120; 134). We are returned here to a formulation that first appeared in a text Halimi undoubtedly read: Fanon's lucid commentary on the ripping of the Algerian woman's veil in the colonist's rape dream as a "double deflowering." This violence, and its potential for an eroticized sensationalism akin to the harem fantasies of an earlier Orientalism would become an important tool in the dissemination of Boupacha's story to the broader public. Building this part of the case would require an emphasis on Djamila's girlhood, her beauty, her innocence not just in legal terms, but also in spiritual ones.

Halimi's narrative, including this medical documentation and many months' worth of statements from Djamila Boupacha herself, recounts the rest of the story of the trial in minute detail, offering a vision of the nearly impenetrable, and outlandishly unequal juridical system—a veritable warren of certain failure—in which she pursued Boupacha's case. The accusations against Boupacha would be dropped, and the use of torture admitted, though not punished. By any account, this was an enormous triumph for Halimi, Boupacha, and the independence struggle. Halimi's narrative of the case's technical twists and turns are punctuated with moments of profound feeling, the more poignant for their unexpected appearance in the legal and logistical morass. On Boupacha's arrival in Paris, for example, Halimi describes how she was transported immediately in an ambulance to Fresnes, where she would await her trial. Reunited with her client on more promising soil, she recalls Boupacha's breathless, girlish excitement at having flown in an airplane for the first time, at being in France:

"I kept peering out the window of the 'plane, you know," she told me. "It was my first trip by air. An aeroplane's a wonderful thing. I saw the top of the Eiffel Tower, too. But they used a closed van to bring me here from the airport, and I couldn't see a thing. . . . [D]o you think I'll soon be able to go for a walk with you in Paris? Do you?" (114; 128)

In these moments, Djamila Boupacha is pictured both truthfully and deliberately as a young girl ("do you? do you?"), as wide-eyed and untroubled as Picasso's sketch portrait, completed in 1961, that graces the book's cover. The rhetorical process of her humanization, from militant terrorist to "*jeune fille*," was a crucial and calculated element of the book's impact. Even as they disavowed the moral laziness of simply feeling bad, or finding mere sympathy with the beautiful Algerian without recognizing the complicity of metropolitan readers in the system that tortured and raped her, the salaries they paid to her torturers, the book's authors could not reasonably squander the resource of her beauty, her charisma, her compelling presence, and the marks of her trauma that heightened these qualities. That Djamila, as well as her sister Nefissa—also imprisoned for collaborating with the FLN—and her mother, were already "unveiled" Algerian women before the accusations and trial came to light both made this aesthetic case easier and also necessitated the deeper violation of putting the text of her sex before the world in all its legibility. For a girl already unveiled, another kind of forcible denuding would have to substitute.

The public shock caused in France, the "vast wave of sympathy" her story elicited, the signing of letters on her behalf by what looks now like a roster in an introduction to critical theory—not just Sartre and Beauvoir, but also Jean Amrouche, Germaine Tillion, Michel Leiris, André Schwarz-Bart, Aimé Césaire, Maurice Merleau-Ponty, Jacques Lacan, and Édouard Glissant among many, many others—also reached American shores, where the translation into English by Peter Green was published the same year.[60] In recognizing the requirements of a system of colonial medicine *as* the colonial state for compliance, submission, access, and cooperation as a strategy she might deploy in her own interests and those of her countrymen, Boupacha took the insights of the FLN's inversion of epidemic metaphoricity to its limit, offering her own body as its sacrificial collateral in ways that exceed the ordinary expectations that the militant put her body on the line. In this way, she replicates the strategy Beauvoir notes as the cruelly necessary mode in which Halimi set herself to work in the scandalously unjust French legal system. Djamila Boupacha's story, anchored in her rape at the hands of French paratroopers, renders visible the logic of infinite penetration and serial violation that upholds the colonial fantasy of caregiving and domination as two sides of the same coin. This story, it seems, is impossible to tell—impossible even to envision in the case of Muslim women in their shrouds—without the demand that even their inner tissues be held apart by the speculum, under the fluorescent lights and the "scientific" gaze of exam room, shabbily redecorated from its former use as a torture chamber. We are not yet free of this double-bind.

The Afghan Girl

The Argentine journalist Adolfo Gilly's introduction to *A Dying Colonialism* identifies Frantz Fanon's attention to the problem of sympathy in garnering international support for decolonial movements in the collected essays, noting that even in the fifth year of the bloody revolution, Fanon

> doesn't dwell on the torture, the pain, and the suffering of the Algerian people, rather he emphasizes their life and inner strength . . . [A]bove all, he doesn't want to arouse compassion for the Algerian people, but rather confidence in their strength. In this he dissociated himself from numerous "defenders" of the revolution—in Algeria or elsewhere—who assumed a protective and compassionate tone and invited us to take pity on embattled people and to cease the atrocities.[61]

This strategy is resonant with much of what Fanon had already written about the subjectivity of the colonizer in *Black Skin, White Masks* and would go on to develop in *The Wretched of the Earth*. It also goes some way toward explaining the absence of his name on any of the pleas and amicus briefs circulating around the Boupacha case. Fanon refused, in this instance and others, to circuit his protest against the system of profit-extracting colonialism through its very institutions of disciplinarity.

In her essay "Ethics and Violence: Simone de Beauvoir, Djamila Boupacha, and the Algerian War," Judith Surkis suggests that Beauvoir manages to avoid the kind of sentimentalizing trap to which Fanon was objecting when he wrote in "Concerning a Plea" (1957),

> After the fruitful struggle that [France] waged two centuries ago for the respect of individual liberties and the rights of man, it finds itself today unable to wage a similar battle for the rights of peoples. This explains the feverish concentration on individual cases and the vain hope of stirring the interest of the French people in the whole problem on the basis of extreme situations. The extreme situation is neither [Djamila] Bouhired, nor Zeddour, nor even the Philippeville stadium. The extreme situation is the will of twelve million men. That is the only reality. And it cannot be simplified.[62]

Writing in 1957, Fanon could not of course have been aware of the tortures to which Djamila Boupacha would be subjected in 1960, but his comments on the case of another young woman accused of terrorism, Djamila Bouhired, one whose case had gone public in France, would serve as a prescient warning against the desire to romanticize the woman militant in Orientalist terms. He goes on:

> It does no good to present Djamila Bouhired as a poor girl who is the victim of wickedness. Djamila Bouhired is a conscious Algerian patriot, organized within the FLN. She asks neither for commiseration nor for pity. Djamila Bouhired's extraordinary fortitude, her obstinate determination to remain upright, not to speak, her need to smile in the face of death, constitute essential characteristics of the national attitude of the Algerian people.[63]

Standing accused and given the death sentence along with Djamila Bouhired was the nineteen-year-old Djamila Bouazza; the three would come to be known as "Djamilate el Jazair" and "les belles d'Alger."[64] Boupacha would later enact the same refusal in the form of a disturbing laugh during court proceedings, a fact that would have to be fought against in the soft-focus depiction of her character in Halimi's memoir. This extract from Fanon's occasional essay, a response to Georges Arnaud's bid to the French people for compassion toward Algerians, stands as a challenge to the standard line on the philosopher's regressive gender politics in a number of ways. He insists here (as he often does, given the foundational and ever-present project of repairing the schizoid effects of colonial ontology) on the agential, nonspontaneous, deliberate function of Djamila Bouhired as a patriot, a political actor, a vertical rather than a supine being. Recalling his comments on the role of work and mediation in the production of revolutionary violence, we must also understand this essay as preparatory work for "Algeria Unveiled." In "Concerning a Plea," Fanon forcefully resists the French-facing matrix of torture-victim pornography and imperial sexual-submission paternalism he sees as being cynically or instrumentally deployed by Arnaud in *Pour Djamila Bouhired*, his humanizing plea on behalf of the "girl," as he pointedly calls her.[65]

If we take Boupacha's trial, and the centrality of her medical examination in it, as a significant model for the costs of working through colonial regimes of the evidentiary in the postwar years, and further, if we understand the importance of this moment on American self-fashioning in the War on Terror, we must insist on centering the inscribed violation of the woman's body as that which makes both the juridical system and public opinion go. To fight through the avenues of legitimacy is to don the patient's gown; to play the compliant subject of care is to remove it. It is important to recall that the army flatly refused over the course of the trial to show Boupacha photographs of her torturers "with their faces uncovered."[66] When Beauvoir writes that "what is exceptional, in the Boupacha affair, is not the facts, but their unveiling," and that the investigation removed "the curtain of night and fog protecting routine horror," she is also inadvertently pointing to the ransoming of the unveiled nation on the body of the ungowned girl.[67]

Halimi and Beauvoir's framing of Djamila Boupacha's story may avoid some of the worst pitfalls of Arnaud's classically imperialist endeavor to save brown women (from everyone), but they are not entirely absent. The affective parameters of Boupacha's testimonial are strongly shaped by the paratextual artifacts of Picasso's portrait and Beauvoir's introduction, which begins with the same figure of vulnerability: "An Algerian girl of twenty-three."[68] In Picasso's sketch, the girl is softened further, a faint smile on her lips, shoulders bare in classical bust style, her hair coiffed and eyes heavy with the luxurious eyelashes of storied harem girls. Her dark eyes, the open lines of her features, are both frank and present, honest and compliant. It is not the portrait of a young militant, nor is it a meditation, as I read it, on the dissimulating disguises Pontecorvo would later make famous. It is, rather, a powerfully humanizing depiction of the face whose sweetness the testimony would violate—a frame or overture placed with care and a devastating sense of emotional contrast to exacerbate the pain the reader would be primed to experience within. The strokes of Picasso's resolutely representational portrait—he eschews here the possible mistakes of interpretation proper to more radical modes of abstraction and cubism—act as a recuperative reinscription of the marks on the girl's body and her hymen. Other artists would take interest in Djamila Boupacha as well: the Italian composer Luigi Nono composed a concert piece for solo soprano in her voice for his 1962 cycle *Canti di vita e d'amore*, which also begins with an image of unveiling ("remove this fog of the centuries from my eyes, I want to see the world like a child"), the Chilean artist Roberto Matta followed his painting after Alleg's *La question* with one called *Le supplice de Djamila* (1962), and the painter Robert Lapoujade's sketches of her narrative would appear inside the French edition of the book, though not in the English translation (figure 5.6).[69] Lapoujade's sketches approach Boupacha's pain and disfigurement more directly than Picasso's, revealing the body and the screaming face in challenging and fragmentary lines that suggest the disintegration of personhood under torture in uncompromising terms. This approach, unsurprisingly, also renders her nude.

Western regimes of scopic power, from the commissioned portrait

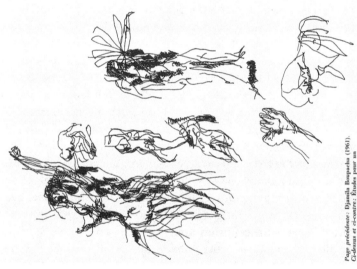

5.6 Robert Lapoujade, *Études pour un "Hommage à Djamila Boupacha"* (1961). © 2019 Artists Rights Society, New York / ADAGP, Paris.

Page précédente: Djamila Boupacha (1961). *Ci-dessus et ci-contre:* Études pour un « Hommage à Djamila Boupacha », par Robert Lapoujade.

to the mugshot, have rarely dealt easily with the racial other, and particularly poorly with the Muslim woman. If the portrait in Western art
addresses itself to both subject and viewer as, in the words of Jean-Luc
Nancy, "the un-representable of the face . . . the dis- or trans-figuration of
the figure . . . the indeterminate slippage of a face barely glimpsed," then
the portrait of the Muslim woman un-represents, dis- and trans-figures
exponentially that which is—by virtue of the specific fugitivity of her visibility in Orientalist painting and literature—"barely glimpsed."[70] The
portrait of the Muslim woman as a genre in the public eye made an important reappearance in 2002, following the US invasion of Afghanistan,
when *National Geographic* sent the photographer Steve McCurry in search
of the young girl—an Afghani refugee living in Pakistan—whom he had
photographed for the cover of its June 1985 issue. The article describing
his journey in search of the girl, whose name he did not know, was published in April 2002, a year before the Pentagon screening of *The Battle
of Algiers*. From its very title, "A Life Revealed," the piece is a study in the
unlearned lessons of postcolonial critique. The tag line of the article
reads, "Her eyes have captivated the world since she appeared on our
cover in 1985. Now we can tell her story."[71] Sharbat Gula, the woman in
question, stands beneath this text in a purple burqa, the crocheted portion intended for covering her face and eyes pulled up onto her forehead.
She holds in her hands a copy of the magazine with her younger self
on its cover. The author, Cathy Newman, frames the girl's childhood in
Pakistan as a flight from the violence of Soviet invaders ("by day the skies
bled terror"), and writes in foreboding tones of her return to Afghanistan,
where she now lives in the mountains of Tora Bora. Her musings on the
original McCurry photograph speak of the girl's eyes as "haunted and
haunting . . . in them you can read the tragedy of a land drained by war";
a caption beneath a present-day portrait of Sharbat Gula speaks to the
impact of the picture, noting that her face alone inspired millions to fight
for the aid of refugees.[72]

Newman suggests that she was difficult to find, though the article does
not say how or when she was looked for, only reminds its readers that
"stories shift like sand in a place where no records exist."[73] She became
known around the office as "the Afghan Girl," reports Newman, "and
for 17 years no one knew her name."[74] Barring the likelihood that many
people—her family and community—in fact knew her name, the article
continues in this vein of myopic mystification, noting frequently the
woman's anger and ferocity, her Pashtun background ("that most warlike
of Afghan tribes"), her illiteracy, her accelerated aging, her "leather"-like
skin, her devout adherence to Islam, her flat affect, in order to amplify
the power of the story's drama and humanism, which culminates—of

course—in her unveiling. Beneath another contemporary photograph of Gula, Newman reports that "she only agreed to be photographed again—to appear unveiled, without her burka—because her husband told her it would be proper."[75] Gula herself explains, "[I]t's a beautiful thing to wear, not a curse." Lest we forget the specific parameters under which the Muslim woman is allowed these fragmentary humanizations in a colonial discursive regime, we are reminded that Gula "has never known a happy day . . . except perhaps the day of her marriage."[76]

In a moment when American attention was hyperfocused on Afghanistan, this story made a splash. The perennial Muslim woman in need of saving—this time from the jihadis and the embers of Islamic fundamentalism fanned by American forces during the cold war—had been found, could be freed, if only for a moment, from her woven prison. Sharbat Gula's reappearance reminded an American public not of its responsibilities in the War on Terror, nor of its complicity in the renewed violence in far-off lands, but rather of the archetypal subject of ultra-vulnerability that subtends the imperial project, an object of pity continually contrasted in the space between Orientalizing gestures of beauty and inscrutability without unincorporability. Djamila Boupacha repurposed these expectations, and the cruel care of the colonial state, to her own ends. Despite her sacrifices of both body and belief, the dismembering effect of empire's medical metaphorics and the material realities upon which they were based never went away. Her mother's words, freighted with desperation at her daughter's plight, bear the extractive logic and sacrificial economy of colonial medicine forward, into the space of the juridical, into the realm of public consumption during the last months of the Algerian war of independence, and into our own political present: "I would give my eyes to save Djamila."[77] Haunted or haunting like the Afghan girl's, these eyes bear ghosts of imperial violence premised on rape, disbelief, alienation, murder, and torture; in the neocolonial rhetorical program of Newman's writing, and so many think pieces on Muslim women since the start of the War on Terror, we must also recognize them as the ghosts of an unreconstructed Orientalism that haunted the Pentagon screening room, and that linger with us now.

PART III: VIRAL DIASPORA AND GLOBAL SECURITY

CHAPTER 6

Selfistan

Terrorism is a pathological copy of the organism it attacks, a retrovirus created from the latter's cells. It is thus deceptive to think that the enemy comes from without, for there is no location outside of our network of global relationships from which any impulse, human or inhuman, could come. The threat of terrorism is omnipresent—like the telephone.

HANS MAGNUS ENZENSBERGER, "THE RESURGENCE OF HUMAN SACRIFICE"

We share the belief that terrorism is a cancer on the human condition and we intend to oppose it wherever it is.

DONALD RUMSFELD, "BRIEFING ON ENDURING FREEDOM"

The conflict over Kashmir, one of the most militarized zones in the world, stretches back at least to the botched mechanics of the partition of British India, when hopes of Kashmiri autonomy were undone by a period of indecision on the part of Maharaja Hari Singh, the Hindu ruler of the predominantly Muslim princely state of Jammu and Kashmir, and the incursion of an armed phalanx from Pakistan's North West Frontier Province that caused the maharaja to accede—temporarily, in theory—to the new state of India.[1] Violence in Kashmir has erupted in periodic waves of intensity around the Indo-Pakistani wars in 1965 and 1971, the surge of killings by armed secessionists in 1989, and the nuclearization of Pakistan and India in 1998. Terrorism in the region—a term that encompasses both Kashmiri separatist insurgency and Pakistan-backed militant operations and jihadi activity—saw a marked increase at the start of the US-led War on Terror and again in 2010 after a spate of border crossings from the north led to fatal confrontations between youth protestors and Indian security forces.[2]

In the years leading up to the lockdown and suspension of Kashmir's special status (enshrined in Article 370 of the Indian Constitution) that began in the fall of 2019, protests in the largely Muslim state became more widespread and more frequent, provoking continued violence and suppression tactics on the part of the Indian army.[3] One of the watershed moments in this period was the targeted killing of twenty-two-year-old Kashmiri militant Burhan Wani by Indian armed forces in the summer of 2016, which led to unprecedented public mourning and mass protests across Kashmir.[4] In an article called "An Epidemic of 'Dead Eyes' in Kashmir," Ellen Barry, reporting for the New York Times, observed, "[T]he stone-throwing crowds have no political leaders, put forward no specific demands and metastasized with alarming speed."[5] The 2016 protests were widely portrayed in the Indian press and major Western media outlets as violent, malignant, senseless riots perpetrated by "angry mobs"—the lack of discernable political leadership and specific demands collapsing easily with the organicizing figure of a malignant cancer.[6] Many Kashmiris, however, saw it as a moment of hope, gesturing toward the renewed promise of the long-delayed plebiscite on accession that led in the first place to a divided Kashmir and to the open laceration known as the Line of Control. Kashmiri novelist Mirza Waheed, for example, called the response of his countrymen a "furious civilian uprising," and "a full-scale popular revolt."[7] Indian security forces responded swiftly, using a variety of so-called nonlethal weapons to disperse the crowds, most notoriously the high-velocity pump-action pellet guns that spray iron bird shot out of cartridges, each containing from four hundred to six hundred tiny bullets. When sprayed indiscriminately into crowds as a method of dispersal, they rupture the corneas and retinas of the eye, blinding people with horrific efficiency.[8]

In the wake of this suppression tactic and its pointed use in Kashmir, eye doctors found themselves among the policy experts and officials, military strategists and diplomats who have weighed in on the conflict. A senior ophthalmologist at Shri Maharaja Hari Singh Hospital in Srinagar reported that "in just four months we have seen security forces using a weapon that has caused injuries in 1,178 eyes. This, by any means, is an epidemic of blindness."[9] More pointedly, Waheed has called it "the world's first mass blinding."[10] "Walking in the hospital hallway," writes Barry, "you see a handful of young men in blackout goggles. Then you see them everywhere."[11] In the narrative of contemporary geopolitics and the twenty-first-century reshaping of the international order, in the power plays between India and Pakistan—themselves crucial but nonsovereign bit players in the War on Terror—Kashmir and Kashmiris are both blind spot and blinded, the source of metastasizing riots, and also the dead retinal bodies that suffer from them, clouded and reflective like the valley's innumerable mirror lakes. If in the words of both its most proximate witnesses and its distant observers this recent episode of mass blinding is also coded as an epidemic, then it is an epidemic unlike the infectious diseases of the choleric and plague imaginaries that lent their shape to the literary and discursive projection of sick colonial space in the late nineteenth and mid-twentieth centuries. This epidemic is deliberate, noncontagious, tethered to the state and its putatively legal suppression of insurgency. It intersects therefore not just in continuous but also in transformative ways with the figural history of epidemic violence as an insurgent phenomenon in colonial historiography.

The previous two sections of this book have accounted for the ways in which the archival and literary record of violence that falls outside of the framework of classical warfare—particularly anticolonial violence during and in the aftermath of the Indian Mutiny and the postwar independence movement in Algeria—consolidates the language of insurgency, anticolonialism, terror, and terrorism around the figure of epidemic. These histories make it not just possible, but unremarkable, expected, a matter of common sense that the same article can refer in one moment to the "epidemic" of blindness unleashed by the occupying Army's security tactics, and in the next to the "metastasizing" protests of Kashmiri separatists and Kashmiris under occupation that seem to have called it forth. With regard to Kashmir and the legacy of imperial disease poetics, the idea of the "metastasization" of protests reiterates the stable analogy of rapidly spreading sickness with rebellious, mutinous, insurgent, or irregular violence, here again by largely Muslim populations. Such depictions of popular revolt, eviscerated of political content and deaf to the demands of those who cry loudly and continually for freedom, are kept quarantined outside of a concept of just war, thereby expanding and further grounding theories and legal definitions of terrorism as a particularly virulent species of nonstate or antistate violence. Despite the waves of state-sponsored terror that define the very parameters of political modernity, these figures of disease, I have suggested, have most often been associated with the non-West, with colonial and former colonial subjects, with failed states, and with the "problem" of Islam-qua-terror in contemporary geopolitics.

I have argued that the trope of an "epidemic of terrorism," as well as its various metaphorical elaborations—a global cancer, a plague on reason and progress, an embedded and insidious retrovirus, an ideological contagion—typically works to maintain a clash-of-civilizations thesis of the kind popularized by Samuel Huntington in his 1996 book of the same name. Parts 1 and 2 of this book detailed how commentators on the Indian Mutiny of 1857, the dismantling of the Ottoman empire, and the Algerian revolution set the terms for the recording of anti- and postcolonial histories through the poetics of disease. This discursive practice inflects not just the conflict in Kashmir, but also, as I will demonstrate here in part 3, the Iranian Revolution, Islam as an ongoing and ineradicable plague on the Indian state and the South Asian diaspora, the War on Terror, and the global migration crisis with the ascendant image of an epidemic of militant Islamism. This picture, ever lurking on the horizon of development and modernity, shores up a notion of the healthy civilizations of the Global North while constructing the Global South, postcolonial states, and the "Muslim world"—terms that are used in strategically imprecise ways—as zones of rampant infection, roiling virality, and raging epidemic, poised to break out at any moment and fell the global order. As we saw in early 2020, these politically expedient metaphorical epidemics persist and overdetermine our responses to actual global pandemics even as they unfold in real time.

This chapter investigates both paradigmatic examples and counter-paradigms in the ongoing legacy of imperial disease poetics. The case of Kashmir's "epidemic" of blindness reminds us of the extent to which state-sponsored terror can also be cast in the organicizing mold of natural catastrophe, which works most often to depoliticize that which is being figured. In Guha's investigation, outlined in chapter 1 of this book, this naturalization dehumanizes the poor and recodes peasant revolt by wresting agency and political claims away from its actors. In the Kashmir example, the dehumanization works both consonantly and in reverse, depicting the Indian army's nonlethal force as a blight from on high, beyond the political machinations of nations—beyond good and evil. To call the outcomes of nonlethal protest suppression tactics in Kashmir an "epidemic" of blindness both draws sympathetic attention to the uniquely horrific plight of wounded Kashmiris in the language of international humanitarian aid (epidemics draw dollars), while also eclipsing the responsibility of those wielding the pellet guns, and the central government in Delhi that protects them under the brutal provisions of the Armed Forces Special Powers Act and the so-called Public Safety Act.[12]

At the same time, a rhetoric that figures the protests against military and police brutality in Kashmir as a "metastasizing" social and political movement draws on a deep history of suppressing and evading antistate and insurgent political demands by way of epidemic neutralization. The danger of a rising community is thus rewritten as a terror-beyond-the-human, prejustifying sterilization, "surgical" extraction, and care in the form of development funds in the interest of a more broadly conceived public health. This public, with its strategically shifting borders, is defined concentrically outward from the mountainous regions of Northern India, Afghanistan, and Pakistan, to the states themselves and eventually to the farthest corners of the globe in South Asia's mobile, multiconfessional diasporic populations. The regional dynamics and narratives I will examine in this chapter reshape colonial relations according to a new map of global security. The instance of Kashmir emerges in the redrafted map of postcolonial imperialism as both exemption and paradigm for the uneven redistribution of imperial and anti-imperial uses of force and narratives of violence with the Indian army and police functioning as an occupying force in Kashmir.

The twenty-first century's media landscape in both its tempo and its forms bears little resemblance to the archive of dispatches produced by colonial medical bureaucracies and the state-sponsored journalism apparatuses that set the narrative and epistemological terms of both the Indian and Algerian independence movements. Given the ever-broadening distribution of real-time historical authorship in the form of social media and a proliferating, multilingual local press, it is difficult to construct a steady enough picture of the ongoing disruptions in Kashmir to serve as the foundation of a lucid analysis in a longer historical frame. This difficulty was compounded by the total media blackout imposed by the Indian government in late 2019. Suvir Kaul's translations and essays about the conflict up to 2014 in *Of Gardens and Graves* offer an extraordinary and compelling range of testimony, from poetic witness to photographs to music.[13] Such utterances and intimate documentation form the warp and weft of resistance and its record—the "very *language*," Kaul writes, "with which to imagine futures different from, and more humane and equitable than, those pasts and indeed our present."[14] I will return to some of these counterhegemonic forms, but I have also been interested in this book in maintaining a focus on the still-open question of popular fiction and crossover literary texts' indebtedness to and re-foundationalizing of colonial imaginaries. While the culture at large reflects discernable patterns of figuration with reference to Islam and terrorism, categories that are habitually collapsed to devastating effect, the authorship of such representations can also be linked to specific writers—in particular to makers of fiction in the largely Anglophone market called "world literature." This chapter reconstructs how one such writer, Salman Rushdie, imagines and projects Kashmir as an exemplary case of the raging plague of contemporary Islamism, extending an intellectual and rhetorical through-line in his career that has deep roots in his reimagining of Muslim history and peoples beginning in the late 1980s.

Since the publication of *The Satanic Verses* in 1988 and the subsequent fatwa calling for the writer's assassination, Rushdie, arguably the most pivotal figure in turn-of-the-century postcolonial Anglophone writing, has joined the now-innumerable experts on terrorism and its genesis in postcolonial failed states in advancing a denunciation of radical Islam and militant Islamisms in the language of epidemic. This chapter follows the rhetorical flow of such thinking as it coalesces in three of Rushdie's most politically influential works: *The Satanic Verses*, *Shalimar the Clown*, and *Joseph Anton*, and filters out into the broader discourses of terrorism and global Islam. Where *The Satanic Verses* resists the association of epidemic with Islamist violence, and provides instead the tools for a critique of the figure of terror-as-disease, *Shalimar the Clown*, whose titular character is a circus-tight-rope-walker-turned-terrorist-assassin, participates in the naturalization of terrorism as a category of identity and being, rather than of action, one that exists outside of and as an enemy of humanity, like and as a plague on the paradisal valley of Kashmir, which in turn functions as a kind of "patient zero" for the geopolitical contagion of post-postcolonial nationalisms—an affliction Rushdie jokingly calls "Selfistanism." Through the historiographic metonym of plague, *Shalimar the Clown* seeks to connect the chauvinism and myopia of postwar American foreign policy to the contemporary epidemic of terrorism as a side effect of a misguided zeal for self-determination. What it does not do is illustrate, or in any significant way critique, the symmetrical operations of the counterterrorism, intelligence, and international security tactics that have burgeoned both in response to and in prophylactic anticipation of Muslim migration and terrorist attacks.

The evolution of Rushdie's thinking about radical Islamism in epidemic terms is even more evident in *Joseph Anton*, the memoir of his years in hiding, which prophesies that "the fanatical cancer spreading through Muslim communities . . . would, in the end, explode into the wider world."[15] Here, we can observe the twenty-first century's opening of epidemic figuration to include not just contagious illness, but also metastatic "autoimmunity," a conceptual touchstone of political philosophy and biopolitical theory from Derrida's work in the early 1990s to the present.[16] This shift indicates not only the perennial slipperiness of the epidemic figure, but also an evolving set of assumptions about the imagined parameters of the collective body, and the measures necessary to protect it. By styling himself an anonymized, third-person confessor requiring a personal security detail in what he dreams is an international Republic of Letters, Rushdie lends the use of his imaginative representations of South Asia and its diaspora to the reconfigurations of global security discourse and US foreign policy.[17]

Although it begins harrowingly with a suicide bomber on a plane, *The Satanic Verses* stands as a counterparadigm, overturning the habits of imperial disease poetics by tracking the positive, community-building effects of two different diseases, one literal and one figurative, on contemporary communities in India and Britain. What Rushdie offers in place of the pathologization of Islam in *The Satanic Verses* is a counterfactual history that decenters the monotheistic and patrilineal origins of the religion and deploys the unruly concepts of contagion, errancy, and mutation to show how a more plural, less dogmatic Islam may have been—indeed may still be—possible. Although this radical, impossible future of early Islamic origins and praxis is a troubled one in the novel, it suggests an alternative present in which the telos of militant Islamism and contemporary jihad, what Rushdie will refer to later as "actually ex- isting Islam," might well have been written out.[18] Situating these three works alongside the events of the 1989 fatwa, Rushdie's years in hiding, and the September 11 attacks points up how Rushdie's hugely impactful writings evolve an ever more jaundiced view of the lost solidarity and radical aspirations of a political Islam and a Muslim people. Given the writer's profound influence on globally significant narratives of South Asia and the cultures of Islam, I argue that Rushdie's growing propensity for avowing the epidemic metaphor of Islamist terrorism authorizes in the Anglophone imagination—postcolonial, Indian, American, British, and beyond—both its dehumanizing effects and the forms of security this dehumanization invites under the aegis of global quarantine and liberal care.

Both the Houses: Postnational Allegory

In a 1999 op-ed for the *New York Times*, Rushdie, still in the prime of his career, referred to the nuclear standoff between Pakistan and India in Kashmir as a "dialogue of the deaf . . . more dangerous than ever before," and called down the famous curse of *Romeo and Juliet*'s Mercutio: "I say: a plague on both their houses."[19] Commenting on the renewed tensions in Kashmir in 2002, Rushdie interrogated the international communi- ty's panic that Pakistan might draw the nuclear trigger first: "Is it really likely . . . that Pakistan would, so to speak, strap a nuclear weapon to its belly, walk into the crowded bazaar that is India and turn itself into the biggest suicide bomber in history?"[20] Both these figures—the state as a disabled body, deaf and vulnerable to an infectious curse, and the state as potential suicide bomber—appear redrafted, again and again, in vari- ous guises in Rushdie's oeuvre. The capacious metaphor of plague is one he also uses to describe his years in hiding: in a slant citation of Defoe, Rushdie entitles the dispatches collected during this period, "Messages From the Plague Years."[21] This figure, as we will see, becomes an unruly concept metaphor for, among other things, Islamist violence and tribal incursions from the Pakistani side of the Kashmiri Line of Control in *Shalimar the Clown*. Through its reprisal of colonial-era disease poetics, *Shalimar* imagines the possible motives and operations of Islamism, communalism, nationalism, global network development, and terrorism more completely—if not more successfully—than any other work of fiction of its stature in the Anglophone world written since the 2001 attacks.

Novelist and critic Amitava Kumar has suggested that Rushdie is an "academic writer," more concerned with breathless games of literary allusion, intertextuality, and historical synchronicity than with the development of subtle political positions or deep characterization.[22] This characterological circumscription deflects psychological realism in favor of the novels' mythic, historical, and political horizons. This is especially true for those characters overdetermined by their national origin, exemplary status, and sense of belonging.[23] Even as they render their intimate plots geopolitical (characters struggle to inhabit freighty names like "India/Kashmira") Rushdie's novels obviate the architecture of allegory and in some instances mock the quaint notion of depth, of a referent outside of textuality, partly because their surfaces are so virtuosically allusive, metafictional, heteroglossic, and hypermobile, and partly because the territories they seem to imagine are constantly crumbling underfoot. Rushdie often begins this play in his epigraphs. *Shalimar the Clown* opens with the Kashmiri poet Agha Shahid Ali, whose lines paint a Kashmir beyond life with the poet as its Orpheus.

I am being rowed through Paradise on a river of Hell;
Exquisite ghost, it is night.
The paddle is a heart; it breaks the porcelain waves.[24]

In Shahid's imaginary, Kashmir is already gone—navigable only by way of a stygian tour, the fragile reflection of the Himalayas shattering at every beat or stroke of the poet's heart. The tragic prophecy is redoubled in the novel's second epigraph, a line revisited from the 1999 op-ed in the form of Mercutio's "a plague on both your houses" curse. *Shalimar the Clown* presents a profusion of possibilities for thinking the status of the "houses" on which the plague has been called down: cities, villages, dwellings, and interior spaces both reinforce and explode the viability of the nation—of warring India and Pakistan—as political concepts by offering lineage, territory, home, and even mind as spaces vulnerable to the imprecations of plague.

A famously cosmopolitan writer, Rushdie expresses suspicion with regard to the depth-based metaphorics of rootedness, even in the works most grounded in national politics and contexts.[25] The narrator of the Pakistan novel *Shame* (1983), a minimally modified Rushdie, claims the space of the sky, the "conquest of the force of gravity," as the rightful inheritance of *mohajirs*, Muslims that migrated from India to Pakistan

during partition: "We have performed the very act of which all men an-
ciently dream, the thing for which they envy the birds; that is to say, we
have flown. I am comparing gravity," he continues, "with belonging."[26]
In both resistance and necessity, postcolonial South Asian writers, particularly those in the Muslim and Urdu-speaking traditions, have not
infrequently turned to the sky and its inhabitants for a model of migrant
survival and supranational belonging.[27] In his reading of Bano Qudsia's
1981 Urdu novel *Raja Gidh* (*The King Buzzard*), Masood Ashraf Raja associates the aerial with the figure of the global *ummah* or Muslim community, a postnational but not entirely religious basis for identification
drawn from prenational political forms. In Qudsia's novel, this model is
specifically adapted from Farid ud-Din Attar's epic, *The Conference of the
Birds*—also the source text for Rushdie's first novel, *Grimus*—reworked as
an allegory for the formation of the Muslim Khilafat in India to oppose
the dismantling of the Ottoman empire, and doubly as an allegory of
the crisis of Pakistani nationalism under Zia's military regime.[28] In his
reading of *Raja Gidh*, Raja posits the inadequacy of national imaginaries
in postcolonial Muslim writing:

> [R]eliance on historical mythologies to justify the nation might seem a
> perfect strategy for metropolitan European nation-states, but when it
> is applied to the Islamic periphery, the same nation-making histories
> tend to complicate the idea of modern Islamic nations, and nation-
> states. This happens . . . because Islamic histories and historical my-
> thologies are supranational, and any modern approaches to territorial
> nationalism are built upon the exclusion of this supranational my-
> thology. . . . [T]he creation of most postcolonial Muslim nation-states
> involved an abandonment of the Muslim universal idea of the *Ummah*
> for the nation-state.[29]

Raja's conception of the *ummah* as a diasporic, but nevertheless political or pluripolitical form is drawn primarily from Abdullah al-Ahsan ("a
community of law and custom"), Abul-A'la Maududi ("neither material
nor territorial, but spiritual"), and Muhammad Iqbal ("Ours is China and
Arabia, ours is Hindustan / For we are Muslims and the whole world is
our country"), all of whom sought to interrogate the immanence of the
nation-state form in the postwar era as a means of social justice and,
in the latter two cases, a form of protest against the three-world system and the intractable globalization of capitalist exploitation and economic liberalism.[30] Rushdie's critique of the nation-form in *Shame* plays
loosely with political Islam's prevailing ideas, but largely previews the
later writings' rejection of any political formation other than the entirely

and wholly "secular," a concept untethered from history. Speaking of *mohajirs*, and an ever-more-untenable political climate in Zia's Pakistan, Rushdie writes,

> We have floated upwards from history, from memory, from Time. I may be such a person. Pakistan may be such a country. . . . Pakistan, the peeling, fragmenting palimpsest, increasingly at war with itself, may be described as the failure of the dreaming mind. Perhaps the pigments used were the wrong ones, impermanent, like Leonardo's; or perhaps the place was just *insufficiently imagined*, a picture full of irreconcilable elements . . . a miracle that went wrong.[31]

The novel was published the same year as Anderson's *Imagined Communities*.[32]

Ironizing Fredric Jameson's preferred mode of reading "third world" literature, *Shalimar*'s first part is titled simply "India" not after a nation, but rather a woman.[33] Set largely between Kashmir and Los Angeles, the book's tragic players come not from two rival ancestral houses, nor from rival nations, but rather from many intersecting lines and many exploded territories, few of which are in any meaningful sense national. India is named for the country where her father was—for a time—ambassador. Shalimar is named for the famed Mughal garden in Srinagar where he was born but never resided. The lines of flight that occasion their constitution and begetting of one another originate in more intimate and indeterminate spaces that, at different moments in history, become sites of contagion for the unfolding of a violent, multigenerational epidemic of terror. Shalimar, even after he kills her father, taps a deep vein of recognition in India, an embodiment of the Kashmir valley.[34] "His hair was a mountain stream," she muses, "there were narcissi from the banks of rushing rivers and peonies from the high meadows growing on his chest, poking out through his open collar. Around him there raucously echoed the sound of the *swarnai*," the famed string instrument played by Kashmiri bards (*SC* 11). In Shalimar, historical desire is compressed into the form of a person—India sees in him not just her surrogate father and personal reaper, but also manifestly as the lost valley, her lost mother, the lost home. In their first encounter, India describes herself as a "conduit," a "crystal ball," "an abstraction," "the channel, the medium" (*SC* 13, 15). Much later, as he attempts to escape from prison, Shalimar inhabits her:

> [S]he had begun to hear his voice inside her head. Or not exactly a voice but a disembodied, nonverbal transmission, like a wild screech full

of static and internal dissension, hatred and shame, repentance and threat, curses and tears; like a werewolf howling at the moon. (*SC* 340)

India's capacity to hear Shalimar's transmissions inverts the shape of the Indian occupation of Kashmir; here it is Shalimar, garden, clown, or both, who has taken up residence in India. This mode of telegraphing the vastness of the world (global transmission systems reprised, to be sure, from *Midnight's Children*) and the miniscule goings-on of the territory of the mind, the interconnectedness of people, place, ethnicities, languages, and the lovingly rendered details of the hybrid particulars, are perhaps Rushdie's most well-known traits as a novelist, leading critics like James Wood to identify in his busy prose a tendency toward hysteria.[35] In India's words, "Everywhere was now a part of everywhere else. . . . Our lives, our stories, flowed into one another's, were no longer our own, individual, discrete . . . This unsettled people. There were collisions and explosions. She thought of Housman in Shropshire. *That is the land of lost content*" (*SC* 37). In a text filled with name-changing, transnational characters—all of them forgers, *passeurs*, posers, performers, or spies— Housman's lines read, on one level, as a lost contentment, or happiness, but also—and more importantly for the novel—as a loss of content, substance, or personhood. Echoing the reductions of people to carriers, mediums, and later, disease vectors, the unauthorized melding of India's brain with Shalimar's in the novel's final section raises the question of autonomy at two levels: the personal, and through the vanishing geography of names, the national and postnational.

In its basic architecture, *Shalimar* advances ideas of territory, nation, city, dynasty, sovereignty, and identity that might be understood through the binary—the both—set forth in the curse. Still, it continuously escapes the binary structure of antagonism and the dialectical unfolding of history, and suggests a series of third terms to the coextensive questions of ontology and sovereignty not through the mechanisms of classical conflict and its implicit bilateralism, but rather through the mechanisms of infection, circulation, and spread.[36] Musing on what will be her father's legacy, India

tried to believe that the global structures he had helped to build, the pathways of influence, money, and power, the multinational associations, the treaty organizations, the frameworks of cooperation and law whose purpose had been to deal with a hot war turned cold, would still function in the future that lay beyond what he could foresee. She saw in him a desperate need to believe that the ending of his age would be

happy, and that the new world which would come after would be better than the one that would die with him. . . . a world without walls, a
frontierless newfound land of infinite possibility. (*SC* 20)

The character who holds these beliefs is called Max Ophuls, after the
German filmmaker. Rushdie's penchant for name puns finds no exception in the ambassador's outsized chivalry and tragic foolishness (or
phul-ishness) setting him up as a foil for the Clown, his rival Shalimar.
The fictional Max, who will later serve as US counterterrorism chief, also
hails from Alsace, the disputed territory between Germany and France.
In Kashmir, he thinks, "Could any two places have been more different . . . could any two places have been more the same?" (*SC* 180).

Max pilots his way out of Nazi-occupied Strasbourg and into a career as
an architect of the postwar international order not in his native Europe,
but rather in the land of promise and novelty, the new imperial super-
power: America. At the fictionalized version of the historic Bretton Woods
conference, he masterminds the open market postwar global economic
"restructuring," which, in actuality, included the creation of the International Bank for Reconstruction and Development and the International
Monetary Fund. Finally, he decamps to New York, where he begins his
ascent to an embassy position, and eventually US counterterrorism chief.
It is these "pathways," "global structures," "treaty organizations," and
"frameworks of cooperation and law" that India invokes as her father's
unfortunate objects of nostalgia and his limited vision for the future.
Inasmuch as they carry with them the germs of Max's own history, they
are also the pathways of transmission of a life-threatening scourge in the
form of a postwar politics of nationhood. Such an infectious world order,
even imagined by a man for whom not one but two formerly autonomous
valley regions—Alsace and Kashmir—function as imaginary homelands,
would depend on the stability of the nation to uphold a right and just
internationalism. If his daughter is his dream, then India's given name
confirms its shape as the dream of the cooperative, multiethnic nation in
an operable community of nations—Nehru's secular India, the multilingual France of the resistance, the America of summit meetings, surfaces,
and revelation. His political fantasies are not shared by his daughter's
mother. Boonyi Kaul, his Hindu consort

decide[s] that the term "Indian armed forces" would secretly refer to
the ambassador himself, she would use the Indian presence in the
valley as a surrogate for the American occupation of her body, so, "Yes,
that's it," she cried, "The 'Indian armed forces,' raping and pillaging.
How can you not know it? How can you not comprehend the humili-

ation of it, the shame of having your boots march all over my private fields?" (*SC* 197)

Shalimar's revenge is symmetrically overdetermined by the ever-present political erotics: the Clown's years of working for global terror networks find him in North Africa, where an agent of the FIS (Front Islamique du Salut), an Algerian militant organization critical during the civil war of the 1990s, arranges his first assassination. Instead of the efficient single shot he's supposed to deliver, he uses the FIS's trademark technique of *égorgement*, reprised from the Algerian revolution: "[H]e wanted to know what it would feel like when he placed the blade of his knife against the man's skin, when he pushed the sharp and glistening horizon of the knife against the frontier of the skin, violating the sovereignty of another human soul, moving beyond taboo, toward the blood" (*SC* 274). These geopolitical metaphors—the "horizon of the knife," the "frontier of the skin," "the sovereignty of another human soul," violated by Shalimar's incision—develop the novel's insistence on the continuity between body and land, self and self-governance. When India finds her father dead at her doorstep in an extravagant incarnadine lake, "his throat had been slashed so violently that the weapon, one of his own Sabatier kitchen knives, which had dropped beside his corpse, had all but severed his head" (*SC* 40). Later, when Shalimar stands trial for the assassination of Max Ophuls, his lawyers wager on a "Manchurian defense," implying that Shalimar, a fool, had fallen into a kind of hypnosis by terrorist masterminds, that he had, without consciousness or will, a "new, senseless kind of sense" (384). India sits quietly through Shalimar's trial until it comes to her mother's death: "In a single, brief statement, made with an executioner's calm, she unmade the defense's case. 'That wasn't how my mother died,' she said. 'My mother died because that man, who also killed my father, cut off her beautiful head'" (*SC* 386).

Casting the story in intimate sexual terms, India's revelation both de-politicizes Shalimar's actions and invalidates his "Manchurian" defense by identifying a personal grievance as the source of his bloodlust, rather than nationalist zeal or terrorist mind control. By identifying a broken heart—not the invasion of Kashmir—as the source of Shalimar's homi-cides, the novel disavows the geopolitical dimensions of its own story, running from politics into the secular novel's favorite tropes of love, loss, and a thwarted *Bildung*.[37] Boonyi's murder, and its reductive implications of serial, terrorist violence rooted in wounded masculine pride and the vengeance of a humiliated Muslim man against his Hindu wife and Jew-ish rival are undercut by reminders of the thoroughgoing militarization of the valley and the sudden appearance of suicide bombing tactics. Fleeing the scene of his wife's murder, Shalimar "was on his way down the pine-forested hill with tears in his eyes when he heard the explosion in Shirmal and guessed the rest" (*SC* 318). If body bombs, throat slashing, and blazing temple fires are plaguing Kashmir, and the history and territory around it, the novel seems to paint a remedial picture of armed security as a salve and a hope. *Shalimar*'s thesis is inchoate, but consequential: terror is plague—horrible, inhuman, amoral, cyclical, and nonagental. Counterterror is equally nonagental, procedural and prophylactic, like quarantine. It follows that today's "epidemic" of blinding in Kashmir— one instance of countless global instances of state-sanctioned terror—is no one's fault. It's merely a function of a cruel and unaccountable nature.

The Plague of Nations

Kashmir saw an epidemic of plague in the winter of 1903–1904 that killed between 1,300 and 1,500 people.[38] Although there was no previous written record of a plague epidemic, A. Mitra, then the chief medical officer of Kashmir, notes in his *Report on the Outbreak of Plague in Kashmir* that since "one of the common abuses used by the Kashmiris is '*Piyoi Toun*,' or 'plague take you' [it] makes one think, that the people had some previous experience of this deadly disease."[39] An anecdote in Mitra's report identifies a ne'er-do-well police constable as a possible critical disease vector. In a section titled "A Mystery," Mitra recounts,

> I have heard a story but it is not confirmed by any eye-witness. This constable, probably with the connivance of his brother, who was the hospital attendant on the plague case, went into the tent and handled the dead-body for the purpose of stealing anything which could have been found. It is further said that he put his mouth on the finger of the deceased to bring out a ring biting it with his teeth. If this story is correct, which I believe it to be, plague commenced in Kashmir from a crime![40]

In the follow-up section titled "Another Mystery," he writes, "In bringing this matter to the notice of the police, I asked them to take the same steps as they would take to find out the whereabouts of a murderer, and pointed out, that this man wherever he was, would probably infect the country."[41] Mitra's text reveals the chief medical officer as an improvisatory judiciary in advance of the crime, with sanitary measures, village inspections, traveler examinations, quarantine (the term he uses is "segregation"), and body disposal serving as forms of policing under extreme

circumstances in which the sick are always already criminal, even or perhaps especially when they are, themselves, the police.[42]

In *Shalimar the Clown*, Rushdie leaves this real outbreak hanging as a
specter over the novel's present, and instead uses plague to describe the
violence befalling the region and also as a catalyst for a theory of history
in which the resurgence of epidemic—both physical and metaphysical—
connects disparate times and places in a leaping, multiemergent, and
nonlinear manner. Through its historical juxtapositions with the Second World War and—in debt to Camus's famous allegory, its literature—
plague figures contemporary violence in Kashmir as a reemergence of
the fascism of Nazi Germany, which the novel understands as a precursor
for the communalism and violent extremism of the "the iron mullahs,"
scrap metal radicals of post-Soviet decay. At the same time, and without
mounting a fully theorized critique of the nation-state form, *Shalimar*
shows how Islamist radicalism intertwines itself with both nationalism
and the logic of the nationalist world order that grew up in the wake of
the two world wars.

It is instructive to consider how *Shalimar's* Alsatian-American ambassador understands and brings about these resonances; Ophuls's is the
kind of amplified humanism the novel ironizes as the outmoded optimism of a bygone era. He is seized by wistful optimism as he stands on
the Kashmiri cease-fire line, thinking of Alsace, of "the history of his
hometown, and the whiplash movements of the Franco-German frontier
across its people's lives" (*SC* 180). He tropes universal: "Human nature,
the great constant, surely persisted in spite of all the surface differences.
One snaking frontier had made him what he was . . . [H]ad he come here,
to another such unstable twilight zone, in order to be unmade?" (*SC* 180).
The question marks the sense of vulnerability implicit in universality;
through sameness, the menaces of the ambassador's own history of religious persecution must loom heavily on the Kashmiri horizon. Reflecting on the lingering effects of postwar nationalist movements, and in a
moment of pique over the putatively absurd suggestion of Kashmiri independence, another of *Shalimar's* architects of post–Cold War political
order, an Indian army colonel known—to himself—as "Hammer," quips,

Kashmir for the Kashmiris, a moronic idea. This tiny landlocked valley
with barely five million people to its name wanted to control its own
fate. Where did that kind of thinking get you? If Kashmir, why not
also Assam for the Assamese, Nagaland for the Nagas? And why stop
there? Why shouldn't towns or villages declare independence, or city
streets, or even individual houses? Why not demand freedom for one's

bedroom, or call one's toilet a republic? Why not draw a circle around
your feet and name that Selfistan? (101–102)

Rushdie's melancholy joke points to the dismembering effects of the
swords and guns of communalism, inherited, to be sure, from the carv-
ing up of the subcontinent on the eve of independence, and from the
arming of the Afghan rebels. Self-determination in this paradigm also
"goes viral," associated by way of the historical outcome of the world
wars with the untrammeled proliferation of nations and nationalism.
In juxtaposing the lament over the slippery slope to Selfistanism with
the ambassador's dreams of autonomy and his role in the establishment of twentieth-century internationalism, *Shalimar* reconceptualizes
the legacy of the League of Nations—the outcome of the dismantling of
empires and the establishment of the mandate system as much as of a
war-reordered world—as a plague of nations.

It's worth remembering that contemporary internationalism is grafted
from the start to a concept of public health and the institutionalization
of epidemic surveillance: both the League of Nations and the United Nations recognized epidemic and global public health alongside war as one
of the most basic threats to freedom and lived existence in an increasingly globalized world, and included in each of their charters a provision for the establishment of international health governance.[43] These
organizations were seen from the start as strategic guarantors of international peace, "an important factor in the promotion of international
stability . . . [and] the development of international amity."[44] The first
head of the league's Epidemics Commission was Norman White, formerly sanitary commissioner with the government of India, for which he
drafted a linchpin report on the 1918–1919 influenza pandemic.[45] White
stands as something of a real-world counterpart for *Shalimar*'s Max—
who participates, fictionally, in the real historical event of the Bretton
Woods agreement—as the kind of war-era public servant or diplomat
who moved easily between colonial governance and international regula-
tory bodies, inevitably carrying the assumptions, approaches, and prejudices of the one into the realm of the other (figure 6.1). In channeling the
histories of previous epidemics and the resources marshalled to combat
them, the plague epidemic also instantiates a historical method in *Shalimar the Clown*. In Rushdie's historical fictions, the past is often couched
in the pluperfect or the epithetical in nested subordinate clauses, which
are often nestled next to low-voiced, parenthetical announcements of
large-scale world historical events. The following describes Shalimar's
parents, his father also a performer:

6.1 Frank G. Boudreau, *Ancient Diseases—Modern Defences* (League of Nations, 1939) (front cover).

The Alexandrian fantasy of Firdaus Noman, which caused her to insist that her fair hair and blue eyes were a royal Macedonian legacy, had provoked her most vehement quarrels with her husband, who opined that conquering foreign monarchs were pestilences as undesirable as malaria, while simultaneously, and without conceding that his behavior was in any way contradictory, reveling in his own portrayals of the arriviste pre-Mughal and Mughal rulers of Kashmir. (*SC* 73)

Here, Rushdie catalogues three historical epochs of Northern Indian conquest (Macedonian, pre-Mughal, Mughal) and connects them to the intimate history of a marriage and its patterns in a continuity of public and private, epoch and counterepoch. This discontinuous but connected series of ruptures and events creates a sense in the novel of history as a form of organicism, rendering the Kashmiri past apprehensible through the laws and dynamics of biotic life.

The critic Pheng Cheah has suggested that the inheritance of an organismic concept of nationalism from German idealism complicates the status of the nation as a revolutionary, life-bearing vehicle to freedom in the postcolonial period, and argues that postcolonial nationalism "performs the undoing of organismic vitalism."[46] While Cheah's claim that "the most apposite metaphor for freedom today is not the organism but the haunted nation" might be brought into productive conversation with the major texts of postcolonial literature and national allegory, including *Shalimar*, the concept of "organism" he works with excludes the microorganic dominions of the virus and the microbe.[47] In Rushdie's novel, the microorganism is precisely that which haunts the nation: the pestilences of foreign conquest that Abdullah Noman describes are consequently naturalized as a part of history, and history, in turn, is rendered as a body, vulnerable to the infections and imprecations of other bodies and other histories. A mass funeral for Kashmir, which takes place outside a planned night of theater in the novel's fictional 1988, the start of the real so-called Kashmir insurgency, bears this out. As a rising protest mounts in the streets, with 400,000 people "clogging up the roads," shouting "*Azadi! Freedom!*" (*SC* 281). Abdullah Noman, the star of the evening's entertainments, asks his bus driver what is going on. The driver answers flatly "It's a funeral. . . . They have come to mourn the death of our Kashmir" (*SC* 281). Politics here takes place outside the empty theater as a spectacle of regional anthropomorphic imagination—a ritual mourning of the land of Kashmir, recast as a plague victim. At the same time as it registers a universal vulnerability in the organic unfolding of history, this subordinated pluperfect narrative technique offers us a way of thinking about history as mimetic, multilateral emergence—as cyclical, resurgent pestilential spread.

In *Shalimar the Clown*, plague as a material condition upon which can be predicated a kind of historiographical causality explicitly connects the exterminating violence of the Holocaust to the present-day cataclysms of Kashmir. Max recalls the months leading up to his flight from his native Strasbourg: "history stopped being theoretical and musty and became personal and malodorous instead" (*SC* 138). Rushdie transposes this sentiment—some twenty years later—into the mouth of Pyarelal Kaul, a Hindu pandit in the novel's central village of Pachigam, who is also the father of Max's lover and Shalimar's wife, Boonyi Kaul. Once again, violence is ratcheting up in the region. The aging man calls his daughter close to him after a series of violent attacks on Hindu places of worship and explains, "In the time of Sikander the Iconoclast . . . Muslim attacks on the Kashmiri Hindus were described as falling locust swarms upon the helpless paddy crops. I am afraid that what is beginning now will make Sikander's time look peaceful by comparison" (*SC* 294). What the novel describes as a "Muslim insurgency against Indian rule" accelerates from here and seems to sicken the entire valley. Once the terror has killed the livestock, the plague moves on, in other forms, to other victims. Pyarelal is old, his orchards are failing and his bees grow weaker as his Muslim neighbors' grow stronger. He buries his face in his hands and weeps: "Our story is finished. . . . It is no longer the story of our lives, but the story of a plague year in which we have the misfortune to be around to grow buboes in our armpits and die unclean and stenchy deaths" (*SC* 295). Pyarelal describes a malodorous history, plaguey and personal like Max's before him, a fascism migrating east, proliferating in the new nations. "We are no longer protagonists, only agonists," he laments; the narrator tells us that "the exodus of the pandits of Kashmir had begun" (*SC* 295). As Pyarelal describes it, to suffer this plague is to involuntarily cede one's status as actor to the infection itself, and to be demoted to mere agonist, a function of one's religion, an agent without agency. Rushdie's representation of postwar political history here, populated with agonists, rather than protagonists, both unseats the promised rationalism of the postwar liberalism—the seemingly inevitable logic of nations, borders, and treaties, monetary exchange—and also indexes a broader tension between history as heroic and agential on the one hand and inevitable and organic, even organismic, on the other.

This tension stretches across the novel and its multiple historical and geographic sites. *Shalimar* repeatedly represents a series of identificatory politics, including nationalism, but also communalism, dynasty, religious ideology, and even professional affiliation, as varieties of a "malodorous," suppurating, "stenchy" plague. As the novel reconstructs the origin of this pestilence, a sharper picture of the figure's pointed critique of the Pakistani state and Islamism come into focus. In the lush, dreamy past of the Kashmiri villages of Pachigam and Shirmal, the portents of the coming sickness take the form of incursions from outside, each of which demands that the residents of these villages, happy in their *Kashmiriyat*, or Kashmiriness, marked by a deep history of syncretism and cooperation, state their identity and pick a side.[48] The political history of Kashmir in the period between Indian and Pakistani independence in 1947 and the Indo-Pakistani war in 1965 is described in simplified terms in the novel, but the basics follow a well-documented account: Hari Singh, the Hindu maharaja of Kashmir, a majority-Muslim state, failed to declare accession into either India or Pakistan at the time of partition.[49] Muslim militias believed to be armed by the Pakistani military entered the valley to try to force incorporation into the new Muslim nation. At the request of the maharaja, with an understanding that nationality would subsequently be determined by a popular referendum, the Indian army pushed the Islamist militants into the mountainous areas of Gilgit, Hunza, and Baltistan, thereby establishing a de facto line of control and militarizing the region. This context is important to the characters in Rushdie's novel as well as to the development of his structural metaphor of plague.

Each ratcheting up of communalism serves to sicken the valley and its inhabitants further. As if in response to the historical suffering unfolding in the shadow of the ancient Himalayas, the land grows sick, too: "In the paddies, fear grew thickly beneath the surface of the shallow water, and in the saffron fields, fear like bindweed strangled the delicate plants. Fear clogged the rivers like water hyacinth, and sheep and goats in the high pasture died for no apparent reason. . . . Terror was killing livestock, like a plague" (SC 119). Cordon-and-search operations grow careless and people die. Sons of the villages slip away into the night to join terrorist organizations. The Iron Mullah descends on the neighboring village of Shirmal and begins pronouncing the duties of the faithful from his scrap-metal pulpit. "The character of the political echelon had changed," explains the narrator. "Its new belief . . . held that the introduction of Islam in the classical period had been uniformly deleterious, a cultural calamity, and that centuries of overdue corrections needed to be made" (SC 290). Some months later, as the "rumble of convoys was heard, and the overhead roar of jets" which signify the Indo-Pakistani war of 1965, it becomes clear that "[f]ear was the year's biggest crop," and the Islamist separatists were its sowers (SC 119).

The series of crises leading up to a series of breaking points in *Shalimar* is complex and retreating, each offering itself up, at the moment of narration, as *the* crisis point. The book is structured as a synoptic historical braid, divided into chapters named for each of the main characters and returning repeatedly to the same events from different perspectives. The story returns to these punctuating events in order to approach, in a concentric fashion, the question of origin, cause, or, to use the language of epidemic, index case or etiology. The most consequential of these scenes is one that Rushdie draws from history: the elaborate feast in the Shalimar Bagh in Srinagar, during which both Shalimar the clown and

Boonyi, his future Hindu bride, are born, and which seems to set into motion the postpartition catastrophe of Kashmir. The residents of Pachigam have prepared an enormous feast and an evening of performance for the maharaja and his family and retinue. An unseasonable but not insurmountable snow begins to swirl and it is at first unclear why no one is turning up for the highly anticipated event. But rumor, compounded by anxious waiting for an audience that never arrives, warns of some great calamity. . . . The maharaja has run away; a shepherd was crucified for sending warring tribals in the wrong direction; a darkness is coming. The time of horrors is here.

In his characteristically maximalist style, Rushdie anthropomorphizes rumor, describing its prismatic character and rapid dissemination in terms both social and biological:

> In the absence of the great majority of guests, all manner of rumors came into the Shalimar Bagh, hooded and cloaked to shield themselves against the elements, and filled the empty places around the *dastarkhan*: cheap rumors from the gutter as well as fancy rumors claiming aristocratic parentage—an entire social hierarchy of rumor lounged against the bolsters, created by the mystery that enveloped everything like the blizzard. The rumors were veiled, shadowy, unclear, argumentative, often malicious. They seemed like a new species of living thing, and evolved according to the laws laid down by Darwin, mutating randomly and being subjected to the amoral winnowing processes of natural selection. The fittest rumors survived, and began to make themselves heard above the general hubbub and in the hissed or murmured noises emanating from these survivors, the loudest, most persistent, most puissant rumor, the single word *kabailis* was heard, over and over again. (*SC* 85)

For Rushdie, rumor sits alongside not only the modes of transmission associated with the insurgent "illegitimate writing . . . of law," as Gayatri Spivak has described it, but also alongside the transmissibility and reproduction of the rapidly evolving organism.[50] The rumor feast acts as a mirror not just for the social universe of Kashmir on the brink of suffering and death, but also for the novel's representation of infectious disease—the rapidly evolving contagions that threaten collective health and life—together with, and in some ways indistinguishable from Islamist terror. The *kabailis*, the most "malicious," "persistent," "puissant" of rumors, seems to knock the others out in its struggle to survive, and although Rushdie doesn't translate the word directly, it is a crucial one:

the *kabailis*, Muslim tribal people from Northern Pakistan, are identified once again as the source of this new organism, which the book calls, in no uncertain terms, a rumor, a terror, and a plague.

And then, the lights go out on the feast. "On the seventh beat of [the magician's] drum, the power station at Mohra was blown to bits by the Pakistani irregular forces and the whole city and region of Srinagar was plunged into complete darkness . . . Abdullah Noman experienced the bizarre sensation of living through a metaphor made real. The world he knew was disappearing: this blind, inky night was the incontestable sign of the times" (*SC* 88). Here, in what might be understood as the proximate source of the present suffering, the figure of plague—unleashed by "irregulars," taken up by terrorists—loosens into a Manichean inversion of the black death, becoming, instead, a death in utter blackness. The blind inky night joins the pestilence in the novel's symbolic order as figure, as condition, as metaphor-made-real. Rushdie marks this blinding horror as a legacy of fallen *Kashmiriyat*, no longer alive in the limpid lakes, the "ice blue eyes, the golden eyes, the emerald eyes" of the Kashmiri girls (*SC* 99). When the village of Pachigam falls in the novel's 1991—a punishment for the terrorist activities of the Noman brothers, among other offenses—we are told by the narrator that "[w]hat happened that day in Pachigam need not be set down in full detail, because brutality is brutality and excess is excess and that's all there is to it. There are things that must be looked at indirectly because they would blind you if you looked them in the face, like the fire of the sun. So to repeat: there was no Pachigam anymore. Pachigam was destroyed. Imagine it for yourself" (*SC* 309).

In an interview with the *Paris Review* following *Shalimar*'s publication, Rushdie explained the novel's historical juxtaposition of Nazi-occupied France and Indian-occupied Kashmir like this: "The resistance, which we think of as heroic, was what we would now call an insurgency in a time of occupation. Now we live in a time when there are other insurgencies that we don't call heroic—that we call terrorist. I didn't want to make moral judgments. I wanted to say: That happened then, this is happening now, this story includes both those things, just look how they sit together."[51] Seen through the lens of plague, however, the novel does seem to make moral judgments. Whether the beliefs expressed about Islam as the source of fear, terror, and plague are those of a retrenched and ideologically motivated Indian occupying force, or those of the Hindu villagers, or the narrator, or the author himself is of course ambiguous. What is not ambiguous is that such beliefs, ramified and elaborated in the culture at large, become themselves a kind of plague on the region in discursive terms.

What becomes of Rushdie's figural system in light of the actually existing epidemic of blindness, of eye injuries and wounds currently being inflicted on Kashmiri protesters by Indian Security forces? If the figure of plague, as in *Shalimar*, can connect various histories of fascism, nationalism, communalism, and interethnic violence by evoking the threat of contagion and the shared bodily experience it entails, then how do we conceptualize, understand, and theorize a noncontagious epidemic unleashed by the state? If, in Rushdie's imagination, the plague of Islamism induces a universal night, a collective blinding, an inky undoing of syncretism and peaceful cohabitation, how do we read the scandalous literalization of his metaphor from another point of view?

In a *nazm* (topical poem) called "Eye Bank," from the collection *Nabeena Sheher mein Aieena* (*Mirror in Blind City*), the Pakistani poet Ahmad Faraz considered the material substrate of political horror as it is imprinted in the body, on the eye. The poem was written in 1983, on the occasion of a visit to the ocular transplant unit at Johns Hopkins Medical Center during a period of the poet's self-imposed political exile from Pakistan, following his arrest for writings critical of Zia ul-Haq's military regime. The poem, also called "Eye Bank" in Urdu, reads:

I shudder at this sorry sight
How many are like this
jealous of vision
In whose portion will be no riches of witness
Whose fate to see no celebration nor celebrant
Who thirst to see the rays stream down
Who say it isn't the alighting
look to the road
Tell them come take my eyes
Before my body gives out
Before this soul of dust is also gone
Before some great calamity befalls

Save my eyes from becoming a notion
Put my eyes in their faces
Who will be able to bear though
the ruin my eyes have seen
Who will be brave enough
keep eyes open always
Even as chimeras roll down
the branches of their lashes
Even as shrapnel twists
and encamps in the breath

Even as life cries out
for the rest of life[52]

In a counterfactual literary historical mood, we might imagine this *nazm* as an answer to the increasingly dehumanizing, depoliticizing effects of Rushdie's poetics of disease. In place of omniscient distance, of knowing historical sweep, of inherited and inheritable allegories of insurgency, Faraz gives us the radical intimacy of the organ as a text of personal and public histories, handed gingerly from one body to another. In this library of eyes, each bearing its own invisible wounds, the poet cleaves closely to the material in the metaphor of dark days, dark times. The shards or shrapnel of his experience will be the inescapable curse, settling in the *rooh*—the spirit or breath—accompanying the gift of sight because the ruin he speaks of seeing—the plague of nations, of nationalism, of communal violence, of military coup and exile—is not, or ought not be confined or quarantined to an over-there, the dark zones of war-torn failed postcolonial states, whose endemic violence periodically breaks out in worldwide pandemic. There is a dark humor in this seemingly sentimental threnody, amplified by the poet's choice to render the title in transliterated English (*aiee baanak*): the pitiable sightless are not *exactly* American, but they are not *not* American either. As I read it, the whisper of a revenge fantasy slithers through the *nazm*, reminding the blind of the West that with sight, with real vision, comes the terror of what is wrought in distant places, in their name, on their watch. Such a model of historico-political epigenesis insists that the healthy body—individual or collective—is a destructive myth, an ideology that upholds projections of a global polity that can be constituted only by its unhealthy, ruinous, disabled outside. Faraz wasn't writing about the present mass blinding in Kashmir, but it is difficult not to hear his words in the voice of today's Kashmiris. When asked by the *Times* whether she was grateful to the Indian government for paying for her eight-year-old son's eye surgery, Wazira Banwo, an avid protester in her own day, answered: "Not a single person from the government has come to help. If any one of them come to me, I will tell them 'Give me your eyes, I will put them in my child.'"[53]

Rushdie's recent memoir of his years in hiding, *Joseph Anton*, establishes a more complete picture of how the figure of epidemic operates in his writing not just as an analogy for terrorism, but also, and perhaps more importantly, as the crystallization of an epidemiological episteme that relies on assumptions about the unquestioned priority of security, in both personal and global terms, and suggests forms of soft power and population sciences that derive from colonial practices of demography, sanitation, and population management.

Imaginary Homeland Security

The displacement of traditional warfare with so-called security measures is a well-documented phenomenon in the twenty-first century, with a preponderance of left and decolonial analyses building from Foucault's extensive lectures on security and biopower.[54] Apart from its philological relationship to care and the removal or banishment thereof, security is the predominant language—a simple euphemism—for the War on Terror. Counterterrorism and counterinsurgency practices have taken a variety of noninnocuous forms over the last two decades, including disputably "legal" warfare in multiple nations and regions in Africa, the Middle East, and South and Southeast Asia—international security interventions in accordance with the Responsibility to Protect doctrine, the United States' so-called signature strikes and other targeted assassinations, domestic surveillance, the suspension of civil liberties, including the Miranda rights, under Department of Justice safety exemptions, the rise of unmanned drones and drone casualty measures that categorize all military-aged men as enemy combatants. This incomplete list, to be sure, could go on.

One of the most visible and consequential ways in which discourses of global health and counterinsurgency have become bound to one another in recent years is in the conflation of and data sharing between apparatuses of biosecurity, both national and international, and counterterrorism intelligence. The United States Department of Homeland Security, for example, has not only articulated among its goals the prevention of bioterrorism, but also, in naming the Rutgers-based Center for Dynamic Data Analysis as a center of excellence in 2009, brought the study of epidemics under its purview.[55] National and international responses to epidemic outbreaks, like swine and avian influenza, have become paradigmatic of the ways in which both national and international health-monitoring apparatuses—most prominently the United States Centers for Disease Control and Prevention and the United Nations' World Health Organization and Global Influenza Surveillance Network—have collaborated with security organizations and branches of national governments to secure borders that are permeable in both material and rhetorically continuous ways to viruses and terror networks.[56]

That these mechanisms for monitoring public health are shared by the Department of Homeland Security and the Centers for Disease Control and Prevention renders acutely visible the institutionalization, legal frameworks, and mandates of biopower in the twenty-first century. The epistemological outcomes for assessing insurgent and irregular violence are no less transformative in the study of terrorism as an epidemic: the epidemiology of mortality and injury sustained during terrorist attacks is now its own, well-established branch of contemporary epidemiological research, and is not limited to the modes of Islamist violence that most often make waves in North American and European news.[57] What is perhaps more surprising is how the banality of surveillance routed through the mechanisms of security discourse co-create these two classes of threat by way of the vast likelihood of non-eventality and innocuousness. This arithmetic, represented in the sublimely large collation of normal data, is nevertheless animated by the tiny but spectacular statistical chance of malignancy. This overwhelming balance toward the ordinary—and all the sacrifices "necessary" to maintain it—is one of the most important features of security states as they are critiqued and theorized in contemporary rights discourses.

Rushdie has described personal security in similar terms: "Security was the art of making nothing happen. . . . Boredom was good. You didn't want things to get interesting. Interesting was dangerous. The whole point was to keep everything dull."[58] This observation marks the difference between the way *Shalimar the Clown* approaches and historicizes Islamist violence by telling a wild, evental story in which a great deal happens, and the way Rushdie's nonfictional writings have veered further into seamless, flat polemic characterized by an abundance of argument and philosophizing, by turns petty and thoughtful. Security, in both theory and practice, forms an important point of intersection between militarization and care in Rushdie's later works. *Shalimar the Clown*'s elaboration of Islamism and terror as a plague on the map of contemporary South Asia and its global diaspora finds its reflection outside of fiction in real-world security measures that miniaturize and localize broader diplomatic disputes and state conflict. In other words, Rushdie's interest in security takes on deeply personal dimensions.

In October 2012, Rushdie published the long-awaited memoir recounting his years in hiding following the Ayatollah Khomeini's 1989 fatwa decreeing his death for the allegedly blasphemous portrayal of the prophet Muhammad and Islam more broadly in *The Satanic Verses*. The state of Iran, first under Khomeini and later under others, upheld this decree and continually threatened to carry it out on British soil or wherever else they might find the offending writer. Other groups joined in the creation and elaboration of a bounty on the writer's head, and in 1993, the Norwegian publisher of the novel was shot three times in an assassination attempt. Earlier, in 1991, the Japanese translator of *The Satanic Verses* was stabbed to death in the face and neck. Taken with these ancillary acts and threats, the fatwa was understood broadly—though to varying degrees by differently motivated actors—as an act of terrorism, galvanized through and arguably further galvanizing radical forms of political Islam around the globe. The trope of terrorism as disease does not appear in the memoir with anything like the robustness or frequency that it does in *Shalimar the Clown*, or even in *The Satanic Verses*, where, as we will see, the treatment is lighter and more oblique. In key moments, however, the figure does some rhetorical heavy lifting, most often when Rushdie is reckoning with his growing disgust and anger with the religion in which he was raised. Following the issuing of the fatwa, he considers his predicament and its implications in the broader currents of world history, writing (in the third person),

> He knew, as surely as he knew anything, that the fanatical cancer spreading through Muslim communities would, in the end, explode into the wider world beyond Islam. If the intellectual battle was lost—if this new Islam established its right to be "respected" and to have its opponents excoriated, placed beyond the pale, and, why not, even killed—then political defeat would follow. (*JA* 346)

Recall the others who have used this metaphor or likened Muslim fanaticism to a cancer or a plague: Rumsfeld, Trump, Roberts, David Cameron, Boris Johnson.[59] As early as 1989, the Egyptian novelist Nawal El Saadawi was referring to the Rushdie case in similar terms: "this bloody terrorism which we're fighting against but which has started to spread its cancer from the arena of politics into the arena of arts and creativity."[60]

If the goal is to divorce murderous militancy from what are imagined to be the core values of Islam, the epidemic metaphor is a convenient way of imagining and representing terror, implying an enlightened view of Islam by isolating its metastasizing and life-threatening form from its putatively "good" parts. At the same time, the historical deployments of imperial disease poetics inform a sanitized, securitized world picture, in which communicability is disabled and political claims—however pernicious—are made obsolete. Rushdie's phrasing above is characteristic of the slipperiness and figural motility of this kind of language. Almost immediately, the metaphor shifts into the much more visually evocative and viscerally frightening image of the terrorist bomb: "the fanatical cancer spreading through Muslim communities would, in the end, explode into the wider world" (*JA* 346). This sentence's imagistic compression suggests that cells have the potential to turn into bombs, that the memory of public history can invoke the painful intimacy of private sickness.[61]

If global space can be anthropomorphized according to the logic of terrorism-as-cancer, what does it mean to try to keep that global body healthy, to remedy its ills? How might we understand the sanitizing language of the "surgical strike"? Where do human actors fall in naturalizing and dehumanizing figures of cellular mutation, bacterial infection, and virality? The mutually reinforcing relationship between the image of the world as single body—a projection that subtends the cancer metaphor—and the image of the world as a collection of innumerable discrete bodies that occupy the territory of the infectious and viral imaginaries produces an extraordinary range of paradoxes both in Rushdie's oeuvre, and more consequentially in Anglophone culture's conceptions of global space. We might begin with a crude schematic: where the metaphor of contagion assumes multiple persons—or in a geopolitical sense, sovereignties, each of which has the capacity to be threatened by ideological microbes and their carriers—it gives onto an idea about internationality that aligns with the possibility of legal modern warfare. The cancer metaphor differently presumes the unity of a single vulnerable body of the globe, and in so doing gives rise to a further militarization of all space, including the enactment of prophylactic strategies on the population as a single whole; the security of all, here, is the security of those who define the global.[62] The latter is in some ways more in keeping with how terrorism has been approached from the point of view of the international community, which, especially during the Obama administration, stressed intelligence and epidemiological approaches. The former, with its shades of ordinary antagonism, quarantine, and war, better represents the most publicly avowed approaches of the United States under the Bush and Trump administrations, with particular reference to Afghanistan and Iraq, as well as increased border control and surveillance at and within national boundaries, including the so-called Muslim ban. In a literary mode, at least, these visions of world space are not mutually exclusive: both tropes and their imaginative landscapes of health are at play in Rushdie's works, as well as those of many of his contemporaries.

The conflicts and discontinuities between these two existing visions of global space represent perhaps the most crucial challenges in defining, investigating, systematizing, and even narrating the prevention of Islamist terrorism.[63] For writers like Rushdie, disease has become a useful metaphor for thinking terrorism because, like acts of violence committed by nonstate actors against civilians within sovereign polities, disease respects no borders within the body or between bodies; because it lies outside of any jurisdiction or ideas about right, thereby making a mockery of the fictions that uphold various social orders; and because in so doing, it seems to defy what the leaders of wealthy secular democracies identify as "human" logic.[64] Recognizing, and in our recognition, ratifying the existence of the global as well as the space of the international and the ideas of international security and justice requires that we operate in agreement with conflicting premises and assumptions, namely that we belong doubly to the nation and to the world. It is a convenient double-bind for documented residents and citizens of North American and European countries, whose sovereignty is rarely under threat. This deep sense of belonging to a world order, in some crucial ways, mirrors the utopian undercurrents of postmodern, postcolonial, and postnational conditions of hybridity, diaspora, and cosmopolitanism whose celebration occupies the wheelhouse of the global English literary market.[65]

In the title and title essay of his 1991 collection of nonfiction, *Imaginary Homelands*, a phrase that had so much traction with other writers that it has become something of a cliché, Rushdie explores the particular fondness, pain, and guilt of having been severed from his native India, and nevertheless building his fiction through his memories of the place:

> It may be that writers in my position, exiles or emigrants or expatriates, are haunted by some sense of loss, some urge to reclaim, to look back, even at the risk of being mutated into pillars of salt. But if we do look back, we must also do so in the knowledge—which gives rise to profound uncertainties—that our physical alienation from India almost inevitably means that we will not be capable of reclaiming precisely that thing that was lost; that we will, in short, create fictions, not actual cities or villages, but invisible ones, imaginary homelands, Indias of the mind.[66]

If the imaginary homelands of fiction are the creations of diasporic and migratory writers who are tethered in some way to their "homes" but also freed of their possible attendant ethno-national myopias through their participation in the civic life of wealthy nations, these imaginary homelands are also populated by writers and artists who have moved away from the demands of telling the "truth," in a literal sense, by virtue of what Rushdie calls the inability to "reclaim precisely that thing that was lost." The emigrant's nostalgia—freed from the practical disruptions of life in the Global South—thus becomes the precondition for the extrapolation of a certain kind of cosmopolitan space, whose most important characteristic is that it gives free, uncensored reign to the imagination.

This same material substrate of cosmopolitanism has become a feature of numerous other kinds of networks of sociality and politics, especially ones with access to capital, including those of the bin Laden–imprinted global jihad, of which the fatwa against Rushdie was an early premonition. In his critical geography of Al Qaeda, *Landscapes of the Jihad*, Faisal Devji has named the phenomenon of supranational affiliation and deterritorialization in Islamism "cosmopolitan militancy." He cites Jacques Derrida's remarks on the way in which, following the September 11 attacks, Middle Eastern oil wells "remain among the rare territories left, among the last nonvirtualizable terrestrial places."[67] In spite of the transformation of oil into capital, the well remains the trace of the real, the punctum in the image of a global jihad that pins supra-regional politics to place. Devji elaborates that the legal status of massive numbers of noncitizens in the oil-rich countries of the Middle East has effectively rendered the category of citizenship, and by extension, nation, obsolete, at least inasmuch as they fail to describe a vast portion of daily interactions, explaining:

> This curious world, which may function in various forms within immigrant and other cosmopolitan enclaves elsewhere, seems to mirror rather closely the world of the jihad itself. It is, after all, the world of the global marketplace, and includes within its ambit not only multinational corporations, or transnational trading networks, but also the international students, economic migrants, illegal aliens and political refugees who form part and parcel of these commercial enterprises. . . . [M]aybe this explains why the jihad re-constitutes the Middle East or Arab world by narratives other than those of the nation or the region as distinct demographic and geographical entities characterized by collective political or economic cultures.[68]

If the rest of the world is indeed becoming more and more smooth, homogeneous, abstract, and, consequently, more imaginary, the problem of how to secure this shared homeland of the imagination follows. In the pathologizing terms of the memoir, we must also consider what such a theory implies in terms of the protection or surveillance of its creators and citizens against the "cancer" of censorious fanaticism, particularly when mere citizenship provides waning protections of all kinds.[69] Finally, who is responsible for protecting this homeland, for its security, if it overlaps in space and time with what Devji calls the new cosmopolitan militancy?

The name of the memoir (*Joseph Anton*) is also the alias Rushdie used during the period in which he was personally under the protection of the British government. To his personal security detail, he was known facetiously, and perhaps with a measure of jovial condescension, as "Joe." The alias honors two of his favorite writers—writers Rushdie identifies as exiles in their own right: Joseph Conrad and Anton Chekov. Other men of literary distinction with whom Rushdie aligns himself and his predicament over the course of the book include Milton, who wrote what is perhaps the best-known anticensorship tract in English, *Areopagitica*; Ovid, exiled by Julius Caesar to the Black Sea; Federico García Lorca, killed by Franco's "thugs"; and Osip Mandelstam, who wrote essays and poetry against Stalin's regime (*JA* 342, 628). In moments of panic over his safety and that of his family, Rushdie finds comfort in the classical dream *ars longa, vita brevis*. "Art," he writes near the end of the book, "could perhaps take care of itself . . . [but] artists needed defenders" (*JA* 628).

The performative juxtaposition of an eternal life of the mind and the grim practicalities of "security"—airlines, low-level politicians, back entrances, and death threats—drives the memoir, which critics lambasted for its arrogance, misogyny, and self-aggrandizement.[70] *Joseph Anton* expands Rushdie's earlier formulation of the imaginary homeland by frequently invoking something like a global Republic of Letters, in which the scene or place of the literary triumphantly transcends national, communal, and otherwise laughably parochial borders.[71] These bards—Ovid, Milton, Mandelstam, Lorca, and Rushdie, as he represents himself—are its honored citizens. He describes the necessity of security in response to a specific terrorist threat, but also as the period in hiding progresses, as itself a kind of ethos: "The security worldview," Rushdie writes, "was impressive, and often persuasive, but it was just one version of the truth. It was one of the characteristics of security forces everywhere in the world to try and have it both ways" (*JA* 601). A pattern emerges in the narrative in which the police discourage the writer from making public appearances, capitulate after one of his trademark temper tantrums, provide outsized security, observe no disruptions, and then claim the lack of disruptions was a direct consequence of the outsized security (and the cost of said security). When he finally returns to his native India, more than ten years after *The Satanic Verses* had been banned there, he describes the experience as a physical one analogous with healing, after having been "infected by the fears of the police" (602). In the fifth year after the fatwa, the International Parliament of Writers in Strasbourg "elected him president and asked him to write a sort of declaration of intent" (419). It was in the speech he gave, his declaration of intent, that he named the "republic of unfettered tongues," as the land of writers: "a territory far greater than that governed by any worldly power" (419). A new imaginary homeland, cancer-free and uninfected, was becoming manifest.

Earlier in the memoir, Rushdie describes his feelings of abandonment by the British government and observes himself veering toward the self-promotional monadic: "He became, having no alternative, in part an ambassador for himself" (355). It is the only instance in the memoir in which he uses this ambassadorial formulation explicitly, but it bears examination for a number of reasons. The "self" he alights on here, and the question of its sovereignty, duplicates *Shalimar*'s central question of Kashmiri independence, as it is lampooned by an officer of the Indian army: a "moronic idea," an overture to the creation of infinite Selfistans (*SC* 102). What was, in the novel a wistful joke applies, too, to Rushdie's feelings about becoming ambassador for his own Selfistan—it's not a desirable outcome. But *Shalimar the Clown*, as we have seen, is deeply interested in the security of a particular ambassador, Max Ophuls, the novel's surrogate for a nostalgic Rushdie. The fictional ambassador—who, it bears repeating, has also served secretly as United States counterterrorism chief—lives under the constant threat of assassination, and indeed is killed by Shalimar, the vengeful Muslim, equally jealous of his liberties and his liberalism. India's thought, in the moments before his murder, points us back to the imaginary Republic of Lost Homelands, the nations of the mind, as yet uninfiltrated by the cancer of terrorism, that Rushdie had been generating with the fervor of an exile for nearly two decades. "Moment by moment," India thinks, "he was leaving her, becoming an ambassador to such unthinkably distant elsewhere" (*SC* 7). This phrase mimics a much earlier locution that appears in *Imaginary Homelands*, where Rushdie describes the subtractive nature of his migrancy: "[Loss] is made more concrete for him by the physical fact of discontinuity, of his present being in a different place from his past, of his being 'elsewhere.'"[72] Prior to Max's assassination, the novel pauses on a peculiar exposition of the details of the ambassador's security arrangement:

> The sidewalk was broad. India's building had an entry-phone system. All this slowed things down, increased his window of vulnerability. There were procedures Max Ophuls knew intimately from his days in the secret job, the job whose name could not be spoken, the job that didn't exist except that it did, but the ambassador was not thinking about those procedures. He was thinking about his daughter. . . . The procedures required advance men to precede him, to block off a parking space right in front of the venue, to pre-enter the address and secure it, to hold the doors open. Any professional in this area knew that the so-called principal was easiest to attack in the space between the door of his vehicle and the door of the location he planned to enter. But the threat assessment against Max Ophuls was not high nowadays and the risk assessment was lower. Threat and risk were not the same. Threat was a general level of presumed danger, while the level of risk was particular to any given activity. It was possible for the threat level to be high while at the same time the risk attached to a given decision, for example, a last-minute whim to go see your daughter, could be negligibly low. (*SC* 39)

Two remarkably similar passages appear in the memoir: in the first, security is described specifically in epidemic terms as "sanitation."

> The most dangerous zone, the zone that could never be sanitized 100 percent, was the space between the exit door of a building and the door of a car . . . when he walked from the door of a car to the door of a building or back again, he consciously slowed down. He would not scuttle. He would try to walk with his head held high. (*JA* 176)

In the second, the author recounts the very earliest days after the issuing of the fatwa:

> The man from the [police] branch would be accompanied by an intelligence officer and they would tell him what security decisions had been made concerning the threat. *Threat* was a technical term, and it was not the same as *risk*. The *threat level* was general, but *risk levels* were specific. The level of threat against an individual might be high—and it was for the intelligence services to determine this—but the level of risk attached to a particular action by that individual might be much lower, for example if nobody knew what he was planning to do, or when. (*JA* 96)

The unmistakable correspondences between the lead-up to the assassination scene in the novel and the musings in the memoir may indicate nothing more than the imprint of a massive biographical fact on Rushdie's writing. Like all writers, he was, during this time, drawing on the peculiarities, lexicons, and conditions that surrounded him. There is more at stake here, however, as the trajectory of Rushdie's writing follows the naturalization of security and its attendant worldview as mechanisms within and between the imaginary homelands he invents and inhabits. Revisiting the disease metaphor that carries across these two texts and points back to the imaginary homelands of the essay, the implications of a securitized world-view that reaches down into territorial, sovereign space as well as up into the space of the "unthinkably distant elsewhere" become clearer: just as the figures of cancer, viruses, and infectious diseases index our fear of those unavoidable, ineradicable threats that defy the logic of law, war, nation, and territory, so too do terrorists. Against both, interstitial spaces require sanitation. To make the point more sharply, Rushdie makes his fictional terrorist succeed, where those who threaten his actual life have not. Shalimar, a double fugitive, simply walks off a prison yard wall onto the gathered air of the night and up into the heavens, "as if he were running up a hill" (*SC* 176).

As it is rendered in the novel, there is a great beauty and sweetness in Shalimar's escape off the boundary wall, even if it achieves for him only a temporary freedom. It reflects some of Rushdie's most ethical moments of thinking in the memoir, as when he writes, "'If you succumb to the security disposition of the world . . . then you will be its creature forever, its prisoner.' . . . This was a thing he would have to remember. *There were only varying degrees of insecurity*" (*JA* 207–208). Shalimar's moment of departure—which literalizes the escape from prison—is both an acknowledgement of the existence and persistence of varying degrees of uncertainty and insecurity, and also a release of something resembling the spirit of the terrorist's character into moral indeterminacy—an escape, in other words, from an outright condemnation that would imprison a reading of this character as simply sexually humiliated and vengeful. What this gathered air makes visible is perhaps one of the most challenging questions of the book. It at once materializes the discontinuous continuity of historical epochs suggested by Rushdie's juxtapositional strategy of putting Second World War liberation movements alongside Kashmiri unrest; the alternating of condensation and dilation—the sense of concrete abstraction that characterizes the space of the sky in the era of air-power and air-travel; the pathways of regional and international networks that sometimes trace bodily itineraries and sometimes just ideological ones; and the invisible vectors of contagion that carry the ancient plagues of violence, of certain forms of politics, and of the sickness of the body itself from time to time and place to place. In short, it is a figure for the transformation of the abstract, or what appears to be abstract, into the manifest and back again, with or sometimes without a trace. Each of these possible indices of vectored flight shuttles in the space of the system or the network that, once again, falls outside of available rubrics of good or evil and instead constitutes the neutrality of relationality and network as such. They have simply come to be; the gathered air that holds things aloft, deterritorializes them, is as neutral—as hijackable—as an airplane.

The Falling Sickness

More than a decade before the publication of Edward Said's *Orientalism*, and more than a decade, too, before the Revolution, the Iranian sociologist and critic Jalal Al-i Ahmad wrote a book-length essay called *Gharbzadegi*, or *Occidentosis: A Plague from the West*, mounting a scathing critique of orientalism, which he claimed was "almost certainly a parasite growing on the root of imperialism."[73] Giving voice to the sources of a growing Marxism in Iran, Al-i Ahmad described his fellow countrymen's blind devotion to Western values, including industrialization, as a form of cultural toxicity akin to "tuberculosis . . . a disease, an accident from without, spreading in an environment rendered susceptible to it. Let us seek a diagnosis for this complaint," he demanded, "and if possible, find its cure."[74] The ending of *Occidentosis* finds kinship, somewhat surprisingly, with a cluster of European modernism's plague and apocalypse narratives: Camus's *The Plague*, Ionesco's *Rhinoceros*, and Bergman's *The Seventh Seal*. In turning to these humanisms and their allegories of disease in order to defend an analogous thesis of the plagues of Western civilization, *Occidentosis* might be understood to simply flip the hierarchy of the epidemic metaphor's dominant East-West paradigm. This is Edward Said's take. Commenting on the work in a survey of the aftermath of his own *Orientalism*, Said derided Al-i Ahmad's argument as "on the whole extremely tiresome and boring," a different and equally bad species of "nativism" to that which it disavowed.[75] He continues, "The same thing"—meaning the nativism of Al-i Ahmad and his ilk—"operates in the Salman Rushdie case."[76] Even as he steps in to defend Rushdie against the attacks on *The Satanic Verses*, Said's criticism of Al-i Ahmad and others' "politics of identity" misses the affordances of *Occidentosis*'s perhaps unconscious but nevertheless powerful intervention in the colonial history of epidemics and their study.[77]

Al-i Ahmad calls Occidentosis "an accident from without, spreading in an environment rendered susceptible to it," and in this gesture, reifies the epidemic as a force of poiesis in the creation of a "without" as much as a "within," the "environment rendered susceptible to it." *Epidemic* means, literally, "that which is upon the people," articulating a distinction between the people, as victims, from that which has befallen them. At the same time, the term raises the question of who counts as the people, and registers an anxiety with regard to the *demos* as a category that requires protection, but that can also turn on itself through the circulation of contagion, or through what Jacques Derrida, in a number of his later works, theorized in the concept of autoimmunity.[78] Although Derridian autoimmunity aims to illuminate the specific mechanisms by which communities turn on themselves, and instantiate "cruelty itself, the autoinfection of autoaffection," Derrida is concerned, especially in the works devoted to terror, with extreme forms of ipseic risk, culminating in the suicide or other forms of the self-annihilation of the democratic state at its own hands, as in the case of the 1992 elections in Algeria.[79] Even when they come from within, in Derrida, as in Rushdie, such epidemics of terror seem constitutively to "befall" a community, suggesting the naturalization of acts of violence as something organic, rather than as political articulations or deliberate acts of faith, however anathema such ideas may be. A theory of terror as autoimmunity thus persists, in the vein of the colonial epidemic imaginary, in ascribing the logic of infection and sickness to acts committed by human agents, even if for Derrida this isn't exactly a depoliticizing move. Even as it unfolds the same paradigm, Al-i Ahmad's work—at least the potential reversal of the dominant directionality of the disease poetics of empire—has important legacies in more fully subverting what we have seen thus far in the colonial and postcolonial archive. Shifting the locus of cultural toxicity and infection to the West may be the move of a dialectician rendered dumb by East-West binaries, but it is also one that opens up the possibility, through the politics Al-i Ahmad wishes to instantiate, of a community of the sick, and political action toward a horizon of both incorporation and a newly defined healability apart from immanence. Such an instantiation is what Roberto Esposito has in mind in the final turn of his remarks on immunity as "a nonexcluding relation with its common opposite. . . . not the enemy of the common, but rather something more complex that implicates and stimulates the common."[80]

As it works in the two books I have thus far discussed, the elaboration of the figure of epidemic terror upholds fantasies of rational mastery through data collection and analysis; projective modeling and historical transposition; the eradication of pathogenic microbes, viruses, and human beings; and the installation and justification of a broad, international security apparatus to defend those privileged citizens of the cosmos, the writers and migrants born of imaginary homelands. The evolution of these tropes in the work of a single writer should not be mistaken as a signal of their insignificance in postcolonial and Anglophone writing. The real-world consequences of Rushdie's fictions are surprisingly direct; the years he spent under government protection in Britain and the United States made his personal opinions about censorship, global Islamist violence, and later the religion of Islam more broadly, fall on the ears of some of the most powerful officials in the world. According to the memoir, politicians requesting signed copies of *The Satanic Verses* was de rigueur. In light of the unlikely confluence Rushdie describes between security strategy, lawmaking, international negotiating, and fiction reading, the stakes of imperial disease poetics in his body of work are not only broad, but profoundly material. It remains unclear to me whether Rushdie was aware of Al-i Ahmad's book, which was translated from the Persian in 1984. He has never commented on it publicly, or, to my knowledge, in the unredacted portions of the journals. In the scenes of *The Satanic Verses* in which the fallen angel Gibreel Farishta dreams the "Imam," a veiled reference to Khomeini during his exile, the unappealing, joyless religious leader declaims, "The habit of power, its timbre, its posture, its way of being with others: it is a disease . . . infecting all who come too near it. If the powerful trample over you, you are infected by the soles of their feet."[81] This scene replicates the flipped dialectic of *Occidentosis*: the Imam maintains a clash-of-civilizations deployment of the epidemic thesis. But in the Ayesha narrative, and in the novel's tropicalization-of-Europe fantasy, *The Satanic Verses* experiments in much more optimistic and open ways than the later books with both the potential for disease to instantiate radical forms of affiliation, as well as for a generative Islamic counterorthodoxy—the novel's imagined legacy of the apocryphal "Satanic" of fallen verses—to open up a secular Muslim path not taken.

In the final section of this chapter, I argue that this opening becomes the greatest resource in the early work of Rushdie, who, unlike Al-i Ahmad in his time, and partly in consequence of the rapid evolution of *The Satanic Verses* into a paragon of antifanatical free speech, has had an enormous global platform and surprisingly material effects on national and international policy. Put simply, *The Satanic Verses* stands as a counterparadigm for the articulation of epidemic terrorism as it appears in *Shalimar the Clown* and *Joseph Anton*. Contrary to the strong correlation between plague and communalism, or cancer and Islamism, in the later books, disease in *The Satanic Verses* performs an ambiguous but largely positive political function. The figure appears in a number of forms, as a swirl of communicable tropical diseases—a punishment Gibreel Farishta calls down on a cold, unfeeling London—and as the noncommunicable conditions of epilepsy and breast cancer, which become transmissible affectively, through acts of prophecy. While sickness is coded as classically tragic, it is also constantly linked to the ideas of recognition, reproduction, and rebirth. Disease, in other words, can lead to suffering, but it is also dedifferentiating and affiliative. This generative counterparadigm of epidemic and disease (which are to some extent differentiated in this book by virtue of the latter's noncommunicability) takes place in two of the novel's major subplots: first in the Ayesha hajj, and second in the "tropicalization" of London at the hands of its dark-skinned warm-climate-derived immigrants.[82]

Like most of Rushdie's novels, *The Satanic Verses* unfolds in multiple historical time periods, even as events, characters, and language ramify across temporal and geographic barriers. The main four strands take place in *jahiliyya* (pre-Islamic times in Mecca and Medina), then-contemporary immigrant London, the fictional Indian village of Titlipur, and the exile of Khomeini in Paris (the novel puts him in London) during the Islamic Revolution in Iran. In Titlipur, the most ordinary of the novel's sites, two women, Mishal and Ayesha, suffer side by side from

246 : CHAPTER 6

noncontagious afflictions, one from breast cancer, and the other from epilepsy, which is also called in the novel "the falling sickness." This nomenclature reflects one of the novel's most evident thematic concerns, the synchronicity of physical and metaphysical falling: devils and angels collide from the start, plummeting together from the upper atmosphere to earth, while a pet secular interpretation holds that the prophet Muhammad's visions of revelation were actually epileptic fits.[83] The two women's ailments—the falling sickness and breast cancer—are noninfectious. The novel's primary narratives of malady and metastasis resist, therefore, the association of disease with contagion and transmissibility.

Instead, *The Satanic Verses* stages a crucial translation from illness to prophecy, such that language and idea become capable of viral spread, and their infectiousness occasions not the untrammeled dissemination of communalism and ideological violence as in Rushdie's later writings, but rather the formation of new communities. In desacralizing the Qur'an by calling its status as sacred transmission into question through transcription errors and texts that function as contagious vectors of communication, the novel evinces an interest in the worldliness of the text—indeed, its embodiment as nonbiological seed or germ. Ideas, even good ideas, are shown to spread through vectors of contact. Through episodes of pilgrimage, conversion, and migration, the novel's configuration of violence and disease holds open the potential of a deracinated, supranational politics of affiliation—a global *ummah*, conceived as anticapitalist, anticaste, and anticlass—which can be understood as distinct from the biological lineages of filiation that have historically structured national and territorial imaginaries of belonging, or, as Said puts it, "natural bonds and natural forms of authority—involving obedience, fear . . . respect, and institutional conflict."[84] In this way, *The Satanic Verses* also disrupts the hegemonic notion of the body politic as "natural" and whole, and the healthy normative body as a model for family, polity, and state, finding potential for revolutionary politics in both illness and disability, even at the risk of romanticizing both.[85]

Rushdie's inquiry into the birth of novel forms—both physical and conceptual—allows for a politically supple critique of religion, belief, and secularism that transcends the category of polemic into which the novel is so often inserted. Islam itself works flexibly in Rushdie's fiction as religion, but also as a word of reproduction and of unorthodox labor, in the sense of work and in the sense of birth. Rushdie makes the meaning of Islam as submission—and the vertical relationality embedded therein—a leitmotif in the novel, using the two words interchangeably. *The Satanic Verses* consistently associates Islam, especially early Islam and South Asian Islam—with disenfranchisement and exile, explaining, "the followers of the new faith of Submission found themselves landless, and therefore poor" (*SV* 375). The early followers of the fictional prophet are depicted as radicals, aiming to overturn the economic structure that oppresses them as a result of their exile: "[T]hey financed themselves," he writes, "by acts of brigandage, attacking the rich camel trains on their way to and from Jahilia" (*SV* 375). Though the novel places them on different sides of an ethical bright line, these brigands—"irregular" foot soldiers fond of ambushing travelers—anticipate and invite comparison to the other forms of "irregular warfare" that appear in the novel, particularly the air-terrorism that appears in the opening hijacking scene, which was modeled after the real-world hijacking and explosion in 1985 of Air India flight 182.

This double sense of submission and its reproduction, submission's ability to be hijacked as an idea, to instantiate an insurgent politics, is embodied in *The Satanic Verses* in the character of Osman, who is born an untouchable and converts to Islam for the practical purpose of gaining access to a well that was forbidden to his touch under Hindu law.[86] Like the *kooan*, the navel in Urdu, which also means well, this point of access serves as both umbilical nourishment and also as the traditional gathering place of the village. Extending the valences of reproduction and renewal, water—in the tradition of Islamic ablutions—works consistently in the novel to purify and to melt away. When Islam takes hold of Osman for mercenary reasons that include the potential for incorporation in a new community, the text stages the spreading of the religion of submission at the originary scene of epidemic dissemination. In the historico-religious imaginary of *The Satanic Verses*, Osman's mercenary conversion is a departure from the realm of the religious and a migration into a narrative of collectivity, of the political, a migration out of untouchability and a fall into belonging.

The novel opens with an iconic free-fall-from-heaven. Two men, one named Gibreel after the angel Gabriel, tumble through the sky in an embrace of intimate necessity; their aircraft, on its way from Bombay to London, has been exploded by a young woman terrorist over the English Channel. Before she pulls the wire attached to an undergarment of explosives—"all those fatal breasts," as the author describes them—concealed beneath her *djellabah*, or robe, Tavleen, the sole female member of the quartet of Sikh separatists who have hijacked the airplane, gently intones the prophecy the text will proceed to fulfill over the course of its many histories (*SV* 89). She says, softly in a voice that is described as "oceanic": "Martyrdom is a privilege. . . . We shall be like stars, like the sun" (*SV* 88). Though Tavleen is a Sikh separatist, in the novel's nod to the Khalistan movement which accelerated in the 1980s and 1990s, she is camouflaged by a *djellabah*, a traditionally Berber garment that invokes the iconography of North African insurgency—especially in Algeria. As she lifts her robe to reveal an arsenal of "fatal breasts," we glimpse the novel's interest in figures of reproduction and maternity adjacent to the violence of communal belief. The airplane that explodes is figured as a reproductive hybrid: in one instance it's described as an exploding "seed pod," scattering its germ and "an egg yielding its mystery" while in another moment it becomes a hyperfertile metal womb aloft, carrying its hostages in a "second gestation," after which they will pass through the birth canal of the freezing, limpid sky to be reborn on the shores of England (*SV* 4, 85). One of the falling men foretells this monstrous dissemination and wonders before the explosion, "[H]ow do you call it when fifty kids come out of the same mother?" (*SV* 85). A more eloquent pair of questions follows: as they fall from the shattered egg womb in the sky, Gibreel Farishta—Farishta is a Farsi loan word for angel—asks, "How does newness come into the world? How is it born?" Versions of these questions, which have become refrains in postcolonial studies to investigate the circulation and transmission of literary and other cultural forms, point to the promise of new political forms as well, the affiliative politics of a diasporic community.[87] They are particularly inflected here by Rushdie's inquiry into the origins of Islam in sixth-century Arabia through the figure of Gibreel and the question of revelation. These questions, "How does newness come into the world? How is it born?" in this exact form, also filter through the novel's fragmented consciousness and come tripping off of the tongues of each of its main characters, who are separated by great distances of space and time.

One such historical leap brings us Ayesha: the Mirza Saeed Akhtar, husband of the recently diagnosed Mishal, looks with longing and befuddlement at an accidental prophetess and asks her, "What kind of idea are you?" Long before he asks her this, the orphan girl sits naked in his garden eating butterflies—in Urdu they are called *titli*, and their abundance in this village gives it its name, Titlipur. Rushdie's Urdu/English pun, the city of butterflies as the city of "tits," plays with the gauzy image of a breast miasmatised as a nourishing cloud of insects. Ayesha, in the moment she appears, is thus parented by the atmosphere of the village, drawing nourishment from the gossamer insects as they funnel down into her mouth. A seizure interrupts her lepidopteric feast—Ayesha, in the long tradition of seers and sufferers touched by God, has been afflicted with epilepsy, or "the falling sickness." These swoons, indistinguishable from Farishta's lucid dreams, give Ayesha access to revelation, even as they contain in repetitious miniature the Miltonic fall from heaven with which the novel begins. The beautiful young mystic forges a friendship with the man's wife, Mishal, from the ore of absent maternity: Ayesha, named for Muhammad's wife who carries the moniker *"umm al mu'uminin"* or "mother of the believers" is an orphan; Mishal is unhappily childless. Mishal is about to learn that she has fatal cancer that has metastasized in both of her breasts, a fact which Ayesha reveals to her alongside other messages she claims to be receiving from the Angel Gabriel, even as the character Gibreel dreams the prophetess into existence. Among these messages is the conviction that Mishal's recovery will be contingent upon a mass pilgrimage to the sea, whereupon the waters will part, and the villagers, including Mishal, will walk to Mecca. Mishal's breasts, riddled with disease, double the "fatal breasts" of the suicide bomber, Tavleen. Taken together, these women constitute the novel's attenuated representation of disease, violence, and the reproducibility of ideas through multiple characters who are reborn in each other through the metonym of their deadly organs of maternal nourishment.

The man, the Mirza Saeed Akhtar, enters his bedroom to find Mishal and Ayesha "facing each other, grey eyes staring into grey, and Mishal's face . . . cradled between Ayesha's outstretched palms" (*SV* 239). Ayesha's embrace of Mishal prefigures the catastrophic end of the pilgrimage they will undertake together: the folding of the sea onto the two women and their cohort, an image of melding, of grey eyes staring into the grey of other eyes, and beyond them, the grey of the sea. Though he would expunge to some extent the religious associations originally attached to it in Romain Rolland's description of the oceanic as a dramatic fall into religious sensation—the notion that one belongs to, and indeed is protected by, a vast receiving body into which one can dive or plunge—it is worth recalling here the Freudian association of the oceanic and the maternal. The ocean of the women's eyes, and the ocean toward which they will undertake their healing pilgrimage—recalling the oceanic voice of Tavleen—serves a dedifferentiating function, rendering the border between bodies permeable, meltingly unified. If for Freud the "oceanic" points to a recognition of suicide's necessary incompleteness—the sense that even when we face a "self-inflicted death," "we shall not fall out of this world. We are in it once and for all"—this incomplete end, disrupted by the immanence of falling, is mirrored in Ayesha's co-pilgrims, who walk into the water, but cannot, within the parameters of the novel's logic, fall out of life, or, as it were, the story.[88]

Mishal and Ayesha's friendship, the linking of their fates, and their increasing indistinguishability from each other prove disastrous both for their village and for Mishal herself. Fog, like the ocean mists displaced, has come to rest over the village and swarms of color-changing butterflies cling to the trees and grasses and people like low, sticky clouds.

Increasingly agitated by her visions and revelations, Ayesha proposes her plan to the *panchayat*—the ruling council of the village—and, Rushdie writes, it was as if "her silence infected everyone" (*SV* 242). Ayesha's infectious silence is a part of her prophecy. As with Muhammad's contested revelations—the so-called Satanic verses—her revelation can go awry, be infected by a presemantic silence, untethered from its source, from explication and elaboration. Gibreel's Miltonic fall in the opening pages of the novel advances an argument against the ordinary uses of the epidemic trope in colonial letters, demonstrating in positive, affiliative terms the capacity of revelatory or prophetic speech to become detached from its source, to mutate and to fall or err, to go rogue. This argument anchors the proliferative movements of the novel in the form of the epigraph from Defoe's *History of the Devil*, which associates Satan's fall with the unmoored migration in the imperium of air and liquid waste: "Satan, being thus confined to a vagabond, wandering, unsettled condition, is without any certain abode; for though he has, in consequence of his angelic nature, a kind of empire in the liquid waste of air, yet this is certainly part of his punishment, that he is . . . without any fixed place, or space, allowed him to rest the sole of his foot upon" (*SV* frontmatter).

The villagers agree to Ayesha's plan, rapt in her prophetic quiet, and anxious for a chance to perform the hajj to Mecca. Mirza Saeed protests in familiar terms: "The devil alone knows what germ this whore has infected the villagers with!" (*SV* 245). The promiscuity of prophetic language aligns here with the promiscuous woman: both, we are reminded, are unreliable media, suspicious proxies or carriers of the divine seed of language. Saeed's invocation of infection anticipates as well the illness and suffering that will occur as a result of their arduous walk. As they walk, "the land browned under rainless skies. The corpses of buses and ancient monuments rott[ed] in the fields beside the crops . . . trees st[ood] on roots exposed by soil erosion . . . looking like huge wooden claws scrabbling for water in the earth" (*SV* 493). Those who remain are, by the time they reach the water, a "lame, tottering, rheumy, feverish, red-eyed bunch," Saeed wonders "how many of them would manage the final few yards to the water's edge" (*SV* 515). Nevertheless, they do this. Muslims, Hindus, untouchables, the young, the old, resisting chaperones, zealous toy-peddlers, even titans of industry: they all catch the Ayesha pathogen—Mirza Akhtar describes it as "an eczema of the spirit that maddened him because there was no way of scratching it"—and walk behind her to the edge of Ma-Bharat, Mother India, to enter the waters.

The pilgrimage is an episode Rushdie adapts from contemporary Pakistani history. In 1983 a young woman named Naseem Fatima lead thirty-eight Shia Muslims to their demise on the Hawke's Bay beach in Karachi with promises of an ocean that would open like a book, and convey them, like lines of prayer, to the holy city of Mecca.[89] As in the novel, the survivors were charged by the police with attempting to emigrate without visas. As we know well from the Rushdie affair, at the base of *The Satanic Verses*'s inquiry into novel forms is the birth of Islam itself. In repeatedly asking Ayesha, "What kind of idea are you?" and "How does newness come into the world? How is it born?," the novel inflects the question of prophetic dissemination with disability as well as with noncontagious epidemic form.[90] The Ayesha episodes offer up an idea—a bad one, sort of, and sort of not—hailing from the land of the pure, plucked from the news, and remodeled and hybridized, "deracinated," as Sara Suleri has put it.[91] In abstracting the identity of the Shias in Pakistan to a more generalized Muslim populace in India, Rushdie creates a parable for the tragic fate of a community that is seen as a metastasizing force on the maternal body of the Subcontinent.

The stakes of this dislocation are highlighted by the nomenclature of pilgrimage. The *padyatra*—foot pilgrimage—draws on the powerful memory of Gandhi's 1930 Salt March, a key moment in the independence struggle in which the Mahatma incited his followers to walk from Ahmedabad to Dandi to protest the British monopoly on salt and the heavy taxes levied on its trade. The Ayesha pilgrimage is thus strongly associated with the activities of a liberatory politics whose horizon was the birth of a democratic nation, but which also contained the seeds of partition of the Subcontinent. Instead of hajj, the word Rushdie uses for the Ayesha pilgrimage is a specifically Sanskrit-derived one: *padyatra* is a foot pilgrimage from an implicitly Hindu standpoint. In the novel, Hindu nationalists and communalists object to the "hijacking" of a long-standing Indian practice: "Padyatra, or foot pilgrimage, is an ancient pre-Islamic tradition of national culture," onlookers object, "not imported property of Mughal immigrants." This Muslim girl, they argue, ought not co-opt a Hindu practice; it's "a flagrant and deliberate inflammation of already sensitive situation" (*SV* 502). *Pad*, they insist, is for Hindu feet, *yatra* is for Hindu pilgrimage. They shout from the roadside "NO ISLAMIC PADYATRA! BUTTERFLY WITCH, GO HOME" (*SV* 503). Still, the prophetess, an oblique figure for Gandhi's slow march toward democracy, welcomes everyone, and an impediment thrown up by Hindu nationalists is washed away by an apocalyptic flood, which has come too late to save the crops, but just in time to save the pilgrims. In the moments before the healing waters arrive, Mirza Saeed muses, "we have suffered from a kind of disease: one of detachment, of being unable to connect ourselves to things, events, feelings" (*SV* 504).

The flood sets the scene for the entering of the maternal ocean—"it was as if God had been saving up the water for just this purpose, letting it build up in the sky until it was as endless as the sea"—and for a double rebirth (*SV* 505). The pilgrims walk calmly into the water. Witnesses attest to diving deeper and deeper to rescue them, only to find the waters parted, like hair, the pilgrims "going along the ocean floor," as Osman puts it, "among the dying fish" (*SV* 518). A police officer, who has arrived at the beach to keep order, greets a wet and desperate Saeed with a simple question: "What is befalling?" he asks (*SV* 517). This question addresses itself not just to the frantic man, but to the novel as a whole, a version of Islamic history in which the "falling sickness" has taken hold of them all. Mishal's mother, another witness to the parting waters, confirms the status of her witnessing as recitation: "Believe, don't believe," she finishes emphatically, "but what my eyes have seen, my tongue repeats" (*SV* 518) (figure 6.2). Like Ayesha's prophetic speech, a symmetrical foil for the errancy of revelation at the hands of the untrustworthy Persian scribe, these acts of witness stage the birth of affiliation as an originary interpen-

6.2 Daisy Rockwell, *Oscar, Wow! III* (2010). Courtesy of the artist.

etration of eye and tongue, of saying and seeing—an act of transmission
in which witness cannot simply be believed or enacted, but must first be
received and interpreted.

The second rebirth occasioned by the Ayesha pilgrimage is Mirza
Saeed's, though it arrives many years later, after his return to Titlipur.
As he sits on his dusty verandah, overlooking his broken land and remembering his wife, Saeed begins to fall out of life, seeing Ayesha under
the water, glorious with "tentacles" of light streaming out of her navel.
He struggles, begins to chop wildly at the radiant umbilical cords, and
they both begin to drown. The gates of paradise, the heavy water, he
thinks, are slamming in his face. At this moment, Saeed "made a different choice," and "his body split apart from his adam's apple to his groin,
so that she could reach deep within him, and now she was open, they all
were, and at the moment of their opening the waters parted" (SV 520–521).
In re-entering each other's bodies through the outflow of umbilical light
in an act of poetic, impossible reproduction, the pilgrims are drawn out
of the depths, are thrown back up into the firmament from which they
fell. In their luminous ascendancy, they have become, as Tavleen with
her arsenal of deadly breasts prophesied, "like stars, like the sun" (SV 88).

The horizon of the pilgrimage and the prophecy of Ayesha is that of
non-filiative reproduction, and of healability: for Mishal, for the village,
for the desiccated land, for the nonbelievers even in their nonbelief, for
the wounds of partition. Ayesha's words, "everything will be required of
us, and everything will be given," contain within them an ambivalence,
and a potential for that which befalls the people—indeed for their falling
itself, for the falling sickness—to occasion such a rebirth (SV 232, 239,
240, 242, 245). In entering the grey waters pointed toward but without
arriving at Mecca, the pilgrims demonstrate the ambiguous status of an
idea that can be hijacked away from religion, an idea that can spread and
metastasize, can be borne, like an illness, but can also be born like new
life, can gather and affiliate, and can also bear them along. In comparison to the rest of the novel, the Ayesha hajj has the virtue of satisfying
readers' thirst—in what is admittedly a drier, more academic climate
than many of Rushdie's other books—for the satisfaction of pain and
fatality transubstantiated, made divine. In this way, the book is far more
imprinted by religious—specifically Abrahamic—iconography than a
reader who came late to Rushdie would be given to expect. In this profane and erotic encounter between the girl-prophet and the godless, age-
ing landowner, *The Satanic Verses* filters across the fragile membrane
between the aesthetic and secular appropriations of religious themes,
and a genuine experiment with the political dimensions of eschatology,
passion, and infinite love.

If the question of revelation, epiphany, and spiritual transformation is made visible in the Ayesha narrative as a traveling vector at odds with the noncontagiousness of epilepsy and breast cancer, *The Satanic Verses* also presents a more explicit political affiliation through the figure of a concrescence of contagious diseases and other afflictions from the third world. This is the novel's depiction of "tropicalization"—a backward glance to the discourses of tropical disease and epidemic in the nineteenth century—repurposed here as a swirling amalgam of radical politics through which minority groups in Britain challenged the dominant agendas of Thatcher-era political liberalism.[92] Fallen Gibreel Farishta finds himself disappeared in London, self-spirited away from a crowd throning with sinister tones. Now in flight above the city, he is aloft in different, more urban air. Hovering over the vast city, armed with his *London A–Z*, he determines that the problem with England is that "they were English: damn cold fish!" (*SV* 363). In response to this problem, and its many violent consequences for the struggling and marginalized migrants of England, Gibreel styles himself the "great Transformer," and, like an unseen pandemic, prepares to bring the city to its knees. "Truth is extreme," he muses, "it is *so* and not *thus*, it is *him* and not *her*, a partisan matter, not a spectator sport. It is in brief *heated*. . . . City," he bellows, "I am going to tropicalize you" (*SV* 365). Among other narrative results, including the famous melting of political effigies in the Hot Wax nightclub, and the coalition of West Indian, African, and South Asian migrants to which this event gives rise, Gibreel's threat of tropicalization is tantamount to reverse colonialism. His new order will be forged from better friendships, from "religious fervour, political ferment, renewal of interest in the intelligentsia," but also "cholera, typhoid, legionnaire's disease, cockroaches, dust, noise, and a culture of excess" (*SV* 365–366).

In coding tropicalization as the touchstone of the novel's politics of extremity, Rushdie offers yet another possibility for the political projection of epidemic as isomorphic with forms of insurgent violence, even as it intersects in some cases with forms of domestic and international terrorism. This is where the productive capacities of the novel's epidemic imaginary begin to break down and point us to the later, more jaundiced Rushdie. To balance the hot optimism of this London boiling, the novel has already given us the monstrous, failed scenes of the Iranian Revolution in images of a throbbing, self-consuming swarm—scenes that certainly played into the ayatollah's objections to the book. Perhaps one of the novel's greatest achievements, particularly when read in light of the later works' intractable pessimism with regard to the potential of political Islam and third-world politics more broadly, is that these representations of affiliation and disease don't fall easily into favorable or unfavorable categories. They are rather juxtaposed with one another in peculiar ways through the trans-historical figure of disease. The practice of writing fiction through the lens of epidemic history invites a perpetual reading and rereading of fictional space as a dynamic interpenetration of surfaces and revelations, agential action and natural affliction. At the same time, perhaps the discovery of likeness in the unlike is another unlucky attempt at humanist universalism: an arrogant, rationalist proposition mired in the epistemologies of depth and truth. Gibreel Farishta entertains this thought:

> When you looked through an angel's eyes you saw essences instead of surfaces, you saw the decay of the soul blistering and bubbling on the skins of people in the street. . . . As he roamed the metamorphosed city he saw bat-winged imps sitting on the corners of buildings made of deceits and glimpsed goblins oozing wormily through the broken tilework of public urinals for men. (SV 331)

Farishta claims to see through London's surface to what lies beneath, an underlayer of gargoyles, devils, parasites, and serpents. He sees the decayed souls of the people erupting like buboes on the skin. Farishta, like Jalal Al-i Ahmad in his Occidentotic vision, sees the "essence" of London, but it is also simply the essence, partially reordered, of the very plague that colonial history has seen before as it gazed on the choleric swamps of Bengal, the swarming casbah in Algiers, the insurgent forts at Delhi, the armed militants creeping into Kashmir, the terrorists in our midst.

CHAPTER 7

Cures from Within

The worst sickness of mankind originated in the way in which they have com-
batted their sicknesses, and what seemed to cure has in the long run produced
something worse than that which it was supposed to overcome.

FRIEDRICH NIETZSCHE, *DAYBREAK*

As we continue to battle against al Qaeda, we must overcome a movement—a
global movement infected by al Qaeda's radical agenda.

GEORGE TENET, STATEMENT TO THE U.S. SENATE COMMITTEE
ON ARMED SERVICES

Even in the midst of a catastrophic global pandemic, there are patterns
in what kinds of societies believe themselves to be subject to infectious
disease, just as there are patterns in what kinds of actors are perceived
to be agents of destruction beyond the parameters of legitimate violence. No legal definition of terrorism today offers enough solidity to
function as anything but a vector toward the question of a bomber's or
a hijacker's or a gunman's ethnicity and religious beliefs. When Cathy
McMorris Rodgers, congresswoman from Washington State and chair
of the House Republican Conference stated in a July 2016 Republican
Leadership Press Conference,

> My heart breaks every time I see these continued attacks around the
> world on people that are doing . . . just going about their daily lives.
> Sadly Paris, Brussels, San Bernardino, Orlando, Syria, Iraq, Turkey . . .
> they're just some of the places impacted by the rise of Islamic terror-
> ism. We have a global terrorism epidemic . . . ,

she defined, once again, a "security archipelago," to borrow Paul Amar's
generative term, that maps on to the global body worth defending against
such epidemics.[1] Implicit here is the nonhumanity of those who do not
rise to the list of the "impacted," or, to stay with McMorris Rodgers's
tired metaphor, the afflicted. The epidemic here, as in Algeria, as in the

Indian anticolonial struggle, is "Islamic terrorism," two words whose binding operation is now a matter of irrevocable discursive history. In the previous chapters, I have shown how the structure of uneven political relations and lopsided sovereignty lends itself, in the age of empire, to an extended and historically significant reconceptualization of colonial and anti-insurgent warfare as a brand of morally and politically neutralized counterepidemic. Epidemic becomes more than a metaphor in this period. It occasions an epistemological revolution in thinking the future of neoimperial armed conflict and international security.

Approaching an "Approaches" Approach to Terrorism

A survey of scholarly and policy writing about terrorism over the last two decades reveals the entrenchment of the epidemiological approach, particularly during the years of the Obama presidency, when the language of civilizational conflict and nativism that marked the Bush administration's response to the September 11 attacks went underground, only to burst forth again in the ultra-protectionist Trump era. A mood of pluralism, progress, and cool-headed rationalism dominated these years, even, as I have argued, in the War on Terror's showiest set pieces, like the 2011 assassination of Osama bin Laden in Pakistan, which rendered the killing legible as an extension of a humanitarian health program.[2] The rise of systematic demography, the expansion of intelligence mandates and international surveillance, and the skyrocketing incidence of drone strikes—even when they involved civilian casualties—branded Obama's War on Terror the leaner, smarter, more dispassionate coda to Bush and Rumsfeld's hot-headed epic of blunders, indefensible excuses, retribution, and greed. When Obama said at an antiwar rally in 2002, "I am not opposed to all wars. I'm opposed to dumb wars," he seemed, before the fact of his own term in office, to call for a more studious and scientific if not less bloody approach to the ostensibly necessary evil of fighting terrorism at home and abroad.[3]

The U.S. Armed Services and foreign policy machines—alongside their adjacent knowledge production industries in the academy and beyond—would take up this task, beginning an intensive nationwide study of the Islamic world bolstered by federally backed scholarships, new degree programs and centers for research, grants for language and cultural study, art exhibitions, and new expert positions across the country.[4] The industrious national and nationalist flourishing of "knowledge" and "expertise" about Islam and the Islamic world in the first two decades of the twenty-first century found its model in the Orientalism of the British and French empires of the eighteenth and nineteenth centuries, that tried and true "Western style for dominating, restructuring, and having authority over the Orient."[5] Also originating in the ascendant period of European colonialism was the complementarity between this knowledge production and the systematic dehumanization of the subjects thus studied. Modeling an approach to the administration of empire in the late nineteenth and early twentieth centuries on the observation, prevention, and eradication of epidemics—especially as they were carried by the mobile Muslim population in South Asia, Southeast Asia, North Africa and the Middle East—allowed new concepts of international humanitarian and security regimes to occlude both the moral imaginary and the legal strictures that for centuries upheld the conventions of classical warfare. The effects of this historic transformation are very much with us today: as Jennifer Terry has argued in her recent study, "War and medicine are in a relationship of mutual provocation. . . . [T]his provocation perpetuates and elaborates processes of militarization through which war comes to be tactically accepted as a necessary condition for human advancement."[6] I take Terry's point a step further. War, as such, no longer exists; its full imbrication with security and medicine in the War on Terror has rendered the concept obsolete under the downward pressure of the "human advancement" model of armed conflict. Since the earliest years of the War on Terror, analysts Paul Stares and Mona Yacoubian of the United States Institute of Peace, in particular, have published a number of well-placed essays, reports, and think pieces advocating for an epidemiological approach to global terrorism. A 2005 "peace brief" written by Stares and Yacoubian argues for "an 'epidemic' conception as a way of thinking—and acting" in response to terrorism, "draw[ing] on the scientific principles and practices of epidemiology as well as insights from a growing body of research on social contagion phenomena such as fads, rumors, and civil violence."[7] Without naming terrorism as an epidemic, but rather pointing to the phenomenological and formal similarities between the two, they refer to the ways in which social scientists have "increasingly look[ed] to epidemiology to understand a variety of contagions . . . [H]ere, Islamist militancy is no different."[8] With the assistance of Yacoubian and Stare's institutional affiliation, we can see how the epidemic approach is offered up as a means of waging "peace," while the war, in fact, continues apace under new guises of rationalism in the interest of a never-defined, but implicitly good and unquestionable world health.

For these two influential analysts, the conceptual reorientation toward "Islamist militancy," the term they prefer, through the lens of epidemic is not a convenient rhetorical flourish designed to retrench familiar forms of xenophobia, but a significant and long-term project to target the threat we commonly think of through the suggestive figure of "cells." In an editorial for the *Washington Post*, "Terrorism as Virus," they outline a "promising new approach [that] builds on the parallels often drawn between terrorism and a mutating virus or metastasizing cancer."[9] To deploy epidemiological strategies only within the scope of "clinical disease," according to their argument, would be to miss what is "undeniably appealing or 'infectious' to many about the ideas and beliefs that motivate terrorists and their many supporters."[10] Stares and Yacoubian unfold the metaphor in strategic terms, asking

> What is the nature of the infectious agent, in this case the ideology? Which transmission vectors—for example mosques, madrassas, prisons, the Internet, satellite TV—spread the ideology most effectively? Who seems to be most vulnerable to its appeal? Why are most Muslims immune?[11]

Their approach has the virtue of a putatively nonbellicose model in "classic counter-epidemic measures" and the admirable goal of "protect[ing] those who are most susceptible and remedy[ing] the key environmental factors that foster it."[12] An epidemiological conception of Islamist militancy is also better suited, they argue, to the "transnational phenomenon propelled by a diverse collection of groups and individuals with different grievances and agendas," in that it provides a glimpse into the "evolving big picture" and encourages a "systematically planned, multi-pronged international effort," akin to the cooperative efforts that have led to the near-eradication of epidemics like polio.[13] This conceptual metaphor when applied to political movements, insurgent operations, and terrorist events (which sometimes overlap and sometimes do not) loses the granularity of the "different grievances and agendas" in the overarching "transnational phenomenon" of Islamism. In other words, the epidemiological vantage point brings into focus a shared set of symptoms (Islam, economic disenfranchisement, political instability, migrancy) over and against disparate and sometimes competing motives, identities, and objectives, projecting in turn a single "disease"—the terrorism epidemic—which consequently becomes the sole guiding principle for legibility and sense-making.

Yacoubian and Stares advocate for "antidotes," "immunizations," "remedies," and "cures," including "foment[ing] internal dissention and defection," promoting counterideology that "offers a positive, more compelling view of the future," and "remedial initiatives that address the key environmental conditions underlying the spread."[14] Environmental factors, in their view, include the conflicts in Iraq, Palestine, Kashmir,

Chechnya, and Afghanistan, the "marginalization" of Muslim migrant communities in Europe, and "stagnation" in Muslim states. In this last turn toward environmental factors, Yacoubian and Stares seem to point toward a remedy for terrorism based on never having begun the War on Terror. Tempting as this circular reasoning may seem, its pragmatic solutionism occludes both the responsibility for these factors, which are far from merely "environmental," and the persistence of the logic of the sanitary or therapeutic empire—what historian Megan Vaughan pointedly calls the colonial project of "curing their ills."[15] If the stakes of this kind of putatively anodyne rhetoric in defense of the spread of liberalism were not clear enough, Stares and Yacoubian spell it out plainly: "Containment initiatives would include controlling the movement of individuals to and from countries of concern [and] cleansing the most hate-filled vectors."[16] Whether we call it war or washing, it becomes less and less difficult to understand how, as the writers of *The 9/11 Commission Report* put it, "Bin Ladin w[o]n thousands of followers and some degree of approval from millions more" by citing the thievery and arrogance of the American empire in the late 1990s.[17]

Stares and Yacoubian have made waves with this undertaking. They are serious about theorizing the effects of metaphorical thinking on political agendas and the waging of war, taking up the casual figure and noting the "visceral appeal" of "disease metaphors," the way "pundits often invoke the image of madrassas and mosques as 'incubators' of a 'virulent' ideology" to point to "a dangerous and darkly insidious threat."[18] In literalizing the metaphor, they also note the way it sets "implicitly . . . a more realistic goal for what counterterrorism efforts can achieve," namely a managed lower-risk environment without complete eradication.[19] In another paper funded by the Ford Foundation, "Terrorism as a Disease," Stares and Yacoubian update their claims in a grammar of overweening passivity, calling for "institution building," "facilitating," and "promoting" "remedial efforts" that will "create a more 'healthy' and integrated" Muslim world. By this, they mean one "integrate[d] more effectively into the broader global economic system."[20] The delicate reorientation of counterinsurgency-as-care turns out to be, once again, an overture to both military intervention as well as "economic reforms that create an environment more appealing to foreign investors."[21] These analysts are joined by dozens of others who both cite their work and respond, often in looser, less theoretically astute ways, to the prevalence of the epidemic or disease metaphor for terrorism. Notable examples include *Terrorism and Public Health*, published by Oxford University Press and the American Public Health Association in 2002, now in its second edition; scholarly papers like "The Infectiousness of Terrorist Ideology: Insights from Ecology and Epidemiology," funded by the NSF and the NIH and "Terrorism as Cancer: How to Combat an Incurable Disease," written by Bryan Price, the director of the Combating Terrorism Center at West Point. Military research enters the fray with Air Force 1st Lieutenant Kjirstin Bentson's master's thesis, "An Epidemiological Approach to Terrorism."[22] Such texts, it should be said, are symptomatic of a period in which colonial discourse finds new avenues in neoimperial praxis. Stares and Yacoubian, and their fellow scholars and analysts, are unlikely to have a profound impact on the historical record of the period, though their military counterparts certainly have an impact on ground operations and the training of future military tacticians and personnel. Far more impactful—historiographically speaking—are the synthetic, consolidating narratives that garner wide readerships and take their place in the canon of millennial global culture.

If terrorism has been the watchword of the twenty-first century for public health analysts and ecologists as much as policy experts and military strategists, the epidemic terrorist narrative will be the genre we bequeath to future generations of readers. How these minor texts feed into and filter out of the period's landmark works of journalism, fiction, and history is not just a question of discourse analysis, it is also a profoundly literary question. Dozens of academic books and hundreds of scholarly articles have focused their attention on 9/11 novels and films, the terrorist plot in millennial fiction and TV, and the "bad Muslim" in popular culture.[23] These studies contribute a great deal to the terms in which we read our literary and cultural present. At the same time, they register (often without interrogating) the ways in which narrative brings its object into being. The translation of epidemic into prose, not least for its diachronicity and potential synopticism, has always stood at the center of a disciplinarily-specific epidemiological examination of disease, which incorporated and in some instances eclipsed the ascendancy of pathological and laboratory data in favor of a fuller, more descriptive, and thus more actionable picture of widespread morbid phenomena. In this way, the production of narrative—the mere putting into words and registering in the archive of clinical charts and epidemic reports—has long been tethered to the ontology of disease. I follow the sharpest historians of colonial medicine in both insisting on the bodily and organismic materiality of infection, contagion, and other syndromic phenomena, and at the same time attending to the function of narrative in bringing such effects into hermeneutic and historical existence.[24] If this is true of real diseases, it is more so of metaphorical ones. The story of Islamist terrorism as an epidemic, in other words, is one of a shockingly consistent collective poiesis. In these final pages, I read *The 9/11 Commission*

Report as a catalyst of a new transnational literary form determined by old colonial psychogeographies, and interrogate its language of malaise, wound, and harm as well as its logic of diagnosis and cure.

The 9/11 Commission Report and the Limits of the Bureaucratic Imagination

The 9/11 Commission Report begins, like any cosmopolitan pastoral, with the weather, with a constellation of placid and ordinary sites, with everyday people waking up and moving into the world.

> Tuesday September 11, 2001, dawned temperate and nearly cloudless in the eastern United States. Millions of men and women readied themselves for work. Some made their way to the Twin Towers, the signature structures of the World Trade Center complex in New York City. Others went to Arlington, Virginia, to the Pentagon. Across the Potomac River, the United States Congress was back in session. At the other end of Pennsylvania Avenue, people began to line up for a White House tour. In Sarasota, Florida, President George W. Bush went for an early morning run.[25]

This distant, high-altitude opening conjures the pulse of American normalcy in graceful scene shifts from New York to Virginia, D.C. to Sarasota, with the busy peace of a shared endeavor unfolding to the industrious rhythm of an American president out for his morning jog. The text's conjured air grows heavier and more silken as the narrative moves south to the Capitol, and further south to the Gulf. The proper names are familiar, steady, comforting; in the Potomac, we hear the echo of George Washington's crossing, in Arlington, the glory of fallen soldiers. In and as her millions, America woke, went to work, paid homage to democracy, attended to her fitness. Replete with sweeping "meanwhile" gestures, one sees immediately what Anderson means by the imagined community, brought into being, once again, in print. It is a masterpiece of patriotism—ekphrastic and lyrical, shimmering with idealism and ideology. The image it presents is that of a healthy nation.

The next paragraph reveals this idyll—as every reader already knows—on the brink of being shattered, the opening lines already an irrecoverable fantasy of innocence. The narrative shifts into a register of quasi-menacing detail, quoting from the bureaucratized speech of commercial airlines, and then zooms further in to focus on two strangers, whose names fall heavily in the prose, an index of their unbelonging:

For those heading to an airport, weather conditions could not have been better for a safe and pleasant journey. Among the travelers were Mohammed Atta and Abdul Aziz al Omari, who arrived at the airport in Portland, Maine. (1)

The *Report* does not persist in this tone or this pastoral projection of American life at the turn of the millennium for very long. Much of the text is technical and didactic, aiming to provide "the fullest possible account of the events surrounding 9/11 and to identify lessons learned" (xvi). But there are, throughout, surprising moments of lyricism, literary deftness, and depth of feeling, even where these sentiments are entirely bizarre and misguided. For a government document, *The 9/11 Commission Report* expresses an almost unsettling profundity and warmth—couched in a marked writerliness—especially around the edges of the chapters. In the preface, Thomas Kean and Lee Hamilton, chair and vice-chair of the commission, express their gratitude to their fellow commissioners, and their "great affection for them," an odd sentiment that marks the *Report* not only as a record of trauma and detection, but of an unexpectedly optimistic national reimagining (xvi).

It also plays, as many readers have noted, with the generic conventions of the thriller, the mystery, and the horror novel and film, punctuating the dry compilation of facts and the sometimes excruciatingly slow pace—the whole first chapter, forty-six densely footnoted pages, covers about twenty minutes on the morning of September 11—with dramatic transcripts from cell-phone conversations and cliffhangers that attenuate the smaller enigmas that flow into the larger events of the day. The *Report*'s novelistic strategy appears to be more than decorative, inviting a newly adventurous and creatively apocalyptic view of the international threats to US security, even as it moves within and through received literary forms. As it shifts into the synthetic assessment suite of chapters toward the end, the commissioners make explicit their concern that "[i]magination is not usually a gift associated with bureaucracies. . . . It is crucial," they write, "to find a way of routinizing, even bureaucratizing, the exercise of imagination" (344). The difficulty of "bureaucratizing imagination," at least in the local history the *Report* offers, however, points inevitably back to imaginaries already inscribed in literary and filmic registers. When the commissioners wonder why no one thought of hijacked aircraft being repurposed as weapons in the years leading up to 9/11—particularly following Al Qaeda's use of "suicide vehicles" like truck bombs and boats, as in the attacks on US embassies in Kenya and Tanzania and the USS Cole—they discover that Richard Clarke, at least according to his own lengthy testimony before the commission, had in fact done so, "but" they note, "he attributes his awareness more to Tom Clancy novels than to warnings from the intelligence community" (347).[26]

The 9/11 Commission Report's first chapter, "We Have Some Planes," unfolds in this Clancian register, with the literarily suspenseful but historically obvious revelation that the story of 9/11 has actually begun percolating at a great—according to the narrative, an almost unimaginable—distance:

> [T]he conflict did not begin on 9/11. It had been publicly declared years earlier, most notably in a declaration faxed early in 1998 to an Arabic-language newspaper in London. Few Americans had noticed it. The fax had been sent from thousands of miles away by the followers of a Saudi exile gathered in one of the most remote and impoverished countries on earth. (46)

The thousands of miles separating the London fax machine from "one of the most remote and impoverished countries on earth" are not just larger in number than the thousands of miles separating Portland, Maine, from Sarasota, Florida. The distance, as the commissioners and their staff conceive it, is augmented by the redoubling of the as-yet-unnamed Saudi's "exile" and the country's "remoteness," here presented not as relative characteristics, but rather as ontic ones. The impoverishment of the region, too, stands to distance it from the earnest and cloudless business taking place in and under the gleaming skyscrapers of New York, which appear, by contrast, to exist in an entirely unconnected temporal order.

If the *Report* treats geospacial dilation as sublime, its contraction is horrific. The middle sections of the *Report*, especially chapter 5, "Al Qaeda Aims at the American Homeland," emphasize the infiltration of foreign nationals into the channels of American progress, and the peace of unsuspecting rural locales. The background narrative of Khalid Sheikh Mohammed is instructive in this regard, emphasizing his proficiency in the migrant's Protean arts, the extent to which he was "equally comfortable in a government office or a terrorist safehouse," where he "applied his imagination, technical aptitude, and managerial skills to hatching and planning an extraordinary array of terrorist schemes" (145). Ethnically Baluch, "KSM," as the narrative refers to him, was raised in Kuwait and wound up at Chowan College, "a small Baptist school in Murfreesboro, North Carolina"—from there, he transferred to the North Carolina Agricultural and Technical State University in Greensboro, where he studied mechanical engineering (145). The following lines "plunge" KSM, postgraduation, into the anti-Soviet Afghani jihad, cutting ominous scenes between Peshawar and cave excavation in Afghanistan. The contrast between Greensboro and Tora Bora is pointedly, strategically uncanny, suggesting an ever-present proximity that is only terrifying in one direction. The next pages detail KSM's connections and operations in the Philippines, Qatar, Brazil, Sudan, Yemen, Malaysia, Saudi Arabia, Israel, Thailand, the Maldives, and more. These details, both of Khalid Sheikh Mohammed's movements and of alleged operations coordinated by or through him are included in the narrative in spite of a boxed disclaimer that the chapter "relies heavily on information obtained from captured Al Qaeda members," and that "[a]ssessing the truth of statements by these witnesses—sworn enemies of the United States—is challenging" (146). The commissioners surmise whether other Al Qaeda operatives interrogated in the post-9/11 arrests might have diminished Mohammed's role in the organization out of "a touch of jealousy" (152).

The oscillation between shrinking-world rhetoric and the human-scale personal intimacies and grievances that destabilize the narrative foundations of the *Report* and highlight its key affects of anxiety and fear on the one hand, and a dilatory representation of the distance between the Islamic breeding grounds of terrorism and the West on the other, is a specific effect of the *9/11 Commission Report* as a literary document. It only partially reflects the distribution of resources between the War on Terror as it was waged abroad and domestic security within the US in the wake of the attacks. As Zareena Grewal has noted in her critical geography *Islam Is a Foreign Country*, the first city-based office of Homeland Security opened not in New York, but in the predominantly Arab Detroit suburb of Dearborn, Michigan.[27] Global space in the *Report* is hardly a matter of cartography; it is, rather, a narrative device determined by the text's twin goals of justification for the War on Terror and a narrative of national healing and bureaucratic reordering. Both are routed through the genre of descriptive landscape, which is offered up as evidence of what a healthy, flourishing society does and does not look like. The first chapter, "We Have Some Planes," ends in a disorientating cliffhanger, with no location named. The unspecified country—"one of the most remote and impoverished on earth," which is the origin of the ominous fax—insists on these landscapes not as specific sites with cultural, political, and economic determinants, but rather as paragons of the ahistorical qualities of "remoteness" and "impoverishment" long associated with the backwards regions of the Orient and other colonized spaces. This picture of a backward and sickly place lingers over the break until it is named in the beginning of the next chapter; once the narrative locates the reader in Afghanistan, the juxtaposition of a primer on Islam (we learn that it "arose in Arabia with what Muslims believe are a series of revelations to the prophet Muhammad from the one and only God") with the diagnosis of a "social and economic malaise" in the oil states, the other Arab nations, and Pakistan is already fixed in the reader's mind as a kind of perfect sense (49, 53). According to the logic laid out by the narrative, Islam—in contrast to the "anticolonial grievances" that fed the "overwhelmingly secular struggles for independence after World War I"—fills in the blank space of the remote and the impoverished "country" from which the threat issues with maladies both social and economic (52).

These sources of malaise include an addiction to subsidized social welfare programs and their entitlements in the "unmodernized oil states," the failure of free enterprise owing to "unprofitable industry, state monopolies, and opaque bureaucracies," stagnant economies with low job growth ("a sure prescription for social turbulence"), and the "repression and isolation of women in many Muslim countries," which "crippled overall economic productivity" (53, 54). Afghanistan's many woes do not even make the list of these symptoms, since it is a place, according to the narrative, "where real economic development has barely begun" (53). If this weren't bad enough, the "secular education reflected a strong cultural preference for technical fields over the humanities and social sciences," such that the exploding population of young Arab men "even if able to study abroad, lacked the perspective and skills needed to understand a different culture" (54). Presumably, the *Report*'s warmly informative tone, textbook style information boxes, and one-paragraph introduction to Islam—the religion of a quarter of the world's population—represents the appropriate "perspective and skills needed to understand a different culture." The malaise here described culminates in a simultaneous diagnosis of the warning signs of "radicalization," and an underhanded defense of the global university and its shallow diversity training as a conduit of development and proper thinking. The picture of the Islamic world as a space of disordered education and nondevelopment locates in it both the agent of a diseased civilization as well as its symptoms. Unmodernity and economic stagnation are also locked in a tautology with the repression of women and crippled productivity—the sanctions and debt structures imposed by US foreign policy appear nowhere. American material and political support of repressive regimes in the Gulf states make no appearance either. But for the unique lexicon of late-capitalist bureaucratese, the list might have come from Josephine Butler's impassioned plea on behalf of her "Indian Fellow Subjects," or Macaulay's Minute on Indian Education—or worse, from the mouth of one Turton or Burton in Forster's satire of late-imperial decline in *A Passage to India*.[28]

The chapter affixes the terminus of its suspense by returning to the menacing fax that served as the previous chapter's cliffhanger, while also playing on a peculiar assonance with bin Laden's name ("bomb-laden"):

> On the morning of August 7, the bomb-laden trucks drove into the embassies roughly five minutes apart—about 10:35 A.M. in Nairobi and 10:39 A.M. in Dar es Salaam. Shortly afterward, a phone call was placed from Baku to London. The previously prepared messages were then faxed to London. (70)

The temporal coordination of the attacks on the East African embassies mimics in sinister reverse the "meanwhile" gestures of the *Report*'s opening pages. The contraction of American space from Maine to New York to D.C. to Florida appears through this lens as a premonition of the seeming instantaneity—the out-of-the-clear-blue-sky-ness—of the planes' collision with the Towers. This narrative technique highlights the terror of global enterprise through a combination of pathetic fallacy and spatial juxtapositions that sound the alarm or—in the *9/11 Commission Report*'s terms—beat the drum of warning. Paradoxically, it is the colonial origin of this discursive history that enables the authors of the *9/11 Commission Report* to meditate on the way in which globalization has "taught us that terrorism against American interests 'over there' should be regarded just as we regard terrorism against America 'over here.' In this same sense," they conclude, "the American homeland is the planet" (362). Nevertheless, the commissioners characterize the "Muslim world" as a monolithic entity—somehow within this American planet—which "has fallen behind the West politically, economically, and militarily for the last three centuries" (362). Such a vision also seems to claim the future as its territory: "because few tolerant or secular Muslim democracies provide alternative models for the future, Bin Ladin's message finds receptive ears" (362).

This characterization further implies that the lack of secular democratic structures leaves people in the "Muslim world" more susceptible or vulnerable to the kinds of ideology with which "Americans cannot bargain or negotiate," namely radical Islam's lack of "respect for life," which the commissioners suggest "can only be destroyed or isolated," as if by inoculation or quarantine (362). What festers over there, such narratives warn, can be here in an instant. It's important to note that these rhetorical features are not present in the majority of bureaucratic and government writing about the events leading up to or resulting from the attacks on 9/11. The CIA Office of the Inspector General's "Report on CIA Accountability With Respect to the 9/11 Attacks," for example, eschews entirely any framing devices or narrative flourishes.²⁹ *The Senate Intelligence Committee Report on Torture*, which I will turn to in this chapter's final section, goes to great pains to both undermine these rhetorical devices, and, I argue, reveal their obscurantism in both dispositional and narrative terms.

A Healing Narrative

A rare document of its kind to receive such an accolade, *The 9/11 Commission Report* was nominated for a National Book Award for nonfiction in 2004.³⁰ It sold more than two million copies in the first year, and was downloaded nearly seven million times.³¹ Literary critic Craig Warren has documented the breathless responses to the *Report*'s publication in 2004, citing its readability and its combination of clarity and elusiveness, and noting its astonishing sales figures in spite of its density. Warren reads the *Report* as a document of immense creative power, observing the ways in which it both instantiates anew an American collectivity and provides succor to the community thus called into being. He highlights the commissioners' impactful choice of the first-person-plural voice, which, in contrast to *The Warren Report* and previous similar documents of "state-sponsored prose," keeps the personhood of the writers in view, while also validating their own conclusions by "the reader's implied participation and consent."³² This, he argues, in spite of its demand that "readers train their interpretive powers not only on the accessible language of the commissioners, but also on the wounds behind that language."³³ In pointing to the wounds behind the language, Warren further reveals the *Report*'s foundations in a shared experience of bodily vulnerability—twinned in the opening paragraphs of the *Report* to the commissioners' affect—as a crucial subtext in the putatively bureaucratic document, which, by extension, becomes a textual salve or cure for those wounds. The effect of this subtextual goal comes through in what critic Benjamin DeMott calls the *Report*'s "undervoice," which, he argues, eschews the explicit task of uncovering lapses in intelligence and security protocols while seeming to whisper, in dulcet tones, "*Let us look to the future. We need to move on.*"³⁴ DeMott perceives in this therapeutic project a sinister and dishonest attempt to "whitewash" the intelligence failures leading up to the attacks and to "defraud" the nation into buying into the wars in Iraq and Afghanistan.³⁵ DeMott's frustration with the sense of blamelessness put forward by the *Report* might be understood as a symmetrical function of the commission's framing of the story of September 11 as one of geography, even geo-ontology, proffered in the narrative's easeful tone and multisite structuring as the unchanging receptacle of civilizational values and forms of life. These, according to the images put forward in the opening passages, equate development and the concentration of wealth with health. The *Report*'s epidemic approach, though it is subtle and attenuated, becomes clearer in its closing sections, where the logic of disease and cure asserts itself in force.

The *9/11 Commission Report*'s synthesizing analysis theorizes the relationship between events, documentation, archive building, imagination, and the writing of state-sponsored history. "In composing this narrative, we have tried to remember that we write with the benefit and the handicap of hindsight. Hindsight can sometimes see the past clearly—with 20/20 vision. But the path of what happened is so brightly lit that it places everything else more deeply into shadow" (339). The process of producing the *Report* appears in this light as a primarily editorial one—a series of decisions about what pieces of the narrative will be relegated to obscurity, and what organizing concepts will emerge as the most efficacious and advantageous to the declared projects of lesson-learning and future action. Filtered in this homiletic chapter through a section called simply "Imagination," the disease metaphor emerges as a considered and hindsight-informed model of intelligence and security "management." The commissioners cite the failure of data sharing between intelligence agencies, broken information handoffs, and ineffective operations as key factors in the failure to prevent the terrorist attacks of September 11, 2001. Then they step back further into the metaphorical, "imaginative" space the text insists, again and again, is the key to both understanding the past and forestalling future catastrophes.

> However the specific problems are labeled we believe they are symptoms of the government's broader inability to adapt how it manages problems to the new challenges of the twenty-first century. The agencies are like a set of specialists in a hospital, each ordering tests, looking for symptoms, and prescribing medications. What is missing is the attending physician who makes sure they work as a team. (353)

Calling back to Foucault's account in *The Birth of the Clinic*, we see in this moment an imaginative attempt to pull back, to access and synthesize the "multiple gaze" required to parse the epidemic's "special, accidental, unexpected qualities."[36] The diagnostic scene works in at least two ways: first, it identifies the bureaucratic systems of American intelligence and national security as subject to the kinds of bodily failures that result in "symptoms." Here, the mechanisms of coordination that have broken down are understood as a failure of a natural system—one that has evolved in accordance with the blueprint of a successfully functioning body. The government's "broader inability to adapt how it manages problems to the new challenges of the twenty-first century" is thus cast as a malfunction in the putative metabolic perfection and perfectibility of the government's organ systems. At the same time, the problem is externalized as one of "adaptability," suggesting that the system's inadequacy is not one of conception or design, but rather of some unaccountable incursion from without. One wonders where the borders of the hospital are, what becomes of the sick who are not admitted. Secondly, and in a slightly different vein, the passage above suggests that the agencies are themselves hyper-focused and overtrained physicians, too specialized and blinkered to perceive holistically the systems-level breakdown that led to the attacks being successfully carried out. Here, "ordering tests, looking for symptoms, and prescribing medications" stands in for the tactical and operational inefficiencies of the CIA's many Al Qaeda and terrorism offices and operatives, which, in this model, both undermine and eclipse the wider strategic concerns. The attending physician in this metaphor is the one with the resources, the plan, the coordination strategy, the level head, the experience unclouded by too many studies and too much data. He—and the image certainly invokes the kind of cool-headed masculinity that provides comfort in chaotic times—is not an army general shouting orders, or an intelligence officer slinking in the shadows, but a brightly lit, scrubbed, white-coated expert whose chief concern is making his patient, that is, us, the readers of this traumatic history, well—getting us back on our feet. Given the placement of this gesture in the overall structure of the *Report* just prior to the two prescriptive chapters, the hospital metaphor casts the commissioners themselves, and their corporate embodiment—five Democrats, five Republicans, and an extensive staff of nonpartisan experts—as the attending physician, innocuously ministering to both broken nation and its broken systems. In light of the scandalous obstruction of the advice of actual doctors and medical professionals and of their work and that of their support staffs of custodial workers, transportation workers, medical technicians, paramedics, and other essential workers during the COVID-19 pandemic in 2020, it is worth highlighting that these imaginary physicians are *only* metaphorical. Their figural status, in a nation of profound anti-intellectualism and hostility to care work must be understood as a sign of the War on Terror's strategic disingenuousness. The self-imagined rational heroism of the commissioners emphatically does not indicate abiding respect for the real work of doctoring. Instead, it indexes an older style of medical moralism as an overture to the abandonment of care. Indeed, the authors suggest in their final recommendations that

the best way to remedy the resentment of America and the West is "toler-
ance, the rule of law, political and economic openness, the extension of
greater opportunities for women—these cures," they write, "must come
from within Muslim societies themselves" (362–363).

Although I have said much already about the politically neutered and
neutralizing figure of the doctor in colonial letters—a figure profoundly
humanized, at great cost, in Camus's postwar allegory of plague—I want
to linger here with this latter-day inflection and its implications for how
we read *The 9/11 Commission Report* as a document of intensely self-
conscious history influenced by and laden with literary concern. In an
essay for the *New Republic*, ominously called "When Government Writes
History," Ernest May, an eminent American historian, explained in helpful detail the motives behind the composition and division of labor on
the commission, centering his own role as a professional writer of American history in the creation of the text's narrative arc and its style.[37] As May
describes it, the architects of the report had two chief characteristics that
set them apart from previous corporate authors of government inquiries:
first, a conception of their own work as politically and culturally neutral,
a quality reflected in the bipartisan composition of the commission and
its staff, as well as the burnished academic credentials of a number of its
consultants. Second, the commission had the benefit of May himself, an
experienced writer of American history, who, according to his account,
convinced "everyone" of the necessity of "bec[oming] a storyteller."[38]

In some senses, May simply describes in compositional terms the process by which the team of experts that appear in the *Report* as a conceit
for a malfunctioning surveillance system reconceive themselves as the
"attending physician" responsible for synthesizing and modifying the
chart or narrative. In this vein, May writes of the work of making a "history," rather than a set of conclusions and recommendations as a bid to
"delay a partisan split within the commission. . . . It was also possible,"
he writes, "to strip away interpretive language, even adjectives and ad-
verbs, so as to assure the reader that we were just reciting the historical
facts."[39] Although he admits that the "documentary base" from which
the *Report* was constructed was "extraordinarily deep but also extraordinarily narrow," and that the results were both "indulgent" to Presidents Clinton and Bush and inattentive to the "alternative argument
that the World Trade Center, the Pentagon, and the Capitol might not
have been targeted absent America's identification with Israel, support
for regimes such as those in Saudi Arabia, Egypt, and Pakistan, and in-
sensitivity to Muslims' feelings about their holy places," he nevertheless
frames these shortcomings as faults that are eclipsed by the triumph of

the *Report*'s accuracy, readability, and future legacy. He closes by noting that the *Report*

> was written in a period of partisanship almost as intense as the 1790s or the 1850s. But the report was dedicated to the idea that a genuine concern for communicating an accurate picture of our reality to future generations may allow us to transcend the passions of the moment. For this reason, I hope that this official report will not be the last government document of its kind. In these perilous times, there will surely be other events that require the principles of historiography allied to the resources of government, so that urgency will sometimes become the friend of truth.[40]

One hardly needs to be a critic of the state, let alone an enemy thereof, to see that May's insistence that the very form of history guarantees the *Report*'s political neutrality, its transcendence of partisan politics—compounded by his acknowledgment and dismissal of the failure to address American foreign policy as a viable field for the study of the causes of terrorist attacks because it would have been "too controversial to be discussed except in recommendations written in the future tense"—is utterly compromised by his claim that a "historiography allied to the resources of government" can produce a document in which "urgency" can "become the friend of truth."[41]

If the commissioners' studied nonpartisanship and insistence on *both* the artistry and the disinterested accuracy of the *Report* did not already point to the textual paradoxes of the genre, then May's narrative of its drafting provides further evidence of the literary maneuvers and the impetus behind them that made the *Report* "novelistically intense" and "one of the most riveting, disturbing, and revealing accounts of crime, espionage and the inner workings of government ever written."[42] May also cites John Updike's felicitous comparison to the King James Bible as "our language's lone masterpiece produced by committee, at least until this year's *9/11 Commission Report*."[43] May wanted to write

> international history, not just American history. None had aspired to deal not only with the immediate past but also with the long background that would be needed if . . . the report was to remain the reference volume on September 11 sitting on the shelves of high school and college teachers a generation hence.[44]

The chair of the commission, Thomas Kean, ratifies this desire, saying that "we want a report that our grandchildren can take off the shelf in

fifty years and say 'this is what happened.'"[45] I cite these passages somewhat abundantly to show the persistent attention paid by May, the commission, and its consultants and staffers to the crafting of the report
as a literary endeavor. The historian's "memoir" of the commission, as
he calls it, gives us invaluable insight into the personalities, disciplinary training, institutional histories, social connections, and motives of
those whose voices make up the voice of the "Government," that, in May's
terms, "Writes History." May was a scholar not just of American history
and postwar isolationism, but also of American imperialism. Written
as the war in Vietnam was cementing itself as a catastrophe of historic
proportions, May's *American Imperialism* was profoundly concerned with
narrative, rhetoric, and their central role in foreign policy.[46] Bearing in
mind the imprint of May's scholarship and narrative influences on the
9/11 Commission Report further grounds our ability to locate it in an archive of colonial-state narrative production, and enables a deeper understanding of its figures and their indebtedness to imperial epistemologies.

Black Boxes: The Muslim Subject

State history doesn't often make itself so appealing. For a casual reader,
the most striking difference between *The 9/11 Commission Report* and *The
Senate Intelligence Committee Report on Torture*, published by the small
literary press Melville House in 2014 and widely known as the "Feinstein
Report" after then-chair of the Senate Select Committee on Intelligence,
Dianne Feinstein, is the omnipresence in the latter of censor bars. The
notes in particular illustrate this difference in disclosure in urgently visual terms, the pages bedecked or marred—depending on the reader's
disposition—with smooth black secrets of geometric regularity. These
censor bars stand as assurances that someone, somewhere, is taking
American safety very seriously. Or, alternatively, that CIA officers who
have committed torture, and the intelligence agents, career bureaucrats, and elected officials who knew about it are working scrupulously
to protect themselves. Names, dates, locations, and case file numbers
that might bear such identifying information are largely blacked out in
the text. In contrast to the *9/11 Report* where classification and clearance
determined the commissioners' access to data, and a pervasive sense of
secrecy and security shaped the narrative behind the scenes in ways that
were largely inapparent to the lay reader, *The Senate Report on Torture*
makes much of what it is not showing visible. The cover of the first-
run paperback is also black, setting a markedly different tone from the
patriotic red, white, and blue of the *9/11 Report*, which was sold at the
accessible price point of ten dollars a copy. In 2006, the esteemed liter-

ary publisher Farrar, Straus and Giroux published a graphic adaptation of *The 9/11 Commission Report* by comic book veterans Sid Jacobson and Ernie Colón (figure 7.1); no such marketing schemes or kid-friendly versions accompanied *The Senate Report on Torture*, despite their similarly violent and disturbing subject matter.

In almost every way, *The Senate Report on Torture* is a radically different record of the period of American history during the first decade of the War on Terror. It is largely free of rhetorical flourishes and novelistic frameworks. There are no cliffhangers or evocative section headings, no pastorals or set pieces, little attention is paid to painting a picture of the enemy, who is, in any case, ourselves or those acting on behalf of our government. The chapter titles of the executive summary exhibit neither narrative clues nor artistry: "Background on the Committee Study" and "Overall History and Operation of the CIA's Detention and Interrogation Program" are exemplary of the document's tone. Compare these to "We Have Some Planes" and "The System Was Blinking Red." There is no palette of Orientalist tropes to draw on; and the text largely eschews characters, motives, and sweeping cultural histories. In keeping with the prose, *The Report on Torture*'s visual performance is one of sobriety, shame, collective guilt, an admission of a systematic violation of the Constitution's core principles of due process and international law. It gives shape, color, and heft to the decade's national unknowing—to a sense of crescendoing ignorance, to a losing war. Even as it attempts to shed light on the horrifically extensive use of torture and "enhanced interrogation," the *Report on Torture* presents itself as a tissue of only partial information, pointing insistently in both its visual dimensions and its rhetoric to that which it does not and cannot reveal.

Also unlike *The 9/11 Commission Report*, *The Senate Report on Torture*'s preface is drafted by a sole author who uses the first person (singular), and states regularly her position on her committee's findings: "[T]hey are highly critical of the CIA's actions, and rightly so. . . . It is my sincere and deep hope that through the release of these Findings and Conclusions and Executive Summary that U.S. policy will never again allow for secret indefinite detention and the use of coercive interrogations."[47] *The Senate Report on Torture*'s appendix B lays out in a handy chart the dizzying array of lies and evasions by former CIA director Michael Hayden—at least those uncovered by the committee's work. Among these are the revelations that the CIA's 119 post-9/11 detainees were regularly stripped, "walled" (thrown into a wall), beaten, slapped and sodomized, fed "liquid diets" of Ensure and water to decrease vomiting during waterboarding, threatened with death and harm to their families, placed in coffin-sized boxes to inflict psychological damage, immersed in ice baths, "walked" and "hung" to

7.1 Excerpt from Sid Jacobson and Ernie Colón, *The 9/11 Report: A Graphic Adaptation* (2006), 116-117. Copyright © 2006 by Castlebridge Enterprises, Inc. Reprinted by permission of Hill and Wang, a division of Farrar, Straus and Giroux. By permission of Frank R. Scatoni, Venture Literary, Inc.

prolong sleep deprivation, and, perhaps most horrifically, medicated by CIA doctors in order to enable further torture.[48] When asked directly "did anyone die," Michael Hayden responds "No." "Not one person?" "No one." Under the CIA TESTIMONY column of the chart, Hayden claims the one person who died in CIA custody did so before the commencement of the interrogation program. On the SAMPLING OF INFORMATION IN CIA RECORDS side of the chart, the Select Committee's rebuttal, we read:

> This testimony is incongruent with CIA records. . . . On November ▮, 2002, Gul Rahman was shackled to the wall of his cell in a short chain position, which required him to sit on the bare concrete. Rahman was wearing a sweatshirt, but was nude from the waist down. On November ▮, 2002, the guards at DETENTION SITE COBALT found Gul Rahman's dead body. Although a CIA employee tried to perform CPR, Gul Rahman remained unresponsive and was declared dead. An autopsy report found that the cause of Gul Rahman's death was "undetermined," but that the clinical impression of the medical officer who conducted the autopsy was that the cause of death was hypothermia.[49]

Even as it exposes the horrific abuses of state secrecy, *The Senate Report on Torture* also lays out in painstaking detail the instability of testimony, documentary evidence, recollection, and, to borrow Warren's useful term, "state-sponsored prose." To read the beginning of each entry in the SAMPLING OF INFORMATION IN CIA RECORDS side of the chart is to confront not just the mendacity and sadism of the CIA leadership and ground personnel, but also to recall queasily the chiming confidence of the 9/11 commissioners and the narrative they constructed, as well as the figures that grounded it (entries separated by points):

- The CIA representation that Abu Zubaydah stopped cooperating with debriefers who were using traditional interrogation techniques is not supported by CIA records.
- The representation that the "requirement to be in the CIA detention program is knowledge of [an] attack against the United States or its interests or knowledge about the location of Usama Bin Laden or Ayman al-Zawahiri" is inconsistent with how the CIA's Detention and Interrogation Program operated from its inception.
- The representation that Abu Zubaydah "would not talk" is incongruent with CIA interrogation records.
- A review of CIA records on this topic identified no records to indicate that al-Qa'ida had conducted "broadly based" interrogation resistance training.

- The CIA testimony is incongruent with internal CIA records and the operational history of the program.
- This testimony is incongruent with CIA records.
- This statement is incongruent with CIA records.
- This testimony is not supported by CIA records.
- This testimony is inaccurate.
- The CIA regularly disseminated intelligence reports based on un-corroborated statements from CIA detainees. The reports, some of which included fabricated or otherwise inaccurate information, required extensive FBI investigations.
- CIA records detail how, throughout the program, CIA medical personnel cleared detainees for the use of the CIA's enhanced interrogation techniques and played a central role in deciding whether to continue, adjust, or alter the use of the techniques against detainees.
- The CIA consistently represented that the interrogation of CIA detainees using the CIA's enhanced interrogation techniques re-sulted in critical and otherwise unavailable intelligence that led to the capture of specific terrorists. . . . These representations were inaccurate.[50]

My aim in serializing these abbreviated statements is not to lionize Dianne Feinstein as a paragon of transparency—she has also publicly called for the censorship of *The Anarchist Cookbook* and Al Qaeda's English-language glossy *Inspire* following a bomb plot by two young American women in 2015.[51] Nor do I wish to posit some essential inac-cessibility of truth where crimes of enormous magnitude and violations of human rights are concerned. I am more interested in the contrasting literary and cultural effects of these two signal documents of the War on Terror. I am particularly interested in how opacity functions in the latter as a corrective to the tone of unanimity and transparency in the former. In the context of the ascendancy of Stares, Yacoubian, and oth-ers' epidemiological approach to terrorism, we must ask to what extent the visual impact of redaction tropes on the black-boxed infection sites of nineteenth-century cartographies of disease. If the medical fantasy of *The 9/11 Commission Report* sustains a faith in the possibility of opening up, reading, understanding, the motive and organizations of contem-porary Islamist terrorism—if it holds out belief in finding "cures from within" and instantiates a torture-based practice for the extraction of information through interrogation—*The Report on Torture* locates such sites of infection firmly within the mechanisms of American intelligence.

Read not just as the record of an investigation but also as a theory of information, even of representation ("the CIA representation is inaccurate"), *The Senate Report on Torture* highlights the relationship in *The 9/11 Commission Report* between positivism and imperialist chauvinism. At the risk of oversimplifying a dramatically complex set of factors, and suppressing the deep continuities between torture in the War on Terror and the long record of US human rights abuses domestically and around the world, I want to hazard that the story told by the second of these twin tomes of the terrorism decades is a direct result of the first. Where *The 9/11 Commission Report* novelizes and medicalizes the War on Terror, *The Senate Report on Torture* interrogates the consequences of this way of thinking, and brings American wrongdoing into sharp relief with a supporting cast of nefarious CIA doctors. In so doing, *The Report on Torture* also subtly recasts its own revelations as proleptic causes for the widespread hatred of American imperialism; recall not just the arming and training of the Afghani jihadis during the Cold War, but also the unconscionable use of the sham vaccination campaign in the capture and killing of Osama bin Laden.

Behind the black boxes of the redaction bars, *The Report on Torture* thus reveals the symmetry of American motives and crimes to the putatively veiled and obscure—the ontologically, culturally, and ethically incommensurable—motives of the terrorist. The black box of Muslim (or Islamic or Islamist or jihadi) subjectivity appears, transfigured, in the black boxes that obstruct a vision of what happens inside a detention cell, inside Guantanamo, at innumerable other black sites. This effect, of course, is not limited to *The Senate Intelligence Committee Report on Torture*—the aesthetics of redaction are an inescapable and visually powerful feature of so many documents provided in response to Freedom of Information Act requests. Pages like the one illustrated in figure 7.2 stand as perverse visual jokes in efforts to bring CIA detainees some measure of justice, even humanity.

Contemporary writers from the Islamic world have responded to the dominant iconography of the Muslim subject as commensurate with the literal black box of downed or hijacked airliners, and the ontological black box of the impenetrable Oriental other, veiled or otherwise, in a variety of ways. In *The Satanic Verses*, Salman Rushdie revisits the archetypal black box of Islam, the Kaaba, recasting it as a site not of swarming obscurity, a cube of horrific secrecy, but as a busy locus of theistic agonism. He begins at the dawn of Islam, in an *Arabian Nights*–esque vein, with shades of Joyce's carnival: "Jahilia today is all perfume. The scents of Araby, of *Arabia Odifera*, hang in the air: balsam, cassia, cinnamon, frankincense, myrrh. The pilgrims drink the wine of the date-palm and wander in the great fair of the feast of Ibrahim."[52] The pilgrims arriving in

Water board

00········

8

CT3 15-8

7.2 CIA, "Other Document 45." Redacted document provided in response to an American Civil Liberties Union Freedom of Information Act request (2003) (www.aclu.org).

Jahilia navigate a town organized in a "series of rough circles . . . houses spreading outwards from the House of the Black Stone" (99). The house will soon be adorned with the seven best verses composed at the annual poetry competition, "nailed up on the walls" like so many Lutheran theses. Rushdie adorns and fills the Kaaba not just with verses, but with conflicting beliefs and political arguments. Inside this structure, and all around it, is the statuary of various gods and goddesses, "a glut of gods, a stone flood to feed the glutton hunger of the pilgrims, to quench their unholy thirst . . . [T]he idols, too, are delegates to a kind of international fair" (101). Here we are given a picture of Islam's origins—blasphemous, to be sure—in which migrancy, multiplicity, and syncretism take the place of an austere and mysterious fundament. Orthodoxy, in typically Rushdian fashion, is made heterodox in the shadow of the sacred cube. In place of monstrous obscurity, the vanishing point for a globe of Mecca-facing Muslims, Rushdie's Kaaba is infused with prismatic light, becoming a kind of terrestrial sun:

> They say in Jahilia that this valley is the navel of the earth; that the planet, when it was being made, went spinning round this point. Adam came here and saw a miracle: four emerald pillars bearing aloft a giant glowing ruby, and beneath this canopy a huge white stone, also glowing with its own light, like a vision of his soul. He built strong walls around the vision to bind it forever to the earth. This was the first House. It was rebuilt many times—once by Ibrahim, after Hagar's and Ismail's angel-assisted survival—and gradually the countless touchings of the white stone by the pilgrims of the centuries darkened its colour to black. Then the time of the idols began; by the time of Mahound, three hundred and sixty stone gods clustered around God's own stone. (101)

The pilgrims congregate most avidly around the three female goddesses, Uzza, Manat, and Al-Lat, "Allah's opposite and equal" (102). The feminist revision enacted in this passage compounds architectural palimpsesting—the history of structures and institutions fallen and rebuilt—with a history of touch. In keeping with the novel's reparative plots of shared sickness, and shared apotheosis, the Kaaba's darkness is recuperated as evidence of rapt generations, of a devoted people, a collective love expressed in *con-tagion*, or co-touching. Returning to the birth of Islam is, for Rushdie, also a way of rewriting the political promise of the Iranian Revolution. In this earlier, more open, less written temporality, he imagines the shift to Mahound's monotheism as both a scriptural site of errancy and as a "revolution of water-carriers, immigrants and slaves" (103). Whether we understand these revisions as acts of devotion or as textual crimes against the God-given origin stories of the prophet, Rushdie's efforts to populate Islam's most sacred site with the banalities of everyday life registers one attempt to challenge the received wisdom in the West of Islam as a cultural and epistemological black box.

The Iranian-American poet Solmaz Sharif has taken up the contemporary resonances of this inherited tropology in more direct ways. Her 2016 collection *LOOK* derives its conceptual vocabulary from the 2007 edition of the *United States Department of Defense Dictionary of Military and Associated Terms*. Sharif's appropriation of military vocabulary—already an exercise in morbid poetry featuring terms like "protected emblems" and "amphibious breaching"—performs the poet's alienation in migrancy and the wounds of imperialist tongues in historically specific ways by returning the language of the War on Terror to the intimate scenes it necessarily infiltrates and often aptly describes, particularly for Americans and immigrants with Muslim roots. In poems like "LOOK," the title piece in the collection, Sharif begins, "It matters what you call a thing," and resituates technical terms from the DOD Dictionary (marked visually in small caps) in the bedroom, in threnodies for ex-lovers, and laments for those killed in drone strikes or detained in court.[53] The word "TORTURE," for example, functions here in both its colloquial and technical senses. A question posed in a conversation with a stranger follows a tender recollection of a former lover, fond of calling the speaker *exquisite*: "*You would put up with* TORTURE. . . ?" Here attached to the commonplace pairing of "exquisite pain" and the ordinary masochisms of love, "TORTURE" points both to the hyperbolic dimensions of intimate language and to the proximity of its specific meaning, of illegal rendition and indefinite detention for anyone mistaken or mistakable for a Muslim. The "THERMAL SHADOW" the speaker invokes later in the poem similarly apostrophizes the heat sensor and the drone as surveillance technologies in order to illustrate the way the body flushes in ardor. The speaker stands rapt at this memory and also trivializes it: "Whereas the lover made my heat rise, rise so that if heat / sensors were trained on me, they could read my THERMAL SHADOW . . ." (3). Although some critics have read Sharif's incorporation of military terminology as a consciousness-raising endeavor, or worse, a didactic reminder of the ongoing wars in the Middle East and Central and South Asia, what these incursions reveal to me is more than an educational conceit. They serve not just as a mnemonic to widen our view of the world, but also a demonstration of the depth of involuntary incorporation and interpellation from which, for American Muslims, there is and can be no escape. Unlike for the questioner above, "the man outside the 2004 Republican National / Convention," TORTURE for the speaker of the poem can never be a metaphor. It is part of a war so long and an attendant discursive regime so pervasive that it restructures every encounter, every memory, appears in every dream.

In "EXPELLEE" she illustrates the devastating effects of "LOOK's" injunction: "Let it matter what we call a thing," as the speaker finds herself, a child, "at the clinic. The doctor's softly / splintered popsicle stick" depressing her tongue, a reminder that the state also silences refugees' refusals and their fear (40). "By five," she writes, "I knew I was / a HEALTH THREAT." The poem describes the clinic as an extension of the Immigration and Naturalization Service's reluctantly proffered care: "The daylong waits, the predawn lines. / Stale taste of toothpaste and skipped breakfast. / The *No* and *Next* metronome of INS. Numbered windows, / numbered tongues hanging out of red dispensers / you pull at the butcher shop" (40). The first line locates us not just in the health care facility, but with a view inside the body: "Chest films taken at the clinic." The short meditation on the nonnaturalized subject, even the minor, as a HEALTH THREAT ends by comparing the serial bureaucratic processing of migrant patients' many tongues (both body parts and languages) to "The ground meat left out / for strays, the sewing needles planted in it." By the poem's final lines, the opening gesture of care is liquidated. The child in the processing center has become both stray and meat, while the decommissioned tools of the surgeon—the needles for sewing clothes or bodies—have burrowed into a generalized and unrecognizable corpse.

In the serial poem "Reaching Guantánamo," Sharif shifts from a method of exposing the violent language of the state to an examination of the suppression and erasure of language as another form of violence, of systematic de-ontology. The poem comprises seven letters, written by an unnamed wife to her husband, Salim. The poem's title, "Reaching Guantánamo," speaks to a hopeful gesture, an attempt to touch, a hand held out, and also to the impossibility of literary arrival under conditions of extreme surveillance, abuse, and isolation. The sixth letter in the series elaborates an actuarial approach to the lives of the detained or the otherwise abandoned, and demonstrates the thoroughgoing failures of an attempt at accountability:

Dear Salim,

The neighbors got an apology
                     and a few thousand dollars.
They calculate   based on
and age. The worth of a   , of a human
                 .   hands shook as she opened
                    . She took it out front
and ripped it   .   a little pile
and set fire to it right there, right in front of

                     .

               says they'll send me
a check   for   . I would

!   !
                    ? Never.
Yours, (50)

    At the level of narrative, this penultimate letter in the series rages against the inadequacy of a bureaucratic response to wrongful detention, or loss of a child in battle, or perhaps some unrelated injustice. If that which is being apologized for is not made explicit, the suggestion of torture is implicit in the poem's framing and its site of arrival in Guantánamo. The promise of a similar compensation offered to the speaker shimmers between the gaps: "says they'll send me   / a check   for   . I would/ !   !/   ? Never." The spacing of the poem thus illustrates an obstinate secrecy that heightens the unspeakable acts for which the neighbors are recompensed. In the context of the letter's destination and recipient, a Muslim husband imprisoned (Salim in Arabic means "safe" or "intact") the white spaces also stand as a noticeably negative replacement for the black bars of redaction. The measurable intervals of the white page invite, to some extent, an imaginative populating, something like the gesture Salman Rushdie undertakes when he peoples (and deities) the Kaaba, renders it black with touch, rather than in essence. The reader cannot help but fill in the gaps, suggest words in order to bring sense to the letter. At the same time, however, Sharif's choice of blankness in place of the obscuring mark reorients our relationship to the referent. In contrast to the aesthetics of secrecy and withholding, it suggests there may be no inside-text, no truth to be unveiled, no subject to bring to light. This is not, as we will see in the final letter of the series, a claim to the unknowability of the Muslim subject, or of the impossibility of the literary as a vessel for the creation thereof. It functions more like a lament for the conditions of erasure under which such a subject is barred from coming into being or remaining present to the world or existing in time as a worlded subject, even object. The seventh letter reads,

Dear Salim,

I read some   Hikmet,
Human   *Country.*
The wife send letters to her
                    like I do. I don't read
now. He was   like you.
I've   the books,
all of them. Can't stomach their

. All
those spines lined up on my shelf. How you
would stand there, smelling the pages.
Them. They all say
the same   story
and none tell ours. (51)

This final letter in the poem's series is unsigned—without the
"Yours,   " of the preceding letters—as if written by some omniscient
being, or a mass collectivity, or by no one. The text to which the poem
alludes in its opening lines is Nâzim Hikmet's 1938 verse novel, *Human
Landscapes from My Country*. Hikmet, imprisoned for his communist beliefs, gave voice to the stories of his countrymen, Muslims in culture, if
not in belief, in a secular Turkey. Sharif's reference to the poet and his
sprawling work bespeaks the letter writer's distress at finding herself separated from her husband under similar circumstances: "I don't read   /
now. He was   like you." The pain of confronting the books once loved
and shared, "How you / would stand there, smelling the pages," is too
much for the writer to bear. "Can't stomach their   " she writes, "   them.
They all say   / the same   story   / and none tell ours" (51). Even more
than in the prior letter, it is difficult to submit to the logic of this letter,
to its blanknesses. On the one hand, the text harbors faith in the existence of a literature produced under different, if not better conditions,
an epic that both tells and doesn't tell "our story." On the other hand, it
makes plain the impossibility of the Muslim subject—and this subject's
prismatic refractions in the Arab, the Turkish, the Iranian subject, and
or as the Gauntánamo detainee—within the discursive parameters and
aesthetic regime of the War on Terror. Though Hikmet once told stories
the pair would read, smell, and appreciate, no literature can inscribe
this, the present story. "He was   like you" is the hinge that connects the
poem's beginning—"I read some"—to its turn "I don't read   now" (51).
Facing the shelves of literary history, the speaker finds resonances, but
also blankness. Amid "all those spines . . . none tell ours." (51)
    In refusing an aesthetics of concealment, Sharif's blank redactions
in the poem "Reaching Guantánamo" displace a long-standing hermeneutics of the Muslim subject—and the black sites of the US torture
machine—that makes its way to us through the epidemiological lens in
the form of the cholera morbidity maps of nineteenth-century London
(figure 7.3), the smallpox charts of the Algerian revolution, and most recently the *Senate Report on Torture*, which in spite of the visual confession
of its own instability and incompleteness as a document (figure 7.4),
retains both its faith in the discoverable truth of the archive as well as

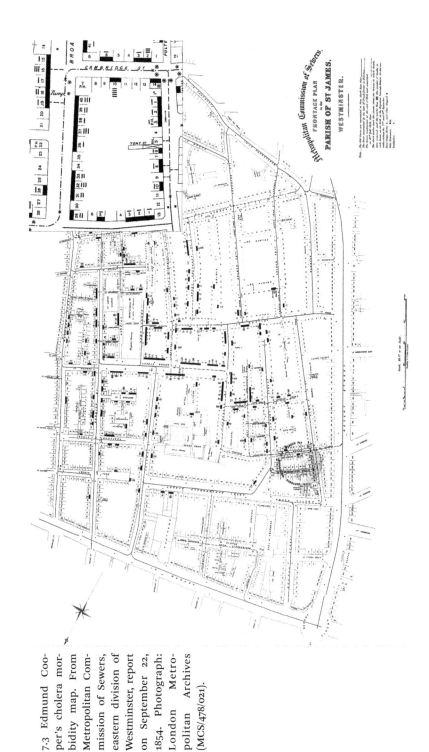

7.3 Edmund Cooper's cholera morbidity map. From Metropolitan Commission of Sewers, eastern division of Westminster, report on September 22, 1854. Photograph: London Metropolitan Archives (MCS/478/021).

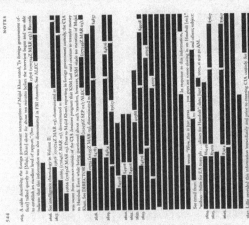

7.4 Two pages from *The Senate Intelligence Committee Report on Torture* (Brooklyn: Melville House Publishing, 2014), 544-545.

its links to an Oriental Gothic legacy of unspeakable, inhuman enmity. Sharif's is a challenge to the overwhelming consistency of a disciplining of the Oriental other through a dialectic of legible illegibility. As I have sought to show throughout these chapters, the consequences of this way of reading "Islam" and the Muslim subject—an epistemological tradition brought into being by the demands of ruling a multiconfessional colonial populace—can be seen in the infinitely expanding parameters of the War on Terror as a revival of the therapeutic empire.

Conclusions

The research undertaken in this book has been motivated by pressing questions about how the disease poetics of empire moves through the exemplary scenes of colonial, anticolonial, and postcolonial politics and cultural production, and how it changes as it moves away from characterizations of national self-determination struggles, such as those in India and Algeria, toward more wide-ranging forms of violence and resistance, and finally toward depictions of global jihad and other forms of contemporary terrorism. Across the texts and discursive fields that my research compasses, I have observed the figure doing two kinds of work—the first opens up nonstate violence to the rational hermeneutics of epidemiological science, and in so doing, attempts to domesticate the radical alterity that presumably constitutes this form of enmity under the auspices of an infinite science of surveillance. The other kind of work the figure does is both contrary to and inextricable from the first: the epidemic figuring of terror obscures motive, agency, and legibility behind a veil of monstrosity and the dehumanizing organicization of the pathogenic other. As an extension of this epistemic confluence, the historically durable recourse to imagining anticolonial insurgency and terror as epidemics depoliticizes nonstate actors, while also sanitizing the prophylactic measures and retaliations of sovereign and governmental actors against them. Such representations, therefore, are also frequently attended by a slippage in the conception of the subject, such that human actors become reconfigured as viral vectors or infectious agents. The figural system of epidemic serves as a programmatic rhetorical justification of any and all acts against these agents—and the places in which they reside—in the interest of defending the unassailable good of the abstraction "global health," even as resources are siphoned away from infectious disease, sanitation, and access to health care. The epidemic method as it operates in the texts I have interrogated here thus consolidates and extends colonial and neoimperial forms of surveillance, quarantine, and care as a delivery system not just of novel xenophobias and a global anti-Islamic movement, but also of endless war.

This book has told a story that I hope carries explanatory force in thinking deeply and systematically about the deep systems that structure our present. It is about the impact and aftershocks of a historical "accident"—the coinciding of the cholera epidemics and the birth of nationalist revolution in India—that gave rise to an epistemic revolution in the administration of empire and the understanding of global public health as an appendage of it. The work of Michel Foucault stands, in very obvious ways, at the base of the research I have undertaken in this book. In closing, I am in mind of the productive reticence in Foucault's work to locate the nineteenth century's systems of biopower along a moral axis. I don't wish to eschew responsibility for what I have sought to show here about the coeval development of Islamophobia and epidemiological approaches to contemporary terrorism, but neither does it strike me as useful to risk condemning the discipline of epidemiology, especially as we witness the unfolding of a global pandemic, nor to dismiss theoretical and practical attempts to understand why Muslims in desperate straits have with some regularity targeted civilians in public spaces in both the Islamic world and in the West. This book is not against colonial science any more than it is against literature. But it is against the scientific packaging of counterinsurgency and the concurrent evisceration of social services, health equity, and care. Its force, I hope, is in tracing the continuities between colonial science and neocolonial war in its many forms. To be a serious Foucauldian is also to attend to the ways in which the very dispersal that structures the epidemic imaginary is also its greatest resource. In the capillary nodes of contact, exchange, and transmission of contagious or otherwise-shared affliction resides a nearly infinite potential for attachment, mutual responsibility, and the redistribution of power. In concluding the previous chapter with Salman Rushdie's counterparadigmatic deployment of the epidemic figure for a politics of affiliation in *The Satanic Verses*, and in attending to the ways in which contemporary writers from the Muslim world have sought to rewrite the interpretive frameworks of Islam and Muslim subjectivity, I am acutely aware of a parallel story that can and indeed ought to be told about the uses of the epidemic imaginary, not for the furtherance of existing structures of biopolitical control, but against them. In other words, discourses of disease and disability can and have been appropriated to revolutionary and affiliative ends.

The cottage industry of terrorism literature is but one small piece of the discursive construction of terrorism epidemics in the contemporary global imaginary, but it is an influential one in setting the terms of an available arsenal of figures, plotlines, and narrative sense-making for reporters, policy makers, and the culture industry at large. Post-9/11 international literary fiction teems with stories that draw on and promulgate these long-standing conventions. The terrorism novels of John Updike, Richard Flanagan, Don DeLillo, Mohsin Hamid, Karan Mahajan, and Amy Waldman among others simply narrow the focus of these pathological presuppositions, looking to crack the code of the pathological psyche of the terrorist or his foil, the "surprisingly" good Muslim.[54] A broad-based cultural apocalyptic approach is also a feature of post-9/11 global fiction: think, for example, of Michel Houellebecq's *Soumission*, a proximate-future speculative account of a France at once relievingly and revilingly overtaken by Arab money and Salafist Islam.[55] Though Houellebecq's novel does not explicitly deploy the figure of disease to describe Muslim conquest in postimperial Europe, it participates in and capitalizes on a broader set of conventions that associates the rise of global Islam with the end of history, a terrible fantasy stoked by the increasingly common use of natural disaster metaphors for Europe's migration crisis.[56] The Global North, in a predictable dialectic, projects itself ever more insistently as the paragon of a "healthy" civilization, where nominally functional democracies serve as an alibi for economic and war crimes in both the national and international arenas. The *9/11 Commission Report*, more than any work of fiction, will carry this projection forward in the historical record of our era.

In constructing a genealogy of the contemporary deployments of epidemic figuration in and around the War on Terror, I have focused my attention on texts that have circulated easily and broadly within the pathways of imperialism and neoimperialism, and in many ways reinforce their ideology. The purview of this book is thus limited in three particular ways. The first is that I have worked primarily with a model of epidemiology that remains wedded to its origins in colonial science. This is not the only model of the discipline, however, which has evolved in significant ways, especially since the outbreak of HIV and AIDS, and has served to instantiate practices of research and care that dramatically decenter the locations of biopower and destabilize its multiple local and global agendas. The second is that I have structured my inquiry around writers and texts whose impact on the evolution of the epidemic figuring of violence is determined by their centrality and continued popularity in canonical Anglophone and Francophone literature. I follow Jed Esty in this regard in insisting on the importance of "famous books," as mediating between the potentially cloistered concerns of the literary and broader social and political movements.[57] As I have shown, these texts are riven with political ambiguity, and their representations of epidemic are neither stable nor ideologically consistent. Nevertheless, Kipling, Stoker, Camus, and Rushdie are writers of global reputation whose texts have earned their place in "world" literature in part because they were written in the vehicular languages of colonialism and published and promoted through the channels of the world literary markets based in London, Paris, and New York. That many other colonial and postcolonial texts and writers participate in the conversation and transformation of epidemic figuration, discourses of pathogenicity and toxicity, and experiments with medical discourse in imaginative writing goes without saying. At the same time, and in spite of whispered critiques that postcolonial criticism has made its point and needs to move on, this book has been animated by an ongoing and indeed increasingly distressing mass of evidence pointing to the unfinished business of colonialism and the unfinished project of reading the ways in which imperialist violence and colonial epistemologies and state-forms continue to define our present. That the War on Terror is a neoimperial war is a matter of common sense on the left; how exactly this translation from small utterances—a metaphor here, pathetic fallacy there—to the organizing principles of twenty-first-century politics takes place is what I have tried to show in these readings.

Since September 11, 2001, political, cultural, and literary criticism in North America and Western Europe has been enormously impacted by research fields and projects that, both implicitly and explicitly, engage with questions of how things have been "since September 11." In this way, despite the dramatically greater number of lives lost in the immediate zones of conflict in the theaters of war in Afghanistan, in Iraq, and now in Syria, the last two decades in literary scholarship, philosophy, and political theory share characteristics with the postwar era in Europe in terms of the urgency with which cosmopolitan subjects—mostly Anglophone and Francophone, though for different reasons this time—have addressed themselves to their own moment in history. The fixation on terrorism, the notion that the entire world has been redefined by the 2001 attack on American soil, is both insular and naïve in ways that range from the quantitative to the qualitative to the broadly epistemic. And yet, it is also true. I think it is fair to point to this phenomenon of cultural periodization that defines a distinct epoch "since September 11" as a myopic one, while also acknowledging the concrete geopolitical effects of this seismic shift—from the outcome of the 2016 American election to the rising white supremacist populisms in Europe to the now-waning arc of ISIS to the expansion of BJP-style Hindu nationalism in India to the catastrophic racial inequities exposed and exacerbated by the COVID-19 pandemic. Such a periodization necessarily makes assumptions about what constitutes the global first-person plural. These conversations—at the level of the production of a public discourse that could be considered in some way global—do not, or did not, characterize dominant political speech anywhere outside of the West/Islam axis, and there, only among a population that was both literate and financially stable enough to have access to modes of publication and dissemination that exceed the local. I acknowledge this limitation as a function of both my institutional training and of my position in the North American academy. I have thus written about the problem of who sets the terms of a global conversation and how the limits of global health are defined as a continuing function of colonialism while also attempting to interrogate the epidemic metaphors through which this globe is figured to accommodate the international security regime that constitutes the twenty-first century's capitalist neoempire.

Acknowledgments

I am grateful to Columbia University, the New York Public Library, Williams College, the City College of New York, the Hellman Foundation, the Heyman Center for the Humanities, the Rose Manuscript, Archives, and Rare Book Library at Emory, the Rosenbach Museum, the Huntington Library, and the University of Toronto for supporting the research and writing of this book. Special thanks go to Mariam Said for her continued commitment to urgent comparative scholarship, and for her endlessly provocative takes.

It would not have been possible to complete this work without the help of an extraordinary group of people who I feel lucky to call my mentors, colleagues, and friends. My greatest debt is owed to Gauri Viswanathan, without whose encouragement I would not have known how to begin finding my place in scholarship; indeed, without whose pathbreaking scholarship such a place may not have existed at all. Gauri, you have taught me more than I can say, perhaps most importantly that the best questions—for scholarship and for friendship—are the ones you want to sit with for years. That you invited me to do so in your company is among the highest compliments I have ever been paid.

Joey Slaughter and Brent Edwards offered wisdom, support, and keen editorial eyes with unwavering generosity and patience over these many years, and I am beyond grateful to them both for their own ambitious and rigorous scholarship and for helping me find my project and my voice. In its early stages, the book benefitted immensely from the guidance of Sarah Cole, Emily Apter, Judith Butler, Sara Suleri, and Elaine Freedgood. At Columbia, Gayatri Spivak, Bob O'Meally, Marcellus Blount, Jenny Davidson, Nicole Wallack, Jennifer Wenzel, and Cassie Fennel helped me think through rough spots in the conception and writing. Since my undergraduate years, the staff at Butler Library has offered extraordinary support and assistance; I am especially indebted to Kerry Saunders for his warmth and affection through difficult stretches.

I am lucky to have been a part of wonderful collaborative spaces at CUNY: both the Humanities Center Seminars and the Beyond Identity Program at City College. Many thanks to Gary Wilder and Nimmi

Gowrinathan for drawing me into the fold, and to the many friends and colleagues at CUNY who have offered their criticism and wisdom.

I could not have finished the manuscript without the assiduous work of my research assistants Stef Hernandez, Erin Hanson, Rachel Clemens, Paul Griffith, Lilika Kukiela, and Leonard Bopp. Thanks especially to Leonard and Stef for seeing it all through, and for your last-minute orchestration of details. To all my beloved students at Columbia, Bard, Williams, City College, and the University of Toronto: you taught me new ways to explain, new ways to care, and new ways to love. I will be forever in your thrall, and I can't wait to see what you all do. I've been fortunate to have the tireless support of Monica Shah, Candace Feldman, and Drew Magidoff; thank you for keeping me alive. Though they did not work directly on this book, my editors at *Poetry*, *The Boston Review*, *Triple Canopy*, *Critical Quarterly*, and *Words Without Borders*—Michael Slosek, Avni Sejpal, Molly Kleiman, Ben Lerner, and Haider Shahbaz—helped my writing grow and find a place in the world.

My friends have made every thought sharper and every pleasure greater. Untold thanks to Amiel Bizé, Steffani Jemison, Nico Muhly, Ariel Bowman, Britt Peterson, and Deb Grossberg for many years of inspiration and collaboration. Graduate school was infinitely better thanks to the kindness and care of Kate Stanley, Anne Diebel, Sherally Munshi, Alvan Ikoku, Musa Gurnis, Bina Gogineni, Ben Parker, Royden Kadyschuk, Sonali Thakkar, Cecelia Watson, Lauren Silvers, and Bill Martin.

The last years have brought enormous surprises and some of the deepest friendships I have known. This book would not exist without the outpouring of love, candor, practical advice, and daily support of Alicia Mireles Christoff, Sonya Posmentier, Heather Cleary, and Valeria Luiselli: the sisters I always dreamed of. My family has grown to include Ryan Moritz, Tanya Agathocleous, Dohra Ahmad, and Ianna Hawkins Owen as well, whose creativity and affection have brightened my thoughts and days. Endless respect and gratitude also to Poulomi Saha, Marina Bilbija, Chris Pye, Emery Shriver, Tony Alessandrini, Karen Swann, Stephen Best, Melanie Micir, Alex Benson, Nancy Leonard, Phoebe Cohen, Leslie Brown, Aruna D'Souza, Aparna Kapadia, Julia Bryan-Wilson, Mel Chen, Ronjaunee Chatterjee, Zarena Aslami, Gemma Sieff, Liz Gately, Nadia Sirota, Janine de Novais, Evans Richardson, Sufjan Stevens, Michael Allan, Kim Calder, Mik Awake, Lisa Kerr, Lindsay Reckson, Anna Thomas, Alex Gillespie, Avery Slater, Sophie Hamacher, Owen Pallett, Zirwat Chowdhury, Dorothy Wang, Laylah Ali, Annie Reinhardt, Brian Martin, Christophe Koné, Will Rawls, Liz Marcus, Jane Hu, Stephanie Hopkins, and Dawn Lundy Martin for necessary rescues, jokes, chats, and more. A duplicate but especially heartfelt thanks to Kate Stanley for her careful eye as I wrote the book's new preface under difficult conditions; I hope we write together always. All my love and thanks to Becky Hope Savitt for carrying me through to the end of this work, and for making the darkest moments radiant and new.

I am beyond lucky to have the unshakeable love and care of my extended family; thank you especially to my cousins Zee, Asad, Akbi, Alia, Zehra, Sakeena, Batool, Musa, Sheher, Lauren, and Jamie for being shady and supportive, loud and proud, and an unending source of hilarity and tenderness. To my parents and my brother—Sughra Raza, James Kolb, and Jaffer Kolb—thank you for everything. Thank you for reading and talking and laughing with me as I've learned how to explain myself. Thank you for being my home no matter where I am, for pushing and for holding me. Your critical acumen and astounding love have made it possible for me to keep learning.

Finally, my experience with the University of Chicago Press has been a dream. Thanks to Randy Petilos, Meredith Nini, Michael Koplow, and most of all Alan Thomas for your patience and guidance. Preparing the index with Josh Rutner was a pleasure. To my anonymous readers: your acuity has made this book stronger and helped it find an ending. Thank you for your care with these ideas, and for believing in the work.

Notes

PREFACE

1. Andrew Cuomo, Televised Address, April 9, 2020, https://www.governor
.ny.gov/news/video-audio-photos-rush-transcript-amid-ongoing-covid-19
-pandemic-governor-cuomo-announces-five.

2. Susan Sontag, *Illness as Metaphor and AIDS and Its Metaphors* (New York:
Picador, 1990).

3. Paul Elie, "(Against) Virus as Metaphor," *New Yorker*, March 19, 2020,
https://www.newyorker.com/news/daily-comment/against-the-coronavirus-as
-metaphor.

4. Elie, "(Against) Virus as Metaphor."

5. See, for example, Davide Lerner, "It's Not Islam That Drives Young Europeans Toward Jihad, France's Top Terrorism Expert Explains," *Haaretz*, August
20, 2017, https://www.haaretz.com/world-news/europe/it-s-not-islam-that-drives
-young-europeans-to-jihad-terrorism-expert-says-1.5477000.

6. Sigal Samuel, "China Is Treating Islam Like a Mental Illness," *The Atlantic*,
August 28, 2018, https://www.theatlantic.com/international/archive/2018/08/
china-pathologizing-uighur-muslims-mental-illness/568525/.

7. Ivan Watson and Ben Westcott, "Watched, Judged, Detained," Cable
News Network, February 2020, https://www.cnn.com/interactive/2020/02/asia/
xinjiang-china-karakax-document-intl-hnk/.

8. Arundhati Roy, "The Pandemic Is a Portal," *Financial Times*, April 3,
2020, https://www.ft.com/content/10d8f5e8-74eb-11ea-95fe-fcd274e920ca. See
also "Tablighi Super Spreaders Cause Covid-19 Explosion in India," *Times of
India*, April 2, 2020, https://timesofindia.indiatimes.com/india/tablighi-super
-spreaders-cause-covid-19-explosion-in-india/articleshow/74956397.cms.

9. Mehdi Hasan, "The Coronavirus Is Empowering Islamophobes—But
Exposing the Idiocy of Islamophobia," *The Intercept*, April 14, 2020, https://
theintercept.com/2020/04/14/coronavirus-muslims-islamophobia/.

10. See Malcolm Surer, "Indonesia's Ramadan Exodus Risks Spreading
Covid-19 across the Country," *France 24*, April 8, 2020, https://www.france24
.com/en/20200408-indonesia-s-ramadan-exodus-risks-spreading-covid-19-across
-the-country; Declan Walsh, "As Ramadan Begins, Muslims (Mostly) Accede
to Pandemic Orders," *New York Times*, April 24, 2020, https://www.nytimes
.com/2020/04/24/world/middleeast/coronavirus-ramadan-2020.html; and "The

Maldives Is Threatened by Jihadism and Covid-19," *The Economist*, March 21, 2020, https://www.economist.com/asia/2020/03/21/the-maldives-is-threatened-by-jihadism-and-covid-19.

11. Erin Cox, "Salt Lake City Mosque Vandalized; Others Remain Closed during Ramadan," Fox 13 Salt Lake City, April 24, 2020, https://www.fox13now.com/news/local-news/salt-lake-city-mosque-vandalized-others-remain-closed-during-ramadan; Sandra E. Garcia, "Man Charged with Hate Crime in Suspected Arson at Islamic Center," *New York Times*, April 28, 2020, https://www.nytimes.com/2020/04/28/us/nicholas-proffitt-missouri-islamic-center-arson.html.

12. See Pien Huang, "Trump and WHO: How Much Does the U.S. Give? What's the Impact of a Halt in Funding?," National Public Radio, April 15, 2020, https://www.npr.org/sections/goatsandsoda/2020/04/15/834666123/trump-and-who-how-much-does-the-u-s-give-whats-the-impact-of-a-halt-in-funding.

13. "President Donald J. Trump Announces Great American Economic Revival Industry Groups," White House Press Release, April 14, 2020, https://www.whitehouse.gov/briefings-statements/president-donald-j-trump-announces-great-american-economic-revival-industry-groups/.

14. See Joseph A. McCartin, "Class and the Challenge of COVID-19," *Dissent*, March 23, 2020, https://www.dissentmagazine.org/online_articles/class-and-the-challenge-of-covid-19, and Adam Serwer "America's Racial Contract Is Killing Us," *The Atlantic*, May 8, 2020, https://www.theatlantic.com/ideas/archive/2020/05/americas-racial-contract-showing/611389/.

15. For an analysis of the contemporary example, see Talia Lavin, "Calling Healthcare Workers War 'Heroes' Sets Them Up to Be Sacrificed," *Gentleman's Quarterly*, April 15, 2020, https://www.gq.com/story/essential-workers-martyrdom. For the historical deployments of this language of sacrifice, see Alan Bewell, *Romanticism and Colonial Disease* (Baltimore: Johns Hopkins University Press, 2003).

16. Ed Yong, "Our Pandemic Summer," *The Atlantic*, April 15, 2020, https://www.theatlantic.com/health/archive/2020/04/pandemic-summer-coronavirus-reopening-back-normal/609940/.

INTRODUCTION

1. Reporter of Decisions, Syllabus, *Trump v. Hawaii* (585 U.S. __, June 26, 2018), 1.

2. For Pershing's own account, in which he relates the practice of burying Moro suicide attackers with the corpse of a pig, see John J. Pershing, *My Life Before the World War, 1860–1917* (Lexington: University Press of Kentucky, 2013), ed. John T. Greenwood, 285.

3. See Patrick Brantlinger, "Kipling's 'The White Man's Burden' and Its Afterlives," *English Literature in Transition, 1880–1920* 50, no. 2 (2007): 172–191.

4. Sotomayor's detailed account includes the following:

[A]t a rally in South Carolina, Trump told an apocryphal story about United States General John J. Pershing killing a large group of Muslim insurgents in the Philippines with bullets dipped in pigs' blood in the early 1900s. In March 2016, he expressed his belief that "Islam hates us . . . [W]e can't allow people coming into this country who have this hatred of the United States . . . [a]nd of people that are not Muslim." That same month, Trump asserted that "[w]e're having problems with Muslims coming into the country." . . . As Trump's presidential campaign progressed, he began to describe his policy proposal in slightly different terms. In June 2016, for instance, he characterized the policy proposal as a suspension of immigration from countries "where there's a proven history of terrorism." He also described the proposal as rooted in the need to stop "importing radical Islamic terrorism to the West through a failed immigration system." . . . A month before the 2016 election, Trump reiterated that his proposed "Muslim ban" had "morphed into a[n] extreme vetting from certain areas of the world." Then, on December 21, 2016, President-elect Trump was asked whether he would "rethink" his previous "plans to create a Muslim registry or ban Muslim immigration." He replied: "You know my plans. All along, I've proven to be right."

Sonia Sotomayor, Dissenting Opinion, *Trump v. Hawaii*, 585 U.S. __ (2018), 5–6. Citations in Sotomayor's text have been expunged for readability.

5. Sotomayor, Dissenting Opinion, 7.

6. John Roberts, Majority Opinion, *Trump v. Hawaii* (585 U.S. __, June 26, 2018), 23.

7. Anthony Zurcher, "What Trump Team Has Said About Islam," *BBC News*, February 7, 2017, https://www.bbc.com/news/world-us-canada-38886496.

8. John W. Kaye, "The Romance of Indian Warfare," *North British Review* 12 (November 1849–February 1850): 205.

9. In both its double hermeneutics and the logic of emergency it instantiates, the epidemic trope is the colonial precursor to the ticking bomb scenario. See Jacques Lezra, *Wild Materialism: The Ethic of Terror and the Modern Republic* (New York: Fordham University Press, 2010), 4–6.

10. Sotomayor, Dissenting Opinion, 9.

11. I'm grateful to my anonymous reader for this phrase.

12. George Lakoff and Mark Johnson, *Metaphors We Live By* (Chicago: University of Chicago Press, 2003), chap. 6, "Ontological Metaphors," 26–32.

13. Donald H. Rumsfeld and Richard B. Myers, "Rumsfeld and Myers Briefing on Enduring Freedom," United States Department of Defense, Office of the Assistant Secretary of Defense, news transcript, October 7, 2001, http://www.defense.gov/transcripts/transcript.aspx?transcriptid= 2011; Martin Amis, "The Age of Horrorism, part three," *Observer*, September 9, 2006, http://www.theguardian.com/world/2006/sep/10/september11

.politicsphilosophyandsociety1; Hans Magnus Enzensberger, "The Resurgence of Human Sacrifice," *Society* 39, no. 3 (March/April 2002), 75; Boris Johnson, "Global Britain Is Helping to Win the Struggle against Islamist Terror," Foreign & Commonwealth Office, Speech Transcript, December 7, 2017, https:www.gov .uk/government/speeches/how-global-britain-is-helping-to-win-the-struggle -against-islamist-terror; Jacques Derrida, "A Dialogue with Jacques Derrida," in Giovanna Borradori, *Philosophy in a Time of Terror: Dialogues with Jürgen Habermas and Jacques Derrida* (Chicago: University of Chicago Press, 2003), 95.

14. W. J. T. Mitchell, "9/11: Criticism and Crisis," *Critical Inquiry* 28, no. 2 (Winter 2002), 568.

15. Niall Ferguson, "War Plans," review of *Terror and Consent* by Philip Bobbitt, *New York Times*, April 13, 2008, http://www.nytimes.com/2008/04/13/books/review/Ferguson-t.html?_r=1&oref=slogin; Cole Moreton, "Philip Bobbitt: The Presidents' Brain," *Independent*, July 20, 2008, http://www.independent.co.uk/news/people/profiles/philip-bobbitt-the-presidents-brain-872412.html.

16. Mona Yacoubian and Paul Stares, "Rethinking the War on Terror," United States Institute of Peace, September 7, 2005, https://www.usip.org/publications/2005/09/rethinking-war-terror.

17. Bernard S. Cohn, *Colonialism and Its Forms of Knowledge: The British in India* (Princeton: Princeton University Press, 1996), 3.

18. Bruce Holsinger usefully elaborates millennial medievalism in "Empire, Apocalypse, and the 9/11 Premodern," *Critical Inquiry* 34 (Spring 2008), 470.

19. According to Pervez Musharraf, then president of Pakistan, this is the threat Richard Armitage, then deputy secretary of state, delivered to a Pakistani intelligence chief in the days following the September 11 attacks. See "US 'Threatened to Bomb' Pakistan," *BBC online*, September 22, 2006, http://news .bbc.co.uk/2/hi/south_asia/5369198.stm.

20. Much longer histories of the concept of terror have been foundational in my thinking, but I circumscribe work here according to the contemporary triad of Islam-epidemic-terror. See Talal Asad, *On Suicide Bombing* (New York: Columbia University Press, 2007), and "Thinking About Terrorism and Just War," *Cambridge Review of International Affairs* 23, no. 1 (December 18, 2009): 3–24; also Susan Buck-Morss *Thinking Past Terror: Islamism and Critical Theory on the Left* (London: Verso, 2003); Retort, "Afflicted Powers: The State, the Spectacle, and September 11," *New Left Review* 27 (May/June 2004): 5–21.

21. United States Department of Homeland Security, Office for Civil Rights and Civil Liberties, "Terminology to Define the Terrorists: Recommendations from American Muslims," January 2008, 1, https://www.dhs.gov/sites/default/files/publications/dhs_crcl_terminology_08-1-08_accessible.pdf.

22. United States Department of Homeland Security, "Terminology."

23. James R. Fox, *Dictionary of International and Comparative Law*, 3rd ed. (New York: Oceana Publications, 2003).

24. United Nations Security Council Resolution 1566 (S/RES/1566 (2004)), October 8, 2004.

25. David Simpson, *States of Terror: History, Theory, Literature* (Chicago: University of Chicago Press, 2019), x.

26. Elleke Boehmer and Stephen Morton, eds., *Terror and the Postcolonial* (London: Wiley Blackwell, 2010), 7. Subsequent references to this work appear in parentheses in the text.

27. Eqbal Ahmad, *Terrorism: Theirs and Ours* (New York: Seven Stories Press, 2001), 13.

28. Adriana Cavarero, *Horrorism: Naming Contemporary Violence*, trans. William McCuaig (New York: Columbia University Press, 2009), 32. Cavarero's invocation of vulnerability draws primarily on Judith Butler's work in *Precarious Life: The Powers of Mourning and Violence* (London: Verso, 2004).

29. Amis, "The Age of Horrorism," part 3.

30. Khaled A. Beydoun, *American Islamophobia* (Berkeley: University of California Press, 2018), 32–44. Subsequent references to this work appear in parentheses in the text.

31. Bernard S. Cohn, *Colonialism and Its Forms of Knowledge: The British in India* (Princeton: Princeton University Press, 1996), 3.

32. Paul Farmer, *Pathologies of Power: Health, Human Rights, and the New War on the Poor* (Berkeley: University of California Press, 2005), xxiv.

33. Barry S. Levy and Victor W. Sidel, eds., *Terrorism and Public Health: A Balanced Approach to Strengthening Systems and Protecting People*, 2nd ed. (New York: Oxford University Press, 2012), 5.

34. *Proclamation by the Queen in Council to the Princes, Chiefs, and People of India* (Allahabad: Office of the Governor General, 1858), https://www.bl.uk/collection-items/proclamation-by-the-queen-in-council-to-the-princes-chiefs-and-people-of-india.

35. Benjamin Guy Babington, Epidemiological Society for the Investigation of Epidemic Diseases, *Transactions of the Epidemiological Society of London*, vol. 1, 1859–1862 (London: John W. Davies, 1863), 6.

36. Babington, *Transactions*, 7.

37. World Health Organization, "Epidemiology," http://www.who.int/topics/epidemiology/en/.

38. World Health Organization, "About WHO," http://www.who.int/about/en/.

39. For Michel Foucault, the shift to biopolitical governmentality includes a growing understanding and study of population's normal ebbs and flows: "its death rates, its incidence of disease, its regularities of accidents. . . . major epidemics," in the interest of "improv[ing] the condition of the population . . . increas[ing] its wealth, its longevity, and its health." Michel Foucault, *Security, Territory, Population: Lectures at the Collège de France 1977–1978*, ed. Michel Senellart, trans. Graham Burchell (New York: Picador, 2007), 104–105. For more on this shift, see 103–110.

40. Margaret Chan, "Welcome to the World Health Organization," introductory letter in World Health Organization, *Working for Health: An Introduction to*

the World Health Organization (Geneva: WHO Press, 2007), 1. http://www.who
.int/about/brochure_en.pdf.

41. See, for example, Limor Aharonson-Daniel et al., "Epidemiology of
Terror-Related Versus Non-Terror-Related Traumatic Injury in Children," *Pedi-
atrics* 112, no. 4 (October 1, 2003); Nick Wilson and George Thomson, "The Epi-
demiology of International Terrorism Involving Fatal Outcomes in Developed
Countries," *European Journal of Epidemiology* 20 (2005): 375–381; and Levy and
Sidel, *Terrorism and Public Health.*

42. Thanks to my anonymous reader for helping me sharpen my intentions
here.

43. Jacques Derrida, "A Dialogue with Jacques Derrida," in Giovanna Borradori, *Philosophy in a Time of Terror: Dialogues with Jürgen Habermas and Jacques
Derrida* (Chicago: University of Chicago Press, 2003), 94.

44. Derrida, "A Dialogue," 94.

45. For an account of this genealogy and its relationship to post-9/11 theory,
see J. Hillis Miller, "Derrida's Politics of Autoimmunity," *Discourse* 30, no. 1/2
(Winter/Spring 2008): 221. See also Roberto Esposito, *Immunitas: The Protection
and Negation of Life*, trans. Zakiya Hanafi (Cambridge: Polity, 2011), 5–7.

46. Derrida, "A Dialogue," 95.

47. Derrida, "A Dialogue," 95 (emphasis in the original).

48. W. J. T. Mitchell, *Cloning Terror: The War of Images, 9/11 to the Present* (Chicago: University of Chicago Press, 2011), 53.

49. Mitchell, *Cloning Terror*, 53.

50. Susan Sontag, *Illness as Metaphor and AIDS and Its Metaphors* (New York:
Picador, 1990), 87. Subsequent references to this work appear in parentheses in
the text.

51. Patricia Clough and Jasbir Puar, "Introduction," *Viral: Women's Studies
Quarterly* 40, no. 1/2 (Spring/Summer 2012), 15.

52. Priscilla Wald, *Contagious: Cultures, Carriers, and the Outbreak Narrative*
(Durham: Duke University Press, 2008), 19.

53. Wald, *Contagious*, 19.

54. Cristobal Silva, *Miraculous Plagues: An Epidemiology of Early New England
Narrative* (New York: Oxford University Press, 2011), 4.

55. Quoted in Wald, *Contagious*, 19–20.

56. See Edward W. Said's account of his own stretching of Foulcauldian
discourse analysis in *Orientalism* (New York: Vintage, 1979).

57. Cited in Ranajit Guha, *History at the Limit of World History* (New York:
Columbia University Press, 2002), 90.

58. Guha, *History at the Limit*, 91.

59. I am thinking in particular of Gayatri Chakravorty Spivak's remarks
on the way in which the distinction between comparative literature and area
studies "infected" comparative literature from the start—an infection that she
proposes to remedy by approaching the "language of the other not only as a

field language . . . but as active cultural media." Gayatri Chakravorty Spivak, *Death of a Discipline* (New York: Columbia University Press, 2008), 8. See also Edward W. Said, *Culture and Imperialism* (New York: Vintage, 1993); Robert J. C. Young, *Postcolonialism: An Historical Introduction* (Oxford: Blackwell, 2001); Peter Hallward, *Absolutely Postcolonial: Writing Between the Singular and the Specific* (Manchester: Manchester University Press, 2001); Joseph Slaughter, *Human Rights Inc.: The World Novel, Narrative Form, and International Law* (New York: Fordham University Press, 2007); and Emily Apter, *Against World Literature: On the Politics of Untranslatability* (London: Verso, 2013).

60. Walter Benjamin, "Theses on the Philosophy of History," *Illuminations*, trans. Harry Zohn, ed. Hannah Arendt (New York: Schocken Books, 1968).

61. Michael Löwy, *Fire Alarm: Reading Walter Benjamin's "On the Concept of History,"* trans. Chris Turner (London: Verso, 2016), 11.

62. Michel Serres, with Bruno Latour, *Conversations on Science, Culture, and Time*, trans. Roxanne Lapidus (Ann Arbor: University of Michigan Press, 1995), 57, 197.

63. World Health Organization, "Declaration of Alma Ata," September 12, 1978, http://www.who.int/publications/almaata_declaration_en.pdf. See also Laurie Garrett, *The Coming Plague: Newly Emerging Diseases in a World Out of Balance* (New York: Penguin, 1995).

CHAPTER 1

1. Saeed Shah, "CIA Organized Fake Vaccination Drive to Get Osama bin Laden's Family DNA," *Guardian*, July 11, 2011, https://www.theguardian.com/world/2011/jul/11/cia-fake-vaccinations-osama-bin-ladens-dna.

2. Matthieu Aikins, "The Doctor, the CIA, and the Blood of Bin Laden," *Gentlemen's Quarterly*, December 19, 2012, https://www/gq.com/story/doctor-cia-blood-of-bin-laden-january-2013/.

3. Aikins, "The Doctor, the CIA, and the Blood of bin Laden."

4. Mark Mazzetti, "Vaccination Ruse Used in Pursuit of bin Laden," *New York Times*, July 11, 2011, http://www.nytimes.com/2011/07/12/world/asia/12dna.html?_r=0.

5. Aikins, "The Doctor, the CIA, and the Blood of bin Laden"; Tim McGirk, "How the bin Laden Raid Put Vaccinators Under the Gun in Pakistan," *National Geographic*, February 25, 2015, http://news.nationalgeographic.com/2015/02/150225-polio-pakistan-vaccination-virus-health/.

6. Anthony Robbins, "The CIA's Vaccination Ruse," *Journal of Public Health Policy* 33, no. 4 (November, 2012) 387–389; McGirk, "How the bin Laden Raid"; "How the CIA's Fake Vaccination Campaign Endangers Us All," *Scientific American*, May 1, 2013, https://www.scientificamerican.com/article/how-cia-fake-vaccination-campaign-endangers-us-all/.

7. Donald G. McNeil Jr., "C.I.A. Vaccine Ruse May Have Harmed the War on

Polio," *New York Times*, July 9, 2012, http://www.nytimes.com/2012/07/10/health/
cia-vaccine-ruse-in-pakistan-may-have-harmed-polio-fight.html?pagewanted
=all&_r=0; World Health Organization, "Circulating vaccine-derived poliovirus type 2—Pakistan," November 28, 2019. https://www.who.int/csr/don/28
-november-2019-polio-pakistan/en/.

8. "Lashkar-e-Islam," Mapping Militant Organizations, Stanford University, last modified August 28, 2012, http://web.stanford.edu/group/mapping
militants/cgi-bin/groups/view/445.

9. Jibran Ahmed, "Pakistani Doctor Who Helped U.S. Find bin Laden
Charged with Murder," Reuters, November 22, 2013, http://www.reuters.com/
article/us-pakistan-afridi-murder-idUSBRE9AL0F720131122. In 2015, Afridi's
former lawyer was shot and killed in Peshawar. "Taliban Faction Kills Lawyer,"
New York Times, March 17, 2015, https://www.nytimes.com/2015/03/18/world/
asia/taliban-faction-kills-lawyer.html.

10. Jason Ukman, "CIA Defends Running Vaccine Program to Find bin
Laden," *Washington Post*, July 13, 2011, https://www.washingtonpost.com/world/
national-security/cia-defends-running-vaccine-program-to-find-bin-laden/2011/
07/13/gIQAbLcFDI_story.html.

11. Leon Panetta, interview by Scott Pelley, *60 Minutes*, CBS News, June 10,
2012, https://www.cbsnews.com/video/the-defense-secretary-leon-panetta-1/.

12. Chris McGreal, "US Cuts Pakistan's Aid in Protest at Jail for Doctor Who
Helped Find bin Laden," *Guardian*, May 24, 2012, http://www.guardian.co.uk/
world/2012/may/24/us-pakistan-aid-doctor-bin-laden. Afridi was reportedly
removed from prison "for security reasons" in April 2018. See "Dr. Shakil Afridi
Moved from Prison 'to Safer Location,'" *Dawn*, April 27, 2018, https://www.dawn
.com/news/1404218.

13. Donald Trump, "Donald Trump on His Foreign Policy Strategy," interview by Bill O'Reilly, *The O'Reilly Factor*, Fox News, April 28, 2016, https://www
.foxnews.com/transcript/donald-trump-on-his-foreign-policy-strategy.

14. Hollie McKay and Mohsin Saleem Ullah, "'Hero' Doctor Shakil Afridi
Who Helped Find bin Laden Launches Hunger Strike behind Bars after 'Losing
Hope for Justice,' Lawyer Says," *Fox News*, March 4, 2020, https://www.foxnews
.com/world/hero-doctor-shakil-afridi-hunger-strike-behind-bars.

15. Ayaz Gul, "Pakistan: Trump Wrong on Jailed Doctor Who Helped Find
bin Laden," Voice of America, May 2, 2016, http://www.voanews.com/east-asia/
pakistan-trump-wrong-jailed-doctor-who-helped-find-bin-laden.

16. Gul, "Pakistan."

17. Gul, "Pakistan."

18. The best analyses of this discursive bleed are Thomas Keenan, "A Language That Needs No Translation, or: Can Things Get Any Worse?," in *Terror
and the Roots of Poetics*, ed. Jeffrey Champlin (New York: Atropos Press, 2013),
92–109, and Faisal Devji, *The Terrorist in Search of Humanity: Militant Islam and
Global Politics* (New York: Columbia University Press, 2008). For bin Laden's
statements, see Bruce Lawrence, ed., *Messages to the World: The Statements of*

Osama bin Laden (London: Verso, 2005). In his introduction to the material, Lawrence draws a different conclusion from the absence of direct references to empire in bin Laden's writings. See xix–xx.

19. Osama bin Laden, *Messages to the World: The Statements of Osama bin Laden*, ed. Bruce Lawrence (London: Verso, 2005), 170.

20. See Frantz Fanon, *The Wretched of the Earth*, trans. Richard Philcox (New York: Grove, 2004), 236–237; Albert Memmi, *The Colonizer and the Colonized*, trans. Howard Greenfeld (Boston: Beacon, 1991), 147; and Jalal Al-i Ahmad, *Occidentosis: A Plague from the West*, trans. R. Campbell (Berkeley: Mizan Press, 1984).

21. See Keenan, "A Language That Needs No Translation," 109; Devji, *The Terrorist in Search of Humanity*, 8.

22. Abu Abdillah Almoravid, "The Blacks in America," *Inspire* 14 (Summer 2015): 23, https://azelin.files.wordpress.com/2015/09/inspire-magazine-14.pdf.

23. See Scott Shane, "The Lessons of Anwar al-Awlaki," *New York Times Magazine*, August 27, 2015, https://www.nytimes.com/2015/08/30/magazine/the-lessons-of-anwar-al-awlaki.html.

24. For a summary of these analyses, see Warren Chin, "Colonial Wars, Post-colonial States: A Debate on the War on Terror," *ReOrient* 1, no. 1 (Autumn 2015): 93–107.

25. See Karl Marx, "The East India Company—Its History and Results," in Karl Marx and Friedrich Engels, *The First Indian War of Independence 1857–1859* (Moscow: Progress Publishers, 1978).

26. Seymour M. Hersh, "The Killing of Osama bin Laden," *London Review of Books*, 37, no. 10 (May 21, 2015): 3.

27. Many critics have made versions of this claim; in the tradition of subaltern studies see David Arnold, "Touching the Body: Perspectives on the Indian Plague," in *Selected Subaltern Studies*, ed. Ranajit Guha and Gayatri Chakravorty Spivak (New York: Oxford University Press, 1988), 391–426, and "Cholera and Colonialism in British India," *Past and Present* 113 (November 1986):118–151. See also Priscilla Wald, *Contagious: Cultures, Carriers, and the Outbreak Narrative* (Durham: Duke University Press, 2008); Alan Bewell, *Romanticism and Colonial Disease* (Baltimore: Johns Hopkins University Press, 2003); Cristobal Silva, *Miraculous Plagues: An Epidemiology of Early New England Narrative* (New York: Oxford University Press, 2011); and Alfred W. Crosby, *Ecological Imperialism: The Biological Expansion of Europe*, 2nd ed. (New York: Cambridge University Press, 2004).

28. Quoted in Sebastian Abbot, "Reported CIA Vaccine Ruse Sparks Fear in Pakistan," *Seattle Times*, July 14, 2011, http://www.seattletimes.com/nation-world/cia-vaccination-ruse-sparks-fear-in-pakistan/.

29. World Health Organization, "Constitution of the World Health Organization," Basic Documents, 45th ed., 2006, http://www.who.int/governance/eb/who_constitution_en.pdf.

30. "Alleged Fake CIA Vaccination Campaign Undermines Medical Care,"

Doctors Without Borders, July 14, 2011, http://www.doctorswithoutborders.org/
news-stories/press-release/alleged-fake-cia-vaccination-campaign-undermines
-medical-care; Caroline Abu Sa'Da, Françoise Duroch, and Bertrand Taithe,
"Attacks on Medical Missions: Overview of a Polymorphous Reality: The Case
of Médicins sans frontières," *International Review of the Red Cross* 95, no. 890
(2013): 325; "How the CIA's Fake Vaccination Campaign Endangers Us All";
"Polio Eradication: The CIA and Their Unintended Victims," *Lancet* 383 (May
31, 2014): 1862; Les F. Roberts and Michael VanRooyen, "Ensuring Public Health
Neutrality," *New England Journal of Medicine* 368 (March, 2013): 1073–1075.

31. Mark Mazzetti, "U.S. Cites End to C.I.A. Ruses Using Vaccines," *New York
Times*, May 20, 2014, http://www.nytimes.com/2014/05/20/us/us-cites-end-to-cia
-ruses-using-vaccines.html?_r=0.

32. See Howard Waitzkin and Rebeca Jasso-Aguilar, "Imperialism's Health
Component," *Monthly Review* 67, no. 3 (July 1, 2005), http://monthlyreview.org/
2015/07/01/imperialisms-health-component/. "Health imperialism" seems
to have appeared around 2008 in public health and epidemiology textbooks
(along with analogous terms like "global medical imperialism") and has
recently been in broader use in social scientific work on the major global
organizations, philanthropic and otherwise, that focus on public health. See
Alfred W. McCoy and Francisco A. Scarano, eds. *Colonial Crucible: Empire in the
Making of the Modern American State* (Madison: University of Wisconsin Press,
2009), especially Nancy Tomes, Part Five: "Introduction," 273–276; Jacob Levich,
"The Gates Foundation, Ebola, and Global Health Imperialism," *American
Journal of Economics and Sociology* 74, no. 4 (September 2015): 704–742; Waitzkin
and Jasso-Aguilar, "Resisting the Imperial Order and Building an Alternative
Future in Medicine and Public Health," *Monthly Review* 67, no. 3 (July 1, 2005),
http://monthlyreview.org/2015/07/01/resisting-the-imperial-order-and-building
-an-alternative-future-in-medicine-and-public-health/.

33. The studies that are most central for me here are Michel Foucault,
Security, Territory, Population: Lectures at the Collège de France 1977–1978, trans.
Graham Burchell, ed. Michel Senellart (New York: Picador, 2007); Michel
Foucault, *The Birth of Biopolitics: Lectures at the Collège de France 1978–1979*,
trans. Graham Burchell (New York: Picador, 2008); and Roberto Esposito, *Bíos:
Biopolitics and Philosophy*, trans. Timothy Campbell (Minneapolis: University of
Minnesota Press, 2008).

34. Ranajit Guha, "The Prose of Counter-insurgency," in *Selected Subaltern
Studies*, ed. Ranajit Guha and Gayatri Chakravorty Spivak (New York: Oxford
University Press, 1988), 45–46.

35. Guha, "The Prose of Counter-insurgency," 69–70.

36. Ernest Jones, *The Revolt of Hindostan*, ed. Snehangshu Kanta Acharyya
(Calcutta: Eastern Trading Co., 1957), 3.

37. On Chartist treatments of empire, see Gregory Vargo, *An Underground
History of Early Victorian Fiction: Chartism, Radical Print Culture, and the Social
Problem Novel* (New York: Cambridge University Press, 2017), chap. 6.

38. Guha, "The Prose of Counter-insurgency," 78.

39. Gautam Chakravarty provides a thorough periodization and contextualization of Mutiny literature and historiography in *The Indian Mutiny and the British Imagination* (Cambridge: Cambridge University Press, 2005), and addresses Kaye's and Malleson's in chap. 1.

40. John W. Kaye, "The Romance of Indian Warfare," *North British Review* 12 (November 1849–February 1850): 205.

41. See Roberto Esposito, *Immunitas: The Protection and Negation of Life*, trans. Zakiya Hanafi (Cambridge: Polity, 2011), 4–20; Jean-Luc Nancy, *L'Intrus* (Paris: Galilée, 2000); Martin Hägglund, *Radical Atheism: Derrida and the Time of Life* (Stanford: Stanford University Press, 2008).

42. Kaye, "The Romance of Indian Warfare," 205.

43. John W. Kaye, "Author's Preface," *Kaye's and Malleson's History of the Indian Mutiny of 1857–8* (London: Longman's, 1906), xi.

44. John W. Kaye and George Bruce Malleson, *Kaye's and Malleson's History of the Indian Mutiny of 1857–8* (London: Longman's, 1906), 436. In the "red pamphlet," Malleson describes each of these council members in some detail, but doesn't identify the speaker of these lines. George Bruce Malleson, *The Mutiny of the Bengal Army: An Historical Narrative By One Who Has Served Under Sir Charles Napier* (London: Bosworth & Harrison, 1857), 13–15.

45. George Bruce Malleson, *The Indian Mutiny of 1857*, 7th ed. (New York: Charles Scribner's Sons, 1898), 43–50, 41.

46. Malleson, *The Mutiny of the Bengal Army*, 5, 9, 27. The attribution of "fanaticism" to Hindus extends to Muslims as well in the later writings.

47. See Gautam Chakravarty, *The Indian Mutiny and the British Imagination* (Cambridge: Cambridge University Press, 2005), 22–32.

48. Karl Marx and Friedrich Engels, *The First Indian War of Independence 1857–1859* (Moscow: Progress Publishers, 1978), 33, 81, 18. Subsequent references to this work appear in parentheses in the text.

49. Hilda Gregg, "The Indian Mutiny in Fiction," *Blackwood's Magazine* 161 (February 1897): 218–231; Patrick Brantlinger, *Rule of Darkness: British Literature and Imperialism, 1830–1914* (Ithaca: Cornell University Press, 1988), 199; Gautam Chakravarty, *The Indian Mutiny and the British Imagination* (Cambridge: Cambridge University Press, 2005), 1.

50. Christopher Herbert, *War of No Pity: The Indian Mutiny and Victorian Trauma* (Princeton: Princeton University Press, 2008), 3.

51. Alex Tickell, *Terrorism, Insurgency, and Indian-English Literature, 1830–1947* (London: Routledge, 2012), 1–21.

52. (Philip) Meadows Taylor, *Seeta* (London: K. Paul, Trench & Co., 1880), 271.

53. Taylor, *Seeta*, 369.

54. Brantlinger reads Taylor's mutineers as "good men goaded to rebellion by the dread of losing caste," and in this way understands the novel to invest the uprising with an overarching cause. Brantlinger, *Rule of Darkness: British Literature and Imperialism 1830–1914* (Ithaca: Cornell University Press, 1988), 212.

55. George Trevelyan, *Cawnpore* (London: MacMillan and Co., 1894), 52.

56. Robert Armitage Sterndale, *The Afghan Knife* (New York: Brentano's, 1889), 31.

57. Julia Stephens, "The Phantom Wahhabi: Liberalism and the Muslim Fanatic in mid-Victorian India," *Modern Asian Studies* 47, no. 1 (January 2013): 24.

58. Jed Esty, *Unseasonable Youth: Modernism, Colonialism, and the Fiction of Development* (London: Oxford University Press, 2011), 18.

59. Rudyard Kipling, *Kim*, ed. Edward W. Said (New York: Penguin, 1989), 100.

60. Kipling, *Kim*, 100.

61. Kipling, *Kim*, 100.

62. Edward W. Said, *Culture and Imperialism* (New York: Vintage, 1993), 141.

63. Said, *Culture and Imperialism*, 153.

64. See David Arnold, "Touching the Body: Perspectives on the Indian Plague 1896–1900," in *Selected Subaltern Studies*, ed. Ranajit Guha and Gayatri Chakravorty Spivak (New York: Oxford University Press, 1988), 391–426; Alan Bewell, *Romanticism and Colonial Disease* (Baltimore: Johns Hopkins University Press, 1999); Wald, *Contagious*; Silva, *Miraculous Plagues*.

65. Kipling, *Kim*, 49.

66. Rudyard Kipling, *The Science of Rebellion* (1901), http://www.kiplingsociety .co.uk/rebellion.htm.

67. Kipling, *The Science of Rebellion*.

68. Rudyard Kipling, *Address: Annual Dinner, Royal College of Surgeons* (London: MacMillan, 1923), 3.

69. "Rudyard Kipling's New Serial," *McClure's Magazine* 16 (November 1900-April 1901): 191.

70. For the definitive account of the collusion of gendered "care" in colonial practice, see Gayatri Chakravorty Spivak, "Can the Subaltern Speak?," in *Can the Subaltern Speak?: Reflection on the History of an Idea*, ed. Rosalind C. Morris (New York: Columbia University Press, 2010), 21–78, particularly the reading of the statement "White men are saving brown women from brown men" (49–50).

71. Rudyard Kipling, "The White Man's Burden," as quoted in Alistair Horne, *A Savage War of Peace: Algeria 1954–1962* (New York: New York Review of Books, 2006), frontmatter.

CHAPTER 2

1. Donald G. McNeil Jr., "Turning the Tide Against Cholera," *New York Times*, February 6, 2017, https://www.nytimes.com/2017/02/06/health/cholera-vaccine -bangladesh.html.

2. Priscilla Wald, *Contagious: Cultures, Carriers, and the Outbreak Narrative* (Durham: Duke University Press, 2008), 27.

3. McNeil, "Turning the Tide Against Cholera."

4. Upamanyu Pablo Mukherjee, *Natural Disasters and Victorian Empire: Fam-*

ines, Fevers, and the Literary Cultures of South Asia (London: Palgrave Macmillan, 2013), 30, 88.

5. R. R. Frerichs, P. S. Keim, R. Barrais, and R. Piarroux, "Nepalese Origin of Cholera Epidemic in Haiti," *Clinical Microbiology and Infection* 18, no. 6 (June 2012): E158–E163.

6. McNeil, "Turning the Tide Against Cholera."

7. David Arnold, *Colonizing the Body: State Medicine and Epidemic Disease in Nineteenth-Century India* (Berkeley: University of California Press, 1993), 9.

8. "History of the Rise, Progress, Ravages, &ct. of the Blue Cholera of India," *Lancet* 1, no. 429 (November 19, 1831): 242.

9. James Jameson, *Report on the Epidemick Cholera Morbus As It Visited the Territories Subject to the Presidency of Bengal in the Years 1817, 1818, and 1819* (Calcutta: Government Gazette Press, 1820), 85.

10. Arnold, *Colonizing the Body*, 192.

11. Jameson, *Report on the Epidemick Cholera Morbus*, ii.

12. Sara Suleri, *The Rhetoric of English India* (Chicago: University of Chicago Press, 1992), 7.

13. Jameson, *Report on the Epidemick Cholera Morbus*, xxix. Subsequent references to this work appear in parentheses in the text.

14. James Kennedy, *The History of the Contagious Cholera; with Facts Explanatory of its Origin and Laws, and of a Rational Method of Cure* (London: James Cochrane and Co., 1831). In the section on quarantine, Kennedy makes plain his mission in defending the "interests of a commercial country," in which "no regulations restrictive of the freedom of maritime enterprise should be adopted without the strongest plea of necessity, and the best founded assurance that they are likely to prove adequate to the accomplishment of their object" (252). Subsequent references to this work appear in parentheses in the text.

15. Alan Bewell, *Romanticism and Colonial Disease* (Baltimore: Johns Hopkins University Press, 1999), 10, 128.

16. Bewell, *Romanticism and Colonial Disease*, 271.

17. Kennedy, *History*, 20.

18. Kennedy, *History*, 28.

19. "Review of James Kennedy, *The History of the Contagious Cholera*," *The Lancet* 1, no. 19 (November 5, 1831): 173. Subsequent references to this work appear in parentheses in the text.

20. "History of the Rise, Progress, Ravages, &ct. of the Blue Cholera of India," 270. Subsequent references to this work appear in parentheses in the text.

21. Arnold, *Colonizing the Body*, 184.

22. G. B. Malleson, *Report on the Cholera Epidemic of 1867 in Northern India* (Calcutta: Office of Superintendent of Government Printing, 1868), 12–13.

23. Malleson, *Report*, 20.

24. See Arnold, *Romanticism and Colonial Disease*, 172; Norman Longmate, *King Cholera: The Biography of a Disease* (London: Hamish Hamilton, 1966);

Christopher Hamlin, *Cholera: The Biography* (Oxford: Oxford University Press, 2009); Pamela K. Gilbert, *Cholera and Nation: Doctoring the Social Body in Victorian England* (Albany: State University of New York Press, 2008); and Erin O'Connor, *Raw Material: Producing Pathology in Victorian Culture* (Durham: Duke University Press, 2000), 21–23.

25. Arnold, *Colonizing the Body*, 193.

26. I am speaking here of dominant Asianizing narratives about cholera. The history, of course, is more complicated. Historian Richard J. Evans points, for example, to the impact of the 1831 Russian military campaign against a Polish rebellion, and the subsequent flight of Polish refugees, on cholera's Westward progress during the second epidemic. Richard J. Evans, "Epidemics and Revolutions: Cholera in Nineteenth-Century Europe," *Past & Present* 120 (August, 1988): 134.

27. *Report to the International Sanitary Conference of a Commission from that Body on the Origin, Endemicity, Transmissibility, and Propagation of Asiatic Cholera*, trans. Samuel L. Abbot (Boston: Alfred Mudge & Son, 1867), 20. Emphasis in the original. Subsequent references to this work appear in parentheses in the text.

28. John Slight, *The British Empire and the Hajj 1865–1956* (Cambridge: Harvard University Press, 2015), 5, 1. Subsequent references to this work appear in parentheses in the text.

29. Samuel Taylor Coleridge, "Cholera Cured Beforehand," *The Complete Poems* (New York: Penguin Books, 2004), 413.

30. Coleridge, "Cholera," 413–414; see also Alan Bewell's reading in *Romanticism and Colonial Disease* (Baltimore: Johns Hopkins University Press, 1999), 256–269.

31. Coleridge, "Cholera," 414.

32. "History of the Rise, Progress, Ravages, &ct. of the *Blue Cholera of India*," 253.

33. "History of the Rise, Progress, Ravages, &ct. of the *Blue Cholera of India*," 253.

34. George Parsons, letter, *Cholera Gazette*, no. 1 (January 14, 1832): 13; William Trotter, letter, *Cholera Gazette*, no. 1 (January 14, 1832): 31.

35. James Bartlett, "Memoranda of the Case of Charles Connell," *Cholera Gazette*, no. 4 (March 3, 1832): 135–136.

36. Bartlett, "Memoranda," 136.

37. Coleridge, "Cholera," 413.

38. See Barbara D. Metcalf and Thomas R. Metcalf, *A Concise History of Modern India* (Cambridge: Cambridge University Press, 1999), 96, 125, 128.

39. Gilbert, *Cholera and Nation*, 115.

40. John Snow, *On the Mode of Communication of Cholera* (London: Wilson and Ogilvy, 1849), 5, 11.

41. Snow, *On the Mode of Communication of Cholera*, 1.

42. Steven Johnson gives a detailed account of the documents and data that

led up to and contributed to the maps in *The Ghost Map: The Story of London's Most Terrifying Epidemic—and How It Changed Science, Cities, and the Modern World* (New York: Riverhead Books, 2006), 192–194.

43. Babington, *Transactions*, 1.

44. Babington, *Transactions*, 1.

45. Arnold, *Colonizing the Body*, 169.

46. Sir Sayyid Ahmad Khan, "The Causes of the Indian Revolt," ed. Frances W. Pritchett, http://www.columbia.edu/itc/mealac/pritchett/00litlinks/txt_sir_sayyid_asbab1873_basic.html. For the standard edition see Sayyid Ahmad Khan, *The Causes of the Indian Revolt* (Benares: Medical Hall Press, 1873).

47. Ahmad Khan, "The Causes of the Indian Revolt."

48. Ahmad Khan, "The Causes of the Indian Revolt."

49. Ahmad Khan, "The Causes of the Indian Revolt."

50. Ahmad Khan, "The Causes of the Indian Revolt."

CHAPTER 3

1. Sandra Laville and Robert Booth, "Khalid Masood: From Kent Schoolboy to Westminster Attacker," *Guardian*, March 25, 2017, https://www.theguardian.com/uk-news/2017/mar/25/khalid-masood-profile-from-popular-teenager-to-isis-inspired-terrorist.

2. Laville and Booth, "Khalid Masood."

3. On the broader phenomenon of the veil-cape association, see Milly Williamson and Gholam Khiabany, "The Veil and the Politics of Racism," *Race and Class* 52, no. 2 (October 1, 2010): 85–96.

4. Frantz Fanon, *A Dying Colonialism*, trans. Haakon Chevalier (New York: Grove Press, 1965), 38; Frantz Fanon, *L'An V de la révolution algérienne* (Paris: François Maspero, 1959), 16.

5. Srinivas Aravamudan makes a formally similar argument about the inseparability of Enlightenment genres and the Oriental tale in *Enlightenment Orientalism: Resisting the Rise of the Novel* (Chicago: University of Chicago Press, 2012) by "follow[ing] the itinerary of European knowledge regarding the East influenced by the utopian aspirations of Enlightenment more than materialist and political interest" (3).

6. The wave of post-9/11 horror is by now widely recognized by scholars in literature, film, and cultural studies and the notable ubiquity of vampire stories in the decade that followed the attacks on the World Trade Center is the subject of several articles and book chapters. See Aviva Briefel and Sam J. Miller, eds., *Horror After 9/11: World of Fear, Cinema of Terror* (Austin: University of Texas Press, 2011); Catherine Spooner, *Post-millennial Gothic: Comedy, Romance and the Rise of Happy Gothic* (London: Bloomsbury Academic, 2017).

7. Peter Kitson, "Oriental Gothic," in *Romantic Gothic: An Edinburgh Companion*, ed. Angela Wright and Dale Townshend (Edinburgh: Edinburgh University Press, 2016), 167–184.

8. Jasbir Puar, *Terrorist Assemblages: Homonationalism in Queer Times* (Durham: Duke University Press, 2007), xxiii.

9. Puar, *Terrorist Assemblages*, xxiii.

10. Jasbir K. Puar and Amit S. Rai, "Monster, Terrorist, Fag: The War on Terrorism and the Production of Docile Patriots," *Social Text* 20, no. 3 (2002): 117.

11. Javed Iqbal, Abbas Khan, Ashraf Jehangir Qazi, and Lt. Gen. Nadeem Ahmed, Untitled a.k.a. "Abbottabad Commission Report," *Al Jazeera* (July 8, 2013), 106, http://www.aljazeera.com/indepth/spotlight/binladenfiles/2013/07/20137814392782246.html.

12. "Living Death-Germs," *Cornhill Magazine* 45 (1882), 303, cited in Tina Young Choi, *Anonymous Connections: The Body and Narratives of the Social in Victorian Britain* (Ann Arbor: University of Michigan Press, 2015), 128.

13. Henry Clerval's study of the Oriental languages and Safie's Turkish background are the two most obvious links to the Orientalism of Shelley's day. See Gayatri Chakravorty Spivak, "Three Women's Texts and a Critique of Imperialism," *Critical Inquiry* 12, no. 1 (1985): 243–261; Sandra M. Gilbert, "Horror's Twin: Mary Shelley's Monstrous Eve," *Feminist Studies* 4, no. 2 (June, 1978): 48–73; and Elizabeth Young, *Black Frankenstein: The Making of an American Metaphor* (New York: New York University Press, 2008).

14. Faisal Devji, *The Terrorist in Search of Humanity: Militant Islam and Global Politics* (New York: Columbia University Press, 2008), x.

15. Devji, *The Terrorist in Search of Humanity*, frontmatter.

16. Devji, *The Terrorist in Search of Humanity*, 27.

17. See Patrick Brantlinger, "Terrible Turks: Victorian Xenophobia and the Ottoman Empire," in *Fear, Loathing, and Victorian Xenophobia*, ed. Marlene Tromp, Maria K. Bachman, and Heidi Kaufman (Columbus: Ohio State University Press, 2013), 208–230; and Lionel Madden, ed. *Robert Southey: The Critical Heritage* (London: Routledge, 1972), 63.

18. John Polidori, "The Vampyre," in *The Vampyre and Other Tales of the Macabre*, ed. Robert Morrison and Chris Baldick (Oxford: Oxford University Press, 2008), 3.

19. Polidori, "The Vampyre," 8.

20. See Anne Williams, *Art of Darkness: A Poetics of Gothic* (Chicago: University of Chicago Press, 1995), especially chap. 6 on "family plots."

21. Burton contends in his preface to the 1870 edition that Boccaccio's *Decameron*—also a plague text—was "inspired" by the tales.

22. According to Jill Galvan, citing Clive Leatherdale, Stoker and Burton exchanged ideas about ancient tales in the 1870s and '80s. Jill Galvan, "Occult Networks and the Legacy of the Indian Rebellion in Bram Stoker's *Dracula*," *History of Religions* 54, no. 4 (May 2015): 444.

23. Mary Shelley, *The Last Man*, ed. Anne McWhir (Peterborough: Broadview Press, 1996).

24. Shelley, *The Last Man*, 150.

25. Stephen D. Arata, *Fictions of Loss in the Victorian Fin de Siècle* (Cambridge: Cambridge University Press, 1996), 107–132. Notable exceptions are Eleni Coundouriotis, "*Dracula* and the Idea of Europe," *Connotations* 9, no. 2 (1999/2000): 143–159; and Patrick Brantlinger, "Terrible Turks: Victorian Xenophobia and the Ottoman Empire," *Fear, Loathing, and Victorian Xenophobia*, ed. Marlene Tromp, Maria K. Bachman, and Heidi Kaufman (Columbus: Ohio State University Press, 2013), 208–230. Attila Viragh also reconstructs the Székely origins of the count, situating his ethnicity in terms of cultural extinction in "Can the Vampire Speak? *Dracula* as Discourse on Cultural Extinction," *English Literature in Transition* 56, no. 2 (2013): 231–245.

26. Isabel Burton's inscription, according to the catalogue, simply read "Bram Stoker, with Isabel Burton's kind regards. Feb. 21, 1879."

27. Barbara Belford, *Bram Stoker and the Man Who Was Dracula* (Cambridge: Da Capo Press, 1996), 128.

28. See Robert Eighteen-Bisang and Elizabeth Miller, eds., *Bram Stoker's Notes for Dracula: A Facsimile Edition* (Jefferson: McFarland & Co., 2008), pt. 3: Typed Research Notes. The other two primary sources are A. F. Crosse, *Round About the Carpathians* (London: Blackwoods, 1878), and William Wilkinson, *An Account of the Principalities of Wallachia and Moldavia* (London: Longman's, 1820). Stoker's notes on both of these other texts also include references to the Islamic legacy of the region (215, 245, 251).

29. E. C. Johnson, *On the Track of the Crescent: Erratic Notes from the Piraeus to Pesth* (London: Hurst and Blackett Publishers, 1885), 205, 317–322.

30. Bram Stoker, *Dracula* (London: Vintage, 2007), 32.

31. Isabella Bird, *The Golden Chersonese and the Way Thither* (London: John Murray, 1883), 452.

32. Stoker, *Dracula* (London: Vintage, 2007), 38. Two such reviews appeared in *The Daily Telegraph* (3 June, 1897) and *Bookman* (August 1897). See Stoker, *Dracula*, ed. Auerbach and Skal, 366; Elizabeth Miller, "Publication History of *Dracula*," in *Bram Stoker's Dracula: A Documentary Volume*, ed. Elizabeth Miller (Detroit: Thomson Gale, 2005).

33. Stoker, *Dracula* (London: Vintage, 2007), 33. Subsequent references to this work appear in parentheses in the text.

34. "General Sherman in Europe and the East," *Harper's New Monthly Magazine*, September 1873, 481–495.

35. Frantz Fanon, "L'Algérie et la crise française," in *Ecrits sur l'aliénation et la liberté*, ed. Jean Khalfa and Robert J. C. Young (Paris: La Découverte, 2015), 467. Fanon, in keeping with his project, flips the figure to name France the "grand malade" of Europe in the late 1950s. See also Christopher de Bellaigue, "Turkey's Hidden Past," *New York Review of Books* (March 8, 2001).

36. Stoker's preparatory papers for Dracula include notes on Mme. E. de Laszowska Gerard's "Transylvanian Superstitions," *Nineteenth Century*, July 1882, 130–150, with a gloss of the term "dschuma" as "spirit of plague," as well

as a transcription of a news story from *New York World*, "Vampires in New England," with a section called "Vampirism: A Plague," in Eighteen-Bisang and Miller, *Bram Stoker's Notes for Dracula*, 125, 187.

37. Friedrich Kittler, "Dracula's Legacy," trans. William Stephen Davis, in *Literature, Media, Information Systems: Essays*, ed. John Johnston (Amsterdam: Overseas Publishers Association, 1997), 50–84. See also Franco Moretti, "Dialectic of Fear," in *Signs Taken for Wonders: Essays in the Sociology of Literary Forms* (London: Verso, 1983); Martin Willis, "'The Invisible Giant,' *Dracula*, and Disease," *Studies in the Novel* 39, no. 3 (Fall 2007): 301–326; David Glover, *Vampires, Mummies, and Liberals: Bram Stoker and the Politics of Popular Fiction* (Durham: Duke University Press, 1996); Laurence A. Rickels, *The Vampire Lectures* (Minneapolis: University of Minnesota Press, 1999); and Galvan, "Occult Networks and the Legacy of the Indian Rebellion in Bram Stoker's *Dracula*."

38. George Harley, *The Life of a London Physician* (London: Scientific Press, 1899), was published two years after *Dracula*; Stoker's interest was abiding.

39. See especially "The Adventure of the Dying Detective" (1913) and "The Adventure of the Sussex Vampire" (1924). Arthur Conan Doyle, *Sherlock Holmes: The Complete Novels and Stories*, vol. 2 (New York: Bantam Classics, 2003). Robert Morrison and Chris Baldick point to the importance of *Blackwoods Magazine* in setting the terms of Victorian horror, particularly the "exploitation of public curiosity about the grisly secrets of the medical profession." See "Introduction," *The Vampyre and Other Tales of the Macabre*, ed. Robert Morrison and Chris Baldick (London: Oxford University Press, 2008), xvii.

40. Willis, "'The Invisible Giant,' *Dracula*, and Disease"; Choi, *Anonymous Connections*, 142–144; Jens Lohfert Jørgensen, "Bacillophobia: Man and Microbes in *Dracula*, *The War of the Worlds*, and *The Nigger of the 'Narcissus*,'" *Critical Survey* 27, no. 2 (2015): 36–49.

41. Christopher Hamlin, *Cholera: The Biography* (Oxford: Oxford University Press, 2009), 43, 4.

42. Hamlin, *Cholera*, 4.

43. See Barbara Belford, *Bram Stoker: A Biography of the Author of Dracula* (New York: Knopf, 1996); Maurice Hindle, "Introduction," in Bram Stoker, *Dracula*, ed. Maurice Hindle (New York: Penguin, 2003); Harry Ludlam, *A Biography of Bram Stoker Creator of Dracula* (New York: Foulsham, 1962); David J. Skal, *Something in the Blood: The Untold Story of Bram Stoker, the Man Who Wrote Dracula* (New York: Liveright, 2016).

44. Charlotte Stoker, letter to Abraham [Bram] Stoker, Caen, France, May 6, 1873, Stoker Family Papers, private collection, reprinted in Stoker, *Dracula*, ed. Hindle, 412. Subsequent references to this work appear in parentheses in the text.

45. Bram Stoker, "Memo," in Eighteen-Bisang and Miller, *Bram Stoker's Notes for Dracula*, 15.

46. Bram Stoker, "The Invisible Giant," *Under the Sunset* (London: Sampson Low, Marston, Searle, and Rivington, 1882), 56.

47. Stoker, "The Invisible Giant," 55.

48. Stoker, "The Invisible Giant," 61–62.

49. Robert Koch, a German bacteriologist, would identify the *Vibrio cholerae* during an investigative trip to Calcutta in 1884. See Norman Howard-Jones, "Robert Koch and the Cholera Vibrio: A Centenary," *British Medical Journal* 288 (February 4, 1984): 379–381.

50. See Willis, "'The Invisible Giant,' *Dracula*, and Disease," and Erin O'Connor, *Raw Material: Producing Pathology in Victorian Culture* (Durham: Duke University Press, 2000), 41.

51. Bram Stoker, "The Invisible Giant," in *Under the Sunset* (London: Sampson Low, Marston, Searle, and Rivington, 1882), 64.

52. Stoker, "The Invisible Giant," 65.

53. See also Rickels, *The Vampire Lectures*, and Gil Anidjar, *Blood: A Critique of Christianity* (New York: Columbia University Press, 2014).

54. Halford John Mackinder, "The Geographical Pivot of History," *Geographical Journal* 23, no. 4 (April 1904): 421–437.

55. See Roman Jakobson's classic definition in "Two Aspects of Language and Two Types of Aphasic Disturbances," in Roman Jakobson, *Language in Literature*, ed. Krystyna Pomorska and Stephen Rudy (Cambridge: Belknap Press of Harvard University Press, 1987).

56. Stoker, *Dracula* (London: Vintage, 2007), 190, 49. Subsequent references to this work appear in parentheses in the text.

57. The ghost ship legend appears to be colonial in origin. It rose to prominence during the Dutch dominance of the seas and the height of the Dutch East India Company in the seventeenth century with the story of the Flying Dutchman, a warship cursed to be tossed forever in the squalls off the Cape of Good Hope, South Africa. Historian and folklorist Willard Bonner cites German folktales as a proto-source, connecting the ghost ship curse to Faustian bargains. Willard Hallam Bonner, "The Flying Dutchman of the Western World," *Journal of American Folklore* 59, no. 233 (July–September 1949): 283. See also John MacDonald, *Travels in Various Parts of Europe, Asia, and Africa, During a Series of Thirty Years and Upward* (London: J. Forbes, 1790), 276.

58. Major outbreaks of typhus, cholera, smallpox, and dysentery were recorded on the coffin ships. See L. A. Clarkson and E. Margaret Crawford, *Feast and Famine: A History of Food and Nutrition in Ireland 1500–1920* (Oxford: Oxford University Press, 2001), 158; and Tyler Anbinder, "Lord Palmerston and the Irish Famine Emigration," *Historical Journal* 44, no. 2 (June 2001): 441–469. Scholars disagree on whether the moniker "coffin ship," pointing toward not just starvation but also fever, is deserved. See also Cormac Ó Gráda, *Black '47 and Beyond: The Great Irish Famine in History, Economy, and Memory* (Princeton: Princeton University Press, 1999), 106.

59. Edward Laxton, *The Famine Ships: The Irish Exodus to America* (New York: Henry Holt, 1998), 103.

60. Belford, *Bram Stoker*, 13.

61. See Jarlath Killeen, "Consuming Bodies: Transubstantiation, Incarnation, and the Politics of Cannibalism in Jonathan Swift," in *Gothic Ireland: Horror and the Irish Anglican Imagination in the Long Eighteenth Century* (Dublin: Four Courts Press, 2005).

62. James Anderson, letter, May 19, 1849, in *Hansard's Parliamentary Debates* v. CV, May 8–June 11, 1849 (London: G. Woodfall and Son, 1849), 1033.

63. Cited in Ó Gráda, *Black '47 and Beyond*, 38. See also Patrick O'Sullivan, ed., *The Meaning of the Famine* (London: Leicester University Press, 1997).

64. L. A. Clarkson and E. Margaret Crawford, *Feast and Famine: A History of Food and Nutrition in Ireland 1500–1920* (Oxford: Oxford University Press, 2001), 159.

65. Catherine Gallagher, "The Potato in the Materialist Imagination," in *Practicing New Historicism*, ed. Catherine Gallagher and Stephen Greenblatt (Chicago: University of Chicago Press, 2000).

66. See Glover, *Vampires, Mummies, and Liberals*.

67. Stoker, *Dracula*, 324, 331.

68. Stoker's posthumously published short story, "Dracula's Guest," adapted from the novel's opening chapters, further crystalizes the novel's interest in the guest-host relationship as it is inflected by both Catholic doctrine and theories of disease. Bram Stoker, *Dracula's Guest and Other Weird Stories*, ed. Kate Hebblethwaite (New York: Penguin Classics, 2006), 5–17.

69. Stoker, *Dracula*, 334.

70. Stoker, *Dracula*, 334.

71. See John Snow, *On the Mode of Communication of Cholera* (London: Wilson and Ogilvy, 1849).

72. Pamela K. Gilbert, *Cholera and Nation: Doctoring the Social Body in Victorian England* (Albany: State University of New York Press, 2008), 122.

73. Stoker, *Dracula*, 331.

74. Stoker, *Dracula*, 133–135, 141, 148, 164.

75. Stoker, *Dracula*, 65. On the novel's sexual politics, see in particular Talia Schaffer, "'A Wilde Desire Took Me': The Homoerotic History of *Dracula*," *English Language History* 61 (1994): 381–425; and Kathleen L. Spencer, "Purity and Danger: *Dracula*, the Urban Gothic, and the Late Victorian Degeneracy Crisis," *English Language History* 59 (1992): 197–225.

76. Stoker, *Dracula* (London: Vintage, 2007), 63, 64, 65. Subsequent references to this work appear in parentheses in the text.

77. See Leslie Klinger, "Dracula After Stoker: Fictional Accounts of the Count," in Bram Stoker, *The New Annotated Dracula*, ed. Leslie Klinger (New York: W. W. Norton & Company, 2008), 532.

78. Most scholars agree that the key data on fibrin and coagulation inhibitors was Alexander Schmidt's, published in 1872. See J. A. Marcum, "Defending the Priority of 'Remarkable Researches': The Discovery of Fibrin Ferment," *History and Philosophy of the Life Sciences* 20, no. 1 (January, 1998), 51–76; and Susan E. Lederer, *Flesh and Blood: Organ Transplantation and Blood Transfusion*

in Twentieth-Century America (Oxford: Oxford University Press, 2008), 150. On the history of blood typing, see Catherine Waldby and Robert Mitchell, *Tissue Economies: Blood, Organs, and Cell Lines in Late Capitalism* (Durham: Duke University Press, 2006), pt. 1; conclusion.

79. George Henry Lewes, *The Physiology of Common Life*, vol. 1 (Edinburgh: William Blackwood, 1859), 239.

80. Stoker, *Dracula*, 156.

81. See Aspasia Stephanou, "A 'Ghastly Operation': Transfusing Blood, Science, and the Supernatural in Vampire Texts," *Gothic Studies* 15, no. 2 (November 2013): 53–65, and Jean-Paul Lallemand-Stempak, "'What Flows Between Us': Blood Donation and Transfusion in the United States (Nineteenth to Twentieth Centuries)," in eds., *Giving Blood: The Institutional Making of Altruism*, ed. Johanne Charbonneau and André Smith (London: Routledge, 2016), 26.

82. Norman Longmate, *King Cholera: The Biography of a Disease* (London: Hamish Hamilton, 1966), lauds the cholera investigator who "pinpointed the guilty spot . . . precisely: a densely populated low-lying area 40 miles southwest of Calcutta at the confluence of three rivers" (86).

83. See Jules Law, *The Social Life of Fluids: Blood, Milk and Water in the Victorian Novel* (Ithaca: Cornell University Press, 2010), 158.

84. Stoker, *Dracula*, 313.

85. Stoker, *Dracula*, 320. Jill Galvan, "Occult Networks and the Legacy of the Indian Rebellion in Bram Stoker's *Dracula*," 445, argues that this "searing" approximates the bindi worn by married Hindu women.

86. Stoker, *Dracula*, 358. Subsequent references to this work appear in parentheses in the text.

87. See detailed discussion of the bureaucratization of occultism in this period in Gauri Viswanathan, "The Ordinary Business of Occultism," *Critical Inquiry* 27 (Autumn 2000): 1–20.

88. Stoker, *Dracula*, 376, 390, 393.

89. Stoker, *Dracula*, 419.

90. Kittler, "Dracula's Legacy," 80.

91. Bhavani Raman, *Document Raj: Writing and Scribes in Early Colonial South India* (Chicago: University of Chicago Press, 2012), ix.

92. Bernard S. Cohn, *Colonialism and Its Forms of Knowledge: The British in India* (Princeton: Princeton University Press, 1996), 8.

93. Cohn suggests that these methods were often worked out first in the colonies and later imported to the metropole, where they would become further normalized and institutionalized. See also Michel Foucault, *The Birth of Biopolitics: Lectures at the College de France 1978–1979*, trans. Graham Burchell (New York: Picador, 2008), 27–50.

94. Cohn, *Colonialism and Its Forms of Knowledge*, 3.

95. James Bryden, *A Report on the Cholera of 1866–68 and Its Relations to the Cholera of Previous Epidemics* (Calcutta: Office of Superintendent of Government Printing, 1869), 4.

96. Bryden, *A Report on the Cholera*, 4.

97. Stoker, *Dracula*, frontmatter. Subsequent references to this work appear in parentheses in the text.

98. Kittler, "Dracula's Legacy," 73. Subsequent references to this work appear in parentheses in the text.

99. Stoker, *Dracula*, 10, 13.

100. Stoker, *Dracula*, 33.

101. Eve Kosofsky Sedgwick, *The Coherence of Gothic Conventions* (New York: Arno Press, 1980), 14.

102. Sedgwick, *The Coherence of Gothic Conventions*, 15.

103. This particular configuration of Weberian disenchantment, scientific knowledge, and Orientalism as a nexus of tension and literary productivity in the late Victorian period is indebted to Gauri Viswanathan's account of the professionalization and bureaucratization of occult knowledge. Viswanathan, "The Ordinary Business of Occultism," 7.

104. See Lawrence Rothfield, *Vital Signs: Medical Realism in Nineteenth Century Fiction* (Princeton: Princeton University Press, 1992), on medical realism and the pathologically embodied person.

105. Michel Foucault, *The Birth of the Clinic: An Archaeology of Medical Perception*, trans. Alan Sheridan (New York: Vintage, 1994), xiii; Michel Foucault, *Naissance de la clinique* (Paris: Presses Universitaires de France, 1997), ix.

106. Foucault, *The Birth of the Clinic*, ix.

107. Charlotte Stoker, letter, 414.

108. Stoker, *Dracula*, 305.

109. Stoker, *Dracula*, 306–307.

110. Stoker, *Dracula*, 307.

111. Sir William Thornley Stoker, "Memo," in Eighteen-Bisang and Miller, *Bram Stoker's Notes for Dracula*, 179–185.

112. Stoker, *Dracula*, 307.

113. Helaine Selin, ed. *Encyclopaedia of the History of Science, Technology, and Medicine in Non-Western Cultures*, 3rd ed. (Berlin: Springer, 2016), 985.

114. Stoker, *Dracula*, 310.

115. See Moretti, "Dialectic of Fear"; Spencer, "Purity and Danger"; Willis, "'The Invisible Giant,' *Dracula*, and Disease"; David Punter, "Bram Stoker's *Dracula*: Tradition, Technology, Modernity," in *Post/Modern Dracula*, ed. John S. Bak (Newcastle upon Tyne: Cambridge Scholars' Press, 2007), 31–41; J. Halberstam, "Technologies of Monstrosity: Bram Stoker's 'Dracula,'" *Victorian Studies* 36, no. 3 (Spring, 1993): 333–352; Stephen D. Arata, "The Occidental Tourist: Stoker and Reverse Colonization," in *Fictions of Loss in the Victorian Fin de Siecle* (Cambridge: Cambridge University Press, 1996), 107–132; Glover, *Vampires, Mummies, and Liberals*; and Schaffer, "A Wilde Desire Took Me." In a meta-critical mode, David Punter, in *The Literature of Terror: A History of Gothic Fictions from 1765 to the Present Day*, vol. 2 (London: Routledge, 1996), argues that prominent works of the decadent Gothic linked the above series of afflictions

in its entirety to the aging body of the Empire. Stephen D. Arata's *Fictions of Loss in the Victorian Fin de Siecle* (Cambridge: Cambridge University Press, 1996) helpfully deals with a similar set of questions.

116. Stephen D. Arata signals this issue in his review of Joseph Valente's study *Dracula's Crypt: Bram Stoker, Irishness, and the Question of Blood* in *Victorian Studies* 45, no. 3 (Spring 2003): 536–538.

117. Stoker, *Dracula*, ed. Auerbach and Skal.

118. Horace Walpole, *The Castle of Otranto: A Gothic Story*, ed. Frederick S. Frank (Peterborough: Broadview Press, 2003), 5.

119. Waldby and Mitchell, *Tissue Economies*, 1–2.

120. Waldby and Mitchell, *Tissue Economies*, 2.

CHAPTER 4

1. Albert Camus, *Notebooks: 1942–1951*, trans. Justin O'Brien (New York: Alfred A Knopf, 1966), 27; Albert Camus, *Carnets: Janvier 1942–Mars 1951*, vol. 2 (Paris: Gallimard, 1964), 40, emphasis in the original.

2. I cite the English in the standard translation, which is Stuart Gilbert's, and include the French (Albert Camus, *La Peste* [Paris: Gallimard, 1947]), only where major divergences arise. Albert Camus, *The Plague*, trans. Stuart Gilbert (New York: Vintage, 1991), 36. Subsequent references to this work appear in parentheses in the text. English and French edition page numbers are separated by a semicolon.

3. See Hannah Arendt, *Eichmann in Jerusalem: A Report on the Banality of Evil* (New York: Penguin Classics, 2006).

4. See Daniel Guérin, *The Brown Plague: Travels in Late Weimar and Early Nazi Germany* (Durham: Duke University Press, 1994).

5. Tony Judt, "On 'The Plague,'" *New York Review of Books* (November 29, 2001), http://www.nybooks.com/articles/archives/2001/nov/29/on-the-plague/.

6. Richard Lloyd Parry, "Coronavirus: Albert Camus' *Plague* Novel Flies off the Shelves in Japan," *The Times*, April 10, 2020, https://www.thetimes.co.uk/article/coronavirus-albert-camus-plague-novel-flies-off-the-shelves-in-japan-3stjn7lvl.

7. Conor Cruise O'Brien, *Albert Camus: Of Europe and Africa* (New York: Viking, 1970); Herbert R. Lottman, *Albert Camus: A Biography* (New York: Doubleday, 1979); Shoshana Felman, *Reading Narrative: Form, Ethics, Ideology* (Columbus: University of Ohio Press, 1989).

8. Albert Camus, *Algerian Chronicles*, trans. Arthur Goldhammer, ed. Alice Kaplan (Cambridge: Harvard University Press, 2013).

9. Robert Zaretsky, "The Stranger Who Resembles Us," *Chronicle Review* (November 26, 2012), http://chronicle.com/article/Camuss-Restless-Ghost/135874/.

10. See Alice Kaplan, "New Perspectives on Camus's Algerian Chronicles," in Albert Camus, *Algerian Chronicles*, trans. Arthur Goldhammer, ed. Alice Kaplan (Cambridge: Belknap Press of Harvard University Press, 2013), 1–18, and Emily

Apter, "Out of Character: Camus's French Algerian Subjects," *Modern Language Notes* 112, no. 4 (September 1997): 499–516.

11. See Mervyn Susser and Zena Stein, *Eras in Epidemiology: The Evolution of Ideas* (Oxford: Oxford University Press, 2009).

12. I haven't seen evidence in Camus's notebooks or essays that would suggest he was specifically interested in the Oran cholera. This claim has nevertheless become a kind of common wisdom. See Mustapha Marrouchi, "Counternarratives, Recoveries, Refusals," in *Edward Said and the Work of the Critic: Speaking Truth to Power*, ed. Paul A. Bové (Durham: Duke University Press, 2000), 187–228.

13. François Delaporte, *Disease and Civilization: The Cholera in Paris, 1832*, trans. Arthur Goldhammer (Cambridge: MIT Press, 1986), 189, 199–200. Emphasis in the original. Subsequent references to this work appear in parentheses in the text.

14. Andrew R. Aisenberg, *Contagion: Disease, Government, and the "Social Question" in Nineteenth-Century France* (Stanford: Stanford University Press, 1999), 104.

15. Aisenberg, *Contagion*, 104.

16. Aisenberg, *Contagion*, 104. For a complete account of the social and cultural history of asymptomatic carriers, exemplified by New York's "Typhoid Mary," see Priscilla Wald, *Contagious: Cultures, Carriers, and the Outbreak Narrative* (Durham: Duke University Press, 2008), chap. 2, "The Healthy Carrier: 'Typhoid Mary' and Social Being."

17. Quoted in Aisenberg, *Contagion*, 104–105.

18. The passages he transcribes are typically difficult to manage at anything but the most abstract aphoristic level. In one instance, when he is just beginning to make notes toward *La Peste*, he copies Heine's epitaph, which also appears in the *Ideas*, "He loved the roses of the Brenta," and in another, what appears to be a reflection from 1848, "What the world seeks and hopes for now has become utterly foreign to my heart." Albert Camus, *Notebooks: 1942–1951*, trans. Justin O'Brien (New York: Knopf, 1966), 13, 174.

19. Camus, *The Plague*, 200–201; Camus, *La Peste*, 182. Subsequent references to this work appear in parentheses in the text. English and French edition page numbers are separated by a semicolon.

20. Olivier Todd, *Albert Camus: A Life*, trans. Benjamin Ivry (New York: Knopf, 1998), 170.

21. Albert Camus, *Notebooks: 1942–1951*, trans. Justin O'Brien (New York: Knopf, 1966), xx; Albert Camus, *Carnets: Janvier 1942–Mars 1951*, vol. 2 (Paris: Gallimard, 1964), xx.

22. Camus, *Notebooks* xx; Camus, *Carnets*, xx.

23. See Jean Pouillon, "L'Optimisme de Camus," *Les Temps Modernes* 3, no. 26 (November 1947): 921–929, and Roland Barthes, *Le degré zéro de l'écriture* (Paris: Seuil, 1953).

24. See Ronald Aronson, *Camus and Sartre: The Story of a Friendship and the Quarrel That Ended It* (Chicago: University of Chicago Press, 2004), 138; Francis Jeanson, "The Third Man in the Story: Ronald Aronson Discusses the Sartre-Camus Conflict with Francis Jeanson," trans. Basil Kingstone, *Sartre Studies International* 8, no. 2 (2002), 25.

25. See Albert Memmi, "Camus ou le colonisateur de bonne volonté," *La Nef* 12 (December, 1957); Edward W. Said, *Culture and Imperialism* (New York: Vintage, 1993), 172; Connor Cruise O'Brien, *Camus* (Glasgow: Fontana, 1970), 14.

26. O'Brien, *Camus*, 23.

27. Edward Said is critical on this point and its function as a medium for hidden ideology. "[Camus] is a very late imperial figure who not only survived the heyday of empire, but survives today as a 'universalist' writer with roots in a now-forgotten colonialism." Said, *Culture and Imperialism*, 172. On the issue of the adolescent appeal of Camus's philosophical positions, see Peter Brooks, "From Albert Camus to Roland Barthes," *New York Times*, September 12, 1982.

28. Roland Barthes, *Writing Degree Zero*, trans. Annette Lavers and Colin Smith (New York: Hill and Wang, 1967), 77; Barthes, *Le degré zéro de l'écriture*, 56. Subsequent references to this work appear in parentheses in the text. English and French edition page numbers are separated by a semicolon.

29. Camus, *The Plague*, trans. Robin Buss (London: Penguin Books, 2001), frontmatter. Camus, *La Peste*, frontmatter. I draw the English above from the less-canonical Robin Buss translation of *The Plague* because the Gilbert translation omits it. Buss seems to have translated the French translation back to English; the original in Defoe's *Serious Reflections During the Life and Surprising Adventures of Robinson Crusoe* reads, "'tis as reasonable to represent one kind of Imprisonment by another, as it is to represent any Thing that really exists, by that which exists not." Daniel Defoe, *Serious Reflections During the Life and Surprising Adventures of Robinson Crusoe*, ed. W. R. Owens and P. N. Furbank (London: Pickering & Chatto, 2008), 53.

30. Camus, *Notebooks*, 28; Camus, *Carnets*, 41.

31. See Olivier Todd, *Albert Camus: une vie* (Paris: Gallimard, 1996), and Patrick McCarthy, *Camus* (New York: Random House, 1982), esp. chapters 6 & 7.

32. Albert Camus, *Lyrical and Critical Essays*, trans. Ellen Conroy Kennedy, ed. Philip Thody (New York: Knopf, 1967), 339; Albert Camus, "Lettre d'Albert Camus à Roland Barthes sur *La Peste*," in Roland Barthes, *Oeuvres complètes*: vol. 1, *1942–1961* (Paris: Editions du Seuil, 2002), 546.

33. Camus, *Notebooks*, 340; Camus, *Carnets*, 547.

34. Camus, *Notebooks*, 341; Camus, *Carnets*, 547.

35. Shoshana Felman, "Narrative as Testimony: Camus's *The Plague*," in *Reading Narrative: Form, Ethics, Ideology* (Columbus: University of Ohio Press, 1989), 257. Emphasis in the original.

36. In reference to this term's presence in Camus, see Irma Kashuba, "A

Method of Presenting Albert Camus's *The Plague*," in *Approaches to Teaching Camus's* The Plague, ed. Steven G. Kellman (New York: Modern Language Association of America, 1985).

37. See especially the chapter "Writing and Silence," in Barthes, *Writing Degree Zero*; Barthes, *Le degré zéro*.

38. Barthes, *Oeuvres Complètes*, 540–541. Translations mine, emphasis in the original.

39. Barthes, *Oeuvres Complètes*, 541–542.

40. Barthes, *Oeuvres Complètes*, 544.

41. Albert Camus, *Camus at Combat: Writing 1944–1947* trans. Arthur Goldhammer, ed. Jacqueline Lévi-Valensi (Princeton: Princeton University Press, 2006), 250; Albert Camus, *Camus à Combat: Éditoriaux et articles d'Albert Camus*, ed. Jacqueline Lévi-Valensi (Paris: Gallimard, 2002), 594–595.

42. Camus, *Camus at Combat*, 340; Camus, *Camus à Combat*, 547.

43. Camus, *Camus at Combat*, 340; Camus, *Camus à Combat*, 547.

44. Kaplan, "New Perspectives," 14.

45. See Camus, *Notebooks*, entries dated February 17, 1955, to October 17, 1955.

46. Camus, *The Plague*, 3, 6; Camus, *La Peste*, 11, 13.

47. Kaplan, "New Perspectives," 8.

48. Albert Camus, "The New Mediterranean Culture," in *Lyrical and Critical Essays*, 190.

49. Camus, *The Plague*, 5–6; Camus, *La Peste*, 12–13. Subsequent references to this work appear in parentheses in the text. English and French edition page numbers are separated by a semicolon.

50. Visual culture in the papers and the cholera publications is especially obvious in registering this fear—a good deal of this material has been catalogued in Patrice Bourdelais and André Dodin, *Visages du choléra* (Paris: Belin, 1987).

51. Delaporte, *Disease and Civilization*, 43.

52. Giorgio Agamben, *Remnants of Auschwitz: The Witness and the Archive*, trans. Daniel Heller-Roazen (New York: Zone Books, 2002), 44–45. Agamben draws on a large archive, in which Levi, Bettelheim, and Ryn and Klodzinski's monograph on the *Muselmann* play a large role. Subsequent references to this work appear in parentheses in the text.

53. Emily Apter, *Continental Drift: From National Characters to Virtual Subjects* (Chicago: University of Chicago Press, 1999), 502.

54. Alice Kaplan, "Reading Camus in Algeria Today," *The Best American Poetry* (July 5, 2012), http://blog.bestamericanpoetry.com/the_best_american _poetry/2012/07/reading-camus-in-algeria-today-alice-kaplan-blog2.html. Some of this material appears transformed in Kaplan's essay "New Perspectives on Camus's Algerian Chronicles," 10–11. The professor reminds her listeners that Ferouan used a line from *La Peste* as an epigraph in *Le Fils du pauvre*, "Il y a dans les hommes plus de choses à admirer que de choses à mépriser"

("Epilogue" *Le Fils du pauvre* (Alger: ENAG, 2002), 161). In "New Perspectives," Kaplan adds to this anecdote the recent example of Hamid Grine's *Camus dans le narguilé*, in which the narrator learns he is the lost son of Camus, "a stand-in for a lost literary heritage" (11).

55. "Epidemic" is the word that Apter uses in the introduction to *Continental Drift*. She writes, "The epidemic of assassinations of Algerian intellectuals (morbidly dubbed 'intellocide') in 1993 . . . by hard-line *islamistes* has been roundly denounced in the French press, but at the same time the condemnation of *intégrisme* mingles uncomfortably with Western ignorance of Islam and a reflexive sympathy toward members of North Africa's westernized elite" (3). Revisiting this subject in *The Translation Zone*, she notes the rhetoric of coverage in a *New York Times* article about a 1997 massacre outside of Algiers that leans on adjectives like "murky" and "shadowy" to describe power structures in Algeria. Emily Apter, *The Translation Zone: A New Comparative Literature* (Princeton: Princeton University Press, 2006), 95–96.

56. The essays in *The Algerian Chronicles* that appeared in *Combat* had been translated previously, also by Arthur Goldhammer, in a volume introduced by David Carroll, *Camus at Combat: Writing 1944–1947* (Princeton: Princeton University Press, 2006).

57. O'Brien, *Albert Camus: Of Europe and Africa*, 54–55.

58. See Jennifer Johnson, *The Battle for Algeria: Sovereignty, Health Care, and Humanitarianism* (Philadelphia: University of Pennsylvania Press, 2015).

59. Sir MacFarlane Burnet and David O. White, *Natural History of Infectious Disease*, 4th ed. (Cambridge: Cambridge University Press, 1972), 226.

60. Camus, *The Plague*, 12–13; Camus, *La Peste*, 18–19. Subsequent references to this work appear in parentheses in the text. English and French edition page numbers are separated by a semicolon.

61. Alistair Horne, *A Savage War of Peace, Algeria 1956–1962* (London: Mac-Millan, 1977), 25.

62. Kaplan, "New Perspectives," 5.

63. Kaplan, "New Perspectives," 18. Kaplan suggests that he wrote to *Le Monde* immediately to correct what he understood to be a misrepresentation (apparently the original statement in the Stockholm press conference was "En ce moment on lance des bombes dans les tramways d'Alger. Ma mère peut se trouver dans un de ces tranways. Si c'est cela le justice, je préfère ma mère"). Kaplan, "New Perspectives," 18n19.

64. Camus, *Algerian Chronicles*, 184; Camus, *Chroniques algériennes 1939–1958* (Paris: Gallimard, 1958), 212.

65. O'Brien, *Albert Camus: Of Europe and Africa*, 59.

66. O'Brien, *Albert Camus: Of Europe and Africa*, 59.

67. Pierre Macherey, "Depth and Complexity," in *A Theory of Literary Production*, trans. Geoffrey Wall (London: Routledge, 2006), 110. Emphasis in the original. Subsequent references to this work appear in parentheses in the text.

68. Hippocrates and Galen both use the word *krisis* in this way. "Crisis," in

C. T. Onions, ed., *Oxford Dictionary of English Etymology* (New York: Oxford University Press, 1966), 229.

69. See Benjamin Stora, *Les mots de la guerre d'Algérie* (Toulouse: Presses Universitaires du Mirail, 2005), 50.

70. Camus, *Algerian Chronicles*, 90–91; Camus, *Essais*, 942–943.

71. John Foley, "A Postcolonial Fiction: Conor Cruise O'Brien's Camus," *Irish Review* 36/37 (2007): 2.

72. Camus, *Algerian Chronicles*, 70–71; Camus, *Essais*, 928. Subsequent references to this work appear in parentheses in the text. English and French edition page numbers are separated by a semicolon.

73. See Gary Wilder, *Freedom Time: Negritude, Decolonization, and the Future of the World* (Durham: Duke University Press, 2015), chaps. 2 and 6.

74. Camus, *Camus at Combat*, 290; Camus, *Essais*, 321. Subsequent references to this work appear in parentheses in the text. English and French edition page numbers are separated by a semicolon.

75. Camus, *Camus at Combat*, xvi; Camus, "Les Déclarations de Stockholm," *Essais*.

76. Camus, *Algerian Chronicles*, 216.

77. Camus, *Algerian Chronicles*, 216.

78. Camus, *Lyrical and Critical Essays*, 148; Camus, *Essais*, 853. Subsequent references to this work appear in parentheses in the text. English and French edition page numbers are separated by a semicolon.

79. Camus, *The Plague*, 308; Camus, *La Peste*, 279. Subsequent references to this work appear in parentheses in the text. English and French edition page numbers are separated by a semicolon.

80. Camus, *Camus at Combat*, 291; Camus, *Essais*, 323.

81. Judt, "On 'The Plague.'"

CHAPTER 5

1. Michael T. Kaufman, "Film Studies: What Does the Pentagon See in 'Battle of Algiers'?," *New York Times*, September 7, 2003, https://www.nytimes.com/2003/09/07/weekinreview/the-world-film-studies-what-does-the-pentagon-see-in-battle-of-algiers.html.

2. Richard A. Clarke, quoted in *The Battle of Algiers: A Case Study* (2004), in Gillo Pontecorvo, *The Battle of Algiers*, DVD extras (Irvington, N.Y.: Criterion Collection, 2004).

3. Sidney Tarrow, "Preface," in *The World Says No to War: Demonstrations Against the War in Iraq*, ed. Stefaan Walgrave and Dieter Rucht (Minneapolis: University of Minnesota Press, 2010), viii.

4. David Ignatius, "Think Strategy, Not Numbers," *Washington Post*, Tuesday, August 26, 2003, http://www.washingtonpost.com/wp-dyn/articles/A45136-2003Aug25.html. Portions of this copy also appear in the WorldCat summary of the film, suggesting a direct influence of the screening invitation's copy on

subsequent encounters with the film. See http://www.worldcat.org/title/bataille
-dalger-the-battle-of-algiers/oclc/55859304#details-allauthors.

5. Michael Sheehan, in *The Battle of Algiers: A Case Study* (2004), in Gillo
Pontecorvo, director, *The Battle of Algiers*, DVD extras (Irvington: Criterion Collection, 2004).

6. Sheehan, in *The Battle of Algiers*.

7. *Preparing for the War on Terrorism, Hearings Before the Committee on Government Reform*, 107th Cong. 112 (2001) (statement by Christopher Harmon). I
first came across this reference in Tony Shaw's *Cinematic Terror: A Global History of Terrorism on Film* (New York: Bloomsbury, 2015), 100–101.

8. On the relationship between the losses in Indochina and the war in Algeria, see Alistair Horne, *A Savage War of Peace: Algeria 1954–1962* (New York: New
York Review of Books, 2006), 67–69.

9. Ujala Sehgal, "Eight Years Ago, Bush Declared 'Mission Accomplished' in
Iraq," *Atlantic*, May 1, 2011, https://www.theatlantic.com/national/archive/2011/
05/mission-accomplished-speech/350187/.

10. Michael E. O'Hanlon and Adriana Lins de Albuquerque, "Iraq Index:
Tracking Variables of Reconstruction in Post-Saddam Iraq," (Washington, D.C.:
The Brookings Institution, 2004), 8.

11. Ellen Ray, "Foreword," in Henri Alleg, *The Question*, trans. John Calder
(Lincoln: University of Nebraska Press, 2006), x.

12. Pontecorvo, *The Battle of Algiers*, 01:20:07.

13. Pontecorvo, *The Battle of Algiers*, 00:59:05–00:59:13.

14. Pontecorvo, *The Battle of Algiers*, 00:59:17.

15. The phrase "cordon sanitaire" appears so commonly in military strategy
of the period that one could argue that it loses entirely its epidemiological
history and reverts to pure military lexicon. Its ubiquity in writings about
the Algerian war is notable. See, for example, J. N. C. Hill, "Remembering the
War of Liberation: Legitimacy and Conflict in Contemporary Algeria," *Small
Wars and Insurgencies* 23, no. 1 (2012): 4–31, referring to the *"cordon sanitaire*
around the city's *casbah"* (8). Paul Silverstein also refers to the omnipresent
cordons sanitaires in the updated context of the Algerian civil war in "An
Excess of Truth: Violence, Conspiracy Theorizing, and the Algerian Civil War,"
Anthropological Quarterly 75, no. 4 (Fall 2002): 643–674. The "cordons" described
in the U.S. Marine Corps *Small Wars Manual* (1940) seem to refer to both
technical meanings at once in the "Methods of Pacification" section: "The
cordon system—a. this system involves placing a cordon of troops around an
infested area and closing in while restoring order in the area." U.S. Marine
Corps, *Small Wars Manual* (Fleet Marine Force Reference Publication 12-15)
PCN 140 121500 00 (Washington: United States Government Printing Office,
1940), 5–19.

16. Horne, *A Savage War of Peace*, 111.

17. Steven Soderbergh, director, *Contagion* (Los Angeles: Warner Brothers,
2011), 00:31:20-00:31:30.

18. Steven Soderbergh, in *Five Directors*, in Pontecorvo, *The Battle of Algiers*, DVD extras.

19. Horne, *A Savage War of Peace*, cover.

20. These three texts, among others, are touchstones in Ranjana Khanna's *Algeria Cuts: Women and Representation 1830 to the Present* (Stanford: Stanford University Press, 2008). Although Khanna considers the microphone scene (described in the text above) in the context of *The Battle of Algiers*'s politics of voice and silence (she remarks as well on Pontecorvo's disavowal of the scene as one of the film's more unrealistic moments [110]), her concern, channeled through psychoanalysis and trauma theory, is mostly with the failure of Pontecorvo, and third cinema more broadly, to adequately address the problem of gender in revolutionary Algeria.

21. Some key studies of Fanon and Pontecorvo in this tradition are Homi Bhabha's 1986 foreword to *Black Skin, White Masks*, "Remembering Fanon: Self, Psyche, and the Colonial Condition" (London: Pluto, 1986); Danièle Djamila Amrane-Minne, *Les femmes algériennes dans la guerre* (Paris: Plon, 1991); Diana Fuss, "Interior Colonies: Frantz Fanon and the Politics of Identification," *diacritics* 24, no. 2 (1994): 20–42; and Anne McClintock, "'No Longer in a Future Heaven': Gender, Race, and Nationalism," in *Dangerous Liaisons: Gender, Nation, and Postcolonial Perspectives*, ed. Anne McClintock, Aamir Mufti, and Ella Shohat (Minneapolis: University of Minnesota Press, 1997), 89–112.

22. Jacques Lezra usefully unpacks this insistence on the film's balance as a legacy of the fantasy of historical objectivity (or history as a determinant of objectivity) in his chapter on Pontecorvo's film in *Wild Materialism: The Ethic of Terror and the Modern Republic* (New York: Fordham University Press, 2010), 175–177.

23. Pontecorvo, *The Battle of Algiers*, 01:12:45. Lindsey Moore, in a virtuosic reading of the criticism surrounding Pontecorvo's film and Fanon's essay, suggests that the figure of Colonel Mathieu was a composite modeled in part on General Massu. Lindsey Moore, "The Veil of Nationalism: Frantz Fanon's 'Algeria Unveiled' and Gillo Pontecorvo's *The Battle of Algiers*," *Kunapipi* 25, no. 2 (2003): 66.

24. Pontecorvo, *The Battle of Algiers*, 01:13:18.

25. Gillo Pontecorvo, "Marxist Poetry and the Making of the Battle of Algiers," in Pontecorvo, *The Battle of Algiers*, DVD extras.

26. Pontecorvo, *The Battle of Algiers*, 00:57.

27. Pontecorvo, *The Battle of Algiers*, 01:30:11–01:30:18.

28. Soderbergh cites this scene as well in *Contagion*, when a WHO epidemiologist screens surveillance footage of the presumed initial outbreak for her local colleagues in Hong Kong. Soderbergh, *Contagion*, 00:18:35–00:20:12.

29. Moore, "The Veil of Nationalism," 66.

30. Pontecorvo, *The Battle of Algiers*, 01:29:09.

31. Pontecorvo, *The Battle of Algiers*, 01:30:12.

32. Khanna, *Algeria Cuts*, 107.

33. Khanna, *Algeria Cuts*, 105, 108.

34. Jean Martin, in *Marxist Poetry: The Making of the Battle of Algiers*.

35. See Nicholas Harrison, "Yesterday's Mujahiddin: Gillo Pontecorvo's *The Battle of Algiers*," in *Postcolonial Film: History, Empire, Resistance*, ed. Rebecca Weaver-Hightower and Peter Hulme (London: Routledge, 2014), 23–46.

36. Pontecorvo, *The Battle of Algiers*, 01:16:10–01:17:24.

37. Pontecorvo, *The Battle of Algiers*, 00:18:31. According to historian Hugh Roberts, most of the real communiqués were written by Abane Ramdane, a close friend of Fanon's who was assassinated by the movement in Morocco in 1957. Hugh Roberts, interview, in *Remembering History*, in Pontecorvo, *The Battle of Algiers*, DVD extras. Mohammed Harbi's collection of FLN letters and draft proclamations provides useful background and points of textual comparison. The prohibition on alcohol and tobacco in particular is interestingly not framed in the moralizing, self-purging language of Camus's *peste* or *"tous ces fléaux"* as they are called in the film, but rather as "un grand coup à l'éconnomie impérialiste." Mohammed Harbi, *Les archives de la révolution algérienne* (Paris: Jeune Afrique, 1981), 105. Harbi wrote the postface of a 2002 edition of Frantz Fanon's *Les damnés de la terre* (Paris: La Découverte/Poche, 2002).

38. Frantz Fanon, "This Is the Voice of Algeria," in *A Dying Colonialism*, trans. Haakon Chevalier (New York: Grove Press, 1965), 65–97; Pontecorvo, *The Battle of Algiers*, 00:18:11–00:19:04.

39. Pontecorvo, *The Battle of Algiers*, 00:29:00–00:29:28.

40. See Jennifer Johnson, *The Battle for Algeria: Sovereignty, Health Care, and Humanitarianism* (Philadelphia: University of Pennsylvania Press, 2015), especially chap. 2, "Medical Pacification and the Sections Administratives Spécialisées," 38–61.

41. See Sohail Daulatzai, *Fifty Years of* The Battle of Algiers: *Past as Prologue* (Minneapolis: University of Minnesota Press, 2016), xi.

42. Pontecorvo, *The Battle of Algiers*, 01:34:23–01:35:19.

43. Pontecorvo, *The Battle of Algiers*, 00:59:17.

44. Jean-Paul Sartre, "Preface: A Victory," in Henri Alleg, *The Question*, trans. John Calder (Lincoln: University of Nebraska Press, 2006) xxxvi–xxxvii.

45. Nicholas Harrison, "'Based on Actual Events . . . ,' *The Battle of Algiers* Forty Years On," *Interventions* 9, no. 3 (2007): 335–339. See also Khanna, *Algeria Cuts*; Danièle Djamila Amrane-Minne, "Women at War," trans. Alistair Clarke, *Interventions* 9, no. 3 (2007): 340–349; Moore, "The Veil of Nationalism," 56–73. On the mini-film phenomenon of the three women / three bombs scene, see Jacques Lezra, "Three Women, Three Bombs," in *Wild Materialism: The Ethic of Terror and the Modern Republic* (New York: Fordham University Press, 2010), 173–201.

46. For important critiques, see Diana Fuss, "Interior Colonies: Frantz Fanon and the Politics of Identification," *diacritics* 24, no. 2–3 (1994): 20–42; Anne McClintock, "'No Longer in a Future Heaven': Gender, Race, and Nation-

alism," in *Dangerous Liaisons: Gender, Nation, and Postcolonial Perspectives*, ed. Anne McClintock, Aamir Mufti, and Ella Shohat (Minneapolis: University of Minnesota Press, 1997).

47. Fanon, "Algeria Unveiled," in *A Dying Colonialism*, trans. Haakon Chevalier (New York: Grove Press, 1965), 47; Fanon, *L'An V de la révolution algérienne* (Paris: François Maspero, 1959), 27.

48. Frantz Fanon, *The Wretched of the Earth*, trans. Richard Philcox (New York: Grove Press, 2004), 44; Frantz Fanon, *Les Damnés de la terre* (Paris: Gallimard, 1991), 117. Subsequent references to this work appear in parentheses in the text. English and French edition page numbers are separated by a semicolon.

49. Aimé Césaire, *And the Dogs Were Silent*, in *Lyric and Dramatic Poetry 1946–1982*, trans. Clayton Eshleman and Annette Smith (Charlottesville: University Press of Virginia, 1990), quoted in Fanon, *The Wretched of the Earth*, trans. Philcox, 46; Aimé Césaire, *Et les chiens se taisaient* (Paris: Gallimard, 1961), quoted in Fanon, *Les Damnés de la terre*, 121.

50. Fanon, "Algeria Unveiled," 47; Fanon, *L'An V*, 16. Subsequent references to this work appear in parentheses in the text. English and French edition page numbers are separated by a semicolon.

51. Fuss, "Interior Colonies," 27.

52. Frantz Fanon, *Black Skin, White Masks*, trans. Richard Philcox (New York: Grove Press, 2008), 93–94.

53. Pontecorvo, *The Battle of Algiers*, 01:59:00.

54. Pontecorvo, *The Battle of Algiers*, 01:59:00.

55. Eve Kosofsky Sedgwick, "The Character in the Veil: Imagery of the Surface in the Gothic," *PMLA* 96, no. 2 (March 1981): 257–258.

56. Gayatri Chakravorty Spivak, "Can the Subaltern Speak?," in *Can the Subaltern Speak? Reflections on the History of an Idea*, ed. Rosalind Morris (New York: Columbia University Press, 2010), 66.

57. Leila Sebbar's *La seine était rouge* contemplates this episode in novel form (Paris: Actes Sud, 2009); see also Michael Haneke, director, *Caché* (Paris: Canal+, 2005).

58. Frantz Fanon, "Medicine and Colonialism," trans. Haakon Chevalier, in *A Dying Colonialism* (New York: Grove Press, 1965), 121; Frantz Fanon, "Médicine et colonialisme," in *L'An V de la révolution algérienne* (Paris: François Maspero, 1959), 111–112. Subsequent references to this work appear in parentheses in the text. English and French edition page numbers are separated by a semicolon.

59. Simone de Beauvoir and Gisèle Halimi, *Djamila Boupacha: The Story of a Young Algerian Girl Which Shocked Liberal French Opinion*, trans. Peter Green (New York: MacMillan, 1962), 43; Simone de Beauvoir et Gisèle Halimi, *Djamila Boupacha* (Paris: Gallimard, 1962), 40. Subsequent references to this work appear in parentheses in the text. English and French edition page numbers are separated by a semicolon.

60. Beauvoir and Halimi, *Djamila Boupacha*, trans. Green, 70, 90; Beauvoir and Halimi, *Djamila Boupacha*, 84, 102.

61. Adolfo Gilly, "Introduction," trans. Nell Salm, in Frantz Fanon, *A Dying Colonialism*, trans. Haakon Chevalier (New York: Grove Press, 1965), 11.

62. Judith Surkis, "Ethics and Violence: Simone de Beauvoir, Djamila Boupacha, and the Algerian War," *French Politics, Culture & Society* 28, no. 2 (Summer, 2010): 38–55; Frantz Fanon, "Concerning a Plea," *Toward the African Revolution*, trans. Haakon Chevalier (New York: Grove Press, 1967), 74.

63. Fanon, "Concerning a Plea," 75.

64. Amrane-Minne, *Les femmes algériennes dans la Guerre*, chap. 5, "Les camps et les prisons."

65. Georges Arnaud and Jacques Vergès, *Pour Djamila Bouhired* (Paris: Éditions de Minuit, 1957).

66. Surkis, "Ethics and Violence," 49.

67. Simone de Beauvoir, "Introduction," in *Djamila Boupacha*, trans. Green, 10.

68. Beauvoir, "Introduction," 9.

69. First lines of "Djamila Boupacha" in Nono's cycle *Canti di vita e d'amore* translated from the Spanish by Heather Cleary.

70. Jean-Luc Nancy, *Portrait*, trans. Sarah Clift and Simon Sparks (New York: Fordham University Press, 2018), 99.

71. Cathy Newman, "A Life Revealed," *National Geographic*, April 2002, https://www.nationalgeographic.com/magazine/2002/04/afghan-girl-revealed/.

72. Newman, "A Life Revealed."

73. Newman, "A Life Revealed."

74. Newman, "A Life Revealed."

75. Newman, "A Life Revealed."

76. Newman, "A Life Revealed."

77. Beauvoir and Halimi, trans. Green, *Djamila Boupacha*, 51; Beauvoir and Halimi, *Djamila Boupacha*, 47.

CHAPTER 6

1. See Sumit Ganguly, *The Crisis in Kashmir: Portents of War, Hopes of Peace* (Cambridge: Woodrow Wilson Center Press and Cambridge University Press, 1997); and Abdul Gafoor Noorani, *Article 370: A Constitutional History of Jammu and Kashmir* (New Delhi: Oxford University Press, 2011).

2. Kavita Suri, "J&K: Return to Violence?," in *Armed Conflicts in South Asia 2010: Growing Left-wing Extremism and Religious Violence*, ed. D. Suba Chandran and P. R. Chari (New Delhi: Routledge, 2011), 77.

3. Fahad Shah, "'News from Here Doesn't Go Out': Kashmir Simmers Under Lockdown," *The Atlantic*, August 18, 2019, https://www.theatlantic.com/international/archive/2019/08/kashmir-india/596314/.

4. For succinct accounts, see Baba Umar, "Kashmir on Fire," *Diplomat*, July 13, 2016, https://thediplomat.com/2016/07/kashmir-on-fire/; and "Deaths as Indian Troops Open Fire on Kashmir Protesters," *Al Jazeera*, July 10, 2016, https://www.aljazeera.com/news/2016/07/deaths-indian-troops-open-fire-kashmir-protesters-160709125142182.html.

5. Ellen Barry, "An Epidemic of 'Dead Eyes' in Kashmir as India Uses Pellet Guns on Protestors," *New York Times*. August 28, 2016, https://www.nytimes.com/2016/08/29/world/asia/pellet-guns-used-in-kashmir-protests-cause-dead-eyes-epidemic.html.

6. Mukhtar Ahmad, "At Least 20 Killed in Kashmir Clashes after Militant's Death," Cable News Network, July 11, 2016, https://www.cnn.com/2016/07/11/asia/kashmir-unrest/index.html. See also Meenakshi R., "Kashmir on the Boil: A Timeline," *The Hindu*, July 21, 2016, http://www.thehindu.com/news/national/kashmir-unrest-after-burhan-wanis-death/article14596369.ece; and "Jammu and Kashmir Saw Three-fold Increase in Rioting in 2016: State Police Data," *Hindustan Times*, March 5, 2017, https://www.hindustantimes.com/india-news/jammu-and-kashmir-saw-three-fold-increase-in-rioting-in-2016-state-police-data/story-72PBpcZew841nnmpqobgxL.html.

7. Mirza Waheed, "India's Crackdown in Kashmir: Is This the World's First Mass Blinding?," *Guardian*, November 8, 2016, https://www.theguardian.com/world/2016/nov/08/india-crackdown-in-kashmir-is-this-worlds-first-mass-blinding.

8. Qadri Inzamam and Mohammad Haziq, "In Kashmir, 'Non-lethal' Weapons Cause Lethal Damage," *Caravan*, July 12, 2016, http://www.caravanmagazine.in/vantage/kashmir-pellets-non-lethal-weapons-damage; Max Bearak, "In Kashmir, Indian Security Forces Use Pellet Guns That Often Blind Protesters," *Washington Post*, July 12, 2016, https://www.washingtonpost.com/news/worldviews/wp/2016/07/12/in-kashmir-indian-security-forces-use-pellet-guns-that-often-blind-protesters/?utm_term=.858a909a26ef.

9. Zehru Nissa, "In 4 Months, Pellets Damage Eyes of 1178 Persons," *Greater Kashmir*, November 8, 2016, http://www.greaterkashmir.com/news/life-style/story/233000.html.

10. Waheed, "India's Crackdown in Kashmir."

11. Barry, "An Epidemic of 'Dead Eyes.'"

12. "'Everyone Lives in Fear': Patterns of Impunity in Jammu and Kashmir," *Human Rights Watch* 18, no. 11 (September 2006): 29–31.

13. Suvir Kaul, *Of Gardens and Graves: Kashmir, Poetry, Politics* (Durham: Duke University Press, 2017).

14. Kaul, *Of Gardens and Graves*, 148.

15. Salman Rushdie, *Joseph Anton: A Memoir* (New York: Random House, 2012), 346.

16. Peta Mitchell provides a very useful overview of the evolution from Derrida's early work on contamination and virality to the full-fledged theorization

of autoimmunity in "Contagion, Virology, Autoimmunity: Derrida's Rhetoric of Contamination," *Parallax* 23, no. 1 (2017): 77–93.

17. See, for example, Rushdie's account of a conversation organized with the author by the U.S. Senate Committee on Foreign Relations to discuss a resolution against the fatwa. Rushdie, *Joseph Anton*, 330.

18. Rushdie, *Joseph Anton*, 356.

19. Salman Rushdie, "June 1999: Kashmir," reprinted in *Step Across This Line: Collected Nonfiction 1992–2002* (New York: Random House, 2002), 274.

20. Salman Rushdie, "The Most Dangerous Place in the World," *New York Times*, May 30, 2002, A25.

21. Rushdie, *Step Across This Line*, 211–346.

22. Amitava Kumar, "Who Will Break the Sad News to Salman Rushdie?," *Tehelka* (August 6, 2005), http://archive.tehelka.com/story_main13.asp?filename =hub080605who_will.asp.

23. See Natasha Walter, "The Children of Paradise," review of *Shalimar the Clown*, by Salman Rushdie, *Guardian*, September 2, 2005, http://www .theguardian.com/books/2005/sep/03/fiction.salmanrushdie.

24. Agha Shahid Ali, "Farewell," in *The Country Without a Post Office* (New York: W. W. Norton & Co., 1998), 22–23.

25. The narrator of *Shame* scolds, "Look under your feet. You will not find gnarled growths sprouting through the soles. Roots, I sometimes think, are a conservative myth, designed to keep us in our places." Salman Rushdie, *Shame* (New York: Henry Holt, 1983), 84. Rushdie would later backtrack on this claim, asking in *Joseph Anton*, "[W]as it possible to become *good* at being—not rootless, but multiply rooted? Not to suffer from a loss of roots, but to benefit from an excess of then?" Rushdie, *Joseph Anton*, 54.

26. Rushdie, *Shame*, 84.

27. For a recent example, see Mohsin Hamid, *Exit West* (New York: Riverhead Books, 2017), 90–91 and throughout.

28. Masood Ashraf Raja, "The King Buzzard: Bano Qudsia's Postnational Allegory and the Nation State," *Mosaic* 40, no. 1 (March 2007): 95–110. Rushdie characterizes the poem as a "Muslim *Pilgrim's Progress*." Rushdie, *Joseph Anton*, 50. See also Laila Lalami, "Among the Blasphemers: On Salman Rushdie," *Nation*, January 16, 2013, https://www.thenation.com/article/among-blasphemers -salman-rushdie/.

29. Raja, "The King Buzzard," 97.

30. Raja, "The King Buzzard," 97, 99.

31. Rushdie, *Shame*, 85–86 (emphasis in the original).

32. Benedict Anderson, *Imagined Communities* (London: Verso, 1983).

33. See Fredric Jameson, "Third World Literature in the Era of Multinational Capitalism," *Social Text* 15 (Autumn 1986): 65–88; and Aijaz Ahmad, "Literary Theory and 'Third World Literature': Some Contexts," in *In Theory: Classes, Nations, Literatures* (London: Verso, 1992), 43–72.

34. Salman Rushdie, *Shalimar the Clown* (New York: Random House, 2005), 54. Subsequent references to this work appear in parentheses in the text and are labeled *SC*.

35. James Wood, "Human, All Too Inhuman," *New Republic*, July 23, 2000, https://newrepublic.com/article/61361/human-inhuman.

36. This concern is simultaneously localizing, in the sense that it is associated with what Foucault called "the problem of the town" in the eighteenth century, writing that in addition to allowing for surveillance, "it was a matter of organizing circulation, eliminating its dangerous elements, making a division between good and bad circulation, and maximizing the good circulation by diminishing the bad." Michel Foucault, *Security, Territory, Population: Lectures at the Collège de France 1977–1978*, ed. Michel Senellart, trans. Graham Burchell (New York: Picador, 2007), 18.

37. To this point, Faisal Devji explains that "it is because the jihad is concerned neither with the undifferentiated unity of the world's oppressed, nor even with the particular struggles of Muslims, that it has the audacity to engage in a global war . . . [M]odern politics cannot comprehend religion in any terms but its own, which is to say as a kind of emotional front for supposedly real issues like freedom or justice, wealth or power." *Landscapes of the Jihad: Militancy, Mortality, Modernity* (Ithaca: Cornell University Press, 2005), 75–76.

38. A. Mitra counts 1,443 deaths in "A Plague in Kashmir," *Indian Medical Gazette* 42 no. 4 (April 1907): 133–138, 137.

39. A. Mitra, *A Report on the Outbreak of Plague in Kashmir* (Kashmir: Central Jail Press, 1904). For an account of the 1901 epidemic in Jammu, see B. R. Sawhney, *Brief Notes on the Outbreak of Plague in the Jammu Province, Kashmir State, 1901* (Jammu: Ranbir Prakash Press, 1901).

40. Mitra, *A Report on the Outbreak of Plague*, 3.

41. Mitra, *A Report on the Outbreak of Plague*, 3.

42. Mitra also describes police officers Chowkidar and Lambardar concealing plague cases in the area of Woolar Lake, and notes the difficultly of registering death statistics without the full cooperation of the police constabulary. Mitra, *A Report on the Outbreak of Plague in Kashmir*, 5.

43. Javed Siddiqi, *World Health and World Politics: The World Health Organization and the UN System* (Columbia: University of South Carolina Press, 1995), 19.

44. Siddiqi, *World Health and World Politics*, 19; and "The Work of the Health Organization of the League of Nations," *Canadian Medical Association Journal*, 15, no. 11 (November 1925): 1153.

45. "The International Health Organization of the League of Nations," *British Medical Journal* 1, no. 3302 (April 12, 1924): 672–675.

46. Pheng Cheah, *Spectral Nationality: Passages of Freedom from Kant to Postcolonial Literatures of Liberation* (New York: Columbia University Press, 2003), 12–13.

47. Cheah, *Spectral Nationality*, 12.

48. See Ayesha Jalal, "Exploding Communalism: The Politics of Muslim

Identity in South Asia," in *Nationalism, Democracy, and Development: State and Politics in India*, ed. Sugata Bose and Ayesha Jalal (Delhi: Oxford University Press, 1997), 70–103.

49. See chap. 1, "Territorializing Sovereignty," in Mridu Rai, *Hindu Rulers, Muslim Subjects: Islam, Rights, and the History of Kashmir* (Princeton: Princeton University Press, 2004), 28–44.

50. Gayatri Chakravorty Spivak, "Subaltern Studies: Deconstructing Historiography," in *In Other Worlds* (New York: Routledge, 1998), 213. See Stephen Morton, "'There Were Collisions and Explosions. The World Was No Longer Calm': Terror and Precarious life in Salman Rushdie's *Shalimar the Clown*," *Textual Practice* 22, no. 1 (June 2008): 337–355.

51. Salman Rushdie, "The Art of Fiction No. 186," interview by Jack Livings, *Paris Review*, no. 174 (Summer 2005), https://www.theparisreview.org/interviews/5531/the-art-of-fiction-no-186-salman-rushdie.

52. Ahmad Faraz, "Eye Bank," in *Nabeena Sheher Mein Aieena* (Montreal: AMO International, 1983), my translation, originally published in *Guernica*, June 6, 2018, https://www.guernicamag.com/eye-bank/.

53. Barry, "An Epidemic of 'Dead Eyes.'"

54. Isabell Lorey's *State of Insecurity: Government of the Precarious* (London: Verso, 2015) is a key example. John Hamilton's *Security: Politics, Humanity, and the Philology of Care* (Princeton: Princeton University Press, 2013) is by far the most creative and rigorous theoretical book on the subject. On the relationship between global health and security, see Jennifer Terry, *Attachments to War: Biomedical Logics and Violence in Twenty Frist Century America* (Durham: Duke University Press, 2017), and Andrew Lakoff and Stephen Collier, eds., *Biosecurity Interventions: Global Health and Security in Question* (New York: Columbia University Press, 2008). For a useful overview of this epochal shift from largely Italian and French social scientists, see Alessandro Dal Lago and Salvatore Palidda, eds. *Conflict, Security, and the Reshaping of Society* (London: Routledge, 2010). The essays collected by Alex J. Bellamy, Roland Bleiker, Sara E. Davies, and Richard Devetak, eds., in *Security and the War on Terror* (London: Routledge, 2008), remain helpful. See also Paul Amar, *The Security Archipelago: Human-Security States, Sexuality Politics, and the End of Neoliberalism* (Durham: Duke University Press, 2013); Inderpal Grewal, *Saving the Security State: Exceptional Citizens in Twenty-First Century America* (Durham: Duke University Press, 2017); Brad Evans, *Liberal Terror* (Cambridge: Polity, 2013); Julian Reid, *The Biopolitics of the War on Terror* (Manchester: Manchester University Press, 2006); and Michael Dillon and Andrew Neal, eds., *Foucault on Politics, Security, and War* (London: Palgrave Macmillan, 2008).

55. This center, now emeritus, operated under the name the Center for Visualization and Data Analytics, https://www.dhs.gov/publication/st-cvada-fact-sheet.

56. See, for example, Janet Napolitano and John Brennan's joint "Press Briefing on Swine Influenza with Department of Homeland Security, Centers for

Disease Control and Prevention, and White House," April 16, 2009, http://www
.dhs.gov/news/2009/04/26/press-briefing-swine-influenza. Here, Napolitano
outlines the role of TSA and other immigration agents in assessing health factors at the borders.

57. See, for example, Limor Aharonson-Daniel et al., "Epidemiology of
Terror-Related Versus Non-Terror-Related Traumatic Injury in Children," *Pedi-
atrics* 112, no. 4 (October 1, 2003): 280–284; Nick Wilson and George Thomson,
"The Epidemiology of International Terrorism Involving Fatal Outcomes in
Developed Countries," *European Journal of Epidemiology* 20 (2005): 375–381; and
Barry S. Levy and Victor W. Sidel, eds., *Terrorism and Public Health: A Balanced
Approach to Strengthening Systems and Protecting People*, 2nd ed. (New York:
Oxford University Press, 2012).

58. Rushdie, *Joseph Anton*, 207–208. Subsequent references to this work appear in parentheses in the text and are labeled *JA*.

59. U.S. Department of Defense, Donald Rumsfeld, "Rumsfeld and My-
ers Briefing on Enduring Freedom," News Transcript, October 7, 2001, 2:45
PM, https://archive.defense.gov/Transcripts/Transcript.aspx?TranscriptID=
2011; Anthony Zurcher, "What Trump Team Has Said About Islam," *BBC News*,
February 7, 2017, https://www.bbc.com/news/world-us-canada-38886496. ; John
Roberts, Majority Opinion, *Trump v. Hawaii* (585 U.S. __, June 26, 2018), 23;
David Shariatmadari, "Swarms, Floods, and Marauders: The Toxic Metaphors
of the Migration Debate," *Guardian*, August 10, 2015, https://www.theguardian
.com/commentisfree/2015/aug/10/migration-debate-metaphors-swarms-floods
-marauders-migrants; Boris Johnson, "Global Britain Is Helping to Win the
Struggle against Islamist Terror," Foreign & Commonwealth Office, Speech
Transcript, December 7, 2017, https:www.gov.uk/government/speeches/how
-global-britain-is-helping-to-win-the-struggle-against-islamist-terror.

60. Nawal El Saadawi, "Extracts from an Interview with a Swedish Journalist," in Albert Memmi, "For Secularism," *Index on Censorship* 18, no. 6 (May 1,
1989): 16–19, http://ioc.sagepub.com/content/18/5/16.citation.

61. During the time in which Rushdie was in hiding, his second wife,
Clarissa Luard, was diagnosed with breast cancer, from which she would die
in 1999. His first wife, Marianne Wiggins, was also diagnosed with Burkitt's
lymphoma, and the memoir focuses a good deal of attention on the death of
Thomasina, the television chef Nigella Lawson's sister, from breast cancer.

62. Foucault, *Security, Territory, Population*, 11, 55–79.

63. See Talal Asad, "Thinking about Terrorism and Just War," *Cambridge
Review of International Affairs* 23, no. 1 (December 18, 2009): 1, 3–24; and
Thomas Keenan, "'Where Are Human Rights . . . ?': Reading a Communiqué
from Iraq," in *Nongovernmental Politics*, ed. Michel Feher (New York: Zone
Books, 2007).

64. Cf. Yaseen Noorani, "The Rhetoric of Security," *New Centennial Review* 5,
no. 1 (Spring 2005): 13–41. Noorani suggests a symmetry between the way in
which terrorism and the US government *both* function external to "world

order," and that this externality "lies at the foundation of the rhetoric of security by which the U.S. government justifies its hegemonic actions and policies" (14).

65. Gayatri Spivak critiques Rushdie for uncritically celebrating the universalist aspirations of the migrant in her 1989 reading of *The Satanic Verses*: "We must acknowledge that, writing as a migrant, Rushdie still militates against privileging the migrant or the exilic voice narrowly conceived, even as he fails in that very effort. . . . [T]he message and the medium of his book are marked by this conflict" (82). My contention is that the balance of his texts has shifted, since this essay was written, toward the failing side. Gayatri Chakravorty Spivak, "Reading *The Satanic Verses*," *Public Culture* 2, no. 1 (Fall, 1989): 79–99.

66. Salman Rushdie, *Imaginary Homelands* (New York: Vintage, 1991), 10.

67. Devji, *Landscapes of the Jihad*, 71.

68. Devji, *Landscapes of the Jihad*, 73–74.

69. Elsewhere in *Joseph Anton*, Rushdie refers to cultural relativism as yet another cancer: "As 'respect for Islam,' which was fear of Islamist violence cloaked in Tartuffe-like hypocrisy, gained legitimacy in the West, the cancer of cultural relativism had begun to eat away at the rich multicultures of the modern world, and down that slippery slope they all might slide" (*JA* 357).

70. See especially Daisy Rockwell, "All Hail Salman Rushdie, All Hail Joseph Anton," review of *Joseph Anton* by Salman Rushdie, *Bookslut*, November 2012, http://www.bookslut.com/white_chick_with_a_hindi_phd/2012_11_019575.php; and Zoë Heller, "The Salman Rushdie Case," review of *Joseph Anton* by Salman Rushdie, *New York Review of Books*, vfDecember 20, 2012, http://www.nybooks .com/articles/archives/2012/dec/20/salman-rushdie-case/.

71. See Pascale Casanova, *World Republic of Letters*, trans. M. B. DeBevoise (Cambridge: Harvard University Press, 2004).

72. Rushdie, *Imaginary Homelands*, 12.

73. Jalal Al-i Ahmad, *Occidentosis: A Plague from the West*, trans. R. Campbell (Berkeley: Mizan Press, 1984), 98.

74. Al-i Ahmad, *Occidentosis*, 98.

75. Edward W. Said, *Power, Politics, and Culture: Interviews with Edward Said* (New York: Vintage, 2002), 221.

76. Said, *Power, Politics, and Culture*, 221.

77. Said, *Power, Politics, and Culture*, 221.

78. Jacques Derrida, *Rogues: Two Essays on Reason*, trans. Pascale-Anne Brault and Michael Naas (Stanford: Stanford University Press, 2005); "Faith and Knowledge: The Two Sources of 'Religion' at the Limits of Reason Alone," in *Acts of Religion*, ed. Gil Anidjar (New York: Routledge, 2002), 40–101. See also J. Hillis Miller, "Derrida's Politics of Autoimmunity," *Discourse* 30, no. 1–2 (Winter/Spring, 2008): 208–225; and Martin Hägglund, *Radical Atheism: Derrida and the Time of Life* (Stanford: Stanford University Press, 2008).

79. This passage from *Rogues* is highlighted as the culmination point of Hillis Miller, "Derrida's Politics of Autoimmunity," 223.

80. Roberto Esposito, *Immunitas: The Protection and Negation of Life*, trans. Zakiya Hanafi (Cambridge: Polity, 2011), 17–18.

81. Salman Rushdie, *The Satanic Verses* (New York: Henry Holt, 1997), 217. Subsequent references to this work appear in parentheses in the text.

82. A third section of explicitly medical interest in the novel is what Gayatri Spivak has written about as the "hospital section of the book" in "Reading *The Satanic Verses*."

83. See Christopher Hitchens, *God Is Not Great: How Religion Poisons Everything* (London: Atlantic Books, 2008), 135.

84. Edward W. Said, "Secular Criticism," in *The World, The Text, and the Critic* (Cambridge: Harvard University Press, 1983), 20.

85. For a thorough account of the regime of debility in contemporary security-based warfare, see Jasbir Puar, *The Right To Maim: Debility, Capacity, Disability* (Durham: Duke University Press, 2017), especially 21–25.

86. The literary precedent is, I think, Mulk Raj Anand, *Untouchable* (London: Penguin, 1940), 61–63.

87. For the most influential example, see Homi Bhabha, "How Newness Enters the World: Postmodern Space, Postcolonial Times and the Trials of Cultural Translation," in *The Location of Culture* (London: Routledge, 2004), 303–337.

88. Sigmund Freud, *Civilization and Its Discontents*, ed. and trans. James Strachey (New York: W. W. Norton & Co., 1961), 11n3.

89. Sara Suleri, "Contraband Histories: Salman Rushdie and the Embodiment of Blasphemy," in *Reading Rushdie: Perspectives on the Fiction of Salman Rushdie*, ed. M. D. Fletcher (Amsterdam: Rodopi, 1994), esp. 232.

90. Bhabha takes up this question in "How Newness Enters the World."

91. Sara Suleri, "Whither Rushdie?," *Transition* 51 (1991): 210.

92. See Janice Ho, "*The Satanic Verses* and the Politics of Extremity," *Novel: A Forum on Fiction* 44, no. 2 (2011): 208–228.

CHAPTER 7

1. Cathy McMorris Rodgers, remarks at the Republican Leadership Press Conference, July 6, 2016, https://www.gop.gov/global-terrorism-epidemic/; Paul Amar, *The Security Archipelago: Human-Security States, Sexuality Politics, and the End of Neoliberalism* (Durham: Duke University Press, 2013).

2. See further discussion of this incident in chapter 1 of this book.

3. See Paul Rosenberg, "Obama's Error: Getting beyond the 'smart war' syndrome," *Al Jazeera*, September 10, 2013. https://www.aljazeera.com/indepth/opinion/2013/09/20139883212838340.html.

4. See Keith Lawrence, "The Growth of Islamic Studies," and interview with Omid Safi, *Duke Today*, August 11, 2016, https://today.duke.edu/2016/08/growth-islamic-studies. The establishment of the State Department's Critical Language Scholarships program in 2005 is a key example. See http://www

.clscholarship.org/about. For a British perspective, see Tariq Amin-Khan, "New Orientalism, Securitisation, and the Western Media's Incendiary Racism," *Third World Quarterly*, 33, no. 9 (2012): 1595–1610. *The 9/11 Commission Report* remarks on the paucity of trained intelligence officials in the years leading up to the attack, noting that the "total number of undergraduate degrees granted in Arabic in all U.S. colleges and universities in 2002 was six." National Commission on Terrorist Attacks upon the United States, *The 9/11 Commission Report* (New York: W. W. Norton, 2004), 92.

5. Edward W. Said, *Orientalism* (New York: Vintage, 1979), 3.

6. Jennifer Terry, *Attachments to War: Biomedical Logics and Violence in Twenty-First Century America* (Durham: Duke University Press, 2017), 6.

7. Mona Yacoubian and Paul Stares, "Rethinking the War on Terror," United States Institute of Peace, September 7, 2005, https://www.usip.org/publications/2005/09/rethinking-war-terror.

8. Yacoubian and Stares, "Rethinking the War on Terror."

9. Paul Stares and Mona Yacoubian, "Terrorism as Virus," *Washington Post*, August 23, 2005, http://www.washingtonpost.com/wp-dyn/content/article/2005/08/22/AR2005082201109.html.

10. Stares and Yacoubian, "Terrorism as Virus."

11. Stares and Yacoubian, "Terrorism as Virus."

12. Stares and Yacoubian, "Terrorism as Virus."

13. Stares and Yacoubian, "Terrorism as Virus."

14. Stares and Yacoubian, "Terrorism as Virus."

15. Megan Vaughan, *Curing Their Ills: Colonial Power and African Illness* (Stanford: Stanford University Press, 1991).

16. Stares and Yacoubian, "Terrorism as Virus."

17. National Commission on Terrorist Attacks upon the United States, *The 9/11 Commission Report* (New York: W. W. Norton, 2004), 1.

18. Stares and Yacoubian, "Terrorism as Virus."

19. Paul B. Stares and Mona Yacoubian, "Terrorism as a Disease: An Epidemiological Model for Countering Islamist Extremism," working paper, 2007, 5, https://pdfs.semanticscholar.org/3a62/c0105444e2739f40357091f76db6c74f2eff.pdf.

20. Stares and Yacoubian, "Terrorism as a Disease."

21. Stares and Yacoubian, "Terrorism as a Disease."

22. Barry S. Levy and Victor W. Sidel, eds., *Terrorism and Public Health: A Balanced Approach to Strengthening Systems and Protecting People*, 2nd ed. (New York: Oxford University Press, 2012); Kevin D. Lafferty, Katherine F. Smith, and Elizabeth M. P. Madin, "The Infectiousness of Terrorist Ideology: Insights from Ecology and Epidemiology," in *Natural Security: A Darwinian Approach to a Dangerous World*, ed. Raphael D. Sagarin and Terence Taylor (Berkeley: University of California Press, 2008), 186–206; Bryan Price, "Terrorism as Cancer: How to Combat an Incurable Disease," *Terrorism and Political Violence* 29, no. 1 (June 9, 2017): 1–25; Kjirstin Bentson, "An Epidemiological Approach to Terrorism,"

thesis, Air Force Institute of Technology, U.S. Department of Defense, March 2006, http://www.dtic.mil/dtic/tr/fulltext/u2/a446659.pdf.

23. See, for example, Jean Baudrillard, *The Spirit of Terrorism* (New York: Verso, 2013); Ann Keniston and Jeanne Follansbee Quinn, *Literature After 9/11* (New York: Routledge, 2010); Tzvetan Todorov, *The Fear of Barbarians: Beyond the Clash of Civilizations*, trans. Andrew Brown (Chicago: University of Chicago Press, 2010); W. J. T. Mitchell, *Cloning Terror: The War of Images, 9/11 to the Present* (Chicago: University of Chicago Press, 2011); Thomas Stubblefield, *9/11 and the Visual Culture of Disaster* (Bloomington: Indiana University Press, 2014); Aimee Pozorski, *Falling After 9/11: Crisis in American Art and Literature* (New York: Bloomsbury Academic, 2014); Aviva Briefel and Sam Miller, eds. *Horror After 9/11: World of Fear, Cinema of Terror* (Austin: University of Texas Press, 2011); and Mahmood Mamdani, *Good Muslim, Bad Muslim: America, the Cold War, and the Roots of Terror* (New York: Pantheon, 2004).

24. Vaughan, *Curing Their Ills*; David Arnold, *Colonizing the Body: State Medicine and Epidemic Disease in Nineteenth-Century India* (Berkeley: University of California Press, 1993); Alan Bewell, *Romanticism and Colonial Disease* (Baltimore: Johns Hopkins University Press, 2003).

25. National Commission on Terrorist Attacks upon the United States, *The 9/11 Commission Report* (New York: W. W. Norton, 2004), 1. Subsequent references to this work appear in parentheses in the text.

26. Clancy's 1994 novel, *Debt of Honor*—one of the "Jack Ryan" books about an American National Security Advisor—features a Boeing 747 used as a suicide vehicle against the Capitol, where the president and dozens of others are killed, as well as a Somali Muslim villain, Mohammed Abdul Corp., supposedly a stand-in for Mohamed Farah Hassan Aidid, the former military general responsible for the 1992 attacks on UN personnel in Somalia. Clancy, who died in 2013, was a favorite of Republican lawmakers, dedicating a number of books to conservative and Republican politicians including Ronald Reagan. Tom Clancy, *Debt of Honor* (New York: G. P. Putnam's Sons, 1994.) For publication details of *Debt of Honor*, see Christopher Buckley, "Megabashing Japan," *New York Times*, October 2, 1994, https://www.nytimes.com/1994/10/02/books/crime -mystery-megabashing-japan.html. For political context of Clancy's career, see Patrick Anderson, "King of the Techno-thriller," *New York Times*, May 1, 1988, https://www.nytimes.com/1988/05/01/magazine/king-of-the-techno-thriller .html.

27. Zareena Grewal, *Islam Is a Foreign Country: American Muslims and the Global Crisis of Authority* (New York: New York University Press, 2014), 2. See also Sally Howell and Andrew Shryock, "Cracking Down on Diaspora: Arab Detroit and America's 'War on Terror,'" *Anthropological Quarterly* 76, no. 3 (Summer, 2003): 443–462.

28. Josephine Butler, "Our Indian Fellow Subjects," cited in Antoinette Burton, *Burdens of History: British Feminists, Indian Women, and Imperial Culture 1865–1915* (Chapel Hill: University of North Carolina Press, 1994); Thomas

Babington Macaulay, "Minute on Education," cited in Gauri Viswanathan, *Masks of Conquest: Literary Study and British Rule in India* (New York: Columbia University Press, 1989); E. M. Forster, *A Passage to India* (New York: Harcourt, 1984), 51.

29. Central Intelligence Agency, Office of the Inspector General, "Report on CIA Accountability With Respect to the 9/11 Attacks," Executive Summary, June 1, 2005, https://www.cia.gov/library/readingroom/document/0001467964.

30. Edward Wyatt, "National Book Award Finalists Include 9/11 Commission Report," *New York Times*, October 13, 2004, https://www.nytimes.com/2004/10/13/books/national-book-awards-finalists-include-911-commission-report.html.

31. Ernest May, "When Government Writes History," *New Republic*, May 23, 2005, https://newrepublic.com/article/64332/when-government-writes-history.

32. Craig A. Warren, "'It Reads Like a Novel': *The 9/11 Commission Report* and the American Reading Public," *Journal of American Studies* 41, no. 3 (December 2007): 552.

33. Warren, "It Reads Like a Novel," 534.

34. Benjamin DeMott, "Whitewash as Public Service," *Harper's Magazine*, October, 2004, 35–45, 44, 37.

35. DeMott, "Whitewash as Public Service," 37.

36. Michel Foucault, *The Birth of the Clinic: An Archaeology of Medical Perception*, trans. Alan Sheridan (New York: Vintage, 1994), 25.

37. May, "When Government Writes History."

38. May, "When Government Writes History."

39. May, "When Government Writes History."

40. May, "When Government Writes History."

41. May, "When Government Writes History."

42. May, "When Government Writes History."

43. John Updike, "The Great I Am," *New Yorker*, November 1, 2004, https://www.newyorker.com/magazine/2004/11/01/the-great-i-am.

44. May, "When Government Writes History."

45. May, "When Government Writes History."

46. See Ernest May, *American Imperialism; A Speculative Essay* (Chicago: Imprint Publications, 1991), 17.

47. Dianne Feinstein, "Preface," Senate Select Committee on Intelligence, *The Senate Intelligence Committee Report on Torture* (New York: Melville House, 2014), x–xi.

48. "Abu Ja'far al-Iraqi was provided medication for swelling in his legs to allow for continued standing sleep deprivation." *The Senate Intelligence Committee Report on Torture*, 354–356.

49. *The Senate Intelligence Committee Report on Torture*, 358.

50. *The Senate Intelligence Committee Report on Torture*, 340, 342, 343, 344, 345, 346, 347, 354, 348.

51. Julian Hattem, "Feinstein: Take the 'Anarchist Cookbook' and al Qaeda Magazine off the Internet," *The Hill*, April 2, 2015, http://thehill.com/policy/

technology/237749-feinstein-take-anarchist-cookbook-al-qaeda-magazine-off
-internet.

52. Salman Rushdie, *The Satanic Verses* (New York: Henry Holt, 1997), 97. Subsequent references to this work appear in parentheses in the text.

53. Solmaz Sharif, *LOOK* (Minneapolis: Greywolf Press, 2016), 3. Subsequent references to this work appear in parentheses in the text.

54. See John Updike, *Terrorist* (New York: Knopf, 2006); Richard Flanagan, *The Unknown Terrorist* (New York: Grove Press, 2006); Don DeLillo, *Falling Man* (New York: Scribner, 2007); Mohsin Hamid, *The Reluctant Fundamentalist* (New York: Harcourt, 2007); Amy Waldman, *The Submission* (New York: Picador, 2011).

55. Michel Houellebecq, *Soumission* (Paris: Flammarion, 2015).

56. Later in 2015, then–British prime minister David Cameron referred to the "swarm" of migrants crossing the Mediterranean. For a more extensive catalogue of such language in the summer of 2015, see David Shariatmadari, "Swarms, Floods, and Marauders: The Toxic Metaphors of the Migration Debate," *Guardian*, August 10, 2015, https://www.theguardian.com/commentisfree/2015/aug/10/migration-debate-metaphors-swarms-floods-marauders-migrants.

57. Jed Esty, *Unseasonable Youth: Modernism, Colonialism, and the Fiction of Development* (London: Oxford University Press, 2011), 18.

Bibliography

Aalseth, Patricia T. *Medical Coding*. Sudbury: Jones and Bartlett, 2006.

Abbas, Ferhat. *Autopsie d'une guerre: L'aurore*. Paris: Éditions Garnier Frères, 1980.

Abbot, Sebastian. "Reported CIA Vaccine Ruse Sparks Fear in Pakistan." *Seattle Times*, July 14, 2011. http://www.seattletimes.com/nation-world/cia-vaccination-ruse-sparks-fear-in-pakistan/.

Abdallah, Anouar, et al. *For Rushdie: Essays by Arab and Muslim Writers in Defense of Free Speech*. Translated by Kevin Anderson and Kenneth Whitehead. New York: George Braziller, 1994.

Agamben, Giorgio. *Homo Sacer: Sovereign Power and Bare Life*. Translated by Daniel Heller-Roazen. Stanford: Stanford University Press, 1998.

———. *The Open: Man and Animal*. Translated by Kevin Attell. Stanford: Stanford University Press, 2003.

———. *Remnants of Auschwitz: The Witness and the Archive*. Translated by Daniel Heller-Roazen. New York: Zone Books, 2002.

———. *State of Exception*. Translated by Kevin Attell. Chicago: University of Chicago Press, 2005.

Aharonson-Daniel, Limor, et al. "Epidemiology of Terror-Related Versus Non-Terror-Related Traumatic Injury in Children." *Pediatrics* 112, no. 4 (October 1, 2003): 280–284.

Ahmad, Aijaz. *In Theory: Classes, Nations, Literatures*. London: Verso, 1992. Reprint, 2000.

———. "Jameson's Rhetoric of Otherness and the 'National Allegory.'" *Social Text* 17 (Autumn 1987): 3–25.

———. "Literary Theory and 'Third World Literature': Some Contexts." In *In Theory: Classes, Nations, Literatures*, 43–72. London: Verso, 1992.

Ahmad, Eqbal. *Confronting Empire: Interviews with David Barsamian*. Cambridge: South End Press, 2000.

———. *Terrorism: Theirs and Ours*. New York: Seven Stories Press, 2001.

Ahmad, Mukhtar. "At Least 20 Killed in Kashmir Clashes after Militant's Death." Cable News Network, July 11, 2016. https://www.cnn.com/2016/07/11/asia/kashmir-unrest/index.html.

Ahmad Khan, Sayyid, Sir. *The Causes of the Indian Revolt*. Benares: Medical Hall Press, 1873.

———. "The Causes of the Indian Revolt." Edited by Frances W. Pritchett. http://

www.columbia.edu/itc/mealac/pritchett/00litlinks/txt_sir_sayyid_asbab1873
_basic.html.

Ahmed, Jibran. "Pakistani Doctor Who Helped U.S. Find bin Laden Charged with Murder." Reuters, November 22, 2013. http://www.reuters.com/article/us-pakistan-afridi-murder-idUSBRE9AL0F720131122.

Aikins, Matthieu. "The Doctor, the CIA, and the Blood of bin Laden." *Gentlemen's Quarterly*, January 2013. http://www.gq.com/doctor-cia-blood-of-bin-laden-january-2013.

Aisenberg, Andrew R. *Contagion: Disease, Government, and the "Social Question" in Nineteenth-Century France*. Stanford: Stanford University Press, 1999.

Alam, Muzaffar. *The Languages of Political Islam: India 1200–1800*. Chicago: University of Chicago Press, 2004.

Ali, Agha Shahid. *The Country Without a Post Office*. New York: W. W. Norton & Co., 1998.

———. "Farewell." In *The Country Without a Post Office*, 7–10 New York: W. W. Norton & Co., 1998.

———. *The Half-Inch Himalayas*. Middletown: Wesleyan University Press, 1987.

———, ed. *Ravishing DisUnities: Real Ghazals in English*. Middletown: Wesleyan University Press; Hanover: University Press of New England, 2000.

———. *Rooms Are Never Finished*. New York: W. W. Norton & Co., 2002.

Ali, Kazim, ed. *Mad Heart Be Brave: Essays on the Poetry of Agha Shahid Ali*. Ann Arbor: University of Michigan Press, 2017.

Al-i Ahmad, Jalal. *Occidentosis: A Plague from the West*. Translated by R. Campbell. Berkeley: Mizan Press, 1984. https://www.cnn.com/2016/07/11/asia/kashmir-unrest/index.html.

Ali, Wajahat, Eli Clifton, Matthew Duss, Lee Fang, Scott Keyes, and Faiz Shakir. *Fear Inc.: The Roots of the Islamophobia Network in America*. Washington: Center for American Progress, 2011.

Alleg, Henri. *The Question*. Translated by John Calder. Lincoln: University of Nebraska Press, 2006.

"Alleged Fake CIA Vaccination Campaign Undermines Medical Care." Doctors Without Borders. July 14, 2011. http://www.doctorswithoutborders.org/news-stories/press-release/alleged-fake-cia-vaccination-campaign-undermines-medical-care.

Almoravid, Abu Abdillah. "The Blacks in America" *Inspire* 14 (Summer 2015), 19–23. https://azelin.files.wordpress.com/2015/09/inspire-magazine-14.pdf.

Amar, Paul. *The Security Archipelago: Human-Security States, Sexuality Politics, and the End of Neoliberalism*. Durham: Duke University Press, 2013.

Amin-Khan, Tariq. "New Orientalism, Securitisation, and the Western Media's Incendiary Racism." *Third World Quarterly* 33, no. 9 (2012): 1595–1610.

Amis, Martin. "The Age of Horrorism," parts 1–3. *Observer*, September 9, 2006. http://www.guardian.co.uk/world/2006/sep/10/september11.politicsphilosophyandsociety.

———. "The Last Days of Muhammad Atta." *New Yorker*, April 24, 2006, 152–163.

Amrane-Minne, Danièle Djamila. *Les femmes algériennes dans la guerre*. Paris: Plon, 1991.

———. "Women at War." Translated by Alistair Clarke. *Interventions* 9, no. 3 (2007): 340–349.

Anand, Mulk Raj. *Untouchable*. London: Penguin, 1940.

Anbinder, Tyler. "Lord Palmerston and the Irish Famine Emigration." *Historical Journal* 44, no. 2 (June 2001): 441–469.

Anderson, Benedict. *Imagined Communities*. London: Verso, 1983.

Anderson, James. Letter, May 19, 1849. *Hansard's Parliamentary Debates* v. CV May 8–June 11, 1849. London: G. Woodfall and Son, 1849.

Anderson, Patrick. "King of the Techno-Thriller." *New York Times*, May 1, 1988. https://www.nytimes.com/1988/05/01/magazine/king-of-the-techno-thriller .html.

Anidjar, Gil. "Blood." *Political Concepts: A Critical Lexicon* 1 (2011), http://www .politicalconcepts.org/issue1/blood/.

———. *Blood: A Critique of Christianity*. New York: Columbia University Press, 2014.

———. "Blutgewalt." *Oxford Literary Review* 31 (2009): 153–174.

Anonymous. "History of the Rise, Progress, Ravages, &ct. of the Blue Cholera of India." *Lancet* 1, no. 429 (November 19, 1831): 241–284.

Appadurai, Arjun. *Fear of Small Numbers: An Essay on the Geography of Anger*. Durham: Duke University Press, 2006.

Apter, Emily. *Against World Literature: On the Politics of Untranslatability*. London: Verso, 2013.

———. *Continental Drift: From National Characters to Virtual Subjects*. Chicago: University of Chicago Press, 1999.

———. "Out of Character: Camus's French Algerian Subjects." *Modern Language Notes* 112, no. 4 (September 1997): 499–516.

———. *The Translation Zone: A New Comparative Literature*. Princeton: Princeton University Press, 2006.

———. "Weaponized Thought: Ethical Militance and the Group-Subject." *Grey Room* 14 (Winter 2004): 6–24.

Arata, Stephen D. *Fictions of Loss in the Victorian Fin de Siecle*. Cambridge: Cambridge University Press, 1996.

———. Review of *Dracula's Crypt: Bram Stoker, Irishness, and the Question of Blood* by Joseph Valente. *Victorian Studies* 45, no. 3 (Spring, 2003): 536–538.

———. "The Occidental Tourist: *Dracula* and the Anxiety of Reverse Colonization." *Victorian Studies* (Summer 1990): 622–645.

Aravamudan, Srinivas. *Enlightenment Orientalism: Resisting the Rise of the Novel*. Chicago: University of Chicago Press, 2012.

Arendt, Hannah. *Eichmann in Jerusalem: A Report on the Banality of Evil*. New York: Penguin, 2006.

Arnaud, Georges, and Jacques Vergès. *Pour Djamila Bouhired*. Paris: Éditions de Minuit, 1957.

Arnold, David. "Cholera and Colonialism in British India." *Past and Present* 113 (November 1986): 118–151.

———. *Colonizing the Body: State Medicine and Epidemic Disease in Nineteenth-Century India.* Berkeley: University of California Press, 1993.

———. "Touching the Body: Perspectives on the Indian Plague 1896–1900." In *Selected Subaltern Studies*, edited by Ranajit Guha and Gayatri Chakravorty Spivak, 391–426. New York: Oxford University Press, 1988.

Aronson, Ronald. *Camus and Sartre: The Story of a Friendship and the Quarrel That Ended It.* Chicago: University of Chicago Press, 2004.

Asad, Talal. *On Suicide Bombing.* New York: Columbia University Press, 2007.

———. "Thinking about Terrorism and Just War." *Cambridge Review of International Affairs* 23, no. 1 (December 18, 2009): 3–24.

Ásmundsson, Valdimar. *Powers of Darkness: The Lost Version of Dracula.* Translated by Hans Corneel De Roos. New York: Overlook Duckworth, 2016.

Aussaresses, Paul. *The Battle of the Casbah: Terrorism and Counter-Terrorism in Algeria 1955–1957.* New York: Enigma Books, 2002–2010.

Babington, Benjamin Guy, et al. *Transactions of the Epidemiological Society of London v. 1 1859–1862.* London: John W. Davies, 1863.

Baldick, Chris, ed. *Oxford Book of Gothic Tales.* London: Oxford University Press, 2009.

Barrell, John. *The Infection of Thomas De Quincey: A Psychopathology of Imperialism.* New Haven: Yale University Press, 1991.

Barry, Ellen. "An Epidemic of 'Dead Eyes' in Kashmir as India Uses Pellet Guns on Protestors." *New York Times*, August 28, 2016, https://www.nytimes.com/2016/08/29/world/asia/pellet-guns-used-in-kashmir-protests-cause-dead-eyes-epidemic.html.

Barthes, Roland. *Essais Critiques.* Paris: Éditions de Seuil, 1964.

———. *Le degré zéro de l'écriture.* Paris: Éditions du Seuil, 1953.

———. *Writing Degree Zero.* Translated by Annette Lavers and Colin Smith. New York: Hill and Wang, 1967.

Bartlett, James. "Memoranda of the Case of Charles Connell." *Cholera Gazette*, no. 4 (March 3, 1832): 135–136.

Baudrillard, Jean. *The Spirit of Terrorism.* New York: Verso, 2013.

Bearak, Max, "In Kashmir, Indian Security Forces Use Pellet Guns That Often Blind Protesters." *Washington Post*, July 12, 2016, https://www.washingtonpost.com/news/worldviews/wp/2016/07/12/in-kashmir-indian-security-forces-use-pellet-guns-that-often-blind-protesters/?utm_term=.858a909a26ef.

Beauvoir, Simone de, and Gisèle Halimi. *Djamila Boupacha.* Paris: Gallimard, 1962.

———. *Djamila Boupacha: The Story of a Young Algerian Girl Which Shocked Liberal French Opinion.* Translated by Peter Green. New York: MacMillan, 1962.

Belford, Barbara. *Bram Stoker: A Biography of the Author of Dracula.* New York: Knopf, 1996.

——. *Bram Stoker and the Man Who Was Dracula*. Cambridge: Da Capo Press, 1996.

Bellamy, Alex J., Roland Bleiker, Sara E. Davies, and Richard Devetak, eds. *Security and the War on Terror*. London: Routledge, 2008.

Benjamin, Walter. *Illuminations: Essays and Reflections*. Translated by Harry Zohn. Edited by Hannah Arendt. New York: Schocken Books, 1968.

——. "Theses on the Philosophy of History." In *Illuminations*. Translated by Harry Zohn. Edited by Hannah Arendt. New York: Schocken Books, 1968.

Bentson, Kjirstin. "An Epidemiological Approach to Terrorism." Thesis, Air Force Institute of Technology, U.S. Department of Defense, March 2006. http://www .dtic.mil/dtic/tr/fulltext/u2/a446659.pdf.

Beresford, Matthew. *From Demons to Dracula: The Creation of the Modern Vampire Myth*. London: Reaktion Books, 2008.

Berger, John. *Hold Everything Dear: Dispatches on Survival and Resistance*. New York: Vintage, 2007.

Berlant, Lauren. *Cruel Optimism*. Durham: Duke University Press, 2011.

Best, Stephen, and Sharon Marcus. "Surface Reading: An Introduction." *Representations* 108, no. 1 (Fall 2009): 1–21.

Bewell, Alan. *Romanticism and Colonial Disease*. Baltimore: Johns Hopkins University Press, 2003.

Beydoun, Khaled A. *American Islamophobia*. Berkeley: University of California Press, 2018.

Bhabha, Homi K. "How Newness Enters the World: Postmodern Space, Postcolonial Times and the Trials of Cultural Translation." In *The Location of Culture*, 303–337. London: Routledge, 2004.

——. *The Location of Culture*. London: Routledge, 2004.

——. "Remembering Fanon: Self, Psyche, and the Colonial Condition." Foreword to *Black Skin, White Masks* by Frantz Fanon. London: Pluto, 1986.

The Bible: Authorized King James Version. Edited by Robert Carroll and Stephen Prickett. Oxford: Oxford University Press, 2008.

Bird, Isabella. *The Golden Chersonese and the Way Thither*. London: John Murray, 1883.

Bobbitt, Philip. *Terror and Consent: The Wars for the Twenty-First Century*. New York: Knopf, 2008.

Boehmer, Elleke, and Stephen Morton, eds. *Terror and the Postcolonial*. London: Wiley Blackwell, 2010.

Bonner, Willard Hallam. "The Flying Dutchman of the Western World." *Journal of American Folklore* 59, no. 233 (July–September 1949): 282–288.

Borradori, Giovanna. *Philosophy in a Time of Terror: Dialogues with Jürgen Habermas and Jacques Derrida*. Chicago: University of Chicago Press, 2003.

Botting, Fred. *Gothic*. London: Routledge, 1996. Reprint, 2008.

Bourdelais, Patrice, and André Dodin. *Visages du choléra*. Paris: Belin, 1987.

Bourdieu, Pierre. *Sociologie de l'Algérie*. Paris: Presses Universitaires de France, 1963.

Bourg, Julian. "On Terrorism as Human Sacrifice." Review of *The Terrorist in Search of Humanity: Militant Islam and Global Politics* by Faisal Devji and *Sacred Violence: Torture, Terror, and Sovereignty* by Paul W. Kahn. *Humanity* 1, no. 1 (Fall, 2010): 137–154.

Brantlinger, Patrick. "Kipling's 'The White Man's Burden' and Its Afterlives." *English Literature in Transition, 1880–1920* 50, no. 2 (2007): 172–191.

———. *Rule of Darkness: British Literature and Imperialism, 1830–1914*. Ithaca: Cornell University Press, 1988.

———. "Terrible Turks: Victorian Xenophobia and the Ottoman Empire." In *Fear, Loathing, and Victorian Xenophobia*, edited by Marlene Tromp, Maria K. Bachman, and Heidi Kaufman, 208–230. Columbus: Ohio State University Press, 2013.

Bree, Germaine. *Camus*. New Brunswick: Rutgers University Press, 1959.

Brennan, Timothy. *Salman Rushdie and the Third World: Myths of Nation*. New York: St. Martin Press, 1989.

Briefel, Aviva, and Sam. J. Miller. *Horror After 9/11: World of Fear, Cinema of Terror*. Austin: University of Texas Press, 2011.

Brombert, Victor. "Albert Camus, the Endless Defeat." *Raritan* 31, no. 1 (Summer 2011): 24–39.

Brooks, Peter. "From Albert Camus to Roland Barthes." *New York Times*, September 12, 1982.

Brown, Marcia. "Unsanitized: COVID-19 in Our Jails, Prisons, and ICE Detention Centers." *American Prospect* (April 11, 2020). https://prospect.org/coronavirus/unsanitized-covid-19-jails-prisons-ice-detention/.

Brown, Marshall. *The Gothic Text*. Stanford: Stanford University Press, 2005.

Browne, Sir Thomas. *The Major Works*. Edited by C. A. Patrides. New York: Penguin Books, 1977.

Bryden, James. *Cholera Epidemics of Recent Years Viewed in Relation to Former Epidemics: A Record of Cholera in the Bengal Presidency from 1817 to 1872*. Calcutta: Office of the Superintendent of Government Printing, 1874.

———. *A Report on the Cholera of 1866–1868 and Its Relations to the Cholera of Previous Epidemics*. Calcutta: Office of Superintendent of Government Printing, 1869.

Buckley, Christopher. "Megabashing Japan." *New York Times*, October 2, 1994, https://www.nytimes.com/1994/10/02/books/crime-mystery-megabashing-japan.html.

Buck-Morss, Susan. "Aesthetics and Anaesthetics: Walter Benjamin's Artwork Essay Reconsidered." *October* 62 (Autumn 1992): 3–41.

———. *Thinking Past Terror: Islamism and Critical Theory on the Left*. London: Verso, 2003.

Burnet, Sir MacFarlane, and David O. White. *Natural History of Infectious Disease*. 4th ed. Cambridge: Cambridge University Press, 1972.

Burton, Antoinette. *Burdens of History: British Feminists, Indian Women, and Imperial Culture 1865–1915*. Chapel Hill: University of North Carolina Press, 1994.

Burton, Antoinette, ed. *The First Anglo-Afghan Wars: A Reader*. Durham: Duke University Press, 2014.

Burton, Sir Richard. *King Vikram and the Vampire: Classic Hindu Tales of Adventure, Magic, and Romance*. Rochester: Park Street Press, 1893.

Butler, Judith. *Precarious Life: The Powers of Mourning and Violence*. London & New York: Verso, 2004.

Camus, Albert. *Chroniques algériennes 1939–1958*. Paris: Gallimard, 1958.

———. *Algerian Chronicles*. Translated by Arthur Goldhammer. Edited by Alice Kaplan. Cambridge: Harvard University Press, 2013.

———. *Camus à Combat: Éditoriaux et articles d'Albert Camus 1944–1947*. Edited by Jacqueline Lévi-Valensi. Paris: Gallimard, 2002.

———. *Camus at Combat: Writing 1944–1947*. Translated by Arthur Goldhammer. Edited by Jacqueline Lévi-Valensi. Princeton: Princeton University Press, 2006.

———. *Carnets: Mai 1935–Février 1942*. Vol. 1. Paris: Gallimard, 1962.

———. *Carnets: Janvier 1942–Mars 1951*. Vol. 2. Paris: Gallimard, 1964.

———. *Essais*. Paris: Gallimard, 1965.

———. *Exile and the Kingdom*. Translated by Carol Cosman. New York: Vintage, 2006.

———. *The First Man*. Translated by David Hapgood. New York: Penguin, 1996.

———. *L'exil et le royaume*. Paris: Gallimard, 1957.

———. "Lettre d'Albert Camus à Roland Barthes sur *La Peste*." In Roland Barthes, *Oeuvres complètes: Tome I 1942–1961*. Paris: Éditions du Seuil, 2002.

———. *Lyrical and Critical Essays*. Translated by Ellen Conroy Kennedy. Edited by Philip Thody. New York: Alfred A. Knopf, 1967.

———. *Notebooks 1942–1951*. Translated by Justin O'Brien. New York: Knopf, 1966.

———. *Notebooks 1951–1959*. Translated by Ryan Bloom. Chicago: Ivan R. Dee, 2008.

———. *La Peste*. Paris: Gallimard, 1947.

———. *The Plague*. Translated by Stuart Gilbert. New York: Vintage, 1991.

———. *The Plague*. Translated by Robin Buss. London: Penguin Books, 2001.

———. *Le Premier homme*. Paris: Éditions Gallimard, 1994.

Camus, Albert, and Jean Grenier. *Correspondance 1932–1960*. Introduction and notes by Marguerite Dobrenn. Paris: Gallimard, 1981.

Canguilhem, Georges. *Ideology and Rationality in the History of the Life Sciences*. Translated by Arthur Goldhammer. Cambridge: MIT Press, 1988.

Carroll, David. *Albert Camus the Algerian: Colonialism, Terrorism, Justice*. New York: Columbia University Press, 2007.

Casanova, Pascale. *The World Republic of Letters*. Translated by M. B. DeBevoise. Cambridge: Harvard University Press, 2004.

Case, Alison. "Tasting the Original Apple: Gender and the Struggle for Narrative Authority in *Dracula*." *Narrative* 1, no. 3 (October 1993): 223–243.

Cavarero, Adriana. *Horrorism: Naming Contemporary Violence*. Translated by William McCuaig. New York: Columbia University Press, 2009.

Central Intelligence Agency, Office of the Inspector General. "Report on CIA Accountability With Respect to the 9/11 Attacks." Executive Summary, June 1, 2005. https://www.cia.gov/library/readingroom/document/0001467964.

Césaire, Aimé. *Lyric and Dramatic Poetry 1946–1982*. Translated by Clayton Eshleman and Annette Smith. Charlottesville: University Press of Virginia, 1990.

———. *Et les chiens se taisaient*. Paris: Gallimard, 1961.

Chan, Margaret. "Welcome to the World Health Organization." In *Working for Health: An Introduction to the World Health Organization*. Geneva: WHO Press, 2007. http://www.who.int/about/brochure_en.pdf.

Chakravarty, Gautam. *The Indian Mutiny and the British Imagination*. Cambridge: Cambridge University Press, 2005.

Charbonneau, Johanne, and André Smith, eds. *Giving Blood: The Institutional Making of Altruism*. London: Routledge, 2016.

Cheah, Pheng. "Nondialectical Materialism." *diacritics* 38, no. 1–2 (Spring/Summer 2008): 143–157.

———. *Spectral Nationality: Passages of Freedom from Kant to Postcolonial Literatures of Liberation*. New York: Columbia University Press, 2003.

Chin, Warren. "Colonial Wars, Post-colonial States: A Debate on the War on Terror." *ReOrient* 1, no. 1 (Autumn 2015): 93–107.

Clancy, Tom. *Debt of Honor*. New York: G. P. Putnam's Sons, 1994.

Clarkson, L. A., and E. Margaret Crawford. *Feast and Famine: A History of Food and Nutrition in Ireland 1500–1920*. Oxford: Oxford University Press, 2001.

Clough, Patricia, and Jasbir Puar, eds. Special issue, *Viral: Women's Studies Quarterly* 40, no. 1–2 (Spring/Summer 2012).

Cohen, Jeffrey Jerome, ed. *Monster Theory: Reading Culture*. Minneapolis: University of Minnesota Press, 1996.

Cohn, Bernard S. *Colonialism and Its Forms of Knowledge: The British in India*. Princeton: Princeton University Press, 1996.

Coleridge, Samuel Taylor. "Cholera Cured Beforehand." In *The Complete Poems*, 413. New York: Penguin Books, 2004.

Cooke, Jennifer. "Transforming Narrative, Witnessing, and History." In *The Tapestry of Health, Illness and Disease*. Edited by Vera Kalitzkus and Peter Twohig. Amsterdam and New York: Rodopi, 2009.

Coundouriotis, Eleni. "*Dracula* and the Idea of Europe." *Connotations* 9, no. 2 (1999/2000): 143–159.

Cox, Erin. "Salt Lake City Mosque Vandalized; Others Remain Closed during Ramadan." Fox 13 Salt Lake City, April 24, 2020. https://www.fox13now.com/news/local-news/salt-lake-city-mosque-vandalized-others-remain-closed-during-ramadan.

Crosby, Alfred W. *Ecological Imperialism: The Biological Expansion of Europe*. 2nd ed. New York: Cambridge University Press, 2004.

Crosse, A. F. *Round About the Carpathians*. London: Blackwoods, 1878.

Cuomo, Andrew. Televised Address (April 9, 2020). https://www.governor.ny.gov/

news/video-audio-photos-rush-transcript-amid-ongoing-covid-19-pandemic
-governor-cuomo-announces-five.

Dal Lago, Alessandro, and Salvatore Palidda, eds. *Conflict, Security and the Re-shaping of Society*. London: Routledge, 2010.

Daoud, Kamel. *Meursault, contre-enquête*. Paris: Actes Sud, 2014.

Daulatzai, Sohail. *Fifty Years of* The Battle of Algiers: *Past as Prologue*. Minneapolis: University of Minnesota Press, 2016.

Davis, Colin. "Camus's *La Peste*: Sanitation, Rats, and Messy Ethics." *Modern Language Review* 102, no. 4 (October, 2007): 1008–1020.

de Bellaigue, Christopher. "Turkey's Hidden Past." *New York Review of Books*, March 8, 2001.

de Kruif, Paul. *Microbe Hunters: The Classic Book on the Major Discoveries of the Microscopic World*. New York: Harcourt, 1926. Reprint, 1996.

"Deaths as Indian Troops Open Fire on Kashmir protesters." *Al Jazeera*, July 10, 2016, https://www.aljazeera.com/news/2016/07/deaths-indian-troops-open -fire-kashmir-protesters-160709125142182.html.

Decker, Jeffrey Louis. "Terrorism (Un)Veiled: Frantz Fanon and the Women of Algiers." *Cultural Critique* 17 (Winter 1990–1991): 177–195.

Defoe, Daniel. *The History of the Devil*. Boston: Dow and Jackson, 1845.

———. *A Journal of the Plague Year*. Oxford: Oxford University Press, 2010.

———. *Serious Reflections During the Life and Surprising Adventures of Robinson Crusoe*. Edited by W. R. Owens and P. N. Furbank. London: Pickering & Chatto, 2008.

Delaporte, François. *Disease and Civilization: The Cholera in Paris, 1832*. Translated by Arthur Goldhammer. Cambridge: MIT Press, 1986.

———. *Figures of Medicine: Blood, Face Transplants, Parasties*. Translated by Nils F. Schott. New York: Fordham University Press, 2013.

———. *Le savoir de la maladie: Essai sur le choléra de 1832 à Paris*. Paris: Presses Universitaires de France, 1990.

Deleuze, Gilles. "Postscript on the Societies of Control." *October* 59 (Winter 1992): 3–7.

Deleuze, Gilles, and Félix Guattari. *Anti-Oedipus: Capitalism and Schizophrenia*. London: Continuum, 2004.

DeLillo, Don. *Falling Man*. New York: Scribner, 2007.

DeMott, Benjamin. "Whitewash as Public Service." *Harper's Magazine*, October 2004.

Derrida, Jacques. *Acts of Religion*. Edited by Gil Anidjar. New York: Routledge, 2002.

———. *The Gift of Death*. Translated by David Wills. Chicago: University of Chicago Press, 1995.

———. "Of a Newly Arisen Apocalyptic Tone in Philosophy." Translated by John Leavey Jr. In *Raising the Tone of Philosophy*, edited by Peter Fenves. Baltimore: Johns Hopkins University Press, 1993.

———. *Of Grammatology*. Translated by Gayatri Chakravorty Spivak. Baltimore: Johns Hopkins University Press, 1976.

———. *On Cosmopolitanism and Forgiveness*. Translated by Mark Dooley and Michael Hughes. London: Routledge, 2001.

———. *Rogues. Two Essays on Reason*. Translated by Pascale-Anne Brault and Michael Naas. Stanford: Stanford University Press, 2005.

Desrosières, Alain. *The Politics of Large Numbers: A History of Statistical Reasoning*. Translated by Camille Naish. Cambridge: Harvard University Press, 1998.

Devji, Faisal. *Landscapes of the Jihad: Militancy, Morality, Modernity*. Ithaca: Cornell University Press, 2005.

———. *Muslim Zion: Pakistan as a Political Idea*. Cambridge: Harvard University Press, 2013.

———. *The Terrorist in Search of Humanity: Militant Islam and Global Politics*. New York: Columbia University Press, 2008.

Dillon, Michael, and Andrew Neal, eds. *Foucault on Politics, Security, and War*. London: Palgrave Macmillan, 2008.

Doyle, Arthur Conan. *Sherlock Holmes: The Complete Novels and Stories*, vol. 2. New York: Bantam, 2003.

"Dr. Shakil Afridi Moved from Prison 'to Safer Location.'" *Dawn*, April 27, 2018. https://www.dawn.com/news/1404218.

Durkheim, Emile. *Selected Writings*. Translated and edited by Anthony Giddens. Cambridge: Cambridge University Press, 1972. Reprint, 2006.

Eaglestone, Robert. " 'The Age of Reason Is Over . . . an Age of Fury Was Dawning': Contemporary Anglo-American Fiction and Terror." *Wasafiri* 22, no. 2 (July, 2007): 19–22.

Eagleton, Terry. *The Function of Criticism: From* The Spectator *to Post-Structuralism*. London: Verso, 1984. Reprint 2000.

Eburne, Jonathan P. *Surrealism and the Art of Crime*. Ithaca: Cornell University Press, 2008.

Eighteen-Bisang, Robert, and Elizabeth Miller, eds. *Bram Stoker's Notes for Dracula: A Facsimile Edition*. Jefferson: McFarland & Co., 2008.

Elie, Paul. "(Against) Virus as Metaphor." *New Yorker* (March 19, 2020). https://www.newyorker.com/news/daily-comment/against-the-coronavirus-as-metaphor.

Enzensberger, Hans Magnus. "The Resurgence of Human Sacrifice." *Society* (March–April 2002): 75–77.

Epidemiological Society of London. *Transactions of the Epidemiological Society of London v. 1 1859–1862*. London: Epidemiological Society, 1859–1907.

Esposito, Roberto. *Bíos: Biopolitics and Philosophy*. Translated by Timothy Campbell. Minneapolis: University of Minnesota Press, 2008.

———. *Immunitas: The Protection and Negation of Life*. Translated by Zakiya Hanafi. Cambridge: Polity, 2011.

Esty, Jed. *Unseasonable Youth: Modernism, Colonialism, and the Fiction of Development*. London: Oxford University Press, 2011.

Evans, Brad. *Liberal Terror*. Cambridge: Polity, 2013.

Evans, Richard J. "Epidemics and Revolutions: Cholera in Nineteenth-Century Europe." *Past & Present* 120 (August 1988): 123–146.

"'Everyone Lives in Fear': Patterns of Impunity in Jammu and Kashmir." *Human Rights Watch* 18, no. 11 (September 2006): 29–31.

Ewald, Paul W. *Evolution of Infectious Disease*. Oxford: Oxford University Press, 1994.

———. "The Evolution of Virulence." *Scientific American* (April 1993): 86–93.

———. *Plague Time: The New Germ Theory of Disease*. New York: Anchor Books, 2002.

Fanon, Frantz. "Algeria Unveiled." In *A Dying Colonialism*. Translated by Haakon Chevalier, 35–68. New York: Grove Press, 1965.

———. "L'Algérie et la crise française." In *Ecrits sur l'aliénation et la liberté*, edited by Jean Khalfa and Robert J. C. Young. Paris: La Découverte, 2015.

———. *L'An V de la révolution algérienne*. Paris: François Maspero, 1959.

———. *Black Skin, White Masks*. Translated by Richard Philcox. New York: Grove Press, 2008.

———. "Concerning a Plea." In *Toward the African Revolution*, 73–75. Translated by Haakon Chevalier. New York: Grove Press, 1967.

———. *Les Damnés de la terre*. Paris: Gallimard, 1991.

———. *A Dying Colonialism*. Translated by Haakon Chevalier. New York: Grove Press, 1965.

———. "Medicine and Colonialism." In *A Dying Colonialism*, translated by Haakon Chevalier, 121–146. New York: Grove Press, 1965.

———. "Médicine et colonialisme." In *L'An V de la révolution algérienne*. Paris: François Maspero, 1959.

———. *Peau noire, masques blancs*. Paris: Éditions de Seuil, 1952.

———. "This Is the Voice of Algeria." In *A Dying Colonialism*, translated by Haakon Chevalier, 65–97. New York: Grove Press, 1965.

———. *The Wretched of the Earth*. Translated by Constance Farrington. New York: Grove Press, 1963.

———. *The Wretched of the Earth*. Translated by Richard Philcox. New York: Grove Press, 2004.

Faraz, Ahmad. "Eye Bank." In *Nabeena Sheher Mein Aieena*, 17–18. Montreal: AMO International, 1983.

Farmer, Paul. *Pathologies of Power: Health, Human Rights, and the New War on the Poor*. Berkeley: University of California Press, 2005.

Farr, William. "Influence of Elevation on Fatality of Cholera." *Journal of the Royal Statistical Society* 15 (1852): 173–174.

———. *Vital Statistics: A Memorial Volume of Selections From the Reports and Writings of William Farr*. Edited by Noel A. Humphreys. London: Sanitary Institute, 1885.

Feinstein, Dianne. "Preface." Senate Select Committee on Intelligence, *The Senate Intelligence Committee Report on Torture*. New York: Melville House, 2014.

Felman, Shoshana. *Reading Narrative: Form, Ethics, Ideology*. Columbus: University of Ohio Press, 1989.

Fenves, Peter, ed. *Raising the Tone of Philosophy: Late Essays by Immanuel Kant, Transformative Critique by Jacques Derrida*. Baltimore: Johns Hopkins University Press, 1993.

Ferguson, Niall. "War Plans." Review of *Terror and Consent* by Philip Bobbitt. *New York Times*, April 13, 2008, http://www.nytimes.com/2008/04/13/books/review/Ferguson-t.html?pagewanted=all&_r=0.

Flanagan, Richard. *The Unknown Terrorist*. New York: Grove Press, 2006.

Flood, Alison. "Houellebecq's *Soumission* Becomes Instant Bestseller in Wake of Paris Attacks." *Guardian*, January 16, 2015, https://www.theguardian.com/books/2015/jan/16/michel-houellebecq-soumission-bestseller-charlie-hebdo.

Foley, John. "A Postcolonial Fiction: Conor Cruise O'Brien's Camus." *Irish Review* 36/37 (2007): 1–13.

Forster, E. M. *A Passage to India*. New York: Harcourt, 1984.

Foucault, Michel. *The Birth of Biopolitics: Lectures at the Collège de France 1978–1979*. Translated by Graham Burchell. New York: Picador, 2008.

———. *The Birth of the Clinic: An Archaeology of Medical Perception*. Translated by Alan Sheridan. New York: Vintage, 1994.

———. *The History of Sexuality Volume I: An Introduction*. Translated by Robert Hurley. New York: Vintage, 1990.

———. *Naissance de la clinique*. Paris: Presses Universitaires de France, 1997.

———. *Security, Territory, Population: Lectures at the Collège de France 1977–1978*. Translated by Graham Burchell. Edited by Michel Senellart. New York: Picador, 2007.

———. *Society Must Be Defended: Lectures at the Collège de France 1975–1976*. Translated by David Macey. Edited by Mauro Bertani and Alessandro Fontana. New York: Picador, 2003.

Fox, James R. *Dictionary of International and Comparative Law*. 3rd ed. New York: Oceana Publications, 2003.

Freud, Sigmund. *Civilization and Its Discontents*. Translated and edited by James Strachey. New York: W. W. Norton & Co., 1961. Reprint 1989.

Frerichs, R. R., P. S. Keim, R. Barrais, and R. Piarroux, "Nepalese Origin of Cholera Epidemic in Haiti." *Clinical Microbiology and Infection* 18, no. 6 (June 2012): E158–E163.

Fuss, Diana. "Interior Colonies: Frantz Fanon and the Politics of Identification." *diacritics* 24, no. 2 (1994): 20–42.

Gallagher, Catherine. *The Body Economic: Life, Death, and Sensation in Political Economy and the Victorian Novel*. Princeton: Princeton University Press, 2006.

———. "The Potato in the Materialist Imagination." In Catherine Gallagher and Stephen Greenblatt, *Practicing New Historicism*, 110–135. Chicago: University of Chicago Press, 2000.

Gallagher, Catherine, and Stephen Greenblatt. *Practicing New Historicism*. Chicago: University of Chicago Press, 2000.

Galvan, Jill. "Occult Networks and the Legacy of the Indian Rebellion in Bram Stoker's *Dracula*." *History of Religions* 54, no. 4 (May 2015): 434–458.

Gandhi, Mohandas K. *Autobiography: The Story of My Experiments With Truth*. Translated by Mahadev Desai. New York: Dover Publications, 1983.

Ganguly, Sumit. *The Crisis in Kashmir: Portents of War, Hopes of Peace*. Cambridge: Woodrow Wilson Center Press and Cambridge University Press, 1997.

Garcia, Sandra E. "Man Charged with Hate Crime in Suspected Arson at Islamic Center." *New York Times*, April 28, 2020. https://www.nytimes.com/2020/04/28/us/nicholas-proffitt-missouri-islamic-center-arson.html.

Garrett, Laurie. *The Coming Plague: Newly Emerging Diseases in a World Out of Balance*. New York: Penguin, 1995.

Gelder, Ken. "Global/Postcolonial Horror: Introduction." *Postcolonial Studies* 3, no. 1 (2000): 35–38.

"General Sherman in Europe and the East." *Harper's New Monthly Magazine*, September 1873, 481–495.

Gilbert, Pamela K. *Cholera and Nation: Doctoring the Social Body in Victorian England*. Albany: State University of New York Press, 2008.

Gilbert, Sandra M. "Horror's Twin: Mary Shelley's Monstrous Eve" *Feminist Studies* 4, no. 2 (June 1978): 48–73.

Gilly, Adolfo. "Introduction." Translated by Nell Salm. In *A Dying Colonialism*, by Frantz Fanon. Translated by Haakon Chevalier. New York: Grove Press, 1967.

Girard, René. "Camus's Stranger Retired." *PMLA* 79, no. 5 (December 1964): 519–533.

Glover, David. *Vampires, Mummies, and Liberals: Bram Stoker and the Politics of Popular Fiction*. Durham: Duke University Press, 1996.

Goldman, Adam, and Matt Apuzzo. "Phone Call by Kuwaiti Courier Led to bin Laden." Associated Press, May 3, 2011. https://www.yahoo.com/news/phone-call-kuwaiti-courier-led-bin-laden-072643413.html.

Goldberg, Elizabeth Swanson. *Beyond Terror: Gender, Narrative, Human Rights*. New Brunswick: Rutgers University Press, 2007.

Gopnik, Adam. "Facing History: Why We Love Camus." *New Yorker*, April 9, 2012, 70–76.

Gray, Margaret. "Layers of Meaning in *La Peste*." In *The Cambridge Companion to Camus*, edited by Edward J. Hughes, 165–177. Cambridge: Cambridge University Press, 2007.

Gregg, Hilda. "The Indian Mutiny in Fiction." *Blackwood's Magazine* 161 (February 1897): 218–231.

Grewal, Inderpal. *Saving the Security State: Exceptional Citizens in Twenty-First Century America*. Durham: Duke University Press, 2017.

Grewal, Zareena. *Islam Is a Foreign Country: American Muslims and the Global Crisis of Authority*. New York: New York University Press, 2014.

Guérin, Daniel. *The Brown Plague: Travels in Late Weimar and Early Nazi Germany.* Durham: Duke University Press, 1994.

Guha, Ranajit. *History at the Limit of World History.* New York: Columbia University Press, 2002.

———. "The Prose of Counter-insurgency." In *Selected Subaltern Studies*, edited by Ranajit Guha and Gayatri Chakravorty Spivak, 45–84. New York: Oxford University Press, 1988.

Gul, Ayaz. "Pakistan: Trump Wrong on Jailed Doctor Who Helped Find bin Laden." Voice of America, May 2, 2016. http://www.voanews.com/east-asia/pakistan-trump-wrong-jailed-doctor-who-helped-find-bin-laden.

Hägglund, Martin. *Radical Atheism: Derrida and the Time of Life.* Stanford: Stanford University Press, 2008.

Halberstam, J. "Technologies of Monstrosity: Bram Stoker's 'Dracula.'" *Victorian Studies* 36, no. 3 (Spring 1993): 333–352.

Hallward, Peter. *Absolutely Postcolonial: Writing Between the Singular and the Specific.* Manchester: Manchester University Press, 2001.

Hamid, Mohsin. *Exit West.* New York: Riverhead Books, 2017.

———. *The Reluctant Fundamentalist.* New York: Harcourt, 2007.

Hamilton, John. *Security: Politics, Humanity, and the Philology of Care.* Princeton: Princeton University Press, 2013.

Hamlin, Christopher. *Cholera: The Biography.* Oxford: Oxford University Press, 2009.

Haneke, Michael, director. *Caché.* Paris: Canal+, 2005. Film.

Harbi, Mohammed. *Les archives de la révolution algérienne.* Paris: Jeune Afrique, 1981.

———. "Postface." In *Les damnés de la terre*, by Frantz Fanon. Paris: La Découverte/Poche, 2002.

Harley, George. *The Life of a London Physician.* London: Scientific Press, 1899.

Harpham, Geoffrey Galt. "Symbolic Terror." *Critical Inquiry* 28, no. 2 (Winter 2002): 573–579.

Harrison, Nicholas. "'Based on Actual Events . . .' *The Battle of Algiers* Forty Years On." *Interventions* 9, no. 3 (2007): 335–339.

———. "Yesterday's Mujahiddin: Gillo Pontecorvo's *The Battle of Algiers*." In *Postcolonial Film: History, Empire, Resistance*, edited by Rebecca Weaver-Hightower and Peter Hulme, 23–46. London: Routledge, 2014.

Hasan, Mehdi. "The Coronavirus Is Empowering Islamophobes—But Exposing the Idiocy of Islamophobia." *The Intercept*, April 14, 2020. https://theintercept.com/2020/04/14/coronavirus-muslims-islamophobia/.

Hattem, Julian. "Feinstein: Take the 'Anarchist Cookbook' and al Qaeda Magazine off the Internet." *The Hill*, April 2, 2015. http://thehill.com/policy/technology/237749-feinstein-take-anarchist-cookbook-al-qaeda-magazine-off-internet.

Heine, Heinrich. *De la France.* Paris: Gallimard, 1994.

Heller, Zoë. "The Salman Rushdie Case." Review of *Joseph Anton* by Salman Rushdie. *New York Review of Books*, December 20, 2012. http://www.nybooks.com/articles/archives/2012/dec/20/salman-rushdie-case/.

Hempel, Sandra. *The Strange Case of the Broad Street Pump: John Snow and the Mystery of Cholera*. Berkeley: University of California Press, 2007.

Herbert, Christopher. *War of No Pity: The Indian Mutiny and Victorian Trauma*. Princeton: Princeton University Press, 2008.

Hersh, Seymour M. "The Killing of Osama bin Laden." *London Review of Books* 37, no. 10 (May 21, 2015): 3–12.

Hill, J. N. C. "Remembering the War of Liberation: Legitimacy and Conflict in Contemporary Algeria." *Small Wars and Insurgencies* 23, no. 1 (2012): 4–31.

Hillis Miller, J. "Derrida's Politics of Autoimmunity." *Discourse* 30, no. 1–2 (Winter/Spring 2008) 208–225.

Hindle, Maurice. "Introduction." In *Bram Stoker, Dracula*, edited by Maurice Hindle. New York: Penguin, 2003.

Hitchens, Christopher. *God Is Not Great: How Religion Poisons Everything*. London: Atlantic Books, 2008.

Ho, Janice. "*The Satanic Verses* and the Politics of Extremity." *Novel: A Forum on Fiction* 44, no. 2 (2011): 208–228.

Hogan, Patrick Colm. *Imagining Kashmir: Emplotment and Colonialism*. Lincoln: University of Nebraska Press, 2016.

Holloway, David. "The War on Terror Espionage Thriller, and the Imperialism of Human Rights." *Comparative Literature Studies* 46, no. 1 (2009): 20–44.

Holsinger, Bruce. "Empire, Apocalypse, and the 9/11 Premodern." *Critical Inquiry* 34 (Spring 2008): 468–490.

Hong, Cathy Park. "The Slur I Never Expected to Hear in 2020." *New York Times* (April 12, 2020). https://www.nytimes.com/2020/04/12/magazine/asian-american-discrimination-coronavirus.html.

Honig, Bonnie. *Democracy and the Foreigner*. Princeton: Princeton University Press, 2001.

Horne, Alistair. *A Savage War of Peace: Algeria 1956–1962*. London: MacMillan, 1977.

———. *A Savage War of Peace: Algeria 1954–1962*. New York: New York Review of Books, 2006.

Houellebecq, Michel. *Soumission*. Paris: Flammarion, 2015.

———. "Michel Houellebecq: 'Suis-je Islamophobe? Probablement oui.'" *Le Figaro*, September 7, 2015. http://www.lefigaro.fr/livres/2015/09/07/03005-20150907ARTFIG00019-michel-houellebecq-suis-je-islamophobe-probablement-oui.php.

"How the CIA's Fake Vaccination Campaign Endangers Us All." *Scientific American*, May 1, 2013. https://www.scientificamerican.com/article/how-cia-fake-vaccination-campaign-endangers-us-all/.

Howard-Jones, Norman. "Robert Koch and the Cholera Vibrio: A Centenary." *British Medical Journal* 288 (February 4, 1984): 379–381.

Howell, Sally, and Andrew Shryock. "Cracking Down on Diaspora: Arab Detroit and America's 'War on Terror.'" *Anthropological Quarterly* 76, no. 3 (Summer 2003): 443–462.

Huang, Pien. "Trump and WHO: How Much Does the U.S. Give? What's the Impact of a Halt in Funding?" National Public Radio, April 15, 2020. https://www.npr.org/sections/goatsandsoda/2020/04/15/834666123/trump-and-who-how-much-does-the-u-s-give-whats-the-impact-of-a-halt-in-funding.

Huber, Valeska. "The Unification of the Globe By Disease? The International Sanitary Conferences on Cholera 1851–1894." *Historical Journal* 49, no. 2 (2006): 453–476.

Hughes, Edward J., ed. *The Cambridge Companion to Camus*. Cambridge: Cambridge University Press, 2007.

Hughes, William. "Fictional Vampires in the Nineteenth and Twentieth Centuries." In *Companion to the Gothic*, edited by David Punter, 197–210. Oxford: Blackwell, 2000.

Ignatius, David. "Think Strategy, Not Numbers." *Washington Post*, August 26, 2003. http://www.washingtonpost.com/wp-dyn/articles/A45136-2003Aug25.html.

"The International Health Organization of the League of Nations." *British Medical Journal* 1, no. 3302 (April 12, 1924): 672–675.

Inzamam, Qadri, and Mohammad Haziq. "In Kashmir, 'Non-lethal' Weapons Cause Lethal Damage." *Caravan*, July 12, 2016. http://www.caravanmagazine.in/vantage/kashmir-pellets-non-lethal-weapons-damage.

Iqbal, Javed, Abbas Khan, Ashraf Jehangir Qazi, and Lt. Gen. Nadeem Ahmed. Untitled, aka "Abbottabad Commission Report." *Al Jazeera*, July 8, 2013. http://www.aljazeera.com/indepth/spotlight/binladenfiles/2013/07/201378143927822246.html.

Irving, Sarah. *Leila Khaled: Icon of Palestinian Liberation*. London: Pluto Press, 2012.

Jacobson, Sid, and Ernie Colón. *The 9/11 Report: A Graphic Adaptation*. New York: Hill & Wang, 2006.

Jakobson, Roman. *Language in Literature*. Edited by Krystyna Pomorska and Stephen Rudy. Cambridge: Belknap Press of Harvard University Press, 1987.

Jalal, Ayesha. "Exploding Communalism: The Politics of Muslim Identity in South Asia." In *Nationalism, Democracy, and Development: State and Politics in India*, edited by Sugata Bose and Ayesha Jalal, 70–103. Delhi: Oxford University Press, 1997.

———. *Self and Sovereignty: Individual and Community in South Asian Islam Since 1850*. London: Routledge, 2000.

Jameson, Fredric. "Third World Literature in the Era of Multinational Capitalism." *Social Text* 15 (Autumn 1986): 65–88.

Jameson, James. *Report on the Epidemick Cholera Morbus As it Visited the Territories Subject to the Presidency of Bengal in the Years 1817, 1818, and 1819*. Calcutta: Government Gazette Press, 1820.

"Jammu and Kashmir Saw Three-fold Increase in Rioting in 2016: State Police Data." *Hindustan Times*, March 5, 2017. https://www.hindustantimes.com/

india-news/jammu-and-kashmir-saw-three-fold-increase-in-rioting-in-2016
-state-police-data/story-72PBpcZew841nnmpqobgxL.html.

Jeanson, Francis. "The Third Man in the Story: Ronald Aronson Discusses the
Sartre-Camus Conflict with Francis Jeanson." Translated by Basil Kingstone.
Sartre Studies International 8, no. 2 (2002): 20–67.

Johnson, Boris. "Global Britain Is Helping to Win the Struggle against Islamist
Terror." Speech Transcript. Foreign & Commonwealth Office, December 7,
2017. https:www.gov.uk/government/speeches/how-global-britain-is-helping
-to-win-the-struggle-against-islamist-terror.

Johnson, E. C. *On the Track of the Crescent: Erratic Notes from the Piraeus to Pesth.*
London: Hurst and Blackett Publishers, 1885.

Johnson, Jennifer. *The Battle for Algeria: Sovereignty, Health Care, and Humanitarianism.* Philadelphia: University of Pennsylvania Press, 2015.

Johnson, Steven. *The Ghost Map: The Story of London's Most Terrifying Epidemic—
and How It Changed Science, Cities, and the Modern World.* New York: Riverhead, 2006.

Jones, Ernest. *The Revolt of Hindostan.* Edited by Snehangshu Kanta Acharyya.
Calcutta: Eastern Trading Co., 1957.

Jørgensen, Jens Lohfert. "Bacillophobia: Man and Microbes in *Dracula*, *The War of
the Worlds*, and *The Nigger of the 'Narcissus.'*" *Critical Survey* 27, no. 2 (2015): 36–49.

Judt, Tony. "On 'The Plague.'" *New York Review of Books*, November 29, 2001.
http://www.nybooks.com/articles/archives/2001/nov/29/on-the-plague/.

Kant, Immanuel. "On a Newly Arisen Superior Tone in Philosophy." Translated
by Peter Fenves. In *Raising the Tone of Philosophy*, edited by Peter Fenves.
Baltimore: Johns Hopkins University Press, 1993.

Kaplan, Alice. "New Perspectives on Camus's Algerian Chronicles." In Albert
Camus, *Algerian Chronicles*, 1–18. Translated by Arthur Goldhammer. Edited
by Alice Kaplan. Cambridge: Harvard University Press, 2013.

———. "Reading Camus in Algeria Today." *The Best American Poetry*, July 5, 2012.
http://blog.bestamericanpoetry.com/the_best_american_poetry/2012/07/
reading-camus-in-algeria-today-alice-kaplan-blog2.html.

Kashuba, Irma. "A Method of Presenting Albert Camus's *The Plague*." In *Approaches to Teaching Camus's* The Plague, edited by Steven G. Kellman. New
York: Modern Language Association of America, 1985.

Kaufman, Michael T. "Film Studies: What Does the Pentagon See in 'Battle of
Algiers'?" *New York Times*, September 7, 2003. https://www.nytimes.com/2003/
09/07/weekinreview/the-world-film-studies-what-does-the-pentagon-see-in
-battle-of-algiers.html.

Kaul, Suvir. *Of Gardens and Graves: Kashmir, Poetry, Politics.* Durham: Duke University Press, 2017.

Kaye, John W. "Author's Preface." In *Kaye's and Malleson's History of the Indian
Mutiny of 1857–8.* London: Longman's, 1906.

———. "The Romance of Indian Warfare." *North British Review* 12 (November
1849–February 1850): 193–224.

Kaye, John W., and George Bruce Malleson. *Kaye's and Malleson's History of the Indian Mutiny of 1857-8*. London: Longman's, 1906.

Keenan, Thomas. "A Language That Needs No Translation, or: Can Things Get Any Worse?" In *Terror and the Roots of Poetics*, edited by Jeffrey Champlin, 92–109. New York: Atropos Press, 2013.

———. "'Where Are Human Rights . . . ?': Reading a Communiqué from Iraq." In *Nongovernmental Politics*, edited by Michel Feher, 57–71. New York: Zone Books, 2007.

Kellman, Steven G., ed. *Approaches to Teaching Camus's* The Plague. New York: Modern Language Association of America, 1985.

Keniston, Ann, and Jeanne Follansbee Quinn. *Literature After 9/11*. New York: Routledge, 2010.

Kennedy, James. *The History of the Contagious Cholera; with Facts Explanatory of its Origin and Laws, and of a Rational Method of Cure*. London: James Cochrane and Co., 1831.

Kennedy, John Fitzgerald. "Imperialism: The Enemy of Freedom." Speech, July 2, 1957. http://www.jfklink.com/speeches/jfk/congress/jfk020757_imperialism.html.

Khanna, Ranjana. *Algeria Cuts: Women and Representation 1830 to the Present*. Stanford: Stanford University Press, 2008.

Killeen, Jarlath. *Gothic Ireland: Horror and the Irish Anglican Imagination in the Long Eighteenth Century*. Dublin: Four Courts Press, 2005.

Kipling, Rudyard. *Address: Annual Dinner, Royal College of Surgeons* (London: MacMillan, 1923), 3.

———. *Kim*. Edited by Edward W. Said. New York: Penguin, 1989.

———. *The Science of Rebellion*. 1901. http://www.kiplingsociety.co.uk/rebellion.htm.

Kitson, Peter. "Oriental Gothic." In *Romantic Gothic: An Edinburgh Companion*, edited by Angela Wright and Dale Townshend, 167–184. Edinburgh: Edinburgh University Press, 2016.

Kittler, Friedrich. "Dracula's Legacy," translated by William Stephen Davis. In *Literature, Media, Information Systems: Essays*, edited by John Johnston, 50–84. Amsterdam: Overseas Publishers Association, 1997.

———. *Gramophone, Film, Typewriter*. Translated by Geoffrey Winthrop-Young. Stanford: Stanford University Press, 1999.

———. *Literature, Media, Information Systems*. Translated by John Johnston. Amsterdam: Overseas Publishers Association, 1997. Reprint, London: Routledge, 2012.

Klinger, Leslie. "Dracula After Stoker: Fictional Accounts of the Count." In Bram Stoker, *The New Annotated Dracula*, edited by Leslie Klinger, 530–536. New York: W. W. Norton & Company, 2008.

Koch, Robert. *Professor Koch on the Bacteriological Diagnosis of Cholera, Water Filtration and Cholera, and the Cholera in Germany in the Winter of 1892-93*. New York: William R. Jenkins, 1895.

Koch, Tom. *Cartographies of Disease: Maps, Mapping, and Medicine*. New York: ESRI Inc., 2005.

———. *Disease Maps: Epidemics on the Ground*. Chicago: University of Chicago Press, 2011.

Kuhn, Thomas S. *The Structure of Scientific Revolutions*. 3rd ed. Chicago: University of Chicago Press, 1962. Reprint 1996.

Kumar, Amitava. *A Foreigner Carrying in the Crook of His Arm a Tiny Bomb*. Durham: Duke University Press, 2010.

———. "Who Will Break the Sad News to Salman Rushdie?" Review of *Shalimar the Clown*, by Salman Rushdie. *Tehelka*, August 6, 2005. http://archive.tehelka .com/story_main13.asp?filename=hub080605who_will.asp.

Lafferty, Kevin D., Katherine F. Smith, and Elizabeth M. P. Madin. "The Infectiousness of Terrorist Ideology: Insights from Ecology and Epidemiology." In *Natural Security: A Darwinian Approach to a Dangerous World*, edited by Raphael D. Sagarin and Terence Taylor, 186–206. Berkeley: University of California Press, 2008.

Lakoff, George, and Mark Johnson. *Metaphors We Live By*. Chicago: University of Chicago Press, 2003.

Lakoff, Andrew, and Stephen Collier, eds. *Biosecurity Interventions: Global Health and Security in Question*. New York: Columbia University Press, 2008.

Lalami, Laila. "Among the Blasphemers: On Salman Rushdie." *Nation*, January 16, 2013. https://www.thenation.com/article/among-blasphemers-salman -rushdie/.

Lallemand-Stempak, Jean-Paul. "'What Flows Between Us': Blood Donation and Transfusion in the United States (Nineteenth to Twentieth Centuries)," in Johanne Charbonneau and André Smith, eds., *Giving Blood: The Institutional Making of Altruism*, 21–35. London: Routledge, 2016.

Lamb, Alastair. *The Kashmir Problem: A Historical Survey*. New York: Frederick A. Praeger, 1966.

"Lashkar-e-Islam." Mapping Militant Organizations, Stanford University, last modified August 28, 2012. http://web.stanford.edu/group/mappingmilitants/ cgi-bin/groups/view/445.

Last, John M., ed. *A Dictionary of Epidemiology*. 4th ed. Oxford: Oxford University Press, 2008.

Latour, Bruno. *The Pasteurization of France*. Translated by Alan Sheridan and John Law. Cambridge: Harvard University Press, 1998. Reprint, 1993.

———. *We Have Never Been Modern*. Translated by Catherine Porter. Cambridge: Harvard University Press, 1993.

Laville, Sandra, and Robert Booth. "Khalid Masood: From Kent Schoolboy to Westminster Attacker." *Guardian*, March 25, 2017. https://www.theguardian .com/uk-news/2017/mar/25/khalid-masood-profile-from-popular-teenager-to -isis-inpired-terrorist.

Lavin, Talia. "Calling Healthcare Workers War 'Heroes' Sets Them Up to Be

Sacrificed." *Gentleman's Quarterly*, April 15, 2020. https://www.gq.com/story/essential-workers-martyrdom.

Law, Jules. "Being There: Gothic Violence and Virtuality in *Frankenstein, Dracula*, and *Strange Days*." *English Language History* 73 (2006): 975–996.

———. *The Social Life of Fluids: Blood, Milk, and Water in the Victorian Novel*. Ithaca: Cornell University Press, 2010.

Lawrence, Bruce, ed. *Messages to the World: The Statements of Osama bin Laden*. London: Verso, 2005.

Lawrence, Keith. "The Growth of Islamic Studies," and interview with Omid Safi. *Duke Today*, August 11, 2016. https://today.duke.edu/2016/08/growth-islamic -studies.

Laxton, Edward. *The Famine Ships: The Irish Exodus to America*. New York: Henry Holt, 1998.

Ledbetter, Rosanna. "Thirty Years of Family Planning in India." *Asian Survey* 24, no. 7 (1984): 736–758.

Lederer, Susan E. *Flesh and Blood: Organ Transplantation and Blood Transfusion in Twentieth-Century America*. Oxford: Oxford University Press, 2008.

Lefebvre, Jeffrey A. "Kennedy's Algerian Dilemma: Containment, Alliance Politics, and the 'Rebel Dialogue.'" *Middle Eastern Studies* 35, no. 2 (April 1999): 61–82.

Lennon, John J. "I'm Facing the Coronavirus Behind Bars." *The Atlantic* (April 14, 2020). https://www.theatlantic.com/ideas/archive/2020/04/covid-breached -wall-and-killed-man-yesterday/609952/.

Leonard, John. Review of Herbert Lottman, *Albert Camus: A Biography. New York Times*, March 19, 1979.

Lerner, Davide. "It's Not Islam That Drives Young Europeans Toward Jihad, France's Top Terrorism Expert Explains." *Haaretz* (August 20, 2017). https:// www.haaretz.com/world-news/europe/it-s-not-islam-that-drives-young -europeans-to-jihad-terrorism-expert-says-1.5477000.

Levich, Jacob. "The Gates Foundation, Ebola, and Global Health Imperialism." *American Journal of Economics and Sociology* 74, no. 4 (September 2015): 704–742.

Levinas, Emmanuel. "As If Consenting to Horror." *Critical Inquiry* 15 (Winter 1989): 485–488.

Levy, Barry S., and Victor W. Sidel, eds. *Terrorism and Public Health: A Balanced Approach to Strengthening Systems and Protecting People*. 2nd ed. New York: Oxford University Press, 2012.

Lewes, George Henry. *The Physiology of Common Life*. Vol. 1. Edinburgh: William Blackwood, 1859.

Lezra, Jacques. *Wild Materialism: The Ethic of Terror and the Modern Republic*. New York: Fordham University Press, 2010.

Lilla, Mark. "The Riddle of Walter Benjamin." Review of *The Correspondence of Walter Benjamin*, edited and annotated by Gershom Scholem and Theodor Adorno and translated by Manfred Jacobson and Evelyn Jacobson. *New York*

Review of Books, May 25, 1995. https://www.nybooks.com/articles/1995/05/25/the-riddle-of-walter-benjamin/.

Lilienfeld, David E., and Paul D. Stolley. *Foundations of Epidemiology*. 3rd ed. Oxford: Oxford University Press, 1994.

Longmate, Norman. *King Cholera: The Biography of a Disease*. London: Hamish Hamilton, 1966.

Lorey, Isabell. *State of Insecurity: Government of the Precarious*. London: Verso, 2015.

Lottman, Herbert R. *Albert Camus: A Biography*. Garden City: Doubleday & Co, 1979.

Löwy, Michael. *Fire Alarm: Reading Walter Benjamin's "On the Concept of History."* Translated by Chris Turner. London: Verso, 2016.

Ludlam, Harry. *A Biography of Bram Stoker Creator of Dracula*. New York: Foulsham, 1962.

Lund, Guiliana. "A Plague of Silence: Social Hygiene and the Purification of the Nation in Camus's *La Peste*." *Symposium* 65, no. 2 (2011): 134–157.

Lyotard, Jean-François. *The Postmodern Condition: A Report on Knowledge*. Translated by Geoff Bennington and Brian Massumi. Minneapolis: University of Minnesota Press, 1984.

MacDonald, John. *Travels in Various Parts of Europe, Asia, and Africa, During a Series of Thirty Years and Upward*. London: J. Forbes, 1790.

Macherey, Pierre. *A Theory of Literary Production*. Translated by Geoffrey Wall. London: Routledge, 2006.

Mackinder, Halford John. "The Geographical Pivot of History." *Geographical Journal* 23, no. 4 (April 1904): 421–437.

Macnamara, Nottidge C. *A History of Asiatic Cholera*. London: MacMillan and Co., 1876.

Madden, Lionel, ed. *Robert Southey: The Critical Heritage*. London: Routledge, 1972.

Mahajan, Karan. *The Association of Small Bombs*. New York: Viking, 2016.

"The Maldives Is Threatened by Jihadism and Covid-19." *The Economist*, March 21, 2020. https://www.economist.com/asia/2020/03/21/the-maldives-is-threatened-by-jihadism-and-covid-19.

Malik, Kenan. *From Fatwa to Jihad: The Rushdie Affair and Its Aftermath*. New York: Melville House Publishing, 2009.

Malleson, George Bruce. *The Indian Mutiny of 1857*, 7th ed. New York: Charles Scribner's Sons, 1898.

———. *The Mutiny of the Bengal Army: An Historical Narrative By One Who Has Served Under Sir Charles Napier*. London: Bosworth & Harrison, 1857.

———. *Report on the Cholera Epidemic of 1867 in Northern India*. Calcutta: Office of Superintendent of Government Printing, 1868.

Mamdani, Mahmood. *Good Muslim, Bad Muslim: America, the Cold War, and the Roots of Terror*. New York: Pantheon, 2004.

Marcum, J. A. "Defending the Priority of 'Remarkable Researches': The Discovery of Fibrin Ferment." *History and Philosophy of the Life Sciences* 20, no. 1 (January 1998): 51–76.

Marcus, Sharon, and Stephen Best. "Surface Reading: An Introduction." *Representations* 108, no. 1 (Fall 2009): 1–21.

Marrouchi, Mustapha. "Counternarratives, Recoveries, Refusals." In *Edward Said and the Work of the Critic: Speaking Truth to Power*, edited by Paul A. Bové, 187–228. Durham: Duke University Press, 2000.

Marx, Karl. "The East India Company—Its History and Results." In Karl Marx and Friedrich Engels, *The First Indian War of Independence 1857–1859*. Moscow: Progress Publishers, 1978.

Marx, Karl, and Friedrich Engels. *The First Indian War of Independence 1857–1859*. Moscow: Progress Publishers, 1978.

Matos, Timothy Carlo. "Choleric Fictions: Epidemiology, Medical Authority, and *An Enemy of the People*." *Modern Drama* 51, no. 3 (Fall 2008): 353–368.

May, Ernest. *American Imperialism; A Speculative Essay*. Chicago: Imprint Publications, 1991.

———. "When Government Writes History." *New Republic*. May 23, 2005. https://newrepublic.com/article/64332/when-government-writes-history.

Mazzetti, Mark. "U.S. Cites End to C.I.A. Ruses Using Vaccines." *New York Times*, May 20, 2014. http://www.nytimes.com/2014/05/20/us/us-cites-end-to-cia-ruses-using-vaccines.html?_r=0.

———. "Vaccination Ruse Used in Pursuit of bin Laden." *New York Times*, July 11, 2011. http://www.nytimes.com/2011/07/12/world/asia/12dna.html?_r=0.

Mbembe, Achille. "Necropolitics." Translated by Libby Meintjes. *Public Culture* 15, no. 1 (2003): 11–40.

McCarthy, Patrick. *Camus*. New York: Random House, 1982.

McCartin, Joseph A. "Class and the Challenge of COVID-19." *Dissent*, March 23, 2020. https://www.dissentmagazine.org/online_articles/class-and-the-challenge-of-covid-19.

McClintock, Anne. "'No Longer in a Future Heaven': Gender, Race, and Nationalism." In *Dangerous Liaisons: Gender, Nation, and Postcolonial Perspectives*, edited by Anne McClintock, Aamir Mufti, and Ella Shohat, 89–112. Minneapolis: University of Minnesota Press, 1997.

McCoy, Alfred W., and Francisco A. Scarano, eds. *Colonial Crucible: Empire in the Making of the Modern American State*. Madison: University of Wisconsin Press, 2009.

McCulloch, John Ramsay. *A Descriptive and Statistical Account of the British Empire, Exhibiting Its Extent, Physical Capacities, Population, Industry, and Civil and Religious Institutions*. 3rd ed. London: Longman, Brown, Green, and Longmans, 1847.

McGirk, Tim. "How the bin Laden Raid Put Vaccinators Under the Gun in Pakistan." *National Geographic*, February 25, 2015. http://news.nationalgeographic.com/2015/02/150225-polio-pakistan-vaccination-virus-health/.

McGreal, Chris. "US Cuts Pakistan's Aid in Protest at Jail for Doctor Who Helped

Find bin Laden." *Guardian*, May 24, 2012. http://www.guardian.co.uk/world/2012/may/24/us-pakistan-aid-doctor-bin-laden.

McKay, Hollie, and Mohsin Saleem Ullah. "'Hero' Doctor Shakil Afridi Who Helped Find bin Laden Launches Hunger Strike behind Bars after 'Losing Hope for Justice,' Lawyer Says." Fox News, March 4, 2020. https://www.foxnews.com/world/hero-doctor-shakil-afridi-hunger-strike-behind-bars.

McLean, Thomas. "Dracula's Blood of Many Brave Races," in *Fear, Loathing, and Victorian Xenophobia*, edited by Marlene Tromp, Maria K. Bachman, and Heidi Kaufman, 331–346. Columbus: Ohio State University Press, 2013.

McNeil, Donald G., Jr. "C.I.A. Vaccine Ruse May Have Harmed the War on Polio." *New York Times*, July 9, 2012. http://www.nytimes.com/2012/07/10/health/cia-vaccine-ruse-in-pakistan-may-have-harmed-polio-fight.html?pagewanted=all&_r=0.

———. "Turning the Tide Against Cholera." *New York Times*, February 6, 2017. https://www.nytimes.com/2017/02/06/health/cholera-vaccine-bangladesh.html.

Memmi, Albert. "Camus ou le colonisateur de bonne volonté." *La Nef* 12 (December 1957): 95–96.

———. *The Colonizer and the Colonized*. Translated by Howard Greenfeld. Boston: Beacon, 1991.

Metcalf, Barbara D., and Thomas R. Metcalf. *A Concise History of Modern India*. Cambridge: Cambridge University Press, 1999.

Mighall, Robert. *A Geography of Victorian Gothic Fiction*. Oxford: Oxford University Press, 1999.

Miller, Elizabeth. *Bram Stoker's Dracula: A Documentary Volume*, edited by Elizabeth Miller. Detroit: Thomson Gale, 2005.

Miller, J. Hillis. "Derrida's Politics of Autoimmunity." *Discourse* 30, no. 1–2 (Winter/Spring, 2008): 208–225.

Mitchell, Peta. "Contagion, Virology, Autoimmunity: Derrida's Rhetoric of Contamination." *Parallax* 23, no. 1 (2017): 77–93.

Mitchell, W. J. T. "9/11: Criticism and Crisis." *Critical Inquiry* 28, no. 2 (Winter, 2002): 567–572.

———. *Cloning Terror: The War of Images, 9/11 to the Present*. Chicago: University of Chicago Press, 2011.

Mitra, A. "A Plague in Kashmir." *Indian Medical Gazette* 42, no. 4 (April 1907): 133–138.

———. *A Report on the Outbreak of Plague in Kashmir*. Kashmir: Central Jail Press, 1904.

Montagu, Mary Wortley. *Selected Letters*. Edited by Isobel Grundy. London: Penguin Books, 1997.

Moore, Lindsey. "The Veil of Nationalism: Frantz Fanon's 'Algeria Unveiled' and Gillo Pontecorvo's *The Battle of Algiers*." *Kunapipi* 25, no. 2 (2003): 56–73.

Moreton, Cole. "Philip Bobbitt: The Presidents' Brain." *Independent*, July 20,

2008. http://www.independent.co.uk/news/people/profiles/philip-bobbitt
-the-presidents-brain-872412.html.

Moretti, Franco. "Conjectures on World Literature." In *Debating World Literature*, edited by Christopher Prendergast, 148–162. London: Verso, 2004.

———. "Conjectures on World Literature." *New Left Review* (January–February, 2001): 56–68.

———. *Signs Taken for Wonders: Essays in the Sociology of Literary Forms*. London: Verso, 1983.

Morrison, Robert, and Chris Baldick. "Introduction." In *The Vampyre and Other Tales of the Macabre*, edited by Robert Morrison and Chris Baldick, vii–xxii. London: Oxford University Press, 2008.

Morton, Stephen. "'There Were Collisions and Explosions. The World Was No Longer Calm': Terror and Precarious life in Salman Rushdie's *Shalimar the Clown*." *Textual Practice* 22, no. 2 (June 2008): 337–355.

Moseley, Benjamin. *A Treatise on Tropical Diseases; On Military Operations and on the Climates of the West Indies*. 3rd ed. London: G. G. & J. Robinson, 1795.

Mufti, Aamir R. *Enlightenment in the Colony: The Jewish Question and the Crisis of Postcolonial Culture*. Princeton: Princeton University Press, 2007.

Mukherjee, Upamanyu Pablo. *Natural Disasters and Victorian Empire: Famines, Fevers, and the Literary Cultures of South Asia*. London: Palgrave Macmillan, 2013.

Nancy, Jean-Luc. *L'Intrus*. Paris: Galilée, 2000.

———. *Portrait*. Translated by Sarah Clift and Simon Sparks. New York: Fordham University Press, 2018.

Napolitano, Janet, and John Brennan. "Press Briefing on Swine Influenza with Department of Homeland Security, Centers for Disease Control and Prevention, and White House." April 16, 2009. http://www.dhs.gov/news/2009/04/26/press-briefing-swine-influenza.

National Commission on Terrorist Attacks upon the United States. *The 9/11 Commission Report*. New York: W. W. Norton, 2004.

Newman, Cathy. "A Life Revealed." *National Geographic*, April 2002. https://www.nationalgeographic.com/magazine/2002/04/afghan-girl-revealed/.

Nissa, Zehru. "In 4 Months, Pellets Damage Eyes of 1178 Persons." *Greater Kashmir*, November 8, 2016. http://www.greaterkashmir.com/news/life-style/story/233000.html.

Nixon, Rob. *Slow Violence and the Environmentalism of the Poor*. Cambridge: Harvard University Press, 2011.

Noorani, Abdul Gafoor. *Article 370: A Constitutional History of Jammu and Kashmir*. New Delhi: Oxford University Press, 2011.

Noorani, Yaseen. "The Rhetoric of Security." *New Centennial Review* 5, no. 1 (Spring 2005): 13–41.

O'Brien, Conor Cruise. *Albert Camus: Of Europe and Africa*. New York: Viking, 1970.

———. *Camus*. Glasgow: Fontana, 1970.

————. *The Great Melody: A Thematic Biography of Edmund Burke*. Chicago: University of Chicago Press, 1992.

O'Connor, Erin. *Raw Material: Producing Pathology in Victorian Culture*. Durham: Duke University Press, 2000.

Ó Gráda, Cormac. *Black '47 and Beyond: The Great Irish Famine in History, Economy, and Memory*. Princeton: Princeton University Press, 1999.

O'Hanlon, Michael E., and Adriana Lins de Albuquerque. "Iraq Index: Tracking Variables of Reconstruction in Post-Saddam Iraq." Washington: Brookings Institution, 2004.

Ong, Walter J. *Fighting for Life: Contest, Sexuality, and Consciousness*. Ithaca: Cornell University Press, 1981.

Onions, C. T., ed., *Oxford Dictionary of English Etymology*. New York: Oxford University Press, 1966.

Onyedum, Jennifer Johnson. "Humanizing Warfare: The Politics of Medicine, Health Care, and International Humanitarian Intervention in Algeria 1954–62." Unpublished dissertation. Princeton University, 2010.

O'Sullivan, Patrick, ed. *The Meaning of the Famine*. London: Leicester University Press, 1997.

Paglen, Trevor. *I Could Tell You, But Then You Would Have To Be Destroyed by Me: Emblems from the Pentagon's Black World*. Brooklyn: Melville House, 2010.

Panetta, Leon. Interview by Scott Pelley. *60 Minutes*, CBS News, June 10, 2012. https://www.cbsnews.com/video/the-defense-secretary-leon-panetta-1/.

Parker, John. *Who's Who in the Theater: A Biographical Record of the Contemporary Stage*. 3rd ed. London: Pitman, 1916.

Parkin, John. *Epidemiology; or the Remote Cause of Epidemic Diseases in the Animal and in the Vegetable Creation. With the Cause of the Hurricanes, and Abnormal Atmospheric Vicissitudes*. Pt. 2, 2nd ed. London: David Bogue, 1880.

Parry, Richard Lloyd. "Coronavirus: Albert Camus' *Plague* Novel Flies off the Shelves in Japan," *The Times*, April 10, 2020. https://www.thetimes.co.uk/article/coronavirus-albert-camus-plague-novel-flies-off-the-shelves-in-japan-3stjn7lvl.

Parsons, George. Letter. *Cholera Gazette*, no. 1 (January 14, 1832): 13.

Patton, Cindy. *Globalizing AIDS*. Minneapolis: University of Minnesota Press, 2002.

Paulson, Ronald. "Gothic Fiction and the French Revolution." *English Language History* 48 (1981): 532–554.

Pelling, Margaret. *Cholera, Fever, and English Medicine 1825–1865*. Oxford: Oxford University Press, 1978.

Pershing, John J. *My Life Before the World War, 1860–1917*. Edited by John T. Greenwood. Lexington: University Press of Kentucky, 2013.

Polidori, John. "The Vampyre." In *The Vampyre and Other Tales of the Macabre*, edited by Robert Morrison and Chris Baldick, 1–24. Oxford: Oxford University Press, 2008.

"Polio Eradication: The CIA and Their Unintended Victims." *Lancet* 383 (May 31, 2014): 1862.

Pontecorvo, Gillo, director. *The Battle of Algiers*. Irvington: Criterion Collection, 2004.

———, director. *The Battle of Algiers*, DVD extras. Irvington: Criterion Collection, 2004.

Porter, Joseph A. "Mercutio's Brother." *South Atlantic Review* 49, no. 4 (1984): 31–41.

Porter, Roy. *Blood and Guts: A Short History of Medicine*. New York: W. W. Norton & Co., 2002.

———. *The Greatest Benefit to Mankind: A Medical History of Humanity*. New York: W. W. Norton & Co., 1997.

Pouillon, Jean. "L'Optimisme de Camus." *Les Temps Modernes* 3, no. 26 (November 1947): 921–929.

Pozorski. Aimee. *Falling After 9/11: Crisis in American Art and Literature*. New York: Bloomsbury Academic, 2014.

Preparing for the War on Terrorism: Hearings Before the Committee on Government Reform, 107th Cong. 112 (2001). Statement by Christopher Harmon.

"President Donald J. Trump Announces Great American Economic Revival Industry Groups." White House Press Release, April 14, 2020. https://www.whitehouse.gov/briefings-statements/president-donald-j-trump-announces-great-american-economic-revival-industry-groups/.

Press, Joy. "Tragic Realism." Review of *Shalimar the Clown* by Salman Rushdie. *Village Voice*, August 2, 2005. http://www.villagevoice.com/2005-08-02/books/tragic-realism/full/.

Price, Bryan. "Terrorism as Cancer: How to Combat an Incurable Disease." *Terrorism and Political Violence* 29, no. 1 (June 9, 2017): 1–25.

Proclamation by the Queen in Council to the Princes, Chiefs, and People of India. Allahabad: Office of the Governor General, 1858. https://www.bl.uk/collection-items/proclamation-by-the-queen-in-council-to-the-princes-chiefs-and-people-of-india.

Puar, Jasbir K. *The Right to Maim: Debility, Capacity, Disability*. Durham: Duke University Press, 2017.

———. *Terrorist Assemblages: Homonationalism in Queer Times*. Durham: Duke University Press, 2007.

Puar, Jasbir K., and Amit S. Rai. "Monster, Terrorist, Fag: The War on Terrorism and the Production of Docile Patriots." *Social Text* 20, no. 3 (2002): 117–148.

Punter, David. "Bram Stoker's *Dracula*: Tradition, Technology, Modernity." In *Post/Modern Dracula*, edited by John S. Bak, 31–41. Newcastle upon Tyne: Cambridge Scholars' Press, 2007.

———. *The Literature of Terror: A History of Gothic Fictions from 1765 to the Present Day*. Vol. 2. London: Routledge, 1996.

R., Meenakshi. "Kashmir on the Boil: A Timeline." *The Hindu*, July 21, 2016. http://www.thehindu.com/news/national/kashmir-unrest-after-burhan-wanis-death/article14596369.ece.

Radcliffe, Ann. "On the Supernatural in Poetry." *New Monthly Magazine* 16, no. 1 (1826): 145–152.

Rai, Mridu. *Hindu Rulers, Muslim Subjects: Islam, Rights, and the History of Kashmir*. Princeton: Princeton University Press, 2004.

Raja, Masood Ashraf. "The King Buzzard: Bano Qudsia's Postnational Allegory and the Nation State." *Mosaic* 40, no. 1 (March 2007): 95–110.

Ramadan, Tariq. *Western Muslims and the Future of Islam*. New York: Oxford University Press, 2004.

Raman, Bhavani. *Document Raj: Writing and Scribes in Early Colonial South India*. Chicago: University of Chicago Press, 2012.

Ray, Ellen. "Foreword." In Henri Alleg, *The Question*, translated by John Calder, vii–xii. Lincoln: University of Nebraska Press, 2006.

Reid, Julian. *The Biopolitics of the War on Terror*. Manchester: Manchester University Press, 2006.

"Review of James Kennedy, *The History of the Contagious Cholera*." *The Lancet* 1, no. 19. (November 5, 1831): 173–179.

Remnick, David. "The Brothers Tsarnaev/The Culprits." *New Yorker*, April 29, 2013. http://www.newyorker.com/talk/2013/04/29/130429ta_talk_remnick.

Report to the International Sanitary Conference of a Commission from that Body on the Origin, Endemicity, Transmissibility, and Propagation of Asiatic Cholera. Translated by Samuel L. Abbot. Boston: Alfred Mudge & Son, 1867.

Reporter of Decisions. Syllabus, *Trump v. Hawaii*, 585 U.S __, June 26, 2018.

Retort, "Afflicted Powers: The State, the Spectacle, and September 11." *New Left Review* 27 (May/June 2004): 5–21.

Rickels, Laurence A. *The Vampire Lectures*. Minneapolis: University of Minnesota Press, 1999.

Rizzuto, Anthony. *Camus' Imperial Vision*. Carbondale: Southern Illinois University Press, 1981.

Robbins, Anthony. "The CIA's Vaccination Ruse." *Journal of Public Health Policy* 33, no. 4 (November 2012): 387–389.

Roberts, John. Majority Opinion, *Trump v. Hawaii*, 585 U.S. __, June 26, 2018.

Roberts, Les F., and Michael VanRooyen. "Ensuring Public Health Neutrality." *New England Journal of Medicine* 368 (March 2013): 1073–1075.

Robertson, Ann E. *Terrorism and Global Security*. New York: Infobase Publishing, 2007.

Rockwell, Daisy. "All Hail Salman Rushdie, All Hail Joseph Anton." Review of *Joseph Anton* by Salman Rushdie. *Bookslut*, November 2012. http://www.bookslut.com/white_chick_with_a_hindi_phd/2012_11_019575.php.

———. *The Little Book of Terror*. Tipp City: Foxhead Books, 2012.

Rodgers, Cathy McMorris. Remarks at the Republican Leadership Press Conference, July 6, 2016. https://www.gop.gov/global-terrorism-epidemic/.

Rogers, Samuel. *Reports on Asiatic Cholera in Regiments of the Madras Army from 1828–1844*. London: Richardson, 1848.

Rosenberg, Paul. "Obama's Error: Getting beyond the 'Smart War' Syndrome."

Al Jazeera, September 10, 2013. https://www.aljazeera.com/indepth/opinion/
2013/09/20139883212838340.html.

Rothfield, Lawrence. *Vital Signs: Medical Realism in Nineteenth Century Fiction.*
Princeton: Princeton University Press, 1992.

Roy, Arundhati. "The Pandemic Is a Portal." *Financial Times*, April 3, 2020. https://
www.ft.com/content/10d8f5e8-74eb-11ea-95fe-fcd274e920ca.

"Rudyard Kipling's New Serial." *McClure's Magazine* 16 (November 1900–April
1901): 191.

Rumsfeld, Donald H., and Richard B. Myers. "Rumsfeld and Myers Briefing on
Enduring Freedom." United States Department of Defense, Office of the Assistant Secretary of Defense, news transcript, October 7, 2001. https://archive
.defense.gov/Transcripts/Transcript.aspx?TranscriptID=2011.

Rushdie, Salman. "The Art of Fiction No. 186." Interview by Jack Livings. *Paris
Review*, no. 174 (Summer 2005). https://www.theparisreview.org/interviews/
5531/the-art-of-fiction-no-186-salman-rushdie.

———. "The Disappeared." *New Yorker*, September 17, 2012. https//www.newyorker
.com/magazine/2012/09/17/the-disappeared.

———. *East West: Stories*. New York: Vintage, 1994.

———. *Imaginary Homelands*. New York: Vintage, 1991.

———. *Joseph Anton: A Memoir*. New York: Random House, 2012.

———. "The Most Dangerous Place in the World." *New York Times* (May 30,
2002): A25.

———. *The Satanic Verses*. New York: Henry Holt, 1997.

———. *Shalimar the Clown*. New York: Random House, 2005.

———. *Shame*. New York: Henry Holt, 1983.

———. *Step Across This Line: Collected Nonfiction 1992–2002*. New York: Random
House, 2002.

Saada, Emmanuelle. *Empire's Children: Race, Filiation, and Citizenship in the
French Colonies*. Translated by Arthur Goldhammer. Chicago: University of
Chicago Press, 2012.

Saadawi, Nawal El. "Extracts from an Interview with a Swedish Journalist." In
Albert Memmi, "For Secularism." *Index on Censorship* 18, no. 6 (May 1, 1989):
16–19.

Sa'Da, Caroline Abu, Françoise Duroch, and Bertrand Taithe. "Attacks on Medical
Missions: Overview of a Polymorphous Reality: The Case of Médicins sans
frontières." *International Review of the Red Cross* 95, no. 890 (2013): 309–330.

Said, Edward W. "The Clash of Ignorance." *Nation*, October 22, 2001. https:www
.thenation.com/article/archive/clash-ignorance/.

———. *Covering Islam: How the Media and the Experts Determine How We See the
Rest of the World*. New York: Vintage, 1981. Reprint 1997.

———. *Culture and Imperialism*. New York: Vintage, 1993.

———. *Orientalism*. New York: Vintage, 1979. Reprint 1994.

———. *Power, Politics, and Culture: Interviews with Edward Said*. New York: Vintage, 2002.

———. "Representing the Colonized: Anthropology's Interlocutors," *Critical Inquiry* 15, no. 2 (Winter 1989): 205–225.

———. *The World, the Text, and the Critic.* Cambridge: Harvard University Press, 1983.

Samuel, Sigal. "China Is Treating Islam Like a Mental Illness." *The Atlantic* (August 28, 2018). https://www.theatlantic.com/international/archive/2018/08/china-pathologizing-uighur-muslims-mental-illness/568525/.

Sartre, Jean-Paul. *Colonialism and Neocolonialism.* Translated by Azzedine Haddour, Steve Brewer, and Terry McWilliams. New York: Routledge, 2001.

———. "Preface: A Victory." In Henri Alleg, *The Question*, translated by John Calder, xxvii–xliii. Lincoln: University of Nebraska Press, 2006.

Sawhney, B. R. *Brief Notes on the Outbreak of Plague in the Jammu Province, Kashmir State, 1901.* Jammu: Ranbir Prakash Press, 1901.

Scarry, Elaine. *The Body in Pain: The Making and Unmaking of the World.* Oxford: Oxford University Press, 1985.

Schaffer, Howard B. *The Limits of Influence: America's Role in Kashmir.* Washington: Brookings Institution, 2009.

Schaffer, Talia "'A Wilde Desire Took Me': The Homoerotic History of Dracula." *English Language History* 61 (1994): 381–425.

Schofield, Victoria. *Kashmir in Conflict: India, Pakistan, and the Unfinished War.* London: I. B. Tauris & Co., 2000.

Scott, William. *Report on the Epidemic Cholera as It Has Appeared in the Territories Subject to the Presidency of Fort St. George.* Edinburgh: William Blackwood and Sons, 1849.

Sebbar, Leila. *La seine était rouge.* Paris: Actes Sud, 2009.

Sedgwick, Eve Kosofsky. "The Character in the Veil: Imagery of the Surface in the Gothic Novel." *PMLA* 96, no. 2 (March 1981): 255–270.

———. *The Coherence of Gothic Conventions.* New York: Arno Press, 1980.

———. *Epistemology of the Closet.* Berkeley: University of California Press, 1990. Reprint, 2008.

———. *Touching Feeling: Affect, Pedagogy, Performativity.* Durham: Duke University Press, 2003.

Sehgal, Ujala. "Eight Years Ago, Bush Declared 'Mission Accomplished' in Iraq." *Atlantic*, May 1, 2011. https://www.theatlantic.com/national/archive/2011/05/mission-accomplished-speech/350187/.

Selin, Helaine, ed. *Encyclopaedia of the History of Science, Technology, and Medicine in Non-Western Cultures*, 3rd ed. Berlin: Springer, 2016.

Senate Select Committee on Intelligence. *The Senate Intelligence Committee Report on Torture.* New York: Melville House, 2014.

Serres, Michel. *The Parasite.* Translated by Lawrence R. Schehr. Minneapolis: University of Minnesota Press, 1982.

Serres, Michel, with Bruno Latour. *Conversations on Science, Culture, and Time.* Translated by Roxanne Lapidus. Ann Arbor: University of Michigan Press, 1995.

Shah, Fahad. "'News from Here Doesn't Go Out': Kashmir Simmers Under Lockdown." *The Atlantic*, August 18, 2019. https://www.theatlantic.com/international/archive/2019/08/kashmir-india/596314/.

Shah, Idries. *The Sufis*. New York: Anchor Books, 1971.

Shah, Saeed. "CIA Organized Fake Vaccination Drive to Get Osama bin Laden's Family DNA." *Guardian*, July 11, 2011. http://www.guardian.co.uk/world/2011/jul/11/cia-fake-vaccinations-osama-bin-ladens-dna.

Shakespeare, William. *Romeo and Juliet*. Edited by G. Blakemore Evans. Cambridge: Cambridge University Press, 2003.

Shane, Scott. "The Lessons of Anwar al-Awlaki." *New York Times Magazine*. August 27, 2015 https://www.nytimes.com/2015/08/30/magazine/the-lessons-of-anwar-al-awlaki.html.

Shariatmadari, David. "Swarms, Floods, and Marauders: The Toxic Metaphors of the Migration Debate." *Guardian*, August 10, 2015. https://www.theguardian.com/commentisfree/2015/aug/10/migration-debate-metaphors-swarms-floods-marauders-migrants.

Sharif, Solmaz. *LOOK*. Minneapolis: Greywolf Press, 2016.

Shaw, Tony. *Cinematic Terror: A Global History of Terrorism on Film*. New York: Bloomsbury, 2015.

Shelley, Mary. *The Last Man*. Edited by Anne McWhir. Peterborough: Broadview Press, 1996.

Shilts, Randy. *And the Band Played On: Politics, People, and the AIDS Epidemic*. New York: St. Martin's Press, 1987.

Siddiqi, Javed. *World Health and World Politics: The World Health Organization and the UN System*. Columbia: University of South Carolina Press, 1995.

Silva, Cristobal. "Miraculous Plagues: Epidemiology on New England's Colonial Landscape." *Early American Literature* 43, no. 2 (June, 2008): 249–275.

———. *Miraculous Plagues: An Epidemiology of Early New England Narrative*. New York: Oxford University Press, 2011.

Silverstein, Paul. "An Excess of Truth: Violence, Conspiracy Theorizing, and the Algerian Civil War." *Anthropological Quarterly* 75, no. 4 (Fall 2002): 643–674.

Simpson, David. *States of Terror: History, Theory, Literature*. Chicago: University of Chicago Press, 2019.

Skal, David. J. *Something in the Blood: The Untold Story of Bram Stoker, the Man Who Wrote Dracula*. New York: Liveright, 2016.

Slaughter, Joseph. *Human Rights Inc.: The World Novel, Narrative Form, and International Law*. New York: Fordham University Press, 2007.

Slight, John. *The British Empire and the Hajj 1865–1956*. Cambridge: Harvard University Press, 2015.

Snow, John. "The John Snow Archive & Research Companion." http://johnsnow.matrix.msu.edu/work.php?id=15-78-28.

———. *On the Mode of Communication of Cholera*. London: Wilson and Ogilvy, 1849.

Soderbergh, Steven, director. *Contagion*. Los Angeles: Warner Brothers, 2011.

Solomon, Robert C. *Dark Feelings, Grim Thoughts: Experience and Reflection in Camus and Sartre*. Oxford: Oxford University Press, 2006.

Sontag, Susan. *Illness as Metaphor and AIDS and Its Metaphors*. New York: Picador, 1990.

Sotomayor, Sonia. Dissenting Opinion. *Trump v. Hawaii*, 585 U.S. __ (2018).

Soyinka, Wole. *Climate of Fear: The Quest for Dignity in a Dehumanized World*. New York: Random House, 2004.

Spencer, Kathleen L. "Purity and Danger: *Dracula*, the Urban Gothic, and the Late Victorian Degeneracy Crisis." *English Language History* 59 (1992): 197–225.

Spigel, Lynn. "Entertainment Wars: Television Culture after 9/11." *American Quarterly* 56, no. 2 (June 2004): 235–270.

Spivak, Gayatri Chakravorty. "Can the Subaltern Speak?" In *Can the Subaltern Speak? Reflections on the History of an Idea*, edited by Rosalind C. Morris, 21–78. New York: Columbia University Press, 2010.

———. *Death of a Discipline*. New York: Columbia University Press, 2008.

———. *In Other Worlds: Essays in Cultural Politics*. New York: Routledge, 1988.

———. "Reading *The Satanic Verses*." *Public Culture* 2, no. 1 (Fall 1989): 79–99.

———. "Subaltern Studies: Deconstructing Historiography." In *In Other Worlds*, 270–304. New York: Routledge, 1998.

———. "Three Women's Texts and a Critique of Imperialism." *Critical Inquiry* 12, no. 1 (1985): 243–261.

Spooner, Catherine. *Post-millennial Gothic: Comedy, Romance and the Rise of Happy Gothic*. London: Bloomsbury Academic, 2017.

Srigley, Ronald D. *Albert Camus' Critique of Modernity*. Columbia: University of Missouri Press, 2011.

Stadtler, Florian. "Terror, Globalization, and the Individual in Salman Rushdie's *Shalimar the Clown*." *Journal of Postcolonial Writing* 45, no. 2 (2009): 191–199.

Stares, Paul, and Mona Yacoubian. "Terrorism as a Disease: An Epidemiological Model for Countering Islamist Extremism." Working paper, 2007. https://pdfs .semanticscholar.org/3a62/c0105444e2739f40357091f76db6c74f2eff.pdf.

———. "Terrorism as Virus." *Washington Post*, August 23, 2005. http://www .washingtonpost.com/wp- dyn/content/article/2005/08/22/AR2005082201109. html.

Stephanou, Aspasia. "A 'Ghastly Operation': Transfusing Blood, Science, and the Supernatural in Vampire Texts." *Gothic Studies* 15, no. 2 (November 2013): 53–65.

Stephanson, Raymond. "The Plague Narratives of Defoe and Camus: Illness as Metaphor." *Modern Language Quarterly* 48, no. 3 (September 1987): 224–241.

Stephens, Julia. "The Phantom Wahhabi: Liberalism and the Muslim Fanatic in mid-Victorian India." *Modern Asian Studies* 47, no. 1 (January 2013): 22–52.

Sterndale, Robert Armitage. *The Afghan Knife*. New York: Brentano's, 1889.

Stoker, Bram. *Dracula*. London: Vintage, 2007.

———. *Dracula*. Edited by Nina Auerbach and David J. Skal. New York: W. W. Norton & Co., 1997.

———. *Dracula*. Edited by Maurice Hindle. New York: Penguin, 2003.

———. *Dracula's Guest and Other Weird Stories*. Edited by Kate Hebblethwaite. New York: Penguin, 2006.

———. *Famous Imposters*. New York: Sturgis & Walton Company, 1910.

———. *The New Annotated Dracula*. Edited by Leslie Klinger. New York: W. W. Norton & Company, 2008.

———. *Under the Sunset*. London: Sampson Low, Marston, Searle, and Rivington, 1882.

Stoker, Charlotte. "Letter." Appendix 2 in Bram Stoker, *Dracula*, edited by Maurice Hindle, 412–418. New York: Penguin, 2003.

Stoker, Sir William Thornley. "Memo." In *Bram Stoker's Notes for Dracula: A Facsimile Edition*, edited by Robert Eighteen-Bisang and Elizabeth Miller, 178–179. Jefferson: McFarland & Co., 2008.

Stora, Benjamin. *Algeria 1830–2000*. Translated by Jane Marie Todd. Ithaca: Cornell University Press, 2001.

———. *La Gangrène et l'oubli: la memoire de la guerre d'Algérie*. Paris: Éditions la Découverte, 1991.

———. *Les mots de la guerre d'Algérie*. Toulouse: Presses Universitaires du Mirail, 2005.

Stora, Benjamin, and Zakya Daoud. *Ferhat Abbas: une utopie algérienne*. Paris: Éditions Denoël, 1995.

Stubblefield, Thomas. *9/11 and the Visual Culture of Disaster*. Bloomington: Indiana University Press, 2014.

Suhrud, Tridip. "Dandi March and Gandhi's Politics." *Economic and Political Weekly* 40, no. 15 (April 9–15, 2005): 1491–1492. http://www.jstor.org/stable/pdfplus/4416456.pdf?acceptTC=true.

Suleri, Sara. "Contraband Histories: Salman Rushdie and the Embodiment of Blasphemy." In *Reading Rushdie: Perspectives on the Fiction of Salman Rushdie*, edited by M. D. Fletcher, 221–236. Amsterdam: Rodopi, 1994.

———. *The Rhetoric of English India*. Chicago: University of Chicago Press, 1992.

———. "Whither Rushdie?" *Transition* 51 (1991): 198–212.

Surer, Malcolm. "Indonesia's Ramadan Exodus Risks Spreading Covid-19 across the Country." *France 24*, April 8, 2020, https://www.france24.com/en/20200408-indonesia-s-ramadan-exodus-risks-spreading-covid-19-across-the-country.

Suri, Kavita. "J&K: Return to Violence?" In *Armed Conflicts in South Asia 2010: Growing Left-wing Extremism and Religious Violence*, edited by D. Suba Chandran and P. R. Chari, 67–90. New Delhi: Routledge, 2011.

Surkis, Judith. "Ethics and Violence: Simone de Beauvoir, Djamila Boupacha, and the Algerian War." *French Politics, Culture & Society* 28, no. 2 (Summer 2010): 38–55.

Susser, Mervyn, and Zena Stein. *Eras in Epidemiology: The Evolution of Ideas*. Oxford: Oxford University Press, 2009.

"Tablighi Super Spreaders Cause Covid-19 Explosion in India." *Times of India*,

April 2, 2020. https://timesofindia.indiatimes.com/india/tablighi-super
-spreaders-cause-covid-19-explosion-in-india/articleshow/74956397.cms.

Tait, Theo. "The Flame-Broiled Whopper." Review of *Shalimar the Clown,* by
Salman Rushdie. *London Review of Books* 27, no. 19 (October 6, 2005). http://
www.lrb.co.uk/v27/n19/theo-tait/flame-broiled-whopper.

"Taliban Faction Kills Lawyer." *New York Times,* March 17, 2015. https://www
.nytimes.com/2015/03/18/world/asia/taliban-faction-kills-lawyer.html.

Tannen, Deborah. "Agonism in Academic Discourse." *Journal of Pragmatics* 34
(2002): 1651–1669.

Taylor, Keeanga-Yahmatta. "The Black Plague." *New Yorker,* April 16, 2020. https://
www.newyorker.com/news/our-columnists/the-black-plague.

Taylor, (Philip) Meadows. *Seeta.* London: K. Paul, Trench & Co., 1880.

Tarrow, Sidney. "Preface." In *The World Says No to War: Demonstrations Against the
War in Iraq,* edited by Stefaan Walgrave and Dieter Rucht, vii–xi. Minneapolis:
University of Minnesota Press, 2010.

Terry, Jennifer. *Attachments to War: Biomedical Logics and Violence in Twenty-First
Century America.* Durham: Duke University Press, 2017.

Tickell, Alex. *Terrorism, Insurgency, and Indian-English Literature, 1830–1947.* London: Routledge, 2012.

Tillion, Germaine. *Algeria: The Realities.* Translated by Ronald Matthews. New
York: Alfred A. Knopf, 1958.

Todd, Olivier. *Albert Camus: A Life.* Translated by Benjamin Ivry. New York: Knopf,
1998.

———. *Albert Camus: une vie.* Paris: Gallimard, 1996.

Todorov, Tzvetan. *The Fear of Barbarians: Beyond the Clash of Civilizations.* Translated by Andrew Brown. Chicago: University of Chicago Press, 2010.

———. *Introduction to Poetics.* Translated by Richard Howard. Minneapolis: University of Minnesota Press, 1981.

———. *The Poetics of Prose.* Translated by Richard Howard. Ithaca: Cornell University Press, 1977. Reprint, 1987.

Tomes, Nancy. Part Five: "Introduction." In *Colonial Crucible: Empire in the Making of the Modern American State,* ed. Alfred W. McCoy and Francisco A. Scarano, 273–276. Madison: University of Wisconsin Press, 2009.

Townshend, Charles. *Terrorism: A Very Short Introduction.* Oxford: Oxford University Press, 2002.

Trevelyan, George. *Cawnpore.* London: MacMillan and Co., 1894.

Trotter, William. Letter. *Cholera Gazette,* no. 1 (January 14, 1832): 30–31.

Trump, Donald. "Donald Trump on His Foreign Policy Strategy." Interview by Bill
O'Reilly, *The O'Reilly Factor.* Fox News, April 28, 2016. https://www.foxnews
.com/transcript/donald-trump-on-his-foreign-policy-strategy.

Ukman, Jason. "CIA Defends Running Vaccine Program to Find bin Laden."
Washington Post, July 13, 2011. https://www.washingtonpost.com/world/
national-security/cia-defends-running-vaccine-program-to-find-bin-laden/
2011/07/13/gIQAbLcFDI_story.html.

Umar, Baba. "Kashmir on Fire." *Diplomat*, July 13, 2016. https://thediplomat.com/2016/07/kashmir-on-fire/.

United Nations Security Council. United Nations Security Council Resolution 1566 (S/RES/1566 (2004)), October 8, 2004.

Updike, John. "The Great I Am." *New Yorker*, November 1, 2004. https://www.newyorker.com/magazine/2004/11/01/the-great-i-am.

———. *Terrorist*. New York: Knopf, 2006.

U.S. Department of Defense, former secretary of state Donald Rumsfeld. "Rumsfeld and Myers Briefing on Enduring Freedom." News Transcript, October 7, 2001, 2:45 PM. http://www.defense.gov/transcripts/transcript.aspx?transcriptid=2011.

U.S. Department of Homeland Security, Office for Civil Rights and Civil Liberties. "Terminology to Define the Terrorists: Recommendations from American Muslims." January 2008. https://www.dhs.gov/sites/default/files/publications/dhs_crcl_terminology_08-1-08_accessible.pdf.

U.S. Department of State. "Country Reports on Terrorism 2012." May 30, 2013. http://www.state.gov/documents/organization/210204.pdf.

U.S. Marine Corps. *Small Wars Manual*. Fleet Marine Force Reference Publication 12-15. PCN 140 121500 00. Washington: United States Government Printing Office, 1940.

"US 'Threatened to Bomb' Pakistan." *BBC online*, September 22, 2006. http://news.bbc.co.uk/2/hi/south_asia/5369198.stm.

Vargo, Gregory. *An Underground History of Early Victorian Fiction: Chartism, Radical Print Culture, and the Social Problem Novel*. New York: Cambridge University Press, 2017.

Vaughan, Megan. *Curing Their Ills: Colonial Power and African Illness*. Stanford: Stanford University Press, 1991.

Viragh, Attila. "Can the Vampire Speak? *Dracula* as Discourse on Cultural Extinction." *English Literature in Transition* 56, no. 2 (2013): 231–245.

Viswanathan, Gauri. *Masks of Conquest: Literary Study and British Rule in India*. New York: Columbia University Press, 1989.

———. "The Ordinary Business of Occultism." *Critical Inquiry* 27 (Autumn 2000): 1–20.

———. *Outside the Fold: Conversion, Modernity, and Belief*. Princeton: Princeton University Press, 1998.

———. "Religion and the Imagination." Interview with Salman Rushdie. *Hindu*, July 4, 2010. http://www.thehindu.com/todays-paper/tp-features/tp-literaryreview/religion-and-the-imagination/article499139.ece?css=print.

Vulor, Ena. *Colonial and Anti-colonial Discourses: Albert Camus and Algeria, An Intertextual Dialogue with Mouloud Mammeri, Mouloud Feraoun, and Mohammed Dib*. Lanham: University Press of America, 2000.

Waalgrave, Stefaan, and Dieter Rucht, eds. *The World Says No to War: Demonstrations Against the War in Iraq*. Minneapolis: University of Minnesota Press, 2010.

Wade, Amadou Moustapha. *Discours sur* les Versets Sataniques *ou lettre ouverte aux Occidentaux et autres ennemis de l'Islam.* Dakar: Éditions Maguilen, 2007.

Waheed, Mirza. "India's Crackdown in Kashmir: Is This the World's First Mass Blinding?" *Guardian*, November 8, 2016. https://www.theguardian.com/world/2016/nov/08/india-crackdown-in-kashmir-is-this-the-worlds-first-mass-blinding.

Waitzkin, Howard, and Rebeca Jasso-Aguilar, "Imperialism's Health Component." *Monthly Review* 67, no. 3 (July 1, 2005). http://monthlyreview.org/2015/07/01/imperialisms-health-component/.

———. "Resisting the Imperial Order and Building an Alternative Future in Medicine and Public Health." *Monthly Review* 67, no. 3 (July 1, 2005). http://monthlyreview.org/2015/07/01/resisting-the-imperial-order-and-building-an-alternative-future-in-medicine-and-public-health/.

Wald, Priscilla. *Contagious: Cultures, Carriers, and the Outbreak Narrative.* Durham: Duke University Press, 2008.

Waldby, Catherine, and Robert Mitchell. *Tissue Economies: Blood, Organs, and Cell Lines in Late Capitalism.* Durham: Duke University Press, 2006.

Waldman, Amy. *The Submission.* New York: Picador, 2011.

Walpole, Horace. *The Castle of Otranto: A Gothic Story.* Edited by Frederick S. Frank. Peterborough: Broadview Press, 2003.

Walsh, Declan. "As Ramadan Begins, Muslims (Mostly) Accede to Pandemic Orders" *New York Times,* April 24, 2020. https://www.nytimes.com/2020/04/24/world/middleeast/coronavirus-ramadan-2020.html.

Walter, Natasha. "The Children of Paradise." Review of *Shalimar the Clown*, by Salman Rushdie. *Guardian*, September 2, 2005. http://www.theguardian.com/books/2005/sep/03/fiction.salmanrushdie.

Warner, Marina. *Monsters of Our Own Making: The Peculiar Pleasures of Fear.* Lexington: University Press of Kentucky, 1998.

Warren, Craig A. "'It Reads Like a Novel': *The 9/11 Commission Report* and the American Reading Public." *Journal of American Studies* 41, no. 3 (December 2007): 533–556.

Watson, Ivan, and Ben Westcott. "Watched, Judged, Detained." Cable News Network, February 2020. https://www.cnn.com/interactive/2020/02/asia/xinjiang-china-karakax-document-intl-hnk/.

Weber, Samuel. *Targets of Opportunity: On the Militarization of Thinking.* New York: Fordham University Press, 2005.

Wharton, Edith. *The Ghost Stories.* New York: Scribner, 1973.

Wilder, Gary. *Freedom Time: Negritude, Decolonization, and the Future of the World.* Durham: Duke University Press, 2015.

———. *The French Imperial Nation State: Negritude and Colonial Humanism Between the Two World Wars.* Chicago: University of Chicago Press, 2005.

Wilkinson, William. *An Account of the Principalities of Wallachia and Moldavia.* London: Longman's, 1820.

Williams, Anne. *Art of Darkness: A Poetics of Gothic*. Chicago: University of Chicago Press, 1995.

Williamson, Milly, and Gholam Khiabany. "The Veil and the Politics of Racism." *Race and Class* 52, no. 2 (October 1, 2010): 85–96.

Willis, Martin. "The Invisible Giant, *Dracula*, and Disease." *Studies in the Novel* 39, no. 3 (Fall 2007): 301–326.

Wilson, Nick, and George Thomson. "The Epidemiology of International Terrorism Involving Fatal Outcomes in Developed Countries." *European Journal of Epidemiology* 20 (2005): 375–381.

Winslow, Charles-Edward Amory. *The Conquest of Epidemic Disease: A Chapter in the History of Ideas*. Madison: University of Wisconsin Press, 1943. Reprint, 1980.

Wisker, Gina. *Horror Fiction*. New York: Continuum, 2005.

Wood, Gillen D'Arcy. *Tambora: The Eruption That Changed the World*. Princeton: Princeton University Press, 2014.

Wood, James. "Human, All Too Inhuman." Review of *White Teeth* by Zadie Smith. *New Republic*, July 23, 2000. https://newrepublic.com/article/61361/human -inhuman.

"The Work of the Health Organization of the League of Nations." *Canadian Medical Association Journal* 15, no. 11 (November 1925): 1153.

World Health Organization. "About WHO." http://www.who.int/about/en/.

———. "Circulating Vaccine-Derived Poliovirus Type 2—Pakistan." November 28, 2019. https://www.who.int/csr/don/28-november-2019-polio-pakistan/en/.

———. "Constitution of the World Health Organization." Basic Documents, 45th ed., 2006. http://www.who.int/governance/eb/who_constitution_en.pdf.

———. "Declaration of Alma Ata." September 12, 1978. http://www.who.int/ publications/almaata_declaration_en.pdf.

———. "Epidemiology." http://www.who.int/topics/epidemiology/en/.

Worth, Robert F. "Can We Imagine the Life of a Terrorist?" *New York Times Magazine*, June 14, 2013. http://www.nytimes.com/2013/06/16/magazine/can-we -imagine-the-life-of-a-terrorist.html?pagewanted=3&_r=0&ref=magazine.

Wyatt, Edward. "National Book Award Finalists Include 9/11 Commission Report." *New York Times*, October 13, 2004. https://www.nytimes.com/2004/10/13/ books/national-book-awards-finalists-include-911-commission-report.html.

Yacoubian, Mona, and Paul Stares. "Rethinking the War on Terror." United States Institute of Peace, September 7, 2005. https://www.usip.org/publications/ 2005/09/rethinking-war-terror.

Yong, Ed. "Our Pandemic Summer." *The Atlantic*, April 15, 2020. https://www .theatlantic.com/health/archive/2020/04/pandemic-summer-coronavirus -reopening-back-normal/609940/.

Young, Elizabeth. *Black Frankenstein: The Making of an American Metaphor*. New York: New York University Press, 2008.

Young, Robert J. C. *Colonial Desire: Hybridity in Theory, Culture, and Race*. London: Routledge, 1995.

———. *Postcolonialism: An Historical Introduction*. Oxford: Blackwell, 2001.

Young Choi, Tina. *Anonymous Connections: The Body and Narratives of the Social in Victorian Britain*. Ann Arbor: University of Michigan Press, 2015.

Yuhas, Alan, and Mazin Sidahmed. "Is This a Muslim Ban? Trump's Executive Order Explained." *Guardian*, January 31, 2017. https://www.theguardian.com/us-news/2017/jan/28/trump-immigration-ban-syria-muslims-reaction-lawsuits.

Zaretsky, Robert. *Albert Camus: Elements of a Life*. Ithaca: Cornell University Press, 2010.

———. "Camus the Jew." *Tablet*, November 7, 2011. https://www.tabletmag.com/sections/arts-letters/articles/camus-the-jew.

———. "The Stranger Who Resembles Us." *Chronicle Review*, November 26, 2012. http://chronicle.com/article/Camuss-Restless-Ghost/135874/.

Zinsser, Hans. *Rats, Lice, and History: Being a Study in Biography, which, after Twelve Preliminary Chapters Indispensible for the Preparation of the Lay Reader, Deals With the Life History of Typhus Fever*. New York: Blue Ribbon Books, 1935.

Zurcher, Anthony. "What Trump Team Has Said About Islam." *BBC News*, February 7, 2017. https://www.bbc.com/news/world-us-canada-38886496.

Zutshi, Chitralekha. *Languages of Belonging: Islam, Regional Identity, and the Making of Kashmir*. New York: Oxford University Press, 2004.

Index

incompleteness: of death (for the colonized Algerian), 196; of *The Senate Intelligence Committee Report on Torture*, 284, 286; of suicide (Freud), 249

Indian Mutiny of 1857, 3–4, 31, 41–47, 54, 59, 67–69, 72, 78, 80–82, 85, 113, 144, 179, 211. *See also* rebellion

infinite: burdens (of the white man), 53; expansion (of the War on Terror's parameters), 287; growth (of the tapeworm), 174; love (and *The Satanic Verses*), 253; penetration (of the colonial fantasy), 200; science (of the colonizer), 85–86, 123, 188; science (of surveillance), 287; "Selfistans" (Rushdie), 240

influenza, 24, 134; Global Influenza Surveillance Network, 233; war as (Emerson), 129

International Bank for Reconstruction and Development, 220

International Monetary Fund, 220

International Parliament of Writers, and Rushdie, 239

International Red Cross, 37

International Sanitary Conferences, 12; *Report to the International Sanitary Conference*, 69–71. *See also* hygiene; sanitation

Ionesco, Eugène, *Rhinoceros*, 243

Iqbal, Muhammad, on the global *ummah*, 217. See also *ummah*, global

IRA, 177, 181

Irving, Henry, homosexuality of, 121

ISIS, 25, 33–35, 46, 290

Islam: "actually existing" (Rushdie), 215; as "barbaric," 3; as cancer (Trump), 2; as contagious, 3; "demonology" of Islam, 94; empty (in right-wing lexicon), 2; expertise/knowledge about, 257, 336n4; FIS (Front Islamique du Salut), 221; "Islamist militancy," 5, 258–61,

277; as outside "humanity," 17; strategic conversion to, 247; as "submission," 246–47. *See also* Islamophobia

Islamophobia, 83, 122, 174, 288; dialectical, 9

isolation: camps, 153–54; and destruction (in *The Battle of Algiers*), 175; in *Frankenstein*, 90; in *The Plague*, 144, 154; vs. "unrestrained intercourse" in epidemiology, 12; of women in Muslim countries, 266. *See also* cordon sanitaire; quarantine

Jacobson, Sid, *The 9/11 Report: A Graphic Adaptation*, 274–75

Jameson, Fredric, and the reading of "third world" literature, 218

Jameson, James, *Report on the Epidemick Cholera Morbus*, 60–62, 64–65, 69, 74

Jeanson, Francis, 148; on Camus's *The Plague*, 142

jihad, 6, 206, 209, 215, 237–38, 264, 278, 287; in Northern India, 51–52, 72

Johnson, Boris, on terrorism (as "plague"), 4, 235

Johnson, E. C., *On the Track of the Crescent*, 94

Jones, Ernest, *The Revolt of Hindostan* (née *The New World*), 39–40, 47

Joseph Anton (Rushdie), 23, 214, 232, 234–35, 238–42, 244–45, 331n25, 335n69

journalism: and *The Battle of Algiers*, 179–82; Camus's, 162–67

Judt, Tony, resituating of *The Plague* (after 9/11), 131, 161, 169

Kaplan, Alice: on the Algerian recovery of Camus, 132; on Camus's "first exile," 148–49; on Camus's legacy, 155, 161; on Camus's silence

Rushdie, Salman (*continued*)
241; *Grimus*, 217; on "heroic" (vs.
non-heroic) insurgencies, 230;
Imaginary Homelands, 237, 239–41;
Joseph Anton, 23, 214, 232, 234–35,
238–42, 244–45, 331n25, 335n69;
Midnight's Children, 219; on the
migrant, 335n65; on the Pakistan/
India standoff, 215; on personal security, 234; on roots (in *Shame* and
Joseph Anton), 331n25; *The Satanic
Verses*, 23, 213–14, 234–35, 239, 242–
55, 278–80, 283, 288; "Selfistan," 214,
223–24, 240; *Shalimar the Clown*,
214–16, 218–31, 234–35, 240–42, 245;
Shame, 216–18, 331n25. See also
Satanic Verses, The (Rushdie)

Saadawi, Nawal El, on terrorism as
cancer, 235. *See also* terrorism: as
cancer
Saadi, Yacef, 171, 181. See also *Battle of
Algiers, The* (Pontecorvo)
Said, Edward, 19; on Al-i Ahmad's *Occidentosis*, 243; on Camus's writing,
131, 142–43, 155, 321n27; on Kipling's
Kim, 49–50; on natural forms of
authority, 246; *Orientalism*, 242–43
sanitation: and interstitial spaces,
241; and morality, 137–38; and Nazi
rhetoric, 153, 156; sanitary controls,
5, 69; sanitary reforms, 50, 98. *See
also* cordon sanitaire; hygiene
Santal *hool* (1855), 38, 40
Sartre, Jean-Paul: and Boupacha's
memoir, 200; and Camus, 142,
148, 161, 185; invoked in *The Battle
of Algiers*, 179–80; on torture (as a
plague), 185
Satanic Verses, The (Rushdie), 23, 213–
14, 234–35, 239, 242–55, 278–80, 283,
288; and cancer, 245–46, 249; and
cholera, 254; and hajj, 245, 248–55,
278–80, 283; and infinite love, 253;

and noise, 254; and prophecy, 248–
55; and submission, 246–47; and
typhus, 254
sati (widow immolation), 84
Schell, Heather, and the use of material metaphors, 19
Schwarz-Bart, André, and Boupacha's
memoir, 200
science: colonial (Western medicine
in India as), 59; as explaining
"what happens" (Camus), 129,
143, 161, 163; Indian (global health
as), 59; infinite (of the colonizer),
85–86, 123, 188; infinite (of surveillance), 287; and literature, 149;
"new paradigm of" (Kittler), 117;
and progress, 194; and the vampire
terrorist, 84
Sedgwick, Eve Kosofsky: on Gothic
writing, 117; on the veil, 193
*Senate Intelligence Committee Report
on Torture, The*, 24, 268, 273–87. *See
also* torture
September 11, 2001, attacks, 2, 25, 33,
35, 215, 257; and blood donation,
122–25; as novel (for Derrida), 14–
15; and *The Plague*, 169; "since September 11," 290. *See also* Al Qaeda;
bin Laden, Osama; *9/11 Commission Report, The*; *Senate Intelligence
Committee Report on Torture, The*
Serres, Michel, on sickness (as a
noise), 21
Shalimar the Clown (Rushdie), 214–16,
218–31, 234–35, 240–42, 245
Sharif, Solmaz, 24; *LOOK*, 280–87
Sheehan, Michael, on the lesson of
The Battle of Algiers, 171–72, 174
Sheikh Mohammed, Khalid, invoked
in *The 9/11 Commission Report*,
264–65
Shelley, Mary: *Frankenstein*, 85, 88–90,
92; *The Last Man*, 85, 91; and Polidori, 90–91

258; on "Islamist militancy" as "epidemic," 5

Updike, John: on *The 9/11 Commission Report*, 272; and the theme of terrorism, 18, 289

vaccination, 5; and cholera, 57–58; and the targeting of bin Laden, 22, 29–38, 41, 46–47, 53–54, 88, 257, 278. *See also* immunization/immunity

vampire: and black clothing, 83; fiction (since 9/11), 22–23, 85–86, 122; and terrorism, 83–125; as "ultimate other" (Kitson), 87. See also *Dracula* (Stoker)

Vaughan, Megan, on the colonial project of "curing their ills," 260

veil, 193, 199; and Arab women, 84–85, 185–86; "impenetrable" (of cholera research, for J. Jameson), 61; of monstrosity, 287. *See also* "Algeria Unveiled" ("L'Algérie se dévoile") (Fanon)

viral, the, 18

voice: of cholera ("vox cholerica"), 74–75; "oceanic," 247; "This Is the Voice of Algeria" (Fanon), 183; "undervoice" of *The 9/11 Commission Report*, 268. *See also* speech

vulnerability: and immunity, 15; and the imperial project, 206; and terrorism, 8

Waheed, Mirza, on "the world's first mass blinding," 210. *See also* eyes: dead (mass blinding in Kashmir)

Wald, Priscilla, on epidemiology and narrative, 18–19, 55

Waldby, Catherine, on blood donation immediately after 9/11, 123–24

Waldman, Amy, and the theme of terrorism, 289

Walpole, Horace, on "the common life," 122

war: against cancer, 17; colonial, 34; dirty, 155; endless, 288; as epidemic (Emerson), 129; "just," 88, 211; and medicine, 258; neoimperial, 290; as an obsolete concept, 258; of peace (Kipling), 53–54; as plague (in *The Plague*), 134, 168; and progress, 258; and public health, 16, 224; smart, 36, 257. *See also* War on Terror

War on Terror, 16, 23–24, 53–54, 233, 256–91; and *The Battle of Algiers*, 170–77, 191; and Camus scholarship, 132; as a colonial war, 34; and *Dracula*, 23, 86–87, 103; and health imperialism, 30–38, 125; and Kashmir, 209–10; and the killing of bin Laden, 30–38, 257; and migration, 212; as neoimperial, 290; and *The 9/11 Commission Report*, 265; and *The Senate Intelligence Committee Report on Torture*, 274, 278; as strategically disingenuous, 270; and the violation of the woman's body, 202. *See also* Al Qaeda; bin Laden, Osama; *9/11 Commission Report, The*; *Senate Intelligence Committee Report on Torture, The*; September 11, 2001, attacks

Warren, Craig, on *The 9/11 Commission Report*, 268, 276. See also *9/11 Commission Report, The*

Warren Report, The, 268

water: bad, 70; bitter/sweet (in *Dracula*), 95, 104; and blood, 110; and cholera, 67, 79–83, 96, 101; the oceanic, 247–49, 251–53; and purification, 247; sleeping, 96, 102; sleepless, 96, 102; thoughts as, 111

weapon: aircraft as, 263; camera as, 181; "nonlethal," 210–12; nuclear, 215

weather: and cholera, 61–62, 64–69, 100–101; and *The 9/11 Commission Report*, 262–63

CPSIA information can be obtained
at www.ICGtesting.com
Printed in the USA
LVHW080501070521
686765LV00019B/350